*European Society
in the Eighteenth Century*

A volume
in
THE DOCUMENTARY HISTORY
of
WESTERN CIVILIZATION

EUROPEAN SOCIETY
IN THE
EIGHTEENTH CENTURY

edited by

ROBERT AND ELBORG FORSTER

WALKER AND COMPANY
New York

EUROPEAN SOCIETY IN THE EIGHTEENTH CENTURY
Introduction, editorial notes, translations by the editors, and compilation
Copyright © 1969 by Robert and Elborg Forster.

Library of Congress Catalog Card Number: 69-15559.

Printed in the United States of America.

Published in the United States of America in
1969 by Walker and Company, a division of the
Walker Publishing Company, Inc.

Published simultaneously in Canada by
The Ryerson Press, Toronto.

Volumes in this series are published in association
with Harper & Row, Publishers, Inc., from
whom paperback editions are available in Harper
Torchbooks.

Contents

Acknowledgments

The editors wish to thank Professor David Joslyn of Pembroke College, Cambridge, England, for bringing to their attention the *Memoirs of a Scottish Banking-House* and Professor R. Burr Litchfield of Brown University for collecting and translating the Italian material. The other translations in this volume have been done by the editors, unless credit is given otherwise. Finally, the editors wish to thank the outside reader, Mrs. Bonnie Anderson, and the copy editor of Harper & Row, for their painstaking efforts to improve the original manuscript.

Introduction

MUCH HAS been written, and even more said privately, about the plight of the American student of European history: the unpublished sources of European archives are far away; for financial, professional, or family reasons, frequent trips to Europe are not easy to arrange; and adjustment to local conditions, from the peculiarities of archival catalogues to the vagaries of European administration, can consume a large part of an academic year abroad.[1]

The response to this plight, however, need not be a total abandonment of archival research. It might well be a judicious blending of archival discoveries with research in published sources found in this country. Such an approach cannot hope to produce either the massive European doctoral monograph or the broad interpretive synthesis. But it can hope to add new information to the ragged edges of "what we already know" and, by incorporating other monographic material, fashion "suggestive" if not "definitive" interpretations. But whether one opts for the blend or for history based entirely on more accessible materials, he should be familiar with the range, variety, and quantity of published sources. Even the determined archival scholar would do well to look harder at the materials close at hand before he burrows into subseries E of a European archive.

A generation ago, the famous French scholar, Georges Lefebvre, said it was not enough for historians to describe; they must also count. In the last decade considerable attention has been paid to quantification in social history. Of course, the amount of measuring possible depends on the sources available and the kinds of questions one asks of his material. The answers to many meaningful historical questions simply cannot be quantified. Other questions may not be worth the time and effort required to process the data. A historian will hesitate to tabulate

[1] See D. Pinkney, "The Dilemma of the American Historian of Modern France," *French Historical Studies*, I (1958), 11–25.

mountains of tax returns, for example, if the result yields only a few statistical averages. On the other hand, statisticians have taught historians that a wide range of questions can be asked of such sources as tax rolls, price series, land registers, or notarized contracts of all kinds. We now possess highly sophisticated data-processing techniques, making it feasible for the historian to attempt statistical analyses impossible only a decade ago.

Quantification is not always practical or desirable. Will counting sermons or newspaper columns provide a useful measure of social reform? Is it profitable to make an exact count of Bayle's allusions to predestination to indicate a Calvinist bias? Can we ever hope to establish a statistical rate of social mobility for the eighteenth century? On the other hand, it is of considerable value to know the precise numerical changes of population, migration, landholding, prices, wages, income, investments, literacy, or marriages. Economic materials obviously lend themselves most readily to counting, sampling, and measuring. Where there are data from sufficient space and time, quantification can lead to unexpected patterns of aggregate behavior and suggest questions the historians would not otherwise have considered. Statistical tables and graphs cannot make value judgments or answer "why" questions, but they can provoke new lines of inquiry and test certain hypotheses. They may also bring long-accepted generalizations crashing to the ground. These are not insignificant virtues.[2]

Social historians are not only learning to employ the techniques of the statistician, but they are also drawing on the neighboring disciplines of demography, sociology, psychology, and economics.[3] Historical demography, under the impulse of recent research in France and England, has now gone beyond the initial phase of collecting statistics on baptisms, marriages, and burials culled from parish registers. In addition to such aggregate work, demographers are now attempting to reconstitute family histories of entire villages over two or three centuries. From these they hope to establish precise data on changes in fertility, mortality, and

[2] See W. O. Aydelotte, "Quantification in History," *American Historical Review*, LXXI, No. 3 (April, 1966), 803–825.

[3] See Keith Thomas, "The Tools and the Job," *Times Literary Supplement* (April 7, 1966), 275–276, and the entire series entitled "New Ways in History" (April 7, July 28, September 8, 1966).

nuptiality.[4] Strict population history has its own fascination, but its most promising contribution has been to social and economic history. As Professor Wrigley, a pioneer in English historical demography, says:

> Whether one studies the balance between numbers and the supply of cultivable land; the importance of harvest and weather to the community; the frequency of turnover of holdings; the views of contemporaries on the idle poor; the upbringing of children and their relationship to their siblings; the structure of authority in the family; the place of the unmarried and widowed; sexual mores; the relationship of master and man in pre-industrial society; the changes in real wages; in later times the flow of people from country to town; or more specifically demographic issues like the average size of families; the proportion of the "tail" of the population beneath working age; the impact of the great killing diseases; or expectation of life at various ages, a knowledge of the society's demographic character is a part of the proper context of the discussion.[5]

The overlap between social history and sociology is too obvious to require much comment here. The concept of "social class," however, has been of particular interest to students of the Old Régime.[6] Historians and sociologists alike have begun to question the reality of traditional social categories such as "bourgeoisie" or "proletariat," terms adopted from the vocabulary of modern industrial society. In eighteenth-century France, for example, the term "bourgeois" was usually employed to designate a man with an independent income, a *rentier*. Capitalized and linked with a particular town or city—*Bourgeois de Paris*, for example—the term denoted special legal prerequisites of citizenship, such as fixed residence and payment of certain local taxes. In both cases, "bourgeois" had a much more restricted meaning than what is usually included in our broad application of the word.

The problem is not entirely revealed by recalling earlier uses of the term. Is it really enlightening to include so many functional

---

[4] See E. LeRoy Ladurie, "From Waterloo to Colyton," *Times Literary Supplement* (September 8, 1966), 791–796.
[5] E. A. Wrigley, ed., *An Introduction to English Historical Demography* (New York, 1966), pp. 101–102.
[6] See Alfred Cobban, *A Social Interpretation of the French Revolution* (Cambridge, 1964).

groups of people under a single rubric, especially since this conveys a strict economic definition of class? In eighteenth-century society certain important differences, not all economic, among the groups of a finely graded hierarchy are smothered by such omnibus terms. The problem becomes even more obvious when one projects the term "bourgeoisie" into rural areas and includes large tenant farmers, land agents, and resident landlords indiscriminately under the same label.

The same objection pertains to the use of the word "proletariat." A perfectly viable category for an advanced industrial society, it has little validity for the eighteenth century. Terms like "artisan," "journeyman," or "day laborer" are more appropriate, and precise identifications, such as "carpenter," "mason," "wine-grower," or "harvest hand," are even better. In general, the eighteenth century's own vocabulary is more reliable than ours, though as the scope of study broadens, some artificial categories are necessary. The important thing is that the definitions be as explicit as possible and relevant to the social groups under consideration.

Despite the impact of Freudianism on American society since the 1930's, American historians have been hesitant to integrate psychology into their research. There have been many reasons for this. Psychology is still a very young field of study, and its claims to scientific respectability have not been entirely validated. Moreover, among the many schools of modern psychology, which one should the historian choose? Third, can the historian hope to acquire the necessary minimum knowledge of the field without formal, analytical training? Nothing would be gained by adding the historian to those who bandy about Freudian terminology without any real understanding of its meaning. Finally, given the need to know childhood histories in treating the unconscious, is the historian's data ever adequate for the task?

In spite of these obstacles, something can be accomplished. Fortunately, the focus of modern psychology has shifted from the domain of the unconscious to the conscious controls, or "defense mechanisms," that enforce repression and adapt us to reality. This kind of depth psychology the historian is better able to handle, since these mechanisms persist into adult life. Still, this does not solve all problems. The newcomer to the field often runs the risk of overstressing single clues. Napoleon's relations with his brother Louis may or may not reflect latent homosexual feelings. And beyond such problems as these lies the much larger issue of the causal connection between a certain psychological "type" and the actions or policies initiated by the individual. For these reasons, the flirtation of historical biography with depth psychology remains cautious but not unpromising.[7]

On the level of group behavior the temptation to find some of the familiar psychological configurations is great. The semiliterate peasants of isolated hamlets have left few personal records, but since they represent a large part of mankind, the historian must employ what tools he has to bring them back to life. Scholars such as Georges Duby and Robert Mandrou have made imaginative efforts to re-create the psychological pressures and anxieties of the peasant community. Others, like George Rudé and Albert Soboul have attempted to do the same for the crowd and the lower classes of Paris. It matters little whether or not we employ such labels as "collective paranoia" so long as it is clear what is happening to people.

Frequently in the past, social historians have relied too heavily on price and income data to explain group behavior, apparently assuming that sufficient economic precision will explain all subsequent action. This is not to deny the impact of high bread prices and consequent malnutrition on the actions of men. But price and wage data cannot carry the entire burden of explaining group behavior. Because they are difficult to measure, the historian should be especially aware of the influence of ideas, however distorted or simplified. Clusters of ideas need not be philosophic systems or even logically consistent to be important. Slogans, taboos, symbols, even primitive rites may be more appropriate for study than ideas in any formal sense. Remember that the mass of Europeans in the eighteenth century were still closer to millenarianism and witchcraft than to the precepts of Descartes or Locke. That is why it is important to recapture the anxiety of the peasant village before the harvest, the increasing cohesion of a crowd, or the emotional intensity of a religious revival meeting. It

[7] See Bruce Mazlish, "Inside the Whale," *Times Literary Supplement* (July 28, 1966), 667–669; W. L. Langer, "The Next Assignment," *American Historical Review,* LXIII, No. 2 (January, 1958), pp. 283–304.

is the subtle mixture of material conditions, habits, customs, and half-conscious beliefs that helps explain group behavior.[8]

The debt of the social historian to the economist is of long standing. In addition to quantification, economists are especially concerned about the magnitude and distribution of national income and the rate of economic growth. True, eighteenth-century economic sources do not always lend themselves to the rigorous requirements of modern economists.[9] However, the emphasis of the economist on such problems as income structure, cost of living, entrepreneurial activity, capital formation, labor conditions, consumer tastes, or technological development has furnished the historian with a wealth of questions to ask of his material. Moreover, the historian is much less averse to model-building than he once was. Econometric history is now coming into its own, especially in the area of comparative economic growth. The field of economics, even before the historian was aware of demography, social psychology, or sociology, saved social history from a tendency toward quaintness. Its services continue.

It is easy to list the disciplines the social historian now has at his disposal. It is much more difficult to coordinate them intelligently into a readable historical study. An excellent example of this can be found in the recent work of Emmanuel LeRoy Ladurie on the peasants of southern France.[10] Combining a thorough investigation of local physical conditions and agricultural technology with price and demographic changes, LeRoy Ladurie broaches the challenging area of peasant psychology, correlating isolation, illiteracy, and poverty with outbursts of millenarianism or witchcraft, conversion to Calvinism, or antagonism to towns. Such integration is at last becoming fashionable. Increasingly, social history will have not only new rigor and precision, but also a new dimension. Different questions and hypotheses about human action and change are now possible, extending the canvas toward "total history."

---

[8] See Georges Duby and Robert Mandrou, *A History of French Civilization* (New York, 1964), pp. 219ff., and R. Mandrou, *Introduction à la France moderne (1500–1640): Essai de psychologie historique* (Paris, 1961).

[9] See Peter Mathias, "The Social Structure in the Eighteenth Century: A Calculation by Joseph Massie," *Economic History Review*, 2nd series, X (1957), 30–45.

[10] E. LeRoy Ladurie, *Les Paysans de Languedoc* (Paris, 1966).

A number of historical developments in the eighteenth century has made that century particularly rich in source materials. The rapid growth of the bureaucratic state has furnished a wealth of administrative and public documents. Sustained by a burgeoning class of lawyers, the lay state also preserved a prodigious quantity of notarial documents. Commercial growth led to an increasing number of formalized contracts, accounts, manuals, dictionaries, and economic tracts of all kinds. A growing affluence among the upper classes as well as an increasing cosmopolitanism made the century a golden age of the traveler's diary and the memoir. Perhaps most novel, the poor had their spokesmen among a vocal band of "improvers," found especially in England. Something should be said about these various types of sources for social history.

Administrative documents are among the most reliable of sources. Bureaucrats may interpret the local scene euphemistically, but the facts reported are reliable. The local official was rarely an interested party in the sense a lawyer or taxpayer might be. The reports of the royal intendants in France, for example, are excellent sources of local social and economic conditions, clearly presented and supported by statistical inquests. The reports of the Paris police share these qualities, though on a narrower plane. Tax rolls are also very useful to the historian since they can reveal the approximate income structure of a community. The accomplishments of Gregory King and Patrick Colquhoun with hearth taxes and poor rates in their own day (see Document 38) is an example to today's historians. Tax declarations, though more suspect for obvious reasons, can be very enlightening if they are carefully interpreted, sometimes with the help of the comments of the tax assessor or other "outside" sources. A noble's tax declaration, for example, can tell us a great deal about the operation of a rural estate. The famous French cahiers of grievances of 1789 are equal to the best national survey. Despite the amendments of lawyers and townsmen, the cahiers remain an excellent source both of local economic conditions and of popular attitudes and aspirations on the eve of the French Revolution. Unlike the tax rolls, a large number of cahiers have been printed and can be subjected to the most modern computer techniques. Students of French social history are favored here by a unique source not found in other countries.

As compensation, however, students of English history possess the large collections of Parliamentary Papers, including debates and committee reports. More than the French intendant, an English Commons committee may color its report to back a particular bill, but again the facts themselves are reliable. Good common sense can go far toward discounting some of the arguments of the Committee on Enclosures, for example. Although the County Session Papers used so effectively by Dorothy George (*London Life in the Eighteenth Century*) are not available in print, a substantial number of parochial reports have been published by Sir Frederick Eden, giving a variety of information, much of it statistical, on local towns and villages. These reports should be distinguished from the parish registers of baptisms, burials, and marriages so important to the historical demographers. In isolation, the registers have much less interest.

Related to administrative documents are the declarations and regulations of constituted bodies. The acts of Parliament, remonstrances of the French *parlements*, edicts of the Imperial Diet or local guild, and fair regulations are in this category. The value of this kind of source is more readily found in the situation it proposes to treat than in the solution itself. Law and practice are such different things. A remonstrance or edict may also tell us about the procedures, or even ideology, of its formulators. The example of a remonstrance of the Parlement of Paris reveals a vocabulary that may have greater implications than simply the reflection of established formulas of speech.

Fortunately for the social historian, in the eighteenth century a large number of everyday transactions had to be notarized and registered with the public authorities. Among economic documents, one uncovers partnership agreements, charters of joint-stock companies, patents, property leases, sales, purchases, and exchanges of all kinds. Relating more directly to family history are the notarized wills, codicils, marriage contracts, "gifts-in-life," estate settlements, and, occasionally, wardship accounts. Together, these sources compose the notarial archives now being systematically explored by European scholars, especially in France and Italy. Along with the administrative documents alluded to above, these sources have become the basis of a new historical sociology.[11]

[11] See *Vingt-cinq ans de recherche historique en France (1940–1965)* (Paris, 1966).

Much harder to come by are family papers. These collections consist most often of scattered accounts, bundles of receipts, and copies of the notarized legal documents mentioned above. These are useful sources, making it possible to reconstruct at least the financial history of a family. Much scarcer are bundles of letters, so important for any analysis of motivation or for recapturing the intimate details of family life. Printed collections of letters naturally tend to be limited to the correspondence of famous figures like Horace Walpole or Lord Chesterfield. It is extremely difficult to uncover the letters of more ordinary men.

Memoirs cannot really replace intimate correspondence. The difficulty in dating them and their apologetic tendencies present problems enough, while the proclivity toward anecdotes and genealogical biography is even more infuriating. Nevertheless, memoirs have their uses, especially if the author is an obscure, unpretentious person. Thus the cramped reminiscences of a Rouen *abbé* or the more expansive comments of a Scottish banker tell us much about their respective attitudes and callings. Even court souvenirs, judiciously used, have their merit. Despite her own role as courtier, Madame Campan still presents a reasonably fair portrait of Versailles, and Horace Walpole, despite heaps of supper-party trivia, opens a window on high society. The autobiographic writings of literary figures such as Goethe, Goldsmith, or Boswell have an imaginative penetration that often compensates for minor errors of fact. It is well to remember that all of social history cannot be quantified; a certain impressionism in biographical material is not only permissible but desirable.

Travelers' accounts, especially when written by a specialist on some economic or social problem, usually combine range of experience with some comparative analysis. The *Travels* of Arthur Young is a masterpiece of comparative observation, which is not restricted to French and English agriculture. Howard's tour of European prisons, Ségur's melancholy trek across Poland, Defoe's meandering progresses through Britain, or Pöllnitz's *petit tour* of central Europe are all tightly packed with social observations. Besides the travelers and the "improvers" are the more sedentary observers, some semiliterary, some statistically oriented. Eden spent his life establishing the condition of the English poor, while Mercier and Restif de la Bretonne roamed the streets of Paris, trying to capture the world beyond brick and mortar. Historians owe much to the inveterate busybodies.

The century produced a large quantity of manuals, dictionaries, and technical brochures. Campbell's professional manual
informs us about the training and education necessary for all sorts
of careers; Postelthwait's commercial dictionary not only establishes business techniques but also serves as a sounding board for
English commercial interests; and Justus Möser or Jakob Marperger filled reams of paper with reflections on public issues—
from the decline of German trade to the rules at commercial fairs.
The line between manual and tract, between description and
prescription, is often hard to define, but here one will find technical details on education and trade unavailable elsewhere.

In the eighteenth century, the popular press had its greatest
growth in England. After 1760 the island was flooded with new
journals that appealed to an ever-widening audience. This collection contains samples from *The North Briton* and *The Annual
Register*, each distinct in format and appeal, but each reflecting
an increasing concern with current issues and less demand for
literary excellence. On the Continent there was nothing comparable to the English press. The *Ephémérides du Citoyen*, suppressed in 1778, was one of the best examples of French journalism. It criticized current practices in education and slavery with
the help of facts and figures in the manner of English improvers.
But as historical sources, the English newspapers are decidedly
more serviceable. The history of the French press really begins
with the French Revolution.

Here, then, are the main categories of eighteenth-century
sources in social history, and samples of each will be found in this
book. Most documents have been taken from printed sources
available in this country, with a sampling of unpublished material
from France and Italy. Not unexpectedly, the largest number of
documents concern Britain and France, but the reader will also
find substantial selections from German and Italian sources. The
amount of material from eastern Europe is small, but other
volumes in this series are designed to treat this important area.

Editing a collection of documents in European social history
implies a double task. The collection should provide a representative sample of source materials and still offer a comprehensive
survey of the major issues or problems of the period. In this book
various types of materials will be integrated into the historical

survey. The book is divided into eleven sections, each dealing with a particular topic in eighteenth-century social history, such as aristocracy, agriculture, the family, education, or religion. Each of these sections is introduced by a brief review of the topic [12] and contains from five to ten documents of various lengths. Each document is introduced by a short explanation of the nature of the source, placing it in a broader historical context. By employing two levels of introduction, the editors hope to provide an adequate setting and a certain continuity in the material.

[12] No claim is made that these reviews are more than points of departure. For an excellent comprehensive treatment of European social history in the eighteenth century, see Matthew S. Anderson, *Europe in the Eighteenth Century, 1713–1783* (New York, 1961).

I

Town and Country

WHEN ARTHUR YOUNG, the famous English traveler, hesitated to publish his diary, a friend told him: "Depend upon it, Young, these notes you write at the moment are more likely to please than what you will produce coldly." [1] No doubt Young's travel journal commanded more readers than did his detailed observations on agriculture. Indeed, the eighteenth century was a golden age of the traveler's diary, fostered as it was by a reading public increasingly interested in foreign lands and exotic customs. Supplementing the travelers' accounts, the shrewd comments of self-appointed observers such as Louis Sébastien Mercier lend an intensely human dimension to brick and mortar. Equally impressionistic are the autobiographical allusions of literary figures such as Goethe and of memoir writers such as the Count de Ségur. Together these sources provide the physical setting for a social history of eighteenth-century Europe.

The first two documents in this section provide a picture of Europe's two most important urban conglomerations—London and Paris. Both authors are observant, though their talents are different. Hence, the London of Archenholz emerges in regimented detail, beginning with the sumptuous town houses of the West End and ending with the ingenious central heating of the Bank of England. Although falling short of present criteria for quantification in social history, Archenholz has a marked tendency to count and measure. By contrast, Mercier's day in Paris is impressionistic and imaginative. He flits quickly from one image to another, from the processions of legal practitioners—with "wigs, gowns, and brief-bags"—to cab horses' hoofs pawing the pavement during the dinner hour, from the swarms of workmen returning home to the shouts of fish hawkers near the Quai de la Vallée. Yet both descriptions—quantitative and imaginative—evoke the diversity and temper of a great city.

Goethe was, of course, a literary figure. Yet his remarks on Frankfurt are more those of the social observer than the poet. Goethe depicts the town of his youth with its market stalls, *Rathaus*, cathedral,

---

[1] Arthur Young, *Travels in France in 1787, 1788, and 1789* (London, 1794), p. 13.

monastic enclosures, local festivals, and traditions. He reminds us that not all of Europe's towns were burgeoning commercial or industrial centers.

Arthur Young, an agronomist and country squire, was quick to seize the contrast between town and country. Although well aware of the benefits of commerce and industry as well as the pleasures of urban living, Young was ever on guard against the dangers of the city devouring the capital of the countryside. The description of his trip through Brittany reveals this anxiety. He was struck by the contrast between the Breton countryside and the Atlantic port of Nantes. "Three hundred miles of waste, desert, and heather leading to within three miles of the great commercial city . . . no gentle transition from ease to comfort . . . from beggary to profusion in one step," wrote Young. The failure of landlords to invest in farm improvements and their habit of spending instead on the "luxuries of a capital" was the root of the evil, he thought.

To the contrasts between city and town, between town and country, add those within the countryside itself. Could the difference between the Combourg of Chateaubriand and the Chambord of Marshal de Saxe be more striking? Combourg—a collection of mud huts huddled under the conical towers of a medieval manorhouse in a region of forest and heath. Chambord—an enormous pleasure château set in the center of 20,000 acres of park and woodland in the lush Loire Valley. Two *pays*, two worlds—one of a miserable peasantry and an austere gentry, the other of aristocratic opulence, of retainers and hounds, the insulated life of the court nobility.

To these variations must be added the contrast between West and East Europe. To cross the Elbe into Prussia or to leave Budapest for the Transylvanian plains was already to enter another society. But for contemporary western Europeans to travel east of Berlin across the plains of Poland to the steppes of Russia was to enter another civilization. A French aristocrat like Count de Ségur or a German professor like Georg Forster reflect the smug superiority of westerners not a little frightened by the melancholy vastness of the eastern plains. On the other hand, the Englishman William Coxe traveled more widely, probed more deeply, and produced a more balanced, informative picture of Russian society. The images of "gloomy forest" and "scorching plain" are relieved by rural folklore and song, by noble hospitality, and by the charm of St. Petersburg on the banks of the Neva. Yet Coxe's balanced view was probably exceptional. One suspects that Robert Ker Porter's sketches of a primitive, picturesque, and sometimes ridiculous people come closer to a western impression of Russian society.

1. *The Metropolis of London*

ALTHOUGH THERE are many travelers' accounts of London in the eighteenth century, this description of the great metropolis by the assiduous German observer Archenholz is particularly informative. If Archenholz lacks a keen sense of the picturesque or the intimately personal, he is so impressed by the wealth and magnificence of London that he gives us a mass of detail. Archenholz is as much struck by the modern comfort and convenience as he is by artistic beauty and the exterior signs of wealth. Central heating, home plumbing, street lighting, sidewalks, and show-window displays seem to him marvels of modern technique, generations ahead of the rest of Europe—as indeed they were. Everywhere he sees the propulsion of public improvement and of private energies.

The passage tells us something about the observer as well. Archenholz cannot refrain from identifying philistine elements in some of the City's buildings, and there is a patronizing tone to his conclusion that English aristocrats were at last leaving their country estates for a more refined life in the metropolis. Throughout is found the ambivalence between admiration and skepticism so often found in the provincial visitor to the Big City. Yet one major impression pervades all detail—London is the great, growing metropolis of the western world.

Source: J. W. Archenholz, *England und Italien* (Leipzig, 1786), vol. I, pp. 105–112, 115–118, 129–131.

London

THIRTY YEARS ago [1756] people were still arguing about whether London or Paris was the larger town. But Paris has fixed boundaries that must be recognized when buildings are to be built, while London has not yet been subjected to this necessary limitation. Therefore, there can no longer be any question that the English have the misfortune of possessing a larger capital than the French. Furthermore, many large villages consisting usually of farmhouses are contiguous to the city proper and thus form an enormous conglomeration without measure or end. It is estimated that 43,000 houses have been built in London between 1762 and 1779. A number of local patriots tried to control this growing evil. They called it madness to cover the County of Middlesex with bricks until clever Lord North thought it advisable to tax them. But in a way, this only served to encourage the building mania, for the entrepreneurs paid no attention to the tax and made their houses all the more attractive and comfortable since they were sure to find tenants. In the last twenty years there has been a regular migration from the East End to the West End of London. Many people have moved from the East End, where no building is being done, to the West End, where the most delightful fields and gardens have been changed into streets. The East End, especially the quarters along the banks of the Thames, consists of poorly built houses on narrow, crooked and badly paved streets. All the sailors live here, as well as the artisans connected with shipbuilding and most of the town's Jews. Consequently, it forms an extraordinary contrast with the West End, where one sees almost nothing but pretty houses, sumptuous squares, very straight and beautifully lighted streets, and the best pavement in Europe. If all of London were built in this fashion, nothing in the world would be comparable to it.

It is strange—and no traveler has ever commented on it—that the west end of town, comprising more than half of London and completely separated from the City, does not have a name. If they refer to it in the City or elsewhere, they get around this difficulty by simply naming the street, and the whole section is called "the other side of town." Many travelers and geographers call this enormous complex of streets and squares "Westminster," but in reality Westminster only takes up about one tenth of this area. Part of it is called "the Liberties of Westminster" in official documents, but the rest belongs to the County of Middlesex. Since everything in this country is unusual and strange, we must not be surprised that the capital not only is located in different counties but also falls under a number of different jurisdictions. The City, being the smallest section, has its own magistracy, while the rest of the town is under the jurisdiction of justices of the peace, so that we find a considerable difference in matters of police. That of the City is more strict and rigidly enforced and in general its inhabitants are notable for their order and industriousness. Two towns many miles apart could not be more different from each other than the City and the West End of London. They differ in their administration and police, in their privileges, the style of their houses, their streets, their churches, their manners, etc. The City alone, and not the rest of London, has the privilege, among many others, of sending representatives to Parliament. The voting inhabitants of the other sections elect the representatives from Middlesex, Surrey, Kent, and Westminster, according to their residence.

Most of the houses in the City have been built after the terrible fire of 1666, when 13,400 houses, 87 churches, 26 hospitals, etc., were burned to the ground. There was not time to think about regularity or convenience; everyone rushed to find some sort of shelter. This rush is evident everywhere in the many poorly built, ugly, dark houses, the crooked and usually narrow streets, the bad location of churches and other public buildings. All these mistakes have been carefully avoided in the West End. In the City, the churches are clustered together to an unusual degree, since they were rebuilt exactly where they had been before—and one can imagine that in earlier times when convents were so numerous, a town like London was certainly not lacking in churches and convents. But if there are too many of them in the City, there are too few in the West End, where the zeal for building churches has in no way kept up with the rage for building houses, so that in some parts of the town 6,000 and more houses belong to one parish.

At eight in the morning, when all the shops and warehouses in the City are already open and everyone is bustling about, most of the streets in the West End still seem completely dead. Everyone is still asleep, even the servants; one does not hear a single carriage and feels as if he were coming to a deserted place. This difference extends to eating, drinking, distractions, dress, the manner of speaking, etc., and naturally fosters a kind of mutual contempt. The West Londoners are derided by the inhabitants of the City for their idleness, their love of luxury, and their fondness for French manners; but the West Londoners amply repay this derision by depicting the City Englishman as an impolite, uncouth animal who only sees merit in money. The courtiers especially expend a great deal of wit ridiculing them on those solemn occasions when the deputies of the City present messages of gratitude or congratulations and petitions to the king. Usually, the deputation is very large and the king receives it seated upon his throne. Obviously, in such a situation a bourgeois,[1] unfamiliar as he is with court manners, will not act like a courtier for whom the study of court etiquette is the most exalted object of human endeavor. This mutual derision is reflected in street songs and in the theater; it even comes up in Parliament. On such occasions in Italy the daggers would not be idle, but in England there are no dangerous consequences. On the contrary, this sort of thing serves to distract the nation's spleen. However, young people, from the City in particular, when they frequent society in the West End, where they are not known, are careful not to reveal their residence, fearing to arouse suspicion about their fine manners.

The English nobility's old habit of spending the greater part of the year on their estates and only a short time in town is responsible for the scarcity of palaces in London. Even though staying in the capital has become quite attractive of late and many remain considerably longer, Englishmen of rank continue to consider their estates as their real residence and their house in London as a kind of *pied à terre*. Many who have revenues of £20,-000[2] and more live in London houses of hardly a dozen rooms. Consequently, they and their numerous servants are rather crowded. But this situation will soon be remedied since many lords have started to build magnificent houses. I think it can be said that this turn of events has not been influenced by the government, even though a numerous resident nobility is desirable to every court since it enhances splendor and also guarantees the court against the machinations of the great landowners. But in this case the distractions of London alone attract the nobles. They have already become less interested in hunting and more in the arts and all that makes for a more refined way of life. It is likely that the next generation of English nobles will live entirely in London as is the case in Paris. Since this [migration to the capital] became the custom in almost all Europe, the internal disturbances directed against the monarch by the great nobles of all states have ceased. In our century we have seen such occurrences only in England and Poland, where the nobility resides mostly in

[1] The German word here is *Bürger*.
[2] This sum was equivalent to about 400,000 French livres, or about $400,000 in 1968. These are *revenues*.

the country.[3] Therefore, it must be admitted that the love of luxury, so widely criticized, can have beneficial consequences.[4]

This tendency among rich landowners to make London their permanent residence has been the reason why in recent years certain entrepreneurs have built as a speculation wide streets and magnificent squares surrounded by houses the likes of which have never been seen in London. These houses, which might well be called palaces, are very large and extremely comfortable. They have two floors underground, which receive sufficient light from a sort of courtyard in front of every house and contain a number of pleasant rooms. These serve as servant quarters, kitchens, pantries, etc. In this manner, all the rest of the building above ground is reserved for the use of the owner.

The entrepreneurs who built these houses usually rent the terrain for ninety-nine years, after which they transfer the building to the landowner or negotiate a new, short-term lease. Nothing but this custom, based on a property right, accounts for the lack of solidity of the houses and the scarcity of real architectural works of art in London. Had they been built by wealthy private parties this would not have been the case. But this drawback is compensated by the great convenience with which these houses have been designed inside. Moreover, every house is provided with water by means of big underground pipes which run through every street. These are extremely useful in case of fire, since the hoses can be attached to openings in the pipes which are constantly replenished and provide ample supplies of water. Not only water from the Thames is used for this purpose, but also a rather wide river called the New River has been redirected toward the town. The river water is raised by pumps and distributed among a number of canals. . . .

No town in Europe has as many beautiful squares as London. They all are surrounded by large, attractive houses, and no stores or warehouses are seen there. Usually the middle of the square consists of a pretty green area to serve as a promenade. Some of them are ornamented with statues, obelisks, or other decoration.

[3] Archenholz must be referring to the English Civil War and "Glorious Revolution" of the seventeenth century. Poland is more to the point.
[4] Archenholz makes no mention of sessions of Parliament as a lure to London.

Never are these agreeable places disfigured by markets as is the case unfortunately in other countries. (We are so accustomed to this that we no longer realize its unseemliness.) In the squares of London one sees only richness and wealth. Among other benefits, the people who live there breathe a pure air and are not bothered by any noise. The numerous markets of the town have their fixed locations away from all traffic. They are not placed along the main thoroughfares, so that only shoppers frequent them. This police measure should be imitated by all large towns [in Europe].

Among the distinguishing features of London are the stone paving and the lighting. Only twenty years ago no large town in Europe was as badly paved as London. For a long time people were aware of this but nothing was done about it, just as nothing was done about the large, oversized signs which hung in front of all the houses, darkening the streets and often falling and killing people. Two beneficial acts of Parliament, promulgated almost simultaneously, quickly remedied this situation. The signs disappeared promptly and £400,000 was appropriated by Parliament to provide a stone pavement which is still the only one of its kind. Wide side stones, or rather slabs, have been placed along both sides of all the streets, so that the pedestrians can walk in safety and comfort in the most populated areas, even in the greatest confusion of carriages.[5] No coachman may touch these side stones, under fine of 20 shillings. Even if he should be unable to move for hours, he is absolutely prohibited from driving over so much as the edge of these stones. Large sums have been appropriated for the upkeep of this stone pavement. Furthermore, an unusual law has been made whereby all carts, wagons, and other heavy vehicles coming to London must have wheels six inches wide. These serve to anchor the pavement stones and compensate for the damage done by the narrow wheels of coaches and other vehicles. In order to defray the extra costs of the carters and drivers, the government has exempted them from certain taxes.

Since the English are not parsimonious when it comes to public institutions and everything bears the stamp of generosity, street lighting is also outstanding and incomparable to anything of its kind. All the lamps are large crystal balls, each fitted with three or four wicks and fastened to poles standing a few paces apart.

[5] English visitors to Paris complained of the mud splashed by the carriages on helpless pedestrians.—Editors.

Every day and all year round these lamps are lighted at sundown without regard to the seasons or to the state of the moon. Oxford Street alone has more lamps than all of Paris. Even the roads seven to eight miles out of London are bordered by lamps, and since many of them go out in all directions, they provide a marvelous sight out in the fields, especially in the County of Surrey which is laced with roads. In addition, there are fences along these roads and in some places country houses and gardens. Every 500 paces there is a little shed with a bell for the night watchman, who is armed. Since all the shops in town are open until ten o'clock in the evening, and each is provided with lighting, this profusion of light produces an extraordinary effect. The Prince of Monaco once came to England by invitation of the king to attend the funeral of the Duke of York, who had died while visiting him. He arrived in London in the evening and found the illumination so remarkable that he thought it especially prepared in his honor. It was inconceivable to him that it could be like this every evening. When his error became known, it gave rise to a great deal of joking.

For the reasons explained above, London has many large and handsome houses, but few real palaces with *cours d'honneur*, extended wings, and the like. Yet Burlington House, Northumberland House, Somerset House (now being built with such magnificence at public expense), and some others certainly deserve this designation, though English custom denies it. This, no doubt, has to do with the equality of which the English are so proud. The title of "palace" is reserved for the residence of the king, and the largest and most magnificent palaces belonging to any other Englishmen would never be so named, not even the residences of the royal brothers or the Prince of Wales....

Among the other great public buildings of the City are the Stock Exchange and the Bank. The Stock Exchange, though not the largest, is surely the most magnificent of merchants' exchanges in Europe. It is surrounded by innumerable coffeehouses, where more business is transacted than at the Exchange itself. Conveniently near are the post office, the insurance companies, the palace of the Lord Mayor, the houses of the East India and other trading companies, the Bank, the homes of almost all the bankers, the offices of brokers, notaries, and the like.

The Bank of England is splendid indeed, though it consists of only one story. Most of the rooms are lighted from above. It has been thoroughly and artfully equipped with iron stoves with neither openings nor pipes exposed, which are stoked from below the main floor. Each one of these stoves is worth £500. Since the Bank belongs to the entire nation, not only are all the rooms and halls open to everyone, but one large room has been furnished with a great many desks complete with large inkstands, quills, and sand-shakers. These are at the disposal of even the most common citizen who happens to come in from the streets without any business at the Bank. I cannot help but admire such republican ways, even though some may think them trivial.

2. A Day in Paris

LOUIS SÉBASTIEN MERCIER wrote twenty volumes of impressions on life in Paris. The work was without plan and seems to follow the moods of the author, but in these pages Parisians come to life in all their human folly. Here is "daily life" in vivid authenticity, punctuated by shrewd comment and flashes of wit and humor. Mercier was a passionate person, interested in all of man's activities, quirks, failings. He said himself that he survived the Revolution by sheer curiosity. Fortunately, he lacks the pessimistic, cynical quality of Restif de la Bretonne. Mercier clings to the conviction that man is not chained to caprice, that fate is still in his own hands. "This is your behavior, these are the tyrannies, little and great, that you suffer, this is your life. . . ."[1]

But the moralist, the philosopher never intrude. Mercier's descriptions are delightful. His *Tableau de Paris* is a masterpiece of its kind, painting the lives of all classes, trades, and professions with the delicacy of Fragonard and the intensity of Chardin.

Source: Helen Simpson, ed., *The Waiting City: Paris 1782–88.* *Being an Abridgement of Louis-Sebastian Mercier's "Le tableau de Paris,"* trans. Helen Simpson (Philadelphia, 1933), pp. 74–80.

How the Day Goes

IT IS curious to see how, amid what seems perpetual life and movement, certain hours keep their own characteristics, whether

[1] Helen Simpson, ed., *The Waiting City: Paris 1782–88* (Philadelphia, 1933), Preface, p. 14.

of bustle or of leisure. Every round of the clock-hand sets another scene in motion, each different from the last, though all about equal in length.

Seven o'clock in the morning sees all the gardeners wheeling their barrows and empty baskets back out of town again. No carriages are about, and not a presentable soul, except a few neat clerks hurrying to their offices.

Nine o'clock sets all the barbers in motion, covered from head to foot with flour—hence their soubriquet of "whitings"—wig in one hand, tongs in the other. Waiters from the lemonade-shops are busy with trays of coffee and rolls, breakfast for those who live in furnished rooms; while along the boulevards trot would-be horsemen learning to sit on, with a lackey riding behind; it is the passer-by, often, who suffers most from their inexperience.

An hour later the Law comes into action; a black cloud of legal practitioners and hangers-on descend upon the Châtelet, and the other courts; a procession of wigs and gowns and brief-bags, with plaintiffs and defendants at their heels. [*Mercier's note:* The saying goes, you should always take three bags into court; one for your money, one for your brief, and one to stow your patience in.]

Midday is the stockbrokers' hour, and the idlers'; the former hurry off to the Exchange, the latter to the Palais-Royal. The Saint-Honoré quarter, where all the financiers live, is at its busiest now, its streets are crowded with the customers and clients of the great.

At two o'clock those who have invitations to dine set out, dressed in their best, powdered, adjusted, and walking on tiptoe not to soil their stockings. All the cabs are engaged, not one is to be found on the rank; there is a good deal of competition for these vehicles, and you may see two would-be fares carry a cab by assault from different sides, jumping in together and furiously disputing which was first; on which the cabman whips up and drives them both off to the Commissary of Police, who takes the burden of decision off his shoulders.

Three o'clock and the streets are not so full; everyone is at dinner; there is a momentary calm, soon to be broken, for at five o'clock the din is as though the gates of hell were opened, the streets are impassable with traffic going all ways at once, towards the playhouses or the public gardens. Cafés are at their busiest.

Towards seven the din dies down, everywhere and all at once. You can hear the cab-horses' hoofs pawing the stones as they wait —in vain. It is as though the whole town were gagged and bound, suddenly, by an invisible hand. This is the most dangerous time of the whole day for thieves and such, especially towards autumn, when the days begin to draw in; for the watch is not yet about, and violence takes its opportunity. [*Mercier's note:* A man was arrested in 1769, who had killed three persons in six days at this season of the year, mid-October, before he was caught. His weapon was a kind of sling.]

Night falls; and, while scene-shifters set to work at the play-houses, swarms of other workmen, carpenters, masons and the like, make their way towards the poorer quarters. They leave white footprints from the plaster on their shoes, a trail that any eye can follow. They are off home, and to bed, at the hour which finds Madame la Marquise sitting down to her dressing-table to prepare for the business of the night.

At nine this begins; they all set off for the play. Houses tremble as the coaches rattle by, but soon the noise ceases; all the fine ladies are making their evening visits, short ones, before supper. Now the prostitutes begin their night parade, breasts uncovered, heads tossing, colour high on their cheeks, and eyes as bold as their hands. These creatures, careless of the light from shop-windows and street lamps, follow and accost you, trailing through the mud in their silk stockings and low shoes, with words and gestures well matched for obscenity. This sort of thing keeps the pure women safe, that is the cant, the excuse; without these crea-tures there would be more assaults, and the innocent would suffer. Certainly, whether or no this is the reason, rape and assault have become much rarer. But it remains a scandal for all that, and one unthinkable in a provincial town, that these women should ply their trade at the very doors of decent folk, and that honest wives and young girls should be obliged to see them at their business; for it is impossible not to see them, and worse, not to overhear what they say.

Still, by eleven most of these are off the streets. People are at supper, private people, that is; for the cafés begin at this hour to turn out their patrons, and to send the various idlers and workless and poets back to their garrets for the night. A few prostitutes still linger, but they have to use more circumspection, for the watch is about, patrolling the streets, and this is the hour when they "gather 'em in"; that is the traditional expression.

A quarter after midnight, a few carriages make their way home, taking the non-card-players back to bed. These lend the town a sort of transitory life; the tradesman wakes out of his first sleep at the sound of them, and turns to his wife, by no means unwilling. More than one young Parisian must owe his existence to this sudden passing rattle of wheels. Thunder sends up the birth-rate here too, as it does everywhere else.

At one in the morning six thousand peasants arrive, bringing the town's provision of vegetables and fruits and flowers, and make straight for the Halles; their beasts have come some eighteen leagues perhaps, and are weary. As for the market itself, it never sleeps, Morpheus never shakes his poppy-seed there. Perpetual noise, perpetual motion, the curtain never rings down on this enormous stage; first come the fishmongers, and after these the egg-dealers, and after these the retail buyers; for the Halles keep all the other markets of Paris going; they are the warehouse whence these draw their supplies. The food of the whole city is shifted and sorted in high-piled baskets; you may see eggs, pyramids of eggs, moved here and there, up steps and down, in and out of the throngs, miraculously; not one is ever broken.

Then the brandy starts to flow across tavern counters; poor stuff, half water, but laced with raw spirit. Porters and peasants toss down this liquor, the soberer of them drink wine. The noise of voices never stops, there is hardly a light to be seen; most of the deals are done in the dark, as though these were people of a different race, hiding in their caverns from the light of the sun. The fish salesmen, who are the first comers, apparently never see daylight, and go home as the street lamps start to flicker, just before dawn; but if eyes are no use, ears take their place; everyone bawls his loudest, and you must know their jargon, to be able to catch what your own vendor shouts in this bedlam of sound. On the Quai de la Vallée it is the same story; but there hares and poultry take the place of herrings and cuts of salmon.

This impenetrable din contrasts oddly with the sleeping streets, for at that hour none but thieves and poets are awake.

Twice a week, at six, those distributors of the staff of life, the bakers of Gonesse, bring in an enormous quantity of loaves to the town, and may take none back through the barriers; no matter if they cannot sell them at a profit, the town keeps tight hold on all bread that comes its way. And at this same hour workmen take up their tools, and trudge off to their day's labour. Coffee with milk is, unbelievably, the favoured drink among these stalwarts nowadays.

At street-corners, where the pale light from a street lamp falls, the coffee women stand, carrying their tin urns on their backs; they sell their coffee in earthenware cups, two sous a cup, one penny, and not too well sugared at that; but our workmen find it very much to their taste. Incredible as it may sound, the company of confectioners, incorporated by statute and all the rest of it, has put every possible obstacle in the way of this perfectly legitimate trade. They, in their mirrored halls, sell this same coffee at two and a half times the price; but workmen have neither time nor inclination to be looking at themselves in mirrors while they drink.

So coffee-drinking has become a habit, and one so deep-rooted that the working classes will start the day on nothing else. It is not costly, and has more flavour to it, and more nourishment too, than anything else they can afford to drink; so they consume immense quantities, and say that if a man can only have coffee for breakfast it will keep him going till nightfall. They take only two meals in the twenty-four hours; that at midday, and the evening snack of supper, what they call the *persillade*.

Now that it is full morning you may see the prostitutes' clients emerging, white-faced, their clothes in disorder; and as for their expression, it is rather that of apprehension than of remorse; the lees of pleasure taste bitter by day, but pleasure is a habit for all that, a tyrant who will not let them go; they will creep back again to-morrow, and so on till the end.

And what of the gamblers? Out they come, from the exclusive club, or the filthy den, paler even than the prostitutes' victims; some striking their foreheads, cursing their luck, others with bulging pockets, which the next night's play will empty.

Laws are powerless against this devouring passion; the desire for gain is at the root of it, a desire that runs through all classes alike. The Government itself panders to it; what else are lotteries but gambling under another name? Public gambling is licensed, private gambling is illegal; that is how the law at present stands.

If the sybarites of Paris, those who like to lie abed till noon, had their way, there would be no smiths in the city, no horses shod, and no pots and pans mended; all such noise would be banished without the walls, together with those street criers who, it must be admitted, make day hideous with their performances, and against whose voices neither shut windows nor thick walls avail. These, the lie-abeds, would have a dozen trades suppressed or exiled, that they might sleep till noon behind the drawn curtains of their alcoves.

Their complaint is well founded; but if their remedy were followed, and carried to extremes, there would be no hats made in Paris, because of the stink of the felt; no leather tanned, no varnish nor perfume made for the same reason, although they themselves make use of these commodities; nor could they permit the tobacconist to ply his trade, by reason of the snuff that gets in their noses as they pass his door. Privilege would allow no shopwindows, but only porticoes to shelter carriages; would strew straw in the streets from midnight till midday, when Privilege does the world the honour of waking; would have soldiers, as they march to the changing of the guard, muffle their drums till that hour; for only Privilege may be privileged to fill the streets with the clatter of wheels and hoofs and to keep others from sleeping.

On the tenth, twentieth, and thirtieth days of the month, from ten o'clock till midday, you may see messengers bent double under the weight of the sacks they carry, and which are full of money; they run as if Satan were at their heels, or an enemy army at the gates of Paris; and it is a sign of our financial backwardness that we have been able to devise no equivalent for these mounds of metal, some paper token which might represent the transfer, instead of shifting actual cash from one strong-room to another.

Nearly every year, towards the middle of November, influenza and catarrh begin their rounds; the reason is, the sudden drop in temperature, and the fogs which result from it, and which check perspiration. There are always a good many deaths from these two causes; the Parisian, who takes nothing seriously, calls these really dangerous afflictions by pet names, the *grippe*, the *coquette;* and three days later is himself gripped, and coquetted with, and, like as not, buried.

People court danger by going straight out into the night air from some hot room or other; perspiration is suddenly checked; and though this present fashion is a good one, of wearing great cloaks, they are not always donned soon enough to be of use. Women often have to wait while their carriages are called; and these delicate creatures, shivering under a portico or at the top of a flight of steps, would do well not to trust altogether to their cloaks to preserve them from illness.

3. Goethe's Frankfurt

GOETHE's *Dichtung und Wahrheit* is more an autobiographical than a literary work, where the poet's talents seem firmly anchored to objective observation. At the same time, Goethe's romantic sensitivity lends a quaint and warm quality to the description of his native Frankfurt with its walls, moats, crowded quarters, and bustling markets. To see a small boy exploring such venerable buildings as the *Römer* and such time-honored institutions as the *Pfeifergericht*, where Goethe's grandfather presided, adds charm without destroying accuracy.

Source: Johann Wolfgang von Goethe, *Autobiography, Truth and Poetry: From My Life*, trans. John Oxenford (London, 1848), pp. 7ff.

IT WAS properly about this period that I first became acquainted with my native city, which I strolled over with more and more freedom, in every direction, sometimes alone, and sometimes in the company of lively companions. To convey to others in any degree the impression made upon me by these grave and revered spots, I must here introduce a description of my birth-place, as in its different parts it was gradually unfolded to me. I loved more than anything else to promenade on the great bridge over the Maine. Its length, its firmness, and its fine appearance, rendered it a notable structure, and it was, besides, almost the only memorial left from ancient times of the precautions due from the civil government to its citizens. The beautiful stream above and below the bridge, attracted my eye, and when the gilt weathercock on the bridge-cross glittered in the sunshine, I always had a pleasant feeling. Generally I extended my walk through Sachsenhausen, and for a *Kreutzer* was ferried comfortably across the river. I was now again on this side of the stream, stole along to the wine

market, and admired the mechanism of the cranes when goods
were unloaded. But it was particularly entertaining to watch the
arrival of the market-boats, from which so many and such extraordinary figures were seen to disembark. On entering the city,
the Saalhof, which at least stood on the spot where the Castle of
Emperor Charlemagne and his successors was reported to have
been, was greeted every time with profound reverence. One liked
to lose oneself in the old trading town, particularly on market-
days, among the crowd collected about the church of St. Bartholomew. From the earliest times, throngs of buyers and sellers
had gathered there, and the place being thus occupied, it was not
easy in later days to bring about a more roomy and cheerful
arrangement. The booths of the so-called *Pfarreisen* were very
important places for us children, and we carried many a *Batzen*
to them in order to purchase sheets of coloured paper stamped
with gold animals. But seldom, however, could one make one's
way through the narrow, crowded, and dirty market-place. I call
to mind, also, that I always flew past the adjoining meat-stalls,
narrow and disgusting as they were, in perfect horror. On the
other hand, the Roman Hill [*Römerberg*] was a most delightful
place for walking. The way to the New-Town, along by the new
shops, was always cheering and pleasant; yet we regretted that a
street did not lead directly towards the Church of the Holy
Virgin, and that we always had to go a round-about way by the
Hasengasse, or the Catherine Gate. But what chiefly attracted the
child's attention, were the many little towns within the town, the
fortresses within the fortress; viz., the walled monastic enclosures,
and several other precincts, remaining from earlier times, and
more or less like castles—as the Nuremberg Court, the Compo-
stella, the Braunfels, the ancestral house of the family of Stall-
burg, and several strongholds, in later days transformed into
dwellings and warehouses. No architecture of an elevating kind
was then to be seen in Frankfort, and every thing pointed to a
period long past and unquiet, both for town and district. Gates
and towers, which defined the bounds of the old city—then further on again, gates, towers, walls, bridges, ramparts, moats, with
which the new city was encompassed—all showed, but too
plainly, that a necessity for guarding the common weal in disastrous times had induced these arrangements, that all the
squares and streets, even the newest, broadest, and best laid out,

owed their origin to chance and caprice and not to any regulating
mind. A certain liking for the antique was thus implanted in the
Boy, and was specially nourished and promoted by old chronicles
and wood-cuts, as for instance, those of Grave relating to the
siege of Frankfort. At the same time a different taste was developed in him for observing the conditions of mankind, in their
manifold variety and naturalness, without regard to their importance or beauty. It was, therefore, one of our favourite walks,
which we endeavoured to take now and then in the course of a
year, to follow the circuit of the path inside the city walls. Gardens, courts, and back buildings extend to the *Zwinger;* and we
saw many thousand people amid their little domestic and secluded circumstances. From the ornamental and show gardens of
the rich, to the orchards of the citizen, anxious about his necessities—from thence to the factories, bleaching-grounds, and similar establishments, even to the burying-grounds—for a little
world lay within the limits of the city—we passed a varied,
strange, spectacle, which changed at every step, and with the
enjoyment of which our childish curiosity was never satisfied. In
fact, the celebrated Devil-upon-two-sticks, when he lifted the
roofs of Madrid at night, scarcely did more for his friend, than
was here done for us in the bright sunshine and open air. The
keys that were to be made use of in this journey, to gain us a
passage through many a tower, stair and postern, were in the
hands of the authorities, whose subordinates we never failed to
coax into good-humour.

But a more important, and in one sense more fruitful place for
us, was the Council-House, named from the Romans. In its lower
vault-like halls we liked but too well to lose ourselves. We obtained an entrance, too, into the large and very simple session-
room of the Council. The walls as well as the arched ceiling were
white, though wainscotted to a certain height, and the whole was
without a trace of painting, or any kind of carved work; only,
high up on the middle wall, might be read this brief inscription:

> One man's word is no man's word,
> Justice needs that both be heard.

After the most ancient fashion, benches were ranged around
the wainscotting, and raised one step above the floor for the accommodation of the members of the assembly. This readily suggested to us why the order of rank in our senate was distributed

by benches. To the left of the door, on the opposite corner, sat the *Schöffen;* in the corner itself the *Schultheiss,* who alone had a small table before him; those of the second bench sat in the space to his left as far as the wall to where the windows were; while along the windows ran the third bench, occupied by the craftsmen. In the midst of the hall stood a table for the registrar [*Protoculführer*].

Once within the *Römer,* we even mingled with the crowd at the audiences of the burgomasters. But whatever related to the election and coronation of the Emperors possessed a greater charm. We managed to gain the favour of the keepers, so as to be allowed to mount the new gay imperial staircase, which was painted in fresco, and on other occasions closed with a grating. The election-chamber, with its purple hangings and admirably-fringed gold borders, filled us with awe. The representations of animals on which little children or genii, clothed in the imperial ornaments and laden with the insignia of the Empire, made a curious figure, were observed by us with great attention; and we even hoped that we might live to see, some time or other, a coronation with our own eyes. They had great difficulty to get us out of the great imperial hall, when we had been once fortunate enough to steal in; and we reckoned him our truest friend who, while we looked at the half-lengths of all the emperors painted around at a certain height, would tell us something of their deeds. . . .

Half a year had scarcely passed away . . . before the fairs began, which always produced an incredible ferment in the heads of all children. The erection, in so short a time, of so many booths, creating a new town within the old one, the roll and crush, the unloading and unpacking of wares, excited from the very first dawn of consciousness an insatiable active curiosity and a boundless desire for childish property, which the Boy with increasing years endeavoured to gratify, in one way or another, as far as his little purse permitted. At the same time he obtained a notion of what the world produces, what it wants, and what the inhabitants of its different parts exchange with each other.

These great epochs, which came round regularly in spring and autumn, were announced by curious solemnities, which seemed the more dignified because they vividly brought before us the old time, and what had come down from it to ourselves. On Escort-day, the whole population were on their legs, thronging to the

Fahrgasse, to the bridge, and beyond *Sachsenhausen;* all the windows were occupied, though nothing unusual took place on that day; the crowd seeming to be there only for the sake of jostling each other, and the spectators merely to look at one another; for the real occasion of their coming did not begin till nightfall, and was then rather taken upon trust than seen with the eyes.

The affair was thus: in those old, unquiet times, when every one did wrong according to his pleasure, or helped the right as his liking led him, traders on their way to the fairs were so wilfully beset and harassed by waylayers, both of noble and ignoble birth, that princes and other persons of power caused their people to be accompanied to Frankfort by an armed escort. Now the burghers of the imperial city would yield no rights pertaining to themselves or their district; they went out to meet the advancing party; and thus contests often arose as to how far the escort should advance, or whether it had a right to enter the city at all. But, as this took place, not only in regard to matters of trade and fairs, but also when high personages came, in times of peace or war, and especially on the days of election; and as the affair often came to blows when a train which was not to be endured in the city strove to make its way in along with its lord, many negotiations had from time to time been resorted to, and many temporary arrangements concluded, though always with reservations of rights on both sides. The hope had not been relinquished of composing once for all a quarrel that had already lasted for centuries, inasmuch as the whole institution, on account of which it had been so long and often so hotly contested, might be looked upon as nearly useless, or at least as superfluous.

Meanwhile, on those days, the city cavalry in several divisions, each having a commander in front, rode forth from different gates and found on a certain spot some troopers or hussars of the persons entitled to an escort, who with their leaders were well received and entertained. They stayed till towards evening, and then rode back to the city, scarcely visible to the expectant crowd, many a city knight not being in a condition to manage his horse, or keep himself in the saddle. The most important bands returned by the bridge-gate, where the pressure was consequently the strongest. Last of all, just as night fell, the Nuremberg post-coach arrived, escorted in the same way, and always containing, as the people fancied, in pursuance of custom, an old woman. Its arrival, therefore, was a signal for all the urchins to break out into an ear-splitting shout, though it was utterly impossible to distinguish any one of the passengers within. The throng that pressed after the coach through the bridge-gate was quite incredible, and perfectly bewildering to the senses. The houses nearest the bridge were those, therefore, most in demand among spectators.

Another more singular ceremony, by which the people were excited in broad daylight, was the Piper's-court [*Pfeifergericht*]. It commemorated those early times when important larger trading-towns endeavoured, if not to abolish tolls altogether, at least to bring about a reduction of them as they increased in proportion with trade and industry. They were allowed this privilege by the Emperor who needed their aid, when it was in his power to grant it, but commonly only for one year; so that it had to be annually renewed. This was effected by means of symbolical gifts, which were presented before the opening of St. Bartholomew's Fair to the imperial magistrate [*Schultheiss*], who might have sometimes been the chief toll-gatherer; and, for the sake of a more imposing show, the gifts were offered when he was sitting in full court with the *Schöffen*. But when the chief magistrate afterwards came to be no longer appointed by the Emperor, and was elected by the city itself, he still retained these privileges; and thus both the immunities of the cities from toll, and the ceremonies by which the representatives from Worms, Nuremberg, and Old Bamberg once acknowledged the ancient favour, had come down to our times. The day before Lady-day, an open court was proclaimed. In an enclosed space in the great Imperial Hall, the Schöffen took their elevated seats; a step higher, sat the *Schultheiss* in the midst of them; while below on the right hand, were the procurators of both parties invested with plenipotentiary powers. The *Actuarius* begins to read aloud the weighty judgments reserved for this day; the lawyers demand copies, appeal, or do whatever else seems necessary. All at once a singular sort of music announces, if we may so speak, the advent of former centuries. It proceeds from three pipers, one of whom plays an old *shawm*, another a *sackbut*, and the third a *pommer*, or oboe. They wear blue mantles trimmed with gold, having the notes made fast to their sleeves, and their heads covered. Having thus left their inn at ten o'clock, followed by the deputies and their

attendants, and stared at by all, natives and strangers, they enter
the hall. The law proceedings are stayed—the pipers and their
train halt before the railing—the deputy steps in and stations
himself in front of the *Schultheiss*. The emblematic presents,
which were required to be precisely the same as in the old prece-
dents, consisted commonly of the staple wares of the city offering
them. Pepper passed, as it were, for everything else; and, even on
this occasion, the deputy brought a handsomely turned wooden
goblet filled with pepper. Upon it lay a pair of gloves, curiously
slashed, stitched, and tasseled with silk—a token of a favour
granted and received—such as the Emperor himself made use of
in certain cases. Along with this was a white staff, which in
former times was not easily dispensable in judicial proceedings.
Some small pieces of silver money were added; and the city of
Worms brought an old felt hat, which was always redeemed
again, so that the same one had been a witness of these ceremonies for many years.

After the deputy had made his address, handed over his
present, and received from the *Schultheiss* assurance of continued
favour, he quitted the enclosed circle, the pipers blew, the train
departed as it had come, the court pursued its business, until the
second and at last the third deputy had been introduced. For
each came some time after the other; partly that the pleasure of
the public might thus be prolonged, and partly because they were
always the same antiquated *virtuosi* whom Nuremberg, for itself
and its co-cities, had undertaken to maintain and produce annually at the appointed place.

We children were particularly interested in this festival, because we were not a little flattered to see our grandfather in a
place of so much honour; and because commonly, on the selfsame day, we used to visit him, quite modestly, in order that we
might, when my grandmother had emptied the pepper into her
spice box, lay hold of a cup or small rod, a pair of gloves or an old
Räder Albus. These symbolical ceremonies, restoring antiquity as
if by magic, could not be explained to us without leading us back
into past times and informing us of the manners, customs, and
feelings of those early ancestors who were so strangely made
present to us, by pipers and deputies seemingly risen from the
dead, and by tangible gifts, which might be possessed by ourselves.

4. *Arthur Young's Travels in France*

ARTHUR YOUNG possessed little of Mercier's talent for observing intimate human detail or Goethe's feeling for the picturesque. Yet ne had
qualities that made him more than an uninspired agronomist. He was
quite capable of enthusiasms, appreciative of the accomplishments of
Continentals, tolerant of mores and customs that differed from his
own. Doggedly practical and utilitarian, Young could still admire the
artistic legacy of the Medici, the reading clubs of Nantes, or the
superiority of French cuisine. Having resided a long time abroad, he
avoided stereotypes without losing all capacity for judgment. The
Chambord of de Saxe or the Chanteloup of Choiseul were useless follies, but the Liancourt of his friend, La Rochefoucauld-Liancourt
demonstrated to him that French nobles could be enlightened landlords. And Young recognized the regional variety of rural France—
that Breton peasants differed from Norman peasants and that there was
a world of difference between the rich soils of the Garonne Valley and
the limestone mountains of the Auvergne. Young did not approve of
the first acts of violence he witnessed in France in 1789, but he understood the Old Régime infinitely better than other would-be English
experts on French society, such as Edmund Burke. Arthur Young's
Travels in France remains one of the most thorough first-hand accounts of provincial France on the eve of the Revolution.

Source: Arthur Young, *Travels in France During the Years 1787,
1788, and 1789* (London, 1794), pp. 67–68, 97, 102–105.

From Auvergnac to Nantes

TURNED ASIDE to Auvergnac, the seat of the Count de la Bourdonaye, to whom I had a letter from the Duchess d'Anville, as a
person able to give me every species of intelligence relative to
Bretagne, having for five-and-twenty years been first syndic of the
noblesse. A fortuitous jumble of rocks and steeps could scarcely
form a worse road than these five miles: could I put as much faith
in two bits of wood laid over each other, as the good folks of the
country do, I should have crossed myself, but my blind friend,
with the most incredible sure-footedness, carried me safe over
such places, that if I had not been in the constant habit of the

saddle, I should have shuddered at, though guided by eyes keen
as Eclipse's; for I suppose a fine racer, on whose velocity so many
fools have been ready to lose their money, must have good eyes,
as well as good legs. Such a road, leading to several villages, and
one of the first noblemen of the province, shews what the state of
society must be;—no communication—no neighbourhood—no
temptation to the expenses which flow from society; a mere se-
clusion to save money in order to spend it in towns. The count
received me with great politeness; I explained to him my plan
and motives for travelling in France, which he was pleased very
warmly to approve, expressing his surprise that I should attempt
so large an undertaking, as such a survey of France, unsupported
by my government; I told him he knew very little of our government, if he supposed they would give a shilling to any agricultural project or projector; that whether the minister were whig or
tory made no difference, the party of THE PLOUGH never yet had
one on its side; and that England has had many Colberts,[1] but
not one Sully.[2] This led to much interesting conversation on the
balance of agriculture, manufactures, and commerce, and on the
means of encouraging them; and, in reply to his enquiries, I made
him understand their relations in England, and how our husbandry flourished in spite of our ministers, merely by the protection which civil liberty gives to property: and consequently that
it was in a poor situation, comparatively with what it would have
been in, had it received the same attention as manufactures and
commerce. I told M. de la Bourdonaye that his province of
Bretagne seemed to me to have nothing in it but privileges and
poverty; he smiled, and gave me some explanations that are important; but no nobleman can ever probe this evil as it ought to
be done, resulting as it does from the privileges going to themselves, and the poverty to the people. He shewed me his plantations, which are very fine and well thriven, and shelter him thoroughly on every side, even from the S.W. so near to the sea; from
his walks we see Belleisle and its neighbours, and a little isle or
rock belonging to him, which he says the King of England took

[1] Jean-Baptiste Colbert (1619–1683), famous minister of Louis XIV, whose
mercantilist policies were primarily aimed at stimulating French industrial
development.
[2] Duc de Sully (1599–1641), minister of Henry IV, who considered agriculture the basis of national prosperity.

from him after Sir Edward Hawke's victory, but that his majesty was kind enough to leave him his island after one night's possession. ——20 miles.

The 20th. Take my leave of Monsieur and Madame de la Bourdonaye, to whose politeness as well as friendly attentions I am much obliged. Towards Nazaire there is a fine view of the mouth of the Loire, from the rising grounds, but the headlands that form the embouchure are low, which takes off from that greatness of the effect which highlands give to the mouth of the Shannon. The swelling bosom of the Atlantic boundless to the right. Savanal is poverty itself. ——33 miles.

The 21st. Come to an improvement in the midst of these deserts, four good houses of stone and slate, and a few acres run to wretched grass, which have been tilled, but all savage, and become almost as rough as the rest. I was afterwards informed that this improvement, as it is called, was wrought by Englishmen, at the expence of a gentleman they ruined as well as themselves.–I demanded how it had been done? Pare and burn, and sow wheat, then rye, and then oats. Thus it is for ever and ever! the same follies, the same blundering, the same ignorance; and then all the fools in the country said, as they do now, that these wastes are good for nothing. To my amazement find the incredible circumstance, that they reach within three miles of the great commercial city of Nantes! This is a problem and a lesson to work at, but not at present. Arrive—go to the theatre, new built of fine white stone, having a magnificent portico of eight elegant Corinthian pillars in front, and four others, to separate the portico from a grand vestibule. Within all is gold and painting, and *a coup d'œil* at entering, that struck me forcibly. It is, I believe, twice as large as Drury-Lane, and five times as magnificent. It was Sunday, and therefore full. *Mon Dieu!* cried I to myself, do all the wastes, the deserts, the heath, ling, furz, broom, and bog, that I have passed for 300 miles, lead to this spectacle? What a miracle, that all this splendour and wealth of the cities in France should be so unconnected with the country! There are no gentle transitions from ease to comfort, from comfort to wealth: you pass at once from beggary to profusion,—from misery in mud cabins to Mademoiselle St. Huberti in splendid spectacles at 500 liv. a night (21l. 17s. 6d.). The country deserted, or if a gentleman in it, you find him in some wretched hole, to save that money which is lavished with profusion in the luxuries of a capital. ——20 miles.

The 22d. Deliver my letters. As much as agriculture is the chief object of my journey, it is necessary to acquire such intelligence of the state of commerce, as can be best done from merchants, for abundance of useful information is to be gained, without putting any questions that a man would be cautious of answering, and even without putting any questions at all. Mons. Riédy was very polite, and satisfied many of my enquiries; I dined once with him, and was pleased to find the conversation take an important turn on the relative situations of France and England in trade, particularly in the West-Indies. I had a letter also to Mons. Epivent, *consilier* in the parliament of Rennes, whose brother, Mons. Epivent de la Villesboisnet, is a very considerable merchant here. It was not possible for any person to be more obliging than these two gentlemen; their attentions to me were marked and friendly, and rendered a few days residence here equally instructive and agreeable. The town has that sign of prosperity of new buildings, which never deceives. The quarter of the *comedie* is magnificent, all the streets at right angles and of white stone. I am in doubt whether the *hotel de Henri IV* is not the finest in Europe: Dessein's at Calais is larger, but neither built, fitted up, nor furnished like this, which is new. It cost 400,000 liv. (17,-500l. furnished) and is let at 14,000 liv. per ann. (612l. 10s.) with no rent for the first year. It contains 60 beds for masters, and 25 stalls for horses. Some of the apartments of two rooms, very neat, are 6 liv. a day; one good 3 liv. but for merchants 5 liv. per diem for dinner, supper, wine, and chamber, and 35s for his horse. It is, without comparison, the first inn I have seen in France, and very cheap. It is in a small square close to the theatre, as convenient for pleasure or trade as the votaries of either can wish. The theatre cost 450,000 liv. and lets to the comedians at 17,000 liv. a year; it holds, when full, to the value of 120 louis d'or. The land the inn stands on was bought at 9 liv. a foot: in some parts of the city it sells as high as 15 liv. This value of the ground induces them to build so high as to be destructive of beauty. The quay has nothing remarkable; the river is choaked with islands, but at the furthest part next to the sea is a large range of houses regularly fronted. An institution common in the great commercial towns of France, but particularly flourishing in Nantes, is a *chambre de lecture,* or what we should call a book-club, that does not divide its books, but forms a library. There are three rooms, one for reading, another for conversation, and the third is the library; good fires in winter are provided, and wax candles. Messrs. Epivent had the goodness to attend me on a water expedition, to view the establishment of Mr. Wilkinson, for boring cannon, in an island in the Loire below Nantes. Until that well known English manufacturer arrived, the French knew nothing of the art of casting cannon solid, and then boring them. Mr. Wilkinson's machinery, for boring four cannons, is now at work, moved by tide wheels; but they have erected a steam engine, with a new apparatus for boring seven more; M. de la Motte, who has the direction of the whole, shewed us also a model of this engine, about six feet long, five high, and four or five broad; which he worked for us, by making a small fire under the boiler that is not bigger than a large tea-kettle; one of the best machines for a travelling philosopher that I have seen. Nantes is as *enflammeé* in the cause of liberty, as any town in France can be; the conversations I witnessed here prove how great a change is effected in the minds of the French, nor do I believe it will be possible for the present government to last half a century longer, unless the clearest and most decided talents be at the helm. The American revolution has laid the foundation of another in France, if government do not take care of itself. Upon the 23d one of the twelve prisoners from the Bastile arrived here—he was the most violent of them all—and his imprisonment has been far enough from silencing him.

The 25th. It was not without regret that I quitted a society both intelligent and agreeable, nor should I feel comfortably if I did not hope to see Messrs. Epivents again; I have little chance of being at Nantes, but if they come a second time to England, I have a promise of seeing them at Bradfield. The younger of these gentlemen spent a fortnight with Lord Shelburne at Bowood, which he remembers with much pleasure; Colonel Barré and Dr. Priestley were there at the same time. To Ancenis is all inclosed: for seven miles many seats. ――――22 ½ miles.

Combourg

THE 30TH. A fine sea view of the Isles of Chausée, at five leagues distant; and afterwards Jersey, clear at about forty miles, with that of the town of Grandval on a high peninsula: entering the town, every idea of beauty is lost; a close, nasty, ugly, ill built hole: market day, and myriads of triflers, common at a French market. The bay of Cancalle, all along to the right, and St. Michael's rock rising out of the sea, conically, with a castle on the top, a most singular and picturesque object. ——30 miles.

The 31st. At Pont Orsin, enter Bretagne; there seems here a more minute division of farms than before. There is a long street in the episcopal town of Doll, without a glass window; a horrid appearance. My entry into Bretagne gives me an idea of its being a miserable province. ——22 miles.

SEPTEMBER 1ST. To Combourg, the country has a savage aspect; husbandry not much further advanced, at least in skill, than among the Hurons, which appears incredible amidst inclosures; the people almost as wild as their country, and their town of Combourg one of the most brutal filthy places that can be seen; mud houses, no windows, and a pavement so broken, as to impede all passengers, but ease none—yet here is a chateau, and inhabited; who is this Mons. de Chateaubriant, the owner, that has nerves strung for a residence amidst such filth and poverty? Below this hideous heap of wretchedness is a fine lake, surrounded by well wooded inclosures. Coming out of Hedé, there is a beautiful lake belonging to Mons. de Blassac, intendant of Poictiers, with a fine accompanyment of wood. A very little cleaning would make here a delicious scenery. There is a chateau, with four rows of trees, and nothing else to be seen from the windows in the true French style. Forbid it, taste, that this should be the house of the owner of that beautiful water; and yet this Mons. de Blassac has made at Poictiers the finest promenade in France! But that taste which draws a strait line, and that which traces a waving one, are founded on feelings and ideas as separate and distinct as painting and music—as poetry or sculpture. The lake abounds with fish, pike to 36lb. carp to 24lb. perch 4lb. and tench 5lb. To Rennes the same strange wild mixture of desert and cultivation, half savage, half human. ——31 miles.

Chambord

QUIT THE Loire, and pass to Chambord. The quantity of vines is great; they have them very flourishing on a flat poor blowing sand. How well satisfied would my friend Le Blanc be if his poorest sands at Cavenham gave him 100 dozen of good wine per acre per annum! See at one *coup d'œil* 2000 acres of them. View the royal chateau of Chambord, built by that magnificent prince Francis I and inhabited by the late Marechal de Saxe. I had heard much of this castle, and it more than answered my expectation. It gives a great idea of the splendour of that prince. Comparing the centuries, and the revenues of Louis XIV and Francis I, I prefer Chambord infinitely to Versailles. The apartments are large, numerous, and well contrived. I admired the stone stair-case in the centre of the house, which, being in a double spiral line, contains two distinct stair-cases, one above another, by which means people are going up and down at the same time, without seeing each other. The four apartments in the attic, with arched stone roofs, were in no mean taste. One of these Count Saxe turned into a neat well contrived theatre. We were shewn the apartment which that great soldier occupied, and the room in which he died. Whether in his bed or not is yet a problem for anecdote hunters to solve. A report not uncommon in France was, that he was run through the heart in a duel with the Prince of Conti, who came to Chambord for that purpose; and great care was taken to conceal it from the king (Louis XV), who had such a friendship for the marechal, that he would certainly have driven the prince out of the kingdom. There are several apartments modernized, either for the marechal or for the governors that have resided here since. In one there is a fine picture of Louis XIV on horseback. Near the castle are the barracks for the regiment of 1500 horse, formed by Marechal de Saxe, and which Louis XV gave him, by appointing them to garrison Chambord while their colonel made it his residence. He lived here in great splendour, and highly respected by his sovereign, and the whole kingdom.—The situation of the castle is bad; it is low, and without the least prospect that is interesting; indeed the whole country is so flat that a high ground is hardly to be found in it. From the battlements we saw the environs, of which the park or forest forms three-fourths; it contains within a wall about 20,000 arpents, and abounds with all sorts of game to a degree of profusion. Great tracks of this park are waste or under heath, &c. or at least a very imperfect cultivation: I could not help thinking, that if the King of France ever formed the idea of establishing one compleat and perfect farm under the turnip culture of England, here is the place for it.[3] Let him assign the chateau for the residence of the director and all his attendants; and the barracks, which are now applied to no use whatever, for stalls for cattle, and the profits of the wood would be sufficient to stock and support the whole undertaking. What comparison between the utility of such an establishment, and that of a much greater expence applied here at present for supporting a wretched haras (stud), which has not a tendency but to mischief! I may recommend such agricultural establishments, but they never were made in any country, and never will be, till mankind are governed on principles absolutely contrary to those which prevail at present—until something more be thought requisite for a national husbandry than academies and memoirs. ——35 miles.

5. *Poland*

Louis Philippe, Comte de Ségur (1753–1830), a French career diplomat, army officer, and writer, was on his way to Russia, where he would become the French ambassador to the court of Catherine II, when he passed through Poland in 1784. In the same year, Georg Forster (1754–1794), a German scholar whose checkered career is outlined in more detail in the introduction to Document 54, was on his way to Vilna, where he was to become professor of natural history at the university there.

For both the Count de Ségur and Georg Forster, Poland was not part of civilized Europe. Except for a few islands of art, wit, and fine manners like Warsaw, Poland was one vast expanse of melancholy, poverty-stricken countryside. Even the enormous châteaux of the eccentric barons were without friendliness or comfort. While Forster was shocked by the lack of hygiene in Grodno, Ségur mused on Poland's anarchic and chivalric past. Both men reflected the attitude of cultural superiority of the western European toward his "backward neighbors" to the east.

Sources: Document A: Comte de Ségur, *Mémoires, Souvenirs, et Anecdotes*, ed. F. M. Barrière (Paris, 1859), vol. I, pp. 300ff.

[3] Young refers to English crop rotations, which included the planting of root crops such as turnips to reinvigorate the soil as well as to provide cattle fodder. The introduction of such forage crops was fundamental to England's agricultural revolution. (See Document 16 in section on agriculture.)

Document B: Paul Zinke and Albert Leitzmann, eds., "*Georg Forsters Tagebücher*" in *Deutsche Literaturdenkmale des 18. und 19. Jahrhunderts* (Berlin, 1914), vol. CXLIX, pp. 239–240.

A. Comte Ségur on Poland

Crossing the eastern parts of the territory of the King of Prussia, one seems to leave regions ruled by a nature embellished by art and a mature civilization. The eye already receives sad impressions of arid expanses of sand and vast forests.

And as soon as one enters Poland, one leaves Europe altogether, and the sights are entirely new: an immense expanse of land almost completely covered with evergreen, ever melancholy firs interrupted at great intervals by cultivated plains resembling green islands in an ocean; a poor population of slaves, dirty villages, cabins not much better than the huts of savages; everything makes us think that we are living ten centuries ago and are again in the midst of Huns, Scythians, Veneti, Slavs, and Sarmatians, who inundated Europe in tidal wave after tidal wave, pushing before them Bulgars, Goths, Scandinavians, Burgundians, and all the bellicose tribes whose weight had crushed the last remains of the Roman Empire.

And yet some large, wealthy, and populous towns appear amidst these cold and uncultivated regions, and around them, far away from each other, arise châteaux inhabited by a polished, warlike, free, proud, and chivalric nobility.

There the feudal centuries are still being lived; there we hear of honor and liberty; there the traveler is received with venerable and generous hospitality, and in the vast halls he finds courtly warriors and graceful ladies, whose lofty souls and romantic bearing add something heroic to their sweet charm. Seeing and listening to them, one almost expects that they will presently preside over a tournament, withstand a siege, cheer on their husbands or lovers, decorate them with colorful scarves, and crown them after victory to the song of a bard or the sweet tones of a troubadour.

All is contrast in that country: deserts and palaces; the slavery of the peasants and the turbulent liberty of the nobility, which has alone for ages formed the Polish nation; a great wealth of grain and almost no commerce save that which is carried on by a large and active number of Jews, jokingly referred to by Prince Potemkin as "the navigation of Poland."

In almost all the châteaux we see the luxury of a great fortune, although it is badly administered and crumbling under the weight of usurious debts; vast numbers of horses and servants, but almost no furniture; Oriental splendor but none of the comforts of daily life; a sumptuous table open to all travelers, but no beds in the apartments except that of the lord and the lady; a life spent almost entirely in excursions and travels, but in which it is necessary to take everything along, for there are almost no inns, except in some of the cities.

A constant passion for war and an aversion to discipline, a well-founded and continuous fear of the powerful oppressors who surround them and yet no thought and no sacrifices to protect the frontiers by erecting fortresses.

The arts, wit, fine manners, literature, and all the charms of social life in Warsaw rival the sociability of Vienna, London, and Paris, but in the provinces manners are still Sarmatian. All in all, it is an inconceivable mixture of the old and the new, of monarchism and republicanism, of feudal pride and equality, of poverty and wealth, of sensible speeches in the Diet and drawing swords to end discussion, of ardent patriotism and a factious temper which all too frequently leads to foreign interference.

B.   Georg Forster
Spends the Night in Grodno

[November 2, 1784]

I arrived at Grodno at 5:30 P.M. One must pass through a narrow defile in order to reach the banks of the Niemen, which is crossed by a toll bridge. There one must pay three Polish florins as at the bridge near Warsaw. On the other side the road rises just as steeply and then passes through extremely muddy streets among houses of stone or wood, some of them pretty and some of them wretched. It leads to the old castle (Stary Samek) of Count Chreptowics, who had been kind enough to reserve me a room. Herr Tolkmit, his marshal, received me most politely and led me to an open fire in one of the Count's rooms, where I found a very tiny dwarf and the Count's oldest son. After half an hour, His Excellency himself appeared, received me most cordially, embraced me, and sent me to my room, where he wanted me to make myself at home. Herr Tolkmit accompanied me there, and soon the Count himself came to see how I was installed. Later Herr Tolkmit led me to the great dining hall, where a very large table was set. We sat down at a smaller one and dined with the young counts and a number of officers connected with the house. Later we had a glass of punch by the fire and I went to bed at nine o'clock since I was tired and sleepy. My room is large, but all it consists of are dirty walls. Two stools, a bedstead, and a table constitute the only furnishings. Since my window also has to provide the light for an attic above me, the ceiling in the front part of the room was left open so that everything from my room can be heard above and my writing table can even be seen. Nonetheless I am fortunate to have found such a good room in this miserable town where all of Poland has gathered.[1]

[November 3]. Arose at seven o'clock. To satisfy a natural need, I had to cross the courtyard and go to a really very filthy place, the mere thought of which still makes me sick. The only nice part of this excursion was that I saw the Niemen in its deep bed at my feet and on the other bank a church and some houses which, I believe, are part of the town of Grodno.

6. The Russian Countryside

WILLIAM COXE, tutor to the son of an English lord, was an observant traveler in Russia. His descriptions of peasant huts and country roads, as well as of the splendor and misery of the large cities, are more detailed and informative than those of Poland by Ségur. But like Ségur, Coxe is half fascinated, half frightened by the vastness and primitiveness of the eastern plains. To these impressions are added some sketches by Robert Ker Porter, an artist who describes typically Russian scenes in the manner of genre painting.

Source: Peter Putnam, ed., *Seven Britons in Imperial Russia, 1698–1812* (Princeton, N.J., 1952), pp. 256ff., 322ff.*

[1] King Stanislaw Poniatowski had come there for a special meeting of the Diet.

A.   *From William Coxe, Travels in Russia* [1778–1779]

THE ACCOMMODATIONS: PEASANT HUTS

THE COTTAGES . . . are of a square shape; formed of whole trees, piled upon one another, and secured at the four corners with mortises and tenons. The interstices between these piles are filled with moss. Within, the timbers are smoothed with the axe, so as to form the appearance of wainscot; but without are left with the bark in their rude state. The roofs are in a penthouse form, and generally composed of the bark of trees or shingles, which are sometimes covered with mould or turf. The peasants usually construct the whole house solely with the assistance of the hatchet, and cut the planks of the floor with the same instrument, in many parts being unacquainted with the use of the saw: they finish the shell of the house and the roof, before they begin to cut the windows or doors. The windows are apertures of a few inches square, closed with sliding frames, and the doors are so low as not to admit a middle-sized man without stooping. These cottages sometimes, though very rarely, consist of two stories; in which case the lower apartment is a store-room, and the upper the habitable part of the house: the stair case is most commonly a ladder on the outside. Most of these huts are, however, only one story; a few of them contain two rooms; the generality only one. In some of these latter sort I was frequently awakened by the chickens picking the grains of corn in the straw upon which I lay, and more than once by a less inoffensive animal.

THE TRANSPORTATION: PEASANT COACHMEN

The peasants at every post were obliged to furnish us with horses at a fixed and reasonable rate, which had the ill effect of rendering them extremely dilatory in their motions; and as our only interpreter was a Bohemian servant, not perfectly acquainted with the Russian language, his difficulty in explaining, joined to their backwardness in executing our orders, occasioned delays of several hours for a change of horses. The peasants acted in the capacity of coachmen and postillions; they always harnessed four horses a-breast, commonly put eight, and sometimes even ten horses to our carriage; as the stages were for the most part twenty, and sometimes thirty miles, and the roads extremely bad. They seldom used either boots or saddles, and had no sort of stirrup, except a rope doubled and thrown across the horse's back. . . . The method of driving was not in a steady pace, but by starts and bounds, with little attention to the nature of the ground: the peasants seldom trotted their horses, but would suddenly force them into a gallop through the worst roads, and sometimes as suddenly check their speed upon the most level surface. A common piece of rope served them for a whip, which they seldom had any occasion to use, as they urged their horses forwards by hooting and whistling like cat-calls. . . . From the wretched harness, which was continually breaking, the badness of the roads, the length of time we were always detained at the posts before we could procure horses, and other impediments, we were seldom able to travel more than forty or fifty miles a day; although we commenced our journey before sun-rise, and pursued it till it was dark.

The Arrival: Moscow

The road for some way before we came . . . to Moscow was a broad straight avenue cut through the forest. The trees which composed these vast plantations, set by the hand of Nature were oaks, beech, mountain-ash, poplar, pines, and firs mingled together in the most wanton variety. The different shades of green, and the rich tints of the autumnal colours, were inexpressibly beautiful; while the sublime, but uniform expanse of forest, was occasionally relieved by recesses of pastures and corn-fields.

August 30: The approach to Moscow was first announced at the distance of six miles by some spires over-topping an eminence at the extremity of the broad avenue cut through the forest; about two or three miles further we ascended a height, from whence a superb prospect of the vast city burst upon our sight. It stretched in the form of a crescent, to a prodigious extent; while innumerable churches, towers, gilded spires and domes, white, red, and green buildings, glittering in the sun, formed a splendid appearance, yet strangely contrasting by an intermixture of wooden hovels. . . .

It is the largest town in Europe; the circumference within the rampart, which encloses the suburbs, being 39 versts, or 26 miles;

but it is built in so straggling a manner, that the population in no degree corresponds to the extent. . . . Moscow contains within the ramparts 250,000 souls, and in the adjacent villages, 50,000.

If I was struck with the singularity of Smolensko, I was all astonishment at the immensity and variety of Moscow, a city so irregular, so uncommon, so extraordinary, and so contrasted, never before claimed my attention. The streets are in general exceedingly long and broad: some are paved; others, particularly, those in the suburbs, formed with trunks of trees or boarded with planks like the floor of a room; wretched hovels are blended with large palaces; cottages of one story stand next to the most stately mansions. Many brick structures are covered with wooden tops; some of the timber houses are painted, others have iron doors and roofs. Numerous churches present themselves in every quarter, built in the oriental style of architecture; some with domes of copper, others of tin, gilt or painted green, and many roofed with wood. In a word, some parts of this vast city have the appearance of a sequestered desert, other quarters, of a populous town; some of a contemptible village, others of a great capital.

An Hospitable Reception

September 1: This morning we received a card of invitation from Count Osterman, governor of Moscow, to dinner, for the 22d of August; but, as it was the 1st of September, our servant, who took the message, came laughing into the room, and informed us, that we were invited to an entertainment that was past: he had endeavoured, he added, to convince the messenger of the mistake; but the man insisted that the ensuing day was the 22d of August. It was indeed a natural mistake in our servant, who did not know that the Russians still adhere to the old style, and as he passed the 22d of August in Lithuania, it is no wonder that he was surprized at finding it so soon again in Moscow. . . .

Nothing can exceed the hospitality of the Russians. We never paid a morning visit to any nobleman without being detained to dinner: we also constantly received general invitations; but, considering them as mere compliments, were unwilling to intrude ourselves without further notice. We soon found, however, that the principal persons of distinction kept open tables, and were highly obliged by our resorting to them without ceremony. . . .

A Social Call

The house of count Orlof is situated at the extremity of one of the suburbs, upon an elevated spot, commanding a fine view of the vast city of Moscow and the neighbouring country; many separate buildings occupy the large tract of ground. The offices, stables, manage [*manège*, riding school], and other detached structures, are of brick; the foundation and lower story of the dwelling-house are built with the same material; but the upper part is of wood, neatly painted of a green colour. (Wooden houses are by many persons in this country supposed to be warmer and more wholesome than those of brick and stone, which is the reason why several of the Russian nobility chuse that part of their house, which they inhabit themselves to be constructed of wood.) We carried a letter of recommendation from prince Stanislaus Poniatowski, the king of Poland's nephew, to the count, who received us with great frankness, and detained us at dinner....

Sights and Sounds

In this part of our journey, we passed numberless herds of oxen, moving towards Petersburgh; most of them were driven from the Ukraine, the nearest part of which country is distant 800 miles from the metropolis. During this long progress the drivers seldom enter any house; they feed their cattle upon the slips of pasture on each side of the road, and have no other shelter in bad weather than the foliage of the trees. In the evening the still silence of the country was interrupted by the occasional lowing of the oxen, and carols of the drivers; while the solitary gloom of the forest was enlivened with the glare of numerous fires, surrounded by different groups of herdsmen in various attitudes.

In our route through Russia I was surprised at the propensity of the natives to singing. Even the peasants who acted in the capacity of coachmen and prostilions, were no sooner mounted than they began to warble an air, and continued it, without the least intermission for several hours. But what still more astonished me was, that they performed occasionally in parts; I frequently observed them engaged in a kind of musical dialogue, making reciprocal questions and responses, as if chanting (if I may so express myself) their ordinary conversation. The postilions *sing* from the beginning to the end of a stage; the soldiers *sing* during their march; the countrymen *sing* amid the most laborious occupations; public-houses re-echo with their carols; and in a still evening I have frequently heard the air vibrate with the notes of the surrounding villages.

The Slow March of Progress

As we approached Petersburgh, and nearer the civilized parts of Europe, the villagers were better furnished with the conveniences of life, and further advanced in the knowledge of the necessary arts, than those who fell under our notice between Tolitzin and Moscow. The planks were less frequently hewn with the axe, and saw-pits, which we had long considered as objects of curiosity, oftener occurred: the cottages were more spacious and convenient, provided with larger windows, and generally had chimnies; they were also more amply stored with household furniture, and with wooden, and sometimes even earthen utensils. Still, however, their progress towards civilization is very inconsiderable, and many instances of the grossest barbarism fell under our observation.

The Approach to St. Petersburg

Our coach being much shattered by the bad roads, we left it at Novogorod [Novgorod], and continued our journey in *kabitkas*, the common carriages of the country. . . . The road, made of timber, and as straight as an arrow, ran through a perpetual forest, without the least intermixture of hill or dale, and with few slips of cultivated ground. Through this dreary extent, the gloomy uniformity of the forest was only broken by a few solitary villages at long distances from each other, without the intervention of a single house. . . . About ten miles from Itchora [Izhora] we suddenly turned to the right, and the scene instantly brightened; the woods gave way to cultivation, the country began to be enlivened with houses, the inequalities of the timber road were succeeded by the level of a spacious causeway equal to the finest turnpikes of England, the end of each verst was marked with superb mile-stones of granite and marble, and a long avenue of trees was closed at the distance of a few miles with a view of

Petersburgh, the object of our wishes, and the termination of our labours.

An Immense Outline

In walking about this metropolis I was filled with astonishment on reflecting that so late as the beginning of this century, the ground on which Petersburgh now stands was a morass occupied by a few fishermen's huts. The first building of the city is so recent as to be almost remembered by persons now alive; and its gradual progress is traced without difficulty. . . .

Succeeding sovereigns have continued to embellish Petersburgh, but none more than the present empress, who may be called its second founder. Notwithstanding, however, all these improvements, it bears every mark of an infant city, and is still "only an immense outline, which will require further empresses and almost future ages to complete."

The Northern Thames

The views upon the banks of the Neva exhibit the most grand and lively scenes I ever beheld. That river is in many places as broad as the Thames at London; it is also deep, rapid, and as transparent as crystal; and the banks are lined with handsome buildings. On the north side the fortress, the Academy of Sciences, and Academy of Arts, are the most striking objects; on the opposite side are the Imperial palace, the Admiralty, the mansions of many Russian nobles, and the English line, so called because the whole row is principally occupied by the English merchants. In the front of these buildings, on the south side, is the Quay, which stretches for three miles, except where it is interrupted by the Admiralty; and the Neva, during the whole of that space has been lately embanked by a wall, parapet, and pavement of hewn granite; a magnificent and durable monument of imperial munificence. The canals of Catherine and of the Fontanka, which are several miles in length, have been recently embanked in the same manner, and add greatly to the beauty of the metropolis. . . .

I have frequently viewed with surprize the process employed by the Russian workmen, in smoothing the granite. They batter the stone with an iron hammer edged with steel; the quantity which flies off at each stroke, is almost imperceptible; but by repeatedly striking the same place, the prominent parts are worn away, and the stone becomes smooth.

CORDIALITY TO FOREIGNERS

The nobles of Petersburgh are no less than those of Moscow distinguished for hospitality to foreigners. We were no sooner presented to a person of rank and fortune, than we were regarded as domestic visitants. Many of the nobility keep an open table, to which the first invitation was considered as a standing passport of admission. The only form necessary on this occasion, was to make inquiry in the morning if the master of the house dined at home; and if he did, we presented ourselves at his table without further ceremony. The oftener we appeared at these hospitable boards, the more acceptable guests we were esteemed, and we always seemed to confer, instead of receiving a favour. . . .

Several of the nobility also receive company every evening in the most easy manner: the parties usually meet at seven; some sit down to whist, macao, loo, and other games; some converse, others dance. Amid the refreshments tea is handed round no less frequently than in England. At ten supper is brought in, and the party generally breaks up between eleven and twelve. It is no exaggeration to say, that, during our continuance in this city, not one evening passed but we had it in our power to attend an assembly of this sort; and had we always frequented the same, we should always have found the greatest cordiality of reception. From these circumstances, perhaps no metropolis in Europe, excepting Vienna, is rendered more agreeable to foreigners than Petersburgh.

B.   From Robert Ker Porter,
Traveling Sketches in Russia and Sweden, 1805, 1806, 1807, 1808

A SNOWSCAPE

No idea can be formed of the immense plains we traversed, unless you imagine yourself at sea, far, far from the sight of land. The Arabian deserts cannot be more awful to the eye, than the appearance of this scene. Such is the general aspect of the country during the rigours of winter; with now and then an exception of a large forest skirting the horizon for a considerable length of way. At intervals, as you shoot along, you see openings amongst its lofty trees, from which emerge picturesque groups of natives and their one-horse sledges, whereon are placed the different articles of commerce, going to various parts of this empire. They travel in vast numbers, and from all quarters, seldom fewer than one hundred and fifty in a string, having a driver to every seventh horse. The effect of this cavalcade at a distance is very curious; and in a morning, as they advance towards you, the scene is as beautiful as striking. The sun then rising, throws his rays across the snow, transforming it to the sight into a surface of diamonds. From the cold of the night, every man and horse is encrusted with these frosty particles; and the beams falling on them too, seem to cover their rude faces and rugged habits with a tissue of the most dazzling brilliants. The manes of the horses, and the long beards of the men, from the quantity of congealed breath, have a particularly glittering effect.

A LAUGHABLE SPECTACLE

Our unlucky barouche, after a variety of disasters in its journey, here [at Tver] broke fairly down. . . . After much bungling we at length got the vehicle mounted on its skates; and I inquired of the landlord his demand for the share he had in the repairs; he coolly asked *thirty rubles!* . . . At this moment my servant came up. . . . He inquired what was the matter. I told him the extortion of the man, and that I wanted to beat him down. "I'll beat him down!" cried he, catching the poor wretch by the beard and laying upon his shoulders, with all his might, an immense bludgeon large enough to be called a club. As the terrified host swung round at the arm's length of my doughty champion, the blows fell like hail upon his back, while he kept bawling out: "twenty, fifteen, ten, etc." till he reduced his demands to the more reasonable sum of two rubles. On this cry, like the last bidding at an auction, the appraiser was satisfied, and the hammer fell. The poor battered wretch was released; and bowing with a grateful air to his chastiser, turned to me. Almost killed with laughing at so extraordinary a sight, I paid him his rubles. I was no less amused at the stupid indifference with which the standers by regarded the whole transaction. . . . The bow he made to my triumphant valet

entertained me as much as any thing . . . and I was so convulsed
with laughter at the oddity of the group they formed, and the
whole was performed in so short a time, that I declare I had not
power to stir from the spot or speak a word; and so for once
allowed the ridiculous to get the better of my humanity.

A SCORCHING PLAIN

I traveled this very road but a few months ago. In vain I now
look round to recognise any object of my former observations: it
seems totally a new scene. When I last beheld it, it was covered
with snow; now, all is one wide stretch of green landscape. The
one showed Winter in his direst reign; the other Summer, though
I am sorry to say, not in her sweetest charms. All is flat and
uninteresting. The villages boast no little spots cultivated with
Swiss beauty and comfort. No tree, or creeping tendril grows near
the doors and windows of these habitations. The russet cottages
of England, overgrown with the blushing rose and fragrant honey-
suckle; their pretty gardens, and domesticated animals, all are
wanting here. The absence of the snow, and the unveiling of the
grass, seem the only marks that winter has disappeared: at least
the only pleasing assurance, for as to disagreeable proofs, in the
forms of heat and dust, we have enough of them. A burning sun
continually over our heads, scorching our very souls; and the
dust, by way of soothing our pride, while it torments our skin,
eyes, and lungs, makes us, like so many Eneases, always move in a
cloud!

A WATERY INTERLUDE

Amongst our scant complement of entertainment . . . the canal
and falls of Borovitsky [Borovichi] struck across our recollection.
. . . At Vislina Valochock [Vyshniy-Volochok] the canal is first
descried, laden with vessels full of productions from the interior;
human industry having here united the river Twertza [Tvertsa]
with the Meutza [now called Tsna]; connecting . . . the Caspian
with the Baltic Sea. We inquired whether there were any barks
collected at the falls, in one of which we might descend; and
being answered in the affirmative, we hired horses to take us to
these torrents. . . .

We found numbers of craft on the eve of going down, and
placing ourselves in one of them, soon entered on the descent,

which was by no means tremendous, although the rapidity of the motion was surprising. This torrent is a long inclining surface of water of about thirty versts; and to give you an idea of the velocity with which the barks moved, we went twenty-five versts in three quarters of an hour. The most alarming circumstances in the exploit, is to see the constant changes the vessels make in their shapes from the violence of the waters. They bend like paper, and are so admirably constructed, as to take the undulating form of the rising wave. Were they of firmer texture they must inevitably be dashed to pieces. As it is, they bound like a feather on the water, and are carried by its impetuosity safely to the bottom of the fall.

A Peasant Interior

One room is the habitation of all the inmates. . . . One quarter of it is occupied by a large stove or peech, flat at the top; on which many of them take their nocturnal rest; and during the day loll over its baking warmth, for hours. . . . The apartment I am describing, rendered insufferably stifling by the stove, the breaths, and other fumigations, contained the postmaster, his wife, his mother, his wife's mother, an infant, and two men, apparently attached to the post department, as they wore green uniforms. There were others besides, who being rather withdrawn in a dark corner, we could not distinctly observe.

When we entered, the top of the oven was occupied by the three women and child, almost all in a state of nature. . . . A bed with dirty curtains filled one corner of the room; a few benches and a table, completed the furniture. The walls were not quite so barren, being covered with uncouth prints and innumerable daubings. In one spot was placed a picture or effigy of our Saviour and the Virgin, decorated with silver plates.

7. *English and French Mores*

Comparing the customs and style of living of two societies always incurs the dangers of superficiality or downright nonsense. Nevertheless, the observer's choice as to what is worth comparing is in itself informative. No one could accuse the Suffolk country squire, Arthur Young, of superficiality, but we seldom picture him discussing table linen. In this selection he evinces considerable expertise in the art of living and pursues various aspects of the subject—from French cuisine and household furnishings to women's fashion and polite conversation. Less measurable, and surely less important in retrospect than other issues in this collection, these *petites choses* absorbed then, as they do now, the extra time and energy of men. And for a few this was their entire existence.

Source: Arthur Young, *Travels in France During the Years 1787, 1788, and 1789,* pp. 289–292.

ONE OF the most amusing circumstances of travelling into other countries, is the opportunity of remarking the difference of customs amongst different nations in the common occurrences of life. In the art of living, the French have generally been esteemed by the rest of Europe, to have made the greatest proficiency, and their manners have been accordingly more imitated, and their customs more adopted than those of any other nation. Of their cookery, there is but one opinion; for every man in Europe, that can afford a great table, either keeps a French cook, or one instructed in the same manner. That it is far beyond our own, I have no doubt in asserting. We have about half a dozen real English dishes, that exceed any thing, in my opinion, to be met with in France; by English dishes I mean, a turbot and lobster sauce—ham and chicken—turtle—a haunch of venison—a turkey and oysters—and after these there is an end of an English table. It is an idle prejudice, to class roast beef among them; for there is not better beef in the world than at Paris. Large handsome pieces were almost constantly on the considerable tables I have dined at. The variety given by their cooks, to the same thing, is astonishing; they dress an hundred dishes in an hundred different ways, and most of them excellent; and all sorts of vegetables have a savouriness and flavour, from rich sauces, that are absolutely wanted to our greens boiled in water. This variety is not striking, in the comparison of a great table in France with another in England; but it is manifest, in an instant, betweeen the tables of a French and English family of small fortune. The English dinner, of a joint of meat and a pudding, as it is called, or *pot luck,* with a neighbour, is bad luck in England; the same fortune in France gives, by means of cookery only, at least four dishes to one among us, and spreads a small table incomparably better. A regular dessert with us is expected, at a considerable table only, or at a moderate one, when a formal entertainment is given; in France it is as essential to the smallest dinner as to the largest; if it consist of a bunch of dried grapes only, or an apple, it will be as regularly served as the soup. I have met with persons in England, who imagine the sobriety of a French table carried to such a length, that one or two glasses of wine are all that a man can get at dinner: this is an error: your servant mixes the wine and water in what proportion you please; and large bowls of clean glasses are set before the master of the house, and some friends of the family, at different parts of the table, for serving the richer and rarer sorts of wines, which are drunk in this manner freely enough. The whole nation are scrupulously neat in refusing to drink out of glasses used by other people. At the house of a carpenter or blacksmith, a tumbler is set to every cover. This results from the common beverage being wine and water; but if at a large table, as in England, there were porter, beer, cyder, and perry, it would be impossible for three or four tumblers or goblets to stand by every plate; and equally so for the servants to keep such a number separate and distinct. In table-linen, they are, I think, cleaner and wiser than the English: that the change may be incessant, it is every where coarse. The idea of dining without a napkin seems ridiculous to a Frenchman, but in England we dine at the tables of people of tolerable fortune, without them. A journeyman carpenter in France has his napkin as regularly as his fork; and at an inn, the *fille* always lays a clean one to every cover that is spread in the kitchen, for the lowest order of pedestrian travellers. The expence of linen in England is enormous, from its fineness; surely a great change of that which is coarse, would be much more rational. In point of cleanliness, I think the merit of the two nations is divided; the French are cleaner in their persons, and the English in their houses; I speak of the mass of the people, and not of individuals of considerable fortune. A *bidet* in France is as universally in every apartment, as a bason to wash your hands, which is a trait of personal cleanliness I wish more common in England; on the other hand their necessary houses are temples of abomination; and the practice of spitting about a room, which is amongst the highest as well as the lowest ranks, is detestable; I have seen a gentleman spit so near the cloaths of a duchess, that I have stared at his unconcern. In every thing that concerns the stables, the English far exceed the French; horses, grooms, harness, and change of equipage; in the provinces you see cabriolets of the last century; an Englishman, however small his fortune may be, will not be seen in a carriage of the fashion of forty years past; if he cannot have another, he will walk on foot. It is not true that there are no complete equipages at Paris, I have seen many; the carriage, horses, harness, and attendance, without fault or blemish;—but the number is certainly very much inferior to what are seen at London. English horses, grooms, and carriages, have been of late years largely imported. In all the articles of fitting up and furnishing houses, including those of all ranks in the estimate, the English have made advances far beyond their neighbours. Mahogany is scarce in France, but the use of it is profuse in England. Some of the hotels in Paris are immense in size, from a circumstance which would give me a good opinion of the people, if nothing else did, which is the great mixture of families. When the eldest son marries, he brings his wife home to the house of his father, where there is an apartment provided for them; and if a daughter do not wed an eldest son, her husband is also received into the family, in the same way, which makes a joyous number at every table. This cannot altogether be attributed to economical motives, though they certainly influence in many cases, because it is found in families possessing the first properties in the kingdom. It does with French manners and customs, but in England it is sure to fail, and equally so amongst all ranks of people: may we not conjecture, with a great probability of truth, that the nation in which it succeeds is therefore better tempered? Nothing but good humour can render such a jumble of families agreeable, or even tolerable. In dress they have given the *ton* to all Europe for more than a century; but this is not among any but the highest rank an object of such expence as in England, where the mass of mankind wear much better things (to use the language of common conversation) than in France: this struck me more amongst ladies who, on an average of all ranks, do not dress at one half of the expence of English women. Volatility and changeableness are attributed to the French as national characteristics,—but in the case of dress with the grossest exaggeration. Fashions change with ten times more rapidity in England, in form, colour, and assemblage; the vicissitudes of every part of dress are phantastic with us: I see little of this in France; and to instance the mode of dressing the gentlemen's hair, while it has been varied five times at London, it has remained the same at Paris. Nothing contributes more to make them a happy people, than the chearful pliancy of disposition, with which they adapt themselves to the circumstances of life: this they possess much more than the high and volatile spirits which have been attributed to them; one excellent consequence is, a greater exemption from the extravagance of living beyond their fortunes, than is met with in England. In the highest ranks of life, there are instances in all countries; but where one gentleman of small property, in the provinces of France, runs out his fortune, there are ten such in England that do it. In the blended idea I had formed of the French character from reading, I am disappointed as to three circumstances, which I expected to find predominant. On comparison with the English, I looked for great talkativeness, volatile spirits, and universal politeness. I think, on the contrary, that they are not so talkative as the English; have not equally good spirits, and are not a jot more polite: nor do I speak of certain classes of people, but of the general mass. I think them, however, incomparably better tempered; and I propose it as a question, whether good temper be not more reasonably expected under an arbitrary, than under a free government?

II

Aristocracy

In the eighteenth century the ultimate social aspiration was "nobility." For nobility symbolized a whole set of virtues and achievements. Bearing the stamp of a knightly and chivalric tradition, this hereditary elite claimed a special status by right of the illustrious acts of its ancestors. And for those whose genealogies would not produce a crusader or a Renaissance captain, there might still be a more recent chancellor, a high magistrate, or even, if necessary, a town notable, mayor, or *échevin*. Despite internal jealousies, nobilities of sword, robe, and town hall were increasingly bound by common interests and even common blood.

On the Continent nobility possessed more than the "decent, regulated pre-eminence" so lauded by Edmund Burke. It claimed privileges pecuniary and honorific—exemption from most taxes, right of primogeniture and entail, special privileges in the law courts, the right to bear arms, lead processions, exhibit coats of arms. Furthermore, since most nobles were seigneurs, they possessed the prerogatives of seigneurial justice, important marks of prestige everywhere; also associated with legal privilege was an extensive political and social influence. This might take the form of staffing the upper bureaucracy and the army, as in Prussia, or membership in the *parlements* of France or diets of the Hapsburg Empire. Everywhere nobles made up the immediate entourage of princes and exerted a courtier's influence inversely related to the will power of the ruler. Far from moribund, the nobilities of Europe were politically and socially dominant.

The economic position of this European nobility was more variable. Generally prosperous in East Europe—Prussia, Poland, Hungary, Russia—and enormously wealthy in England, the nobilities of western Germany, France, Spain, and northern Italy lived modestly, sometimes frugally. Baron Pöllnitz depicts an affluent Bohemian nobility, spending lavishly in Prague or Vienna, but Sismondi or Mirabeau tell another story. Domains usually under 1,000 acres and seigneurial dues from a few hundred more, produced incomes close to 10,000 livres, scarcely enough to risk a season in a capital like Paris, Madrid, or even Florence or Munich. Sismondi describes the determined efforts of Tuscan country gentlemen to economize most of the year in order to afford a certain display in the provincial towns during the winter.

Yet the lure of the big city was very real, and residence in a capital meant more than a social setting for noble *éclat*. To be close to the Crown was to be near the source of pensions and preferments, and in Paris, Madrid, or Vienna these pensions might well retrieve a great name from obscurity. Furthermore, from what better vantage point could a profitable marriage be negotiated? It was not to Auvergne or the Tirol that a noble family turned to find an eligible banker's daughter. In short, if a noble family could risk the expenses of staying in a capital for a season, the rewards could be appreciable. To remain away from court was to assure solvency, but only by the certain sacrifice of national prominence. Alas, a great family would not live in the country, and the exhortations of a Mirabeau could not change this.

How different was the English aristocracy! A few hundred families owned perhaps a quarter of the arable land in England and Wales. Together with investments in mines, overseas ventures, and the public "funds," this land provided incomes in the neighborhood of £10,000 or 200,000 French livres. The English aristocrats lived on estates of 10,000, 20,000, and even 50,000 acres, dotted with palatial Georgian country houses overlooking broad green lawns and artificial lakes—ten English Chatsworths for every French Chambord. Possessing both enormous wealth and a political power extending from their administration of local justice and poor relief to their seats in both houses of Parliament, this was Europe's smallest aristocracy, perhaps 400 families of great landlords, and its most secure. No wonder that the *milords anglais* were the envy of all nobility. Sir Robert Walpole was their political spokesman for over a generation, and Lord Chesterfield served as their unofficial custodian of proper manners.

Theoretically, the English aristocracy was the most open of all privileged classes of the eighteenth century. Without formal privileges, without insurmountable prejudices against establishing younger sons in trade, and with frequent occasions for contact with the wealthier merchants of the City, entry into its ranks should not have been too difficult. In practice, however, the 400 families seem to have been less open to newcomers than at any time since 1600. Estates, government sinecures, and offices were held tightly in the same hands, and there appears to have been a mounting dislike for men of business on the part of the great landlords.[1]

On the Continent, a wealthy commoner might buy his son an ennobling office, acquire a *seigneurie*, or marry his daughter to an impecunious nobleman. Social ascent need not be slow, and cases of transition from merchant to noble in three generations were not uncommon in western Europe. The process was accelerated by the royal policy of selling offices to obtain supplementary revenues and by the prestige traditionally attached to officeholding. Moreover, the owner-

<hr>

[1] See C. E. Mingay, *English Landed Society in the Eighteenth Century* (London and Toronto, 1963), p. 26ff.

ship of land, a step toward nobility, had the added advantage of providing a secure, regular return that even merchants seemed to prefer to other forms of investment. But most important was the pervasive influence of aristocratic values that held all commerce in contempt and pushed all men of a certain affluence to withdraw from trade and live "nobly" from landed rents and annuities. Hence, even those who could not immediately attain "nobility" were inclined to become *rentiers*, a term used almost interchangeably with *bourgeois* in the eighteenth century. Heinrich Brockes of Hamburg is an example of the mentality of such a bourgeois.

Although the gates to noble status were not closed during the eighteenth century, the passage appears to have narrowed. Partly because more offices were reserved for older noble families, and partly because there were too many new candidates for the offices available, frustrations arose among socially ambitious commoners. How significant this lessening social mobility was, especially in France before 1789, is a subject of considerable debate.[1]

8.   Sir Robert Walpole

THE LIFE of Robert Walpole by Archdeacon Coxe is not quite contemporary biography since it was published a half century after the death of the famous prime minister. It remains a distinguished work, however, superseded only by the recent biography by John H. Plumb.[2]

Although Coxe's biography was essentially a political one, he was not unaware of Sir Robert's personal life. Here he describes Walpole's hospitality at Houghton Hall in Norfolk and a style of life that was characterized by pecuniary carelessness, an expansive well-being, a love of good food, wine, and field sports that left little time for letters or the arts. Other English lords—Bolingbroke, Oxford, Chesterfield, the Dukes of Bedford and Devonshire—had more refined tastes, but Walpole possessed the prodigious wealth, love of magnificence, and confident sense of superiority that were the hallmarks of English aristocracy in the Augustan age.

[1] See E. Barber, *The Bourgeoisie in Eighteenth Century France* (Princeton, N.J., 1955), and F. Ford, *Robe and Sword* (Cambridge, Mass., 1953).
[2] J. H. Plumb, *Sir Robert Walpole* (London, 1956 and 1960, 2 vols.), p. ix. "As I went from country-house to country-house, following Coxe's footsteps," writes Plumb, "I found his neat cardboard folders, often untouched since he first sorted the papers, and my admiration for his scholarly care steadily increased."

Source: William Coxe, *Memoirs of the Life and Administration of Sir Robert Walpole, Earl of Orford* (London, 1798), pp. 758–763.

HE was naturally liberal, and even prodigal. His buildings at Houghton were more magnificent than suited his circumstances, and drew on him great obloquy. He felt the impropriety of this expenditure, and on seeing his brother's house at Wolterton, expressed his wishes that he had contented himself with a similar structure. The following anecdote also shews that he regretted his profusion: Sitting by Sir John Hynde Cotton, during the reign of queen Anne, and in allusion to a sumptuous house which was then building by Harley; he observed, that to construct a great house was a high act of imprudence in any minister. Afterwards, when he had pulled down the family mansion at Houghton, and raised a magnificent edifice, being reminded of that observation by Sir John Hynde Cotton, he readily acknowledged its justness and truth, but added, "Your recollection is too late, I wish you had reminded me of it before I began building, it might then have been of service to me."

His style of living was consonant to the magnificence of his mansion. He had usually two annual meetings at Houghton, the one in the spring, to which were invited only the most select friends and the leading members of the cabinet, continued about three weeks. The second was in autumn, towards the commencement of the shooting season. It continued six weeks or two months, and was called the congress. At this time Houghton was filled with company from all parts. He kept a public table, to which all gentlemen in the county found a ready admission.

The expences of these meetings have been computed at £3,000. Nothing could be more ill-judged than the enormous profusion, except the company for which it was made. The mixed multitude consisted of his friends in both houses, and of their friends. The noise and uproar, the waste and confusion were prodigious. The best friends of Sir Robert Walpole in vain remonstrated against this scene of riot and misrule. As the minister himself was fond of mirth and jollity, the conviviality of their meetings was too frequently carried to excess, and lord Townshend, whose dignity of deportment and decorum of character revolted against these scenes, which he called the Bacchanalian orgies of Houghton, not unfrequently quitted Rainham during their continuance. But notwithstanding these censures, and the impropriety of such conduct, it undoubtedly gained and preserved to the minister numerous adherents, who applauded a mode of living so analogous to the spirit of ancient hospitality.

This profusion would have been highly disgraceful had it been attended with a rapacious disposition. On the contrary, he gave many instances of carelessness and disregard of his private fortune. He expended £14,000 in building a new lodge in Richmond park, and when the king, on the death of Bothmar, in 1738, offered him the house in Downing-street, he refused it as his own property, but accepted it as an appendage to the office of chancellor of the exchequer.

He was, from his early youth, fond of the diversions of the field, and retained this taste till prevented by the infirmities of age. He was accustomed to hunt in Richmond park with a pack of beagles. On receiving a packet of letters he usually opened that from his game-keeper first; and he was fond of sitting for his picture in his sporting dress. He was, like chancellor Oxenstiern, a sound sleeper, and used to say, "that he put off his cares with his cloaths."

His social qualities were generally acknowledged. He was animated and lively in conversation, and in the moment of festivity realised the fine eulogium which Pope has given of him—

> Seen him, I have, but in his happier hour
> Of social pleasure, ill-exchang'd for power;
> Seen him, uncumber'd with the venal tribe,
> Smile without art, and win without a bribe.
>
> *Epilogue to the Satires*

To the virtues of Sir Robert Walpole I feel regret in not being able to add that he was the patron of letters and the friend of science. But he unquestionably does not deserve that honourable appellation, and in this instance his rank in the Temple of Fame is far inferior to that of Halifax, Oxford, and Bolingbroke. It is a matter of wonder that a minister who had received a learned education, and was no indifferent scholar, should have paid such little attention to the muses. Nor can it be denied, that this neglect of men of letters was highly disadvantageous to his administration, and exposed him to great obloquy. The persons employed in justifying his measures, and repelling the attacks of the opposition, were by no means equal to the task of combating Pulteney, Bolingbroke and Chesterfield, those Goliaths of opposition; and the political pamphlets written in his defence are far inferior in humour, argument, and style, to the publications of his adversaries. . . .

The truth is, Sir Robert Walpole did not delight in letters, and always considered poets as not men of business. He was often heard to say, that they were fitter for speculation than for action, that they trusted to theory, rather than to experience, and were guided by principles inadmissible in practical life. His opinion was confirmed by the experience of his own time. Prior made but an indifferent negotiator; his friend Steele was wholly incapable of application, and Addison a miserable secretary of state. He was so fully impressed with these notions, that when he made Congreve commissioner of the customs, he said, "You will find he has no head for business."

Low persons were employed by government, and profusely paid, some of whom not unfrequently propagated in private conversation, and even in public clubs, disadvantageous reports of the minister, and declared that high rewards induced them to write against their real sentiments. Several known disseminators of infidelity were engaged to defend his measures. Many warm remonstrances were frequently made by the minister's friends against employing such low mercenaries, but usually disregarded. Some of these insignificant writers had frequent access to him. Their delusive and encouraging accounts of persons and things were too often more credited than the sincere and free intimations of those who were more capable of giving accurate information. But this seems an error too common in ministers: they prefer favourable accounts to dismal truth, and readily believe what they wish to be true.

It is a natural curiosity to inquire into the behaviour and occupations of a minister retired from business, and divested of that power which he had long enjoyed. Those who admired his talents, while he swayed senates and governed kingdoms, contemplate him, "in their mind's eye," enjoying his retreat with dignity, and passing his leisure hours with calmness and complacency. Yet nothing in general is more unsatisfactory than such an inquiry, or more illusive than such a preconceived opinion. The well-known saying, that "no man is a hero to his valet de chambre," may be applied with strict justice to this case. Sir Robert Walpole experienced the truth of the observation, that a fallen minister is like a professed beauty, who has lost her charms, and to whom the recollection of past conquests but poorly compensates for present neglect.

Though he had not forgotten his classical attainments, he had little taste for literary occupations. He once expressed his regret on this subject to Fox, who was reading in the library at Houghton. "I wish," he said, "I took as much delight in reading as you do, it would be the means of alleviating many tedious hours in my present retirement; but to my misfortune I derive no pleasure from such pursuits."—On another occasion, he said to his son Horace, who, with a view to amuse him, was preparing to read some historical performance, "O! do not read history, for that I know must be false."

His principal amusement consisted in planting, observing the growth of his former plantations, and in seeing his son Horace arrange the fine collection of pictures at Houghton. He had a good taste for painting, and his observations on the style of the respective masters were usually judicious.

A letter which he wrote from Houghton to general Churchill, in 1743, was much admired, as indicating a love of retirement, and contempt of past grandeur. Yet this letter strikes me in a contrary light; it proves that he was weary of that repose which he affected to praise; and that he did not, as much as he professed, taste the charms of the inanimate world. The trite observation, that the beeches do not deceive, proves either that he regretted the times that were past, or that with all his penetration, he had not, when in power, made a just estimate of the deceitfulness and treachery of dependents and courtiers. Houghton had been either the temporary place of retirement from public business, or the scene of friendly intercourse and convivial jollity, and neglect rendered it comparatively a solitude. He saw and felt this desertion with greater sensibility than became his good sense; but in the calm and solitude of total retirement, such disagreeable reflections occur often and sink deep. The season of natural gaiety was irrecoverably past, he laboured under a painful distemper; the ill-assorted marriage of his eldest son, and embarrassed situation of his own affairs preyed on his mind, and increased his dejection.

This state of mind was natural. Every circumstance must have appeared uninteresting to a man, who from the twenty-third year of his age, had been uniformly engaged in scenes of political exertion, who, from the commencement of his parliamentary career, had passed a life of unremitting activity, and made a conspicuous figure in the senate, and in the cabinet.

To him who had directed the helm of government in England, and whose decisions affected the interests of Europe in general, all speculative opinions must have appeared dull. To him who had drawn all his knowledge and experience from practice, all theory must have appeared trifling or erroneous. He who had fathomed the secrets of all the cabinets of Europe, must have considered history as a tissue of fables, and have smiled at the folly of those writers, who affected to penetrate into state affairs, and account for all the motives of action. He who had long been the dispenser of honours and wealth, must have perceived a wide difference between the cold expressions of duty and friendship, and the warm effusions of that homage which self-interest and hope inspire in those who court or expect favours. He must have been divested of human passions, had he not experienced some mortification in finding, that he had been indebted to his situation for much of that obsequious regard which he had fondly thought was paid to his personal qualities.

9. *"Good Society"*

THE DESIRE of parents to have their children enjoy all the advantages it is possible to bequeath them is, of course, constant in all ages. Lord Chesterfield, an accomplished social wit, was especially anxious to see his son, a somewhat oafish individual, master the art of frequenting good society. Alas, from all accounts he seems to have failed. But the persistence with which Chesterfield tried to teach his son the social graces indicates more than the concern of the head of a great house for his successor; it reflects the supreme importance attached to good manners.

Proper behavior in society, Chesterfield believed, was an art to be learned. Good family connections were important, but less so than the social graces. These called for a pleasing exterior, good grooming, a measure of wit, and broad, though not pedantic or tedious, knowledge.

Above all, success in society was a matter of charm and tact. Chesterfield insisted that to smoothe over differences, to flatter everyone's vanity, was not base opportunism but a noble accomplishment worthy of a refined and civilized society.

Source: Charles Strachey, ed., *The Letters of the Earl of Chesterfield to His Son* (New York and London, 1925), vol. I, pp. 280–285.

Letter CLXVI

Bath, *October* 19, *O.S.* 1748

DEAR BOY: Having, in my last, pointed out what sort of company you should keep, I will now give you some rules for your conduct in it; rules which my own experience and observation enable me to lay down, and communicate to you, with some degree of confidence. I have often given you hints of this kind before, but then it has been by snatches; I will now be more regular and methodical. I shall say nothing with regard to your bodily carriage and address, but leave them to the care of your dancing-master, and to your own attention to the best models; remember, however, that they are of consequence.

Talk often, but never long: in that case, if you do not please, at least you are sure not to tire your hearers. Pay your own reckoning, but do not treat the whole company, this being one of the very few cases in which people do not care to be treated, every one being fully convinced that he has wherewithal to pay.

Tell stories very seldom, and absolutely never but where they are very apt and very short. Omit every circumstance that is not material, and beware of digressions. To have frequent recourse to narrative betrays great want of imagination.

Never hold anybody by the button, or the hand, in order to be heard out; for if people are not willing to hear you, you had much better hold your tongue than them.

Most long talkers single out some one unfortunate man in company (commonly him whom they observe to be the most silent, or their next neighbour), to whisper, or at least in a half voice, to convey a continuity of words to. This is excessively ill bred, and in some degree a fraud; conversation-stock being a joint and common property. But on the other hand, if one of these unmerciful talkers lays hold of you, hear him with patience (and at least seeming attention), if he is worth obliging; for nothing will oblige him more than a patient hearing; as nothing would hurt him more than either to leave him in the midst of his discourse, or to discover your impatience under your affliction.

Take, rather than give, the tone of the company you are in. If you have parts, you will show them, more or less, upon every subject; and if you have not, you had better talk sillily upon a subject of other people's than of your own choosing.

Avoid as much as you can, in mixed companies, argumentative, polemical conversations; which though they should not, yet certainly do, indispose, for a time, the contending parties towards each other; and if the controversy grows warm and noisy, endeavour to put an end to it, by some genteel levity or joke. I quieted such a conversation-hubbub once, by representing to them that though I was persuaded none there present would repeat, out of company, what passed in it, yet I could not answer for the discretion of the passengers in the street, who must necessarily hear all that was said.

Above all things, and upon all occasions, avoid speaking of yourself, if it be possible. Such is the natural pride and vanity of our hearts, that it perpetually breaks out, even in the people of the best parts, in all the various modes and figures of the egotism.

Some, abruptly, speak advantageously of themselves, without either pretence or provocation. They are impudent. Others proceed more artfully, as they imagine; and forge accusations against themselves, complain of calumnies which they never heard, in order to justify themselves, by exhibiting a catalogue of their many virtues. *They acknowledge it may, indeed, seem odd, that they should talk in that manner of themselves; it is what they do not like, and what they never would have done; no, no tortures should ever have forced it from them, if they had not been thus unjustly and monstrously accused. But, in these cases, justice is surely due to one's self, as well as to others; and when our character is attacked, we may say in our own justification, what otherwise we never would have said.* This thin veil of Modesty drawn before Vanity, is much too transparent to conceal it, even from very moderate discernment.

Others go more modestly and more slyly still (as they think) to work; but, in my mind, still more ridiculously. They confess themselves (not without some degree of shame and confusion) into all the Cardinal Virtues; by first degrading them into weaknesses, and then owning their misfortune, in being made up of those weaknesses. *They cannot see people suffer, without sympathising with, and endeavouring to help them. They cannot see people want, without relieving them, though, truly, their own circumstances cannot very well afford it. They cannot help speaking truth, though they know all the imprudence of it. In short, they know that, with all these weaknesses, they are not fit to live in the world, much less to thrive in it. But they are now too old to change, and must rub on as well as they can.* This sounds too ridiculous and *outré*, almost, for the stage; and yet, take my word for it, you will frequently meet with it, upon the common stage of the world. And here I will observe, by-the-bye, that you will often meet with characters in nature, so extravagant, that a discreet poet would not venture to set them upon the stage in their true and high colouring

This principle of vanity and pride is so strong in human nature, that it descends even to the lowest objects; and one often sees people angling for praise, where, admitting all they say to be true (which, by the way, it seldom is), no just praise is to be caught. One man affirms that he has rode post an hundred miles in six hours; probably it is a lie: but supposing it to be true, what then? Why he is a very good post-boy, that is all. Another asserts, and probably not without oaths, that he has drunk six or eight bottles of wine at a sitting; out of charity, I will believe him a liar; for if I do not, I must think him a beast.

Such, and a thousand more, are the follies and extravagances, which vanity draws people into, and which always defeat their own purpose; and as Waller says, upon another subject,

> Make the wretch the most despised,
> Where most he wishes to be prized.

The only sure way of avoiding these evils, is never to speak of yourself at all. But when, historically, you are obliged to mention yourself, take care not to drop one single word, that can directly or indirectly be construed as fishing for applause. Be your character what it will, it will be known; and nobody will take it upon your own word. Never imagine that anything you can say yourself will varnish your defects, or add lustre to your perfections!

but, on the contrary, it may, and nine times in ten will, make the former more glaring, and the latter obscure. If you are silent upon your own subject, neither envy, indignation, nor ridicule, will obstruct or allay the applause which you may really deserve; but if you publish your own panegyric upon any occasion, or in any shape whatsoever, and however artfully dressed or disguised, they will all conspire against you, and you will be disappointed of the very end you aim at.

Take care never to seem dark and mysterious; which is not only a very unamiable character, but a very suspicious one too; if you seem mysterious with others, they will be really so with you, and you will know nothing. The height of abilities is to have *volto sciolto* and *pensieri stretti;* that is, a frank, open and ingenuous exterior, with a prudent interior; to be upon your own guard, and yet, by a seeming natural openness, to put people off theirs. Depend upon it nine in ten of every company you are in will avail themselves of every indiscreet and unguarded expression of yours, if they can turn it to their own advantage. A prudent reserve is therefore as necessary, as a seeming openness is prudent. Always look people in the face when you speak to them: the not doing it is thought to imply conscious guilt; besides that you lose the advantage of observing by their countenances what impression your discourse makes upon them. In order to know people's real sentiments, I trust much more to my eyes than to my ears: for they can say whatever they have a mind I should hear, but they can seldom help looking what they have no intention that I should know.

Neither retail nor receive scandal willingly; for though the defamation of others may, for the present, gratify the malignity of the pride of our hearts, cool reflection will draw very disadvantageous conclusions from such a disposition; and in the case of scandal, as in that of robbery, the receiver is always thought as bad as the thief.

Mimicry, which is the common and favourite amusement of little, low minds, is in the utmost contempt with great ones. It is the lowest and most illiberal of all buffoonery. Pray, neither practise it yourself, nor applaud it in others. Besides that the person mimicked is insulted; and as I have often observed to you before, an insult is never forgiven.

I need not (I believe) advise you to adapt your conversation to the people you are conversing with: for I suppose you would not, without this caution, have talked upon the same subject, and in the same manner, to a minister of state, a bishop, a philosopher, a captain, and a woman. A man of the world must, like the Cameleon, be able to take every different hue; which is by no means a criminal or abject, but a necessary complaisance; for it relates only to manners and not to morals.

One word only, as to swearing, and that, I hope and believe, is more than is necessary. You may sometimes hear some people, in good company, interlard their discourse with oaths, by way of embellishment, as they think; but you must observe, too, that those who do so are never those who contribute, in any degree, to give that company the denomination of good company. They are always subalterns, or people of low education; for that practice, besides that it has no one temptation to plead, is as silly, and as illiberal, as it is wicked.

Loud laughter is the mirth of the mob, who are only pleased with silly things; for true wit or good sense never excited a laugh, since the creation of the world. A man of parts and fashion is therefore only seen to smile, but never heard to laugh.

But to conclude this long letter; all the above-mentioned rules, however carefully you may observe them, will lose half their effect, if unaccompanied by the Graces. Whatever you say, if you say it with a supercilious, cynical face, or an embarrassed countenance, or a silly, disconcerted grin, will be ill received. If, into the bargain, *you mutter it, or utter it indistinctly and ungracefully*, it will be still worse received. If your air and address are vulgar, awkward, and *gauche*, you may be esteemed indeed, if you have great intrinsic merit; but you will never please; and, without pleasing, you will rise but heavily. Venus, among the ancients, was synonymous with the Graces, who were always supposed to accompany her; and Horace tells us, that even Youth, and Mercury, the God of Arts and Eloquence would not do without her.

> —*Parum comis sine te Juventas,*
> *Mercuriusque.*

They are not inexorable Ladies, and may be had, if properly and diligently pursued. Adieu.

10. The Provincial Noble

THE MARQUIS de Mirabeau [1] was much disturbed by changes he saw about him. He was upset by the drift of the nobility to Paris, by the appearance of "new men" in the countryside, and by the decline of paternalism and charity on the part of the provincial seigneurs. He was shocked by the crass attitude of the rural lawyers toward the misery of the peasants and disgusted with the "bourgeois" of the small towns who did nothing but complain about the cost of day labor. Mirabeau's writings are long and rambling and no doubt idealize the old blood nobility of the provinces, but his plea for the respectability of agriculture is more than physiocratic propaganda—it is a bitter attack on absenteeism, frivolity, and urbanization. Toqueville at a later date could have cited Mirabeau to substantiate his views that local loyalties to the rural nobility were ebbing away.

Source: Marquis de Mirabeau, *L'ami des hommes ou traité de la population* (Paris, 1756), 1883 edn., pp. 62–66, 80–83, 85–88.

WHATEVER MAY be my opinion about what one should like to call good order and police, but what, I think, is rather similar to what can be seen in the seraglio, it is at least certain that the seigneurs of the old days who lived on their estates, if they annoyed their inhabitants, annoyed them in person, which is certainly better than through an overseer, and that they consumed the fruits of their so-called extortions right on the spot, without permitting anyone else to annoy the people. But those who had a solid intelligence and a charitable character, having less opportunity to indulge superfluous desires and more occasion to pity those around them, sustained, protected, and encouraged the inhabitants of the countryside. The poor and the sick were helped at the château, orphans found their livelihood there by becoming servants. In a word, there was a direct relationship between the seigneur and his subjects, and consequently firmer ties and less wrongdoing on both sides without the interference of outsiders.

Passing through an out-of-the-way region in Quercy, I stopped

[1] Father of the Mirabeau of the Constituent Assembly.

in a fairly large place, where there was a stream or small river, and noticed that it was full of crayfish. I asked the innkeeper how many guards the seigneur had posted in order to keep people from fishing. "Ah, Monsieur," the good man told me, "this belongs to Monsieur le Marquis de D.B. They are the best seigneurs and we have had them for two hundred years. They often come back here, and there is not one of us who, so far from stealing anything, would not be the first to denounce his neighbor in such a case." A man of rank, not far from there, served bread and food to a thousand poor in his barns during the food shortage of 1747, and that was for six months. "Now then, my children," he told them on St. John's Day, "try to earn something. I shall get more for next year if this shortage continues." Certainly this man, even though he is distinguished by his probity and his merits, is a seigneur in the full sense of the word. However, benevolent as he may be, he would never have carried his charity this far had he lived in Paris.

Finally, as I have said, the resident seigneurs did an infinite amount of good by simply giving work to poor people. Everyone knows how strong was the habit, not to say the mania, the inhabitants of the country had of continually giving presents to their seigneurs. In my day I have seen this habit die almost everywhere, and rightly so, because in this life every good deed must be related to something, and if the scales are weighted the heavier side naturally goes to the stronger. The seigneur no longer does anything for the inhabitants, and so it is quite normal that he is forgotten by the people just as he has forgotten them. And let nobody say that this was a carry-over of the old serfdom; this would either be completely mistaken or said in bad faith. In the places where this practice still exists, these good people, even the poorest, would be grievously insulted if their presents were refused or if, by a present of equal or greater value, the seigneur tried to pay them back. I have seen this a hundred times.

The remains of the tyranny of our fathers prove at least that the peasants knew the seigneur and were known by him. And whatever one may say about human malice, it is an accepted axiom, proven by experience, that those who know us and are familiar with us will treat us less badly than others to whom we are total strangers. The experience and reality of this principle is one of the mainsprings of the *dulcis amor patriae*. It follows that

when nobody knows the seigneur of his domain any more, everyone will rob him—and that is as it should be.

Another reason, which is closely related to the first, is the almost constant mutation of fiefs and their coming into the hands of
new men. Just as the constitution of a state is most secure when
its succession is perpetuated in the same family, in a smaller way
this is also true for each of a state's members. Just now I am not
dealing with political considerations, I am engaged in the lowlier
occupation of working the land. But I cannot refrain from saying
in passing, that, all other things being equal, the respect for old
nobility does make for order and subordination among the inhabitants of the countryside. I have seen some examples, which I
could cite, of village communities who have purchased their
rights from their seigneur, who wanted to sell them, only to give
them back to him. I have seen thousands who were most unhappy
at the mere rumor of such a change, and even more who remained quiet and did not argue over anything with their old
seigneur, but engaged in all kinds of lawsuits with the new. And
they will do this all the more readily if the new seigneur is the
grandson of a certain Jacques, by the name of Lafontaine, who
may very well say that his father was called *Monseigneur* when
he was *maître de requêtes*. Peasants have a fine ear and a good
memory, and they will always say that their seigneur is no better
than they are and that, if he is wealthier, he knew better how to
lay his hands on money; as for the rest, let him eat two dinners.

This seed of discontent and contempt will soon give birth to
fraud and plundering, to which they [the peasants] believe themselves entitled. It is unbelievable how such a situation will harm
peaceful enjoyment of the land and its desirability, since it makes
it necessary for our Parisians, today the only rich people in the
kingdom, to have lawsuits far away or to find patronage in Paris,
an unbearable thing for a man of gold who is used to giving
patronage to others.

I shall not examine whether the high taxes on land or the way in
which they are collected are not another reason for their discredit. I have already said that I do not go in for politics, and all
this has so many pros and cons that I would get very involved.
However, by this pro and con I do not mean to say that I personally condone the action of the idiots, or the law people, who say
that the peasant must be miserable in order to work and that

otherwise he becomes lazy and careless. Aside from the shameful inhumanity of such a statement, which, I am ashamed to confess, I have heard in the country more often than in the city, and to which one can only reply as that famous Roman did to his son who offered to take a town at the cost of [only] three hundred men: "Would you like to be one of those three hundred?"—aside from its inhumanity, I say, such a statement is completely false. Misery only leads to discouragement, as we have said, and discouragement to laziness. To that they answer that there must be a middle way. Can you find this middle way, in your miserable blindness? Will you take it upon yourselves to find it? But I can tell you that this middle way has ceased to exist for some time. And then they add that when the peasants are content they no longer want to work. I remember arguing one day about this revolting assertion, which I denied. When I said that I had traveled through Switzerland and found it cultivated to perfection, I was told about the County of Avignon which was only five leagues from there. I went to see it the same day and was surprised that it was like a garden everywhere. Having seen the strength and energy of the laborers, I learned that in the cantons of Provence, which are close by, a day laborer from the county [of Avignon] is paid thirty sous per day, as against fifteen for local laborers. This is the way in which the most erroneous principles are defended and proven by fabricated examples, which are the less disputed the easier it would be to verify their untruthfulness.

But even supposing that a comfortable living keeps peasants from working, working their own property certainly does not. The bourgeois of villages and small towns, people who are referred to as "living on their income," a race which has nothing to do but to backbite and to do evil and of whom I should wish to purge society until they all go to work in some honest profession, if it were not against my principles to advocate violence in anything, when they want to have their land worked, when they want to keep the peasants in subjection, paying for their day's work only at the old rates without considering that, if the price of consumer goods has risen, the price paid to hired labor must also rise—these people, I say, complain that a peasant in comfortable circumstances no longer wants to work. To this I answer, first, that it does not matter much and second, that I offer them consolation for the near future. For it is a fact that the rich peasant brings up a number of children, while those of the poor will come to nothing and return to the earth. These children share and exhaust the wealth of the father, force him to work, and soon will help him; and if there is not enough property they become mercenaries. The Swiss is well-to-do, as I have said, but he is so little opposed to work that he voluntarily devotes himself to the hardest kind of all, namely, to selling his blood and his liberty in a foreign land.

A last, but infinitely less problematic, reason for the discredit of landownership in France is the return on money. Sloth, a sister of luxury, as I shall demonstrate, despite what may be said about it, by proofs in good and due form, as I shall also demonstrate that both are children of city living—sloth, I say, is the reason why all its adherents prefer a fixed interest, which they have collected by a lackey when it comes due, to all the thought and supervision that must be given to land. In the interest of tranquillity they give up the advantages they could derive from time, industriousness, and solidity. But if they can collect high interest rates on their money, these advantages are less considerable. If I wanted to write a book on something about which I know nothing, I should know very well where to find a thousand reasons and as many calculations to prove that the interest rate is too high in our country. And if I were then really convinced of my own opus, I would become a doctor *in utroque iure*. But at this point I am only dealing with what I know, and I do not believe that I am digressing if I establish the principle that any form of income which maintains a part of the population without work and without regulation is harmful and that it is most important to put a stop to the discredit of land, a disparagement which should be transferred to paper assets.

The prosperity of a state is also harmful if it fosters a set of values, a kind of lavishness and decoration, which bring about a dislike and rejection of agriculture.

It is not my intention here to enter into the disadvantages of the general urbanization in any detail, and, even when I come to it, I will not be able to exhaust the topic. Volumes could be written about it. If the countryside is necessary to the cities, the cities are also necessary to the countryside; and later it will be seen from my plan that, once I have populated the countryside with as many people as it can bear, I should like to form towns with what is left, so that the industry of the towns could extract a nourishing stream from abroad. But, according to my plan, the cities would be even larger than they are now, even if their resident inhabitants consisted only of the officers employed in the various law courts, the young people being educated in the schools and universities as well as their teachers, of the bourgeois who own the land within the city limits, and the laborers and artisans who are employed by the inhabitants of the town and its hinterland. It would also include those who, employed in manufactures and local production, enhance the value of the raw materials [of the region] and thus make their living; and by offering their products to foreign commerce these artisans would bring in foreign products for their sustenance, this being the only kind of conquest not against public law.

Considering a country in its original state, in isolation and living on its own substance, it cannot be denied that *all classes and all men of a state live at the expense of the landowners;* this is a universally recognized principle. A source originating above the fields, on high ground, fertilizes a region as far as its water can reach; but a source originating in a hollow only forms a swamp until it has made a way by which it can lose itself in the nearest river, thus being completely useless to the neighboring fields.

The first source I compare to the landowner, who is the pivotal point of all the activities that surround him. If he is the most important producer, as he must be by the nature of his position since nobody has a greater interest in production than he, he brings increased activity to the entire region; or, if the rustic surroundings of the countryside do not permit him to have educated and enlightened views, which today is no longer to be feared, he will still, by his very position, do some of the good that is to be expected from his position. If, on the contrary, he is at the center of consumption, he becomes the low and marshy source and contributes to the inundation of the terrain which is only too humid to begin with.

It is commonly said that a nobleman on his estate lives better on an income of 10,000 livres than he would in Paris on 40,000. Just what is meant in this case by living better? Surely it is not to economize more easily in order to change enameled snuffboxes every month, to have coaches painted by Martin, and so on. If it means to consume more, it is true; but, since one cannot dine more than once, and since one is at least as liable to indigestion in Paris as elsewhere, this greater consumption is not for him. It means, therefore, that he provides a livelihood for more people, and it is a fact that one will more easily maintain fifteen unpolished servants who are dressed and paid according to local customs in the country with 10,000 livres than ten in the city with 40,000 livres. Sixty persons, aside from the family, will therefore live on the 40,000 livre income instead of ten.

It would be useless to object that in the city this man provides a livelihood not only for his servants but also for all the workers who produce what he consumes, namely, the merchants, the manufacturers, lacemakers, saddle and carriage makers, and other workers, as well as the caterers, perfumers, musicians, actors, prostitutes, etc., who, after all, are also part of the people, and that, since I only speak from the point of view of the population, I should make everything equal. . . .

The landowners in their natural state do not provide a livelihood to this supplementary class of society, unless great offices and the liberality of the king place them in the category of wage earners, of whom we shall speak later. Even without them, a wealthy city will have enough consumers, people who have become rich through the process of finance or commerce, young people and spendthrifts of all kinds, whose foolish activity and wild spending will maintain all the parasites of the state.

Let us return to our landlord. Quite aside from the increase in consumption brought about by the residence of the seigneur on his estate, it is only human to become attached to one's abode. Inhabited buildings are necessarily better kept than empty ones —everyone likes to repair and beautify his residence and improve the land he has before his eyes. The first of these enterprises encourages the second. I have in my life visited perhaps a thousand châteaux or manor houses, but I can hardly name three where the landlord has not shown me some embellishment or improvement he had added.

It is rather commonly said that people in the country are drunkards, brutes, and hunters, and nothing else. This is an old reproach which goes back to the days when the townspeople were revelers, gamblers, and idlers. I would not deny, however, that there is a good deal of drinking in provinces where the nobility still lives in the countryside and that there is a lot of hunting, but I do deny that they do only that.

I could establish two paradoxes in this connection: one being that the drinking which is so distasteful to water-drinkers is not harmful, and the second that, all in all (for I must always be permitted to regard the people as human), there is proportionately more drunkenness in Paris than in the country and that it is more harmful in the city.

Far be it from me to preach excess, but I must repeat that the way of life of the old rural nobility, which drank late into the night, slept on old easy chairs or cots, rode horseback and went hunting early in the morning, met on St. Hubert's Day [November 3] and did not separate until well after St. Martin's [November 12], that this way of life, I say, produced few musicians, and still fewer geometricians, poets, and charade players; but the nobility was not needed for that. This nobility willingly led a gay and hard life, did not cost the state much, but produced more for it by residence on and fertilizing the life-giving land than we do today by our taste, our studies, our colics, and our vapors. For we know the rules of the theater and the essential differences between Italian and French music; we make judgments about geometricians and take courses in anatomy or botany which make the specialists laugh; we know something about carriages, lacquers, snuffboxes, and chinaware; we are ignorant neither of lying, nor of intrigues, nor of the art of making deals, nor of asking for charity while wearing red heels, nor, above all, of the value of another man's property, of silver, and silver cabinets. They, on the other hand, made all their science consist of seven or eight articles: to respect religion; not to lie; to keep one's word; to do nothing base; not to put up with anything; to ride a horse properly; to know and to find one's way; not to fear hunger or thirst, heat or cold; and to remember always that if Caesar had not known how to defend himself, even he would not have come through so many hazardous enterprises.

And yet these people, ignorant as they were, served the state well, especially when called upon. At times they possessed rather impressive notions of glory, notions which our philosophy has replaced with the science of calculation, no doubt more useful to the individual but less so, I believe, to the public. Henry IV, for example, who was brought up and lived until he turned gray as a true country nobleman, performed his duties as king as well as anybody else.

So much for the alleged dissoluteness of our forefathers. I have taken the liberty of making this digression, but I did not want to write a book about the subject. As for my second paradox, that there is proportionately more drunkenness in Paris than in the provinces, one only has to see the *guinguettes* [winehouses outside Paris] to be convinced. The entire population of Paris leaves the city on holidays, and even the bourgeoisie is in the habit of flocking there [the *guinguettes*] with the whole family, taking even young children. Half of the people come back drunk, gorged with adulterated wine, paralyzed for three days, and soon blunted for the rest of their lives. The local wine on which the peasant gorges himself does not have these dreadful aftereffects. He comes home drunk on Sunday night, that is true enough (although he is now only too thoroughly cured of this meager luxury), but he finds his wife sober, which makes all the difference in public decency and society as a whole, for this kind of debauchery of the fair sex is the most shameful evil, and early the next morning he goes to work. Is it the same in Paris? I leave the answer to the master artisans. . . .

The luxury of the nobility must necessarily exhaust its landed wealth, for we shall demonstrate that the product from the best-yielding land, reduced to luxury goods, amounts to almost nothing. The nobility surrounds the sovereign and tries to persuade him that, since the wealth of the state exists only to pass from the hands of the prince into those of his subjects, the most worthy way to show liberality is to gratify the nobility. The number of applicants for favors is growing every day. A man who receives a pension of 6,000 livres receives the taxes from six villages. The tax revenue, already diminished by the profits of the tax collectors, is exhausted by such liberalities, and the very nobility which, if it stayed at home, could be the support, strength, and luster of the state, unwittingly acts as its veritable bloodsucker.

11. "Living Nobly"

J. C. L. DE SISMONDI of Geneva was a corresponding member of the
Royal Society of Agriculture of Florence. In his *tableau* of Tuscan
agriculture, Sismondi described the crops, agricultural methods, types
of leases, and the way of life of the peasantry. He came to the conclusion that Tuscan agriculture was hopelessly backward.

Sismondi saw the main reason for this in the absenteeism of the old
Tuscan landowning families, their gravitation to the city, and the desire of new landowners to imitate them. Everyone with a certain capital wanted to live "nobly," that is, to draw rents from the land without
improving farm production or even entering a trade or profession.
Where nobility was unattainable, the status of *rentier* would do. The
emphasis was then placed on economy rather than enterprise. Sufficient
income was saved to be spent on necessary display in town.

Sismondi's praise of contrasting conditions in the French countryside before the Revolution is certainly mistaken. The situation in the
small towns of Tuscany did not differ appreciably from that in the
small towns of France where even small shopkeepers aspired to the
status of *rentier*. Nor did it differ much from west Germany where a
wealthy merchant's son like Heinrich Brockes decided that he would
rather "preserve his liberty" than exercise a profession (see Document 13).

Source: J. C. L. Sismondi, *Tableau de l'agriculture toscane* (Geneva, 1801), pp. 274ff.

People of Means
Do Not Live in the Country

THE CULTURE of the land can be engaged in with taste and intelligence only when the proprietors are people whose fortune and
desire to learn have placed them above the common peasantry.
The countryside must have people of that kind, since they alone
can bring intelligence and openmindedness to the practice of
agriculture. Before the Revolution this class of people were
known as *gentilshommes-campagnards* in France. A republican
government owed this class far more consideration than it has
actually shown, for this class more than any other is interested in

the preservation of liberty. Moreover, the *gentilshommes-campagnards* of France have not been destroyed by the Revolution. Only their name has changed, and the French countryside is still, perhaps more than ever, inhabited by people who are capable of profiting from other people's experience and of making their own experiments serve their compatriots. But in Italy a series of revolutions has completely destroyed the rural nobility, much to the detriment of agriculture, especially to that branch of agricultural science which teaches how to enhance the pleasure and beauty of the countryside.

The well-to-do of every province live in its principal city. Even though their fortunes consist almost exclusively of land, they consume the income without paying the slightest attention to its cultivation and without even so much as going to see it. They take the title of nobility, which for them means hardly more than bourgeois. The most respectable of these "nobles" are the descendants of the old republicans, citizens of the former free towns.[1] Anyone who can trace his geneology back to one of these citizens proves his nobility by this fact alone. But everyone cannot produce such a truly glorious title, and the rural gentlemen especially must content themselves with a patent [of nobility], which they have purchased with a few *écus* as soon as they felt they were wealthy enough to retire from retail trade, the only activity that derogates from nobility.[2] Or else they have procured the title of *chevalier* by spending 5,000 *écus* for the foundation of a religious *commanderie* in the Order of St. Stephen which they and their descendants will retain until the extinction of the male line, when it will revert to the order.

Since small towns and villages also occasionally engage in some trade, a number of wealthy people may live there as well. Because they are not connected with a city, they cannot obtain the title of nobility, but once they have come to the stage where their capital produces a regular income, they too want to live nobly, that is, convert their capital into land, have it worked by peasants, live with small pleasures in their home town, display their wealth, and in fact do nothing. All the well-to-do, from the greatest noble down to the last *petit bourgeois*, are interested in only

[1] Free towns or communes of the late Middle Ages and Renaissance.
[2] Derogation, or loss of nobility, resulted from an act unbefitting a nobleman. Retail trade was explicitly regarded as such an act.

one thing: how to make their small income satisfy their needs for an entire year and permit them the appearance of grandeur, which they desire above everything else. With this goal in mind they economize on conveniences and everyday needs, so that they can spend more on luxuries. They would be able to enrich themselves by honest work with less expense of ingenuity, talent, and care than they expend in making use of the last sou of their modest revenue, not for comfort or pleasure, but for display. Since, however, those who are prodigal go through their capital and since those who are considered careful and economical never accumulate any new capital, the fortunes of all the old houses are declining. Trade in consumer goods, the only interior trade to be found in Italy, is not prosperous enough to accumulate much capital either; and agriculture, at least until the reign of Leopold,[3] only preserved, without increasing, the wealth of the proprietors, doing no more than sustaining the peasantry from day to day without ever permitting any accumulation of capital.

By using quit-rent contracts to a greater extent in the region of the plains, Duke Leopold has shown the peasants that it is possible to acquire a fortune, and at the same time he has made them active and industrious. In twenty years agriculture has created more wealth in Tuscany than commerce produced in a hundred years. The whole aspect of the countryside has changed, and wealthy proprietors now live on domains which they constantly improve. But if a period of twenty years has been enough to change the fortune and the condition of the peasants, it has not been enough to change their character. They have become active, shrewd, and acquisitive, but they have remained gross, ignorant, prejudiced, and different in every way from the former *gentilshommes-campagnards* of France [4] and the present gentlemen-farmers of England. After a few generations perhaps we shall see their children make it a point of honor to learn, to study a theory of agriculture which produces wealth, to communicate their experience to the public, and to profit from the literary world. Perhaps they will have country homes which combine

---

[3] Duke Leopold was interested in agricultural progress and sponsored free trade in grain in Tuscany near the end of the century.

[4] Sismondi idealized the French *gentilshommes-campagnards;* they were quite capable of being "active, shrewd, and acquisitive," and even "ignorant and prejudiced," though perhaps not "gross."

beauty with the profitable necessities of country life and train gardeners and planters not as they do now, simply to furnish food for the towns, but also to decorate their homes, improve the quality of their pleasures, and be able to appreciate the most elegant and most innocent of the arts of luxury.

12. The Patriciate of Nürnberg and the Nobility of Prague

KARL-LUDWIG, Freiherr von Pöllnitz, spent many years traveling all over Europe. Bearing a respectable noble name, Pöllnitz was admitted to all the courts and "best circles" everywhere. The mores of the upper classes, whether at court (see Document 66) or in the city (see below), were the center of his interest.

The Nürnberg patricians to whom Pöllnitz refers with a certain condescension did indeed live on the remnants of great fortunes made from the late Middle Ages to the sixteenth century, when Nürnberg, along with Augsburg and Regensburg (Ratisbon) played a leading role in the spice trade and finance. By the eighteenth century, what new prosperity there was came from the toy industry for which Nürnberg is known to this day. The cramped, medieval town with its relics, its religious prejudice, its proud, but frustrated patriciate, and its old-fashioned, obsequious middle class was not made to please the baron; he qualified it as "the most disagreeable place in Europe."

The splendid, frivolous existence of the wealthy Bohemian aristocracy at Prague was more to such a man's taste. True, their sons were poorly educated, since formal education was usually limited to a superficial grand tour in the company of some rapacious tutor; true, their peasants and servants were miserable—but what great names, what hospitality, what excellent taste in food and wines, what magnificent rounds of balls, operas, gaming, and social gatherings of all kinds! The baron's praise of this existence seems like a nostalgic apologia for the aristocratic *douceur de vivre* of the Old Régime.

Source: *Memoirs of Charles Lewis Baron de Pollnitz* (London, 1757), vol. I, pp. 204ff., 223ff. Anonymous contemporary translation.

Nürnberg

[October, 1729]

So MUCH has already been said by others of the City of Nuremberg that I have very little to add to it. I assure you this Town is the most disagreeable Place in *Europe* to live in. The Patricians are the People of the first Rank here, and lord it like the petty Nobles of Venice. The Government here too has very great Resemblance with the *Venetian* and they have a sort of Doge. In short they are very much like the Frog in the Fable that strove to swell itself to the Size of the Ox. Of these Patricians some are very rich, but they are so rude that no body visits them, and they scarce visit one another. Perhaps you will ask me what I mean by the Term Patrician? 'Tis this; they are Gentlemen: There are Patrician Families old enough to dispute Antiquity with any of the Nobility whatsoever, and who were formerly admitted into all the Chapters. But now the Case is otherwise; for the Nobility not only exclude them out of the Chapters, but dispute their being Gentlemen; pretending that they derogate from the Title by their Magistratical Office. Such is, you know, our *Germanic* Vanity; the Things which are honourable in other Countries, are with us diminutive: The Court, the Sword, and the Church, are the only Professions that a Gentleman can follow; If he has not the Talents proper for one or other of these, or if Fortune frown upon him, he had better be out of the World than take any Offices of the Magistracy upon him, or enter into Trade: He had better beg Alms nobly, than marry beneath himself. But I shall not here set up for a Censor of the *Germanic* Customs. Let us talk of *Nuremberg*. . . .

You know that the Government here is altogether Evangelical, *i.e. Lutheran*. The Catholics have a small Church in the House of the Teutonic Order: The Calvinists go to Church in the Territory of Anspach; but the Jews are not tolerated because 'tis said they formerly poisoned the Wells. They live in a Place not far from *Nuremberg*, but come to Town every Morning, paying something for their Entrance, have an old Woman set over them who is commonly both their Guard and their Guide, and are permitted to trade and trick wherever they can 'till Night, when they are obliged to retire.

In the Church of the Hospital is kept *Charlemain's* Crown, said to weigh fourteen Pounds, the Sceptre and the Globe, in short all the Ornaments of Empire except *Charlemain's* Sword said to have been brought from Heaven by an Angel, the same very likely that carry'd the Holy Vial and the Oriflamb to *France*. That Sword is kept at *Aix la Chapelle*.

The Trade of *Nuremberg* is very much fallen off; for besides that the Toys and Knick-knacks which were formerly made in this City are much out of fashion, especially in *Germany*, the Manufactures which the Margraves of *Bareith* and *Anspach* have settled in their Dominions do considerable Prejudice to *Nuremberg*.

The Inhabitants of this City may be (at least I think them so) the honestest People in the World, but they are the most horrible Complimenters that I know. I could not set my Foot in a Shop, but the Master, the Mistress, the Children and the Apprentices waited on me into the very Street thanking me for the Honour I had done them. My Landlord too who saw me go in and out twenty times a day, receiv'd me always with great Ceremony, and ask'd me how I did. And when I went out he pray'd me not to leave his House long in Contempt, without honouring it with my Presence.

Nuremberg is the richest and most potent Imperial City next to *Hamburgh*. The Domain of *Nuremberg* is even much larger than that of *Hamburgh*, but the latter bears the Bell for Wealth. 'Tis said that *Nuremberg* has seven other Towns in its Territory, with 480 Villages and Parishes. Yet for all this 'tis not a rich City, for the Patricians pocket all the Money and the Citizens are poor.

Prague

IF WE except *Rome*, *Paris*, and *London*, there is no City where there are more Gentry, or a Gentry that is more wealthy: Every body here lives grand; and in no Part of the World do the Nobility keep greater State, or take more Pride in their Substance. They are polite and civil to Strangers, whom they know to be Persons of Quality. For my own part, I like them prodigiously; and, I can safely say it, I have hardly met with a Foreigner who has not the same Notion of *Prague* that I have. . . .

There are no People of Quality in the World more addicted to an expensive way of Living than those of *Prague*, which is the

Reason that for all their immense Revenues they are sometimes
over Head and Ears in Debt; but by good Luck they have a
Settlement which prevents them from total Ruin; For most of
their Lands are intail'd for ever on the eldest Son of the Family, so that he can neither alienate nor incumber them without the
Consent of the whole Family, and of the King himself, which is a
thing very hard to be obtain'd. When the eldest Son of a Family
has squander'd his Freehold, and runs himself more and more in
Debt, the Creditors, and sometimes the Parents themselves,
present a Petition to the King and desire a Sequestration. The
King after being inform'd of the List of the Debts, and of the
Majorat (which is the Name they give here to the Lands that are
intail'd) names Trustees for the Administration of the Estates of
the Spendthrift, who is allow'd a Pension till all the Debts are
paid. There's another very good Establishment here for securing
the Sale of Landed Estates and Mortgages. Every Nobleman
gives in a Particular of his Estate to a Tribunal which is call'd the
Landtaffel, where the same is register'd. When a Person wants to
borrow Money or to make a Sale, the Lender or the Purchaser has
recourse to the *Landtaffel's* Office, where he sees whether the
Lands are incumber'd; and if the Borrower's Debts don't exceed
two Thirds of the Price at which they are rated by the *Landtaffel,*
he may lend his Money very safely.

Tho' the *Bohemians* are brave and good Soldiers, yet they don't
love the Service, I mean the Gentry: Most of them prefer the
Civil to Military Employments, and a private Life to Posts in the
Army or at Court. They are so used to be absolute Masters at
their Estates where the Peasants are their Slaves, and to be
homag'd like petty Sovereigns by the Burghers at *Prague,* that
they don't care to reside at *Vienna,* and to be oblig'd like other
Subjects to pay their Court to the Sovereign and the Ministers. As
soon as a Gentleman of *Bohemia* comes of Age, he is oblig'd to
take an Oath of Fidelity to the Emperor as his King; which is a
Law as much binding on the Nobility as the Gentry; and none of
'em dare to go out of the kingdom without express Leave from
the Emperor, on the Penalty of forfeiting his Estate. When the
Noblemen are return'd from their Travels to *France* and *Italy,*
they put in to be Chamberlains, not so much for the Sake of
engaging themselves to Attendance at Court as to procure a
Precedency for their Wives, it being a Custom with most of 'em to

marry as soon as they come of Age. Afterwards they aim to be Counsellors of State, and Stadtholders, and this is the *Ne plus ultra* of their Preferments. The Counsellors of State challenge the Title of *Excellency:* But this is what those who are not of that Denomination, and of as good Families as themselves, scruple to allow them, so that generally speaking they have it only given them by their Domestics and Dependents. So that one may say of their Excellencies what the Duchess of *Elboeuf* of the *Lorrain* Family said in *France* concerning the Princes of *Bouillon*, that they were *Domestic Highnesses*, because none but their own Servants gave them the Title of *Highness*.

Of all the great and wealthy Families, those of *Lobkowitz*, *Kinski*, *Schlick*, *Collobradt*, and *Martinitz*, are the only ones that make a Figure at the Imperial Court. 'Tis true there are several other Noblemen at *Vienna* who have Lands in *Bohemia*, but then the Families are not originally descended from that Kingdom.

The Kinski's Family is actually the most splendid at Court. There are five Brothers of it in Employments. The eldest is the Great Chancellor of Bohemia. The second who is call'd Count *Stephen*, is Great Marshal of *Bohemia*, a Minister of State, and the Emperor's Ambassador at the Court of France. The third, Count *Philip*, is the Emperor's Minister Plenipotentiary to *Great Britain;* and the two youngest are in the Army, where one of them is a Lieutenant-Colonel. Count *Philip* was sent Ambassador when but twenty-nine Years old. He has demonstrated by his Conduct, that Wisdom does not always stay for Age, and that he is the worthy Son of one of the greatest Ministers that the Emperors *Leopold* and *Joseph* ever had. The City of *Prague* is a very great Loser by his Absence, for he liv'd there with Splendor, and his House was always open, particularly to Foreigners. For my own Part I received such Civilities there as I shall never forget.

As I have told you that the Nobility of *Bohemia* are the richest in the Empire, I must also acquaint you that the Peasants there are miserable to the last Degree; their Persons, and all they have, are at the Command of their Lord. The poor Wretches have often not a Bit of Bread to eat, in a Country which is one of the most plentiful in *Europe* for all Sorts of Provisions. They dare not go from one Village to another to Work, nor learn a Handicraft without their Lord's Consent. So much Subjection keeps the poor Creatures always trembling and humble, so that if you do but speak to 'em they are ready to lick the Dust off your Feet. The Severity with which these People are us'd is really terrible, but 'tis as true on the other hand, that gentle Usage has no Effect upon 'em; for they are excessively lazy and stubborn, and being moreover us'd to harsh Treatment from Generation to Generation, Blows scarce terrify them, tho' tis the only Way to make 'em good for anything.

The *Bohemians* have a great many Talents for Music, so that there's no Village, be it ever so small, but the Music is sung in Concert, and they are very happy at winding the Hunter's Horn.

'Tis certain that this Kingdom is one of the best Countries in the Emperor's Possession, and, next to *Hungary*, brings him in most Money.

Bohemia is a Country of States, whom the Emperor, as King of it, summons every Year to the City of Prague. They consist of the Clergy, Nobility, Gentry, and Towns. The Assembly is opened by a Commissioner of the Emperor's Nomination, who lays before them his Imperial Majesty's Demands. The States, such is their Submission and Zeal, grant the full Demand, which is commonly a very great Sum; yet for all this, the *Bohemians* would not complain of Taxes if the Emperor resided among them; but they are sorry to see their Country exhausted to enrich the *Austrians*, to whom they have a natural Aversion, and the *Austrians* as heartily hate the *Bohemians*.

I own to you I shall be sorry to leave *Prague*. I take the *Bohemians* to be the best People upon Earth, and *Prague* to be one of those Towns of the Empire where a Gentleman may have most Choice of Company. The Ladies here are very amiable. Gaming, which may be call'd the universal Pleasure, is carry'd as high here as they please in Houses of the Quality, where Assemblies of both Sexes are held every Night, with good Cheer, particularly Pheasants and Ortolans in Plenty; and upon Fish-Days, there are Trouts, Salmon, and Cray-fish; and, that there may be nothing wanting, *Bohemia* likewise furnishes good Wine. At the Estate of the young Count Tscherwin at *Melneg*, there is a red sort not inferior to *Burgundy*. Of all these good Things many partake together, and for my Part, I own I am taken more with this Pleasure than any other, because we make it last as long as we will, and then 'tis suited to all Ages.

There is a tolerable *Italian* Opera here. In Winter they have

Races in stately Sledges; there is great Masquerading, and they dance till they are ready to drop to the Ground: For this End there are public Balls, which are extraordinary splendid, and might be compar'd, if any can be compar'd, to the Balls at the *Hay-Market* in *London*.

In the Summer-Time, when there is not so much Company in Town, these Assemblies are thinner. The Gentry meet at Night in a Garden belonging to the Prince de *Schwartzenberg*, where they game, chat, and walk up and down, after which they always go to some House or other to sup. When one has a Mind to go to the Country, we are sure of a good Reception, and the longer one stays the greater Pleasure one gives to the Master of the House. Here they pass the Time in Hunting of all Sorts. Many of the Nobility keep Packs of Hounds, and others Hawks. The Generality keep Musicians in their Service, so that let the Weather be what it will, one may be always amused in this Country. Besides, one enjoys all the Freedom here that can be. After this, Sir, can you blame me for being sorry to leave *Bohemia?*

13. The Respectable Rentier

SOCIAL HISTORY is not primarily concerned with heroic individuals. Bertholdt Heinrich Brockes, son of a wealthy merchant, respectable *rentier*, and later senator in the Free City of Hamburg is the very caricature of the unheroic. Pious, self-righteous, and above all cautious, Herr Brockes pursued his grand tour of central Europe by scrupulously avoiding drink, women, gambling, or anything remotely dangerous, adventurous, or stimulating. His two passions were amateur art collecting and pious poetry. Safely back home in Hamburg, Brockes decided to forego a legal career for the independence of a fixed income, and he carefully laid plans for a rich and respectable marriage. Brockes, like other *bourgeois vivant noblement,* lived in constant dread of overstepping the narrow line between prudent economy and the obligations of new found social status.

Source: Bertholdt Heinrich Brockes, *"Selbstbiographie"* in *Deutsche Selbstzeugnisse,* ed. M. Beyer-Fröhlich (Leipzig, 1933), vol. VII, pp. 199ff.

In the year 1700, with the help of God, I began my travels to the universities. I first went to Halle in the company of Mons. Voigt.

As for myself, I have never cared for drinking, but for the sake of company I have not been able to avoid it altogether. A rather strong sense of pride—for like many young people, I was rather taken with myself—kept me away from loose women at the universities as well as in all my other travels. Therefore, I can state publicly that neither at the universities nor in all my other travels have I had any intimate dealings with a low female. I am of the opinion not only that my abstinence insured me against almost unavoidable troubles and dangers, but also that God—albeit without my merit and purely by His Grace—is granting me, instead of forbidden and ignominious pleasure, pleasure a thousandfold in a happy marriage blessed with healthy children, a blessing for which I cannot thank His Clemency enough. I remember that in my travels I observed one maxim in conversation with women, a maxim which turned out to be quite beneficial to me. Instead of approaching the most beautiful women after the example of most young men and paying the greatest attention to them, I diligently sought out the oldest and the least beautiful, treating them in the most kindly fashion. This was not too difficult for me because, owing to a somewhat exaggerated self-love, I did not feel any special tenderness for women. Therefore, on the one hand, I had almost no rivals, thus avoiding many troubles that would otherwise have ensued, while on the other hand, I gained these women's affection without much effort, profiting from a more reliable company. Moreover, I have often found that the most beautiful women, who would probably have treated me with the same *fierté* they treated others, made more advances to me than one would think, no doubt disturbed that I should have escaped the power of their beauty.

I had not been at Halle long when I traveled to Berlin with Baron Zocha and Mons. Linden in order to see the magnificent wedding of the Crown Princess of Prussia. There I had the opportunity of seeing the most sumptuous cortège and all the festivities. Several times I traveled to the Easter and Michaelmas Fair in Leipzig, and once I went to the Naumburg Fair in the company of several barons and counts. And even though I was involved in gaming on various occasions, God protected me from being seriously harmed. For this as well as for the fact that I lacked a passionate inclination for pernicious gambling, I owe Him infinite gratitude. God likewise protected me from quarrels at the universities and everywhere, and only once did I have to fight a duel, which came off well, causing no damage whatsoever.

Having spent two years at Halle without anything particular happening, in 1702 I decided to visit the Imperial Court of Appeal [*Reichskammergericht*] at Wetzlar and learn something of the law. . . .

During my stay in Nürnberg, I spent a good deal of time in the company of the aforementioned Mons. Sandrat who showed me many curiosities. It was upon his advice that I continued my souvenir book begun in Halle in order to assemble paintings and sketches. Having collected a fair number of paintings requested from good friends, I decided to enlarge the format of my book. This acquainted me with good artists everywhere, who later made it a point of honor to become known in this way and painted several good pieces in my book free of charge. I was even able to set up a regular small gallery when I settled down in Hamburg after my travels, mostly from my souvenir book. I augmented it later, but I was most careful not to spend too much money on it. In view of the mores of the times, expenditures on paintings would have given me a bad name rather than the honor I fancied. God be praised for having provided me with so much good sense and yet having granted me so much honor and pleasure through these paintings! Afterwards in Nürnberg I became acquainted with Baron Bohm, Baron Beer, and Count Oxenstiern. The last two were gamblers, but God in His kindness protected me so that I did not become involved with them. . . .

[Brockes goes to Italy: Venice, Ferrara, Bologna, Loretto, Rome, Venice; then to Paris, Brussels, Antwerp, Rotterdam, Leyden, Amsterdam.]

Thus I left Holland and arrived safely in my hometown [Hamburg] on the first Sunday of Advent, A.D. 1704. God be praised fervently for it and for all the innumerable kindnesses He granted me on my dangerous travels! As can easily be imagined, I was very happily received by my mother. Having paid and received the customary visits, I deliberated with myself as to how I was to arrange my life. Did I want to begin practicing and become a busy lawyer? Or did I want to lead a quiet life and remain independent? I had a natural inclination for the latter, which was more and more confirmed in conversation with various friends. It therefore became my design to arrange a rich marriage aided by my good manners, a project which my youthful vanity made appear easy. I kept the most refined company, gave a concert every week, established a small cabinet of paintings, and the like, seeking to win esteem and popularity in this way. Indeed, I was not unsuccessful. Later, however, experience taught me that, given certain conditions in our city, this was not necessarily without danger. In a place where everybody is interested in commerce, such ways can easily give one the reputation of idler. Even though I did not hold any public office, I did not waste my time. I studied moral philosophy, reading such books as La Bruyère's *Charactères*, Rochefoucauld, the *Pensées* of Pascal, Molière, Boileau, and so forth. And since I had started to read Italian poetry to learn Italian, having even translated some passages, I felt it would be an agreeable pastime to translate several satires from Boileau, as well as some poems of Madame des Houllières. Since I did rather well at this, I began to be more and more interested in poetry. . . .

At the same time, I was also intent upon a rich marriage. I received word from Holland that a very prosperous Dutchman, who was said to have a fortune of more than a million and who had shown me considerable affection when I was in Holland, had expressed himself to the effect that, if I proposed to his daughter, I would not be rejected. I decided not to pass up what I considered to be good fortune. Therefore, I set out for Holland in order to try my luck, provided the situation continued to be favorable. Such, however, must not have been God's plan, for even though I was treated by the whole family with the utmost distinction, I heard through an intimate friend that the young lady was as good as betrothed to a Dutchman. Thereupon, I did not tarry and immediately began my voyage back, arriving—God be thanked!— safely in Hamburg. . . .

In the year 1709 my dear mother, to whom I am most indebted for all her great love and care, died. This death obliged me to pursue my marriage plans somewhat more seriously. In the meantime I dissolved my household to the extent of taking my meals at the Kaysershof and paying my servants for their meals. I also began to improve my townhouse, which was rather old-fashioned, using, among other funds, 250 gulden which I had won in the city lottery. . . .

After I had written the well-known Oratorio of the Passion, I had it performed most solemnly in my house. This being an unusual event, it brought to my house not only all the foreign nobility, the ministers and residents and their ladies, but also most of Hamburg's citizens of rank, so that more than 500 persons were present. This event took place—God be praised for it!—in the best of order, without any confusion, and everyone enjoyed it, so that I derived no small pleasure from it.

Soon after, several good friends advised me to become a candidate for the office of Syndic which had recently become vacant. The late Mayor von Bostel strongly supported my candidacy, and I would probably have obtained the position but for a certain circumstance. However, I have thanked God almost daily for this turn of events since I now see what a heavy burden this office entailed.

About this same time, I had directed my attention toward a very wealthy young lady, but, because of certain circumstances, this project came to nothing even though a good beginning had been made. This made me feel God's direction, and I now recognize that I have every reason to thank Him. For at the very least, had this marriage come about, I should not have married the woman God gave me later, whose fear of God and other exceptional qualities of body and soul are such a great source of satisfaction to me. The same thing happened with respect to another alliance. Even though things were practically settled with the future father-in-law, the marriage was amiably retracted on both sides because of certain special circumstances.

Thereafter, several years passed without significant changes. During this time, I was occupied with the above-mentioned translation of Marini which, with the help of God, I brought to a good end. Through my poetry I made the acquaintance of the present Secret Secretary, Herr König, and through him I met my wife. . . . Given her qualities of body, soul, and fortune, she was one of the most attractive of matches, especially since the recent death of her father. I resolved, in the name of God, to ask for her hand, which—praise be to Him!—I was granted. Hence, I was married

to my bride, Anna Ilsabe Lehmann, in February, 1714, by Pastor
Heinson. The great God from whom all blessings come be praised
fervently for having given me in her person a comely, fruitful,
reasonable, virtuous, and God-fearing spouse, and for having
made that day of my marriage a fountain from which pleasure
has flowed a thousandfold in the last fourteen years. May He in
His mercy, if He deems it beneficial for both of us, grant our
marriage a long duration according to His Holy Will.

14. Conspicuous Consumption

SOCIAL ASPIRATIONS require a certain flair. Obvious, blatant economy
will not do. To cut a good figure in society demands, first of all,
proper equipage. A carriage is better than a fiacre, a fiacre better than a
sedan chair. As the inimitable Mercier suggests, the carriage reassures
the clients of the professional man, facilitates the amorous pursuits of
the rake, and alleviates the boredom of the lady of fashion. Most simply, it is the indispensable sign of social respectability. Like Boswell's
"genteel lodging in a good part of the town, proper breeches, silk
stockings, shoe buckles, and wigs," equipage is a requirement of a
gentleman's station.[1] Fortunate indeed is he who avoids the heavier
social demands of "twenty-one" and "open table."

Source: Helen Simpson, ed., *The Waiting City: Paris 1728–88*,
    *Being an Abridgement of Louis-Sebastian Mercier's "Le tableau
    de Paris."* transl. by Helen Simpson, pp. 36–38.

Pedestrian

AN IGNOBLE creature; that is the definition we are coming to.
Nevertheless, men of genius in all walks of life still stick to shoe-
leather. Wits may be carriage-folk, but genius goes afoot.

When a man, rich in intelligence but pocket-foolish, leaves a
drawing-room where the equipaged still chatter, and crosses the
courtyard, its clean flagstones flecked with foam from the bits of

[1] Frederick A. Pottle, ed., *Boswell's London Journal* (New York, 1956),
Appendix I.

idle champing horses, he must slip, blushing, between the motionless wheels to where his old creaking *fiacre* waits out in the street, and there in its ramshackle carcase hide his shame. If the lamps of emerging gilded chariots light up his unhappy vehicle, no bows are exchanged; he would not dare from his ignominious depth to salute these passing ladies, with whom six minutes back he talked so freely. His coachman's moustaches are enough to damn even a *fiacre* at one-fifty an hour; and damn its passenger too, were he Plato, or Homer's self.

For a carriage is the goal of every man that sets out upon the unclean road to riches. His first stroke of luck buys him a cabriolet, which he drives himself; the next, a *coupé;* the third step forward is marked by a carriage; and the final triumph is a separate conveyance for the wife. As his purse rounds, comes a cabriolet for the son, then one for his man of business; the steward drives in one to market; soon it will be the cook's turn to handle the ribbons; and all these diabolical vehicles, given over each morning to the impudents below-stairs, dash and clatter their way through our footpathless streets as though fiends were at their tails.

A doctor's first move is to set up his carriage. It is nothing to look at, he houses it outside his front door in the portico, which it completely fills; the horses are almost in his very waiting-room, his coachman is turned seventy; no matter, all the quarter knows he keeps his carriage. Out of his door he comes, with his powdered wig and his black coat and his septuagenarian on the box, and indeed until he has driven off there is no getting in or out of his house; again, what matter, he is a carriage-doctor, he will never lack patients.

Nowadays the young man of fashion, instead of investing his capital in a country cottage, or a library, or a mistress, sinks it in a carriage. For a while half his income goes in upkeep; then all at once the carriage becomes cook, cottage and mistress to him; every night he drives out, sees ladies home, escorts them to their boxes, and next day to a race meeting. Twice a week he offers gallantly the loan of his horses, while husbands, that uncivil race, eternally and senselessly busy, monopolize without complaint the conjugal vehicle. A man with a carriage is a made man. He is *liaison* officer for all the picnics; his horses and his person—never simultaneously, however, and for good cause—contribute to the ladies' pleasure. And so wives, since the fashion of husbandly neglect set in, have refused to receive or consider any young man suspected of going on foot; which decision seems reasonable.

For how can a woman exist without horses? In the brief space of twelve little hours she must be seen at the opera, a review of troops, any fair that may be open; must dance, and must gamble, to say nothing of ministerial receptions, which no woman dare miss, any more than she can afford to be ignorant of the latest fashion in dancers. Our women of to-day, eternally restless, eternally on show, have lent to existence something of the mobility of their own features.

Thus a provincial's first duty, on ten thousand francs a year, is to set up his carriage. It will cost him three hundred francs a month to begin with, and he will have no use of it whatever; his friends will see to that. He pays, and continues to walk. Lucky man; for this single display of tactics will so advance him, that taking it all round, he will find his carriage an economy—that is, if he is liberal with it. If, obstinately, he refuses to launch out, to horse himself, that is the end of him.

Certain young men only drive in the winter season; in summer they walk, loudly extolling the weather. The fact is, their budgets will allow no more than a bare eighteen hundred francs for transport. Forced to choose between the seasons, you may see them up aloft in a caped coat on the 1st of December, from which eminence they meekly descend somewhere about the 1st of May, when everyone goes out of town. But it is really none too easy, this problem of which season to choose when one has only eighteen hundred to spend; there are excellent arguments for both, between which there is no deciding. And so the young man combines in his person both Pollux and Castor, now Olympus receives him, and now the gutter with whose mud he alternately spatters and is spattered.

But merit, talent, genius, probity, all the virtues imaginable are nothing if they go on foot. Suppose the contrary, stupidity and all the vices served up in an elegant equipage, and then see the doors fly open, welcomes everywhere and the rank taken for granted. Poor humanity! But this is the way of it.

III

Agriculture

THE DYNAMICS of overseas commerce, the spectacular growth of certain port cities, and the intellectual excitement of Paris and London may make us forget how unchangeable, narrow, and provincial the lives of most Europeans were in the eighteenth century. To travel only a few miles into the hinterland of Bordeaux, Cadiz, Livorno, or Hamburg was to enter the Middle Ages. The wheat fields, the sharecropper's cart, the parish church, the château on the hill, a two-room cottage—these were the signposts of a timeless, routine existence, worlds away from drawing rooms and bustling wharves.

The Elbe River marked a kind of boundary between two types of agrarian organization. West of the Elbe, in France, the Rhine Valley, and northern Italy, small property predominated. The peasantry owned a substantial part of the soil, perhaps half of the arable land. The peasant lots, divided and subdivided under the laws of equal inheritance, were usually very small—under five acres—so that the peasant farmer had to work as tenant or field hand to make ends meet. Significantly, however, a large part of the peasantry had learned the meaning of proprietorship. The domains of the larger landlords—noble, townsman, monastery, or cathedral chapter—existed alongside the tiny peasant holdings, forming clusters of family farms whose combined area rarely exceeded 1,000 acres. The largest landlords in France with their stretches of forest did not own more than 5,000 acres. The seigneurs of France, like those of the Rhine and Po Valleys, claimed quit rents and other seigneurial dues on much larger areas of land. These quit rents varied greatly, sometimes consisting of only a few deniers per acre, but in other cases attaining 12 per cent of the harvest. Fixed by customary law, they could not easily be increased, though they were more rigorously collected in the late eighteenth century.

East of the Elbe, the land was owned in enormous tracts by noble landlords and worked by serf labor. As one moved east over the pine-covered plains of Pomerania and Poland and on to the steppes of Russia, small peasant proprietorship disappeared and with it a sense of property ownership among the dirt farmers. In fact, in the eighteenth century, serfdom represented a grimmer existence than it had even a century before. A serf was now likely to work six rather than three days a week on his lord's land. The nobles, in contrast to their western cousins, held thousands of acres. For a Polish or Russian magnate, the 5,000 acres of a Brandenburg Junker were mediocre, and the few hundred acres of a French marquis laughable. Indeed, the eastern landlord was likely to calculate his landed resources in serfs rather than in acres or farms. Working the land in such large blocks, even with primitive methods and a high ratio of labor per acre, the eastern landowners could produce a marketable surplus of wheat, which they exported regularly from the Baltic ports. Only a trifling number of independent peasants and nonnoble landlords disturbed the simplicity of this rural hierarchy—lord and serf.

England presents a third type of agrarian organization. Here the large landlords—10,000, 20,000, 50,000 acres—existed side by side with a more modest gentry and the independent yeoman farmers. By adding the wealthier gentry to the peerage, the landed aristocracy of England can be estimated at about 400 families, the smallest and richest aristocracy in Europe. Their landed revenue far exceeded those of any Continental noblemen west of the Vistula. Adding the revenues from public bonds and overseas trade, they certainly surpassed even the Russian magnates in wealth. Furthermore, this landed aristocracy was getting richer. High prices meant higher rents, and some of the profits were plowed back into farm improvements. In addition to buying out the smaller gentry, the great English families were increasing their farm productivity by enclosures. Since enclosure necessitated the agreement of a large number of proprietors, the wealthy landlords used their influence in Parliament to pass enclosure acts which forced the smaller proprietors to comply. Many a yeoman, of course, lost his land or was simply unable to compete with more efficient, large-scale agriculture. As a result, the number of landless farm laborers increased. It would be wrong, however, to identify this "proletarianization" with "pauperization," since rural wages in England were high by Continental standards. Nevertheless, English agricultural society, though not so simply stratified as that of eastern Europe, was increasingly characterized by a very small group of great landed families, a much larger group of middling gentry, a substantial number of well-to-do tenant farmers, and a mass of day laborers.

The tenant farmers who ran the estates of the great families were the real agricultural entrepreneurs. Given an encouraging margin of profit on their farms, they developed both a personal loyalty to their landlord and a professional expertise that led to farm improvements. No doubt enclosure was an important element in the English agricultural revolution, but the imagination, talent, and capital of the larger tenant farmers, ably seconded by the estate agent, probably counted for even more. These were the men who planted the clover and the turnips, altered the traditional crop courses, eliminated the fallow field, and improved the livestock.

The near absence of this active, imaginative, well-to-do tenant class on the Continent helps explain the relative stagnation of French and Italian agriculture. The French and Italian estate agents and larger tenants tended to be little more than rent collectors from small peasants. If the French landlord was an absentee, he employed short-term leases and raised his rents so high that by the end of the century there was no margin or incentive left for the local tenant to invest in improvements. Even where such a margin did exist, an improving capitalist farmer would have to persuade the small, routine-minded peasantry to accept land exchanges and to adopt new methods. Suppression of the fallow would threaten the poor with the abolition of communal rights, still very strong in France. Unlike the English Parliament, the French government was inclined to support the poor against enclosure or at least not authorize enclosure except in special cases.

As for the resident landlord, such as the Marquis de Fourquevaux near Toulouse, his estate management was a tight-fisted accounting operation whereby a 200-acre domain was made to yield a maximum rent, which was usually reinvested in more land, not in agricultural experiments. In addition to the reasons suggested above, Arthur Young saw another explanation for this. French landlords were so impressed by rising wheat prices that they considered any scheme that would even temporarily reduce wheat acreage foolish and risky. Why suffer such loss for an uncertain gain in the future? Consequently, without increases in crop yields, population pressure drove the prices of basic foodstuffs ever higher in the years after 1750.[1]

The inadequacy of French agricultural productivity was one ingredient in the Revolution of 1789. Though historians continue to debate its relative importance, there is no doubt about increasing distress, since the majority—probably close to 90 per cent of the French peasants—were "buyers" rather than "sellers" in the rising grain market. The poor townsmen were even worse off, except for a few years between 1778 and 1786. The situation was ripe for rural rioting and perhaps for a rural revolution if leadership and direction could be found and sustained. The role of rural notaries, tenant farmers, and estate agents is important here. Did they direct the frustrations and deprivations of the mass of the peasantry against the rural seigneurs? If so, we should know about these middlemen and why they deserted their old masters for the risks and dangers of a peasant revolution. For rural revolutions must be led. Price, wage, and rent can tell us much, but group attitudes and personal psychology can tell us more. Consequently, even ostensibly statistical material should be used as much as

[1] The work of C. E. Labrousse and his disciples in France is relevant here. Arthur Young saw a relation between population pressure and price rise in 1789 (see Document 16).

possible to determine such attitudes, values, or states of mind. Properly used, a tax declaration, an account book, or a will can sometimes bring even the humblest peasant back to life.

15. Reports of Committees of the House of Commons on Enclosure

THE REPORT of the House Committee on the Improvement of Waste and Uninclosed Lands of 1794 reveals the extraordinary progress of enclosure in England since 1760. About 300,000 acres were enclosed in the first two thirds of the century; about 3 million acres were enclosed in the last third. The tables of the committee report clearly establish this acceleration as well as the geographic distribution of the acreages enclosed. Completely converted to enclosure, the committee constantly associates "improvement" with "inclosure," asserting that "those unable or unwilling to improve their allotments" in the commons will soon follow the example of those who are. To expedite further enclosure, the committee recommends a law permitting individuals to separate out their property rights from the common in order to enclose and urges the "parties interested" to appoint commissioners for this purpose, rather than place additional burdens on the courts. Such legislation further favored the larger property holders and penalized the small, who often relied exclusively on common land for pasturage. For what resources did the small holder have to pay for the legal counsel necessary to defend his common rights before the commissioners? And who could afford the expense of hedging and fencing newly enclosed land? Not the small holder, who either sold out or now had to compete unfavorably with the modernized agricultural methods of the large landlords.

On the other hand, there is no question that in England enclosure was a prerequisite for the development of more productive methods of farming. English landlords, by breaking the open-field system with its communal regulations of crop rotation and cattle grazing, could now freely experiment with new crop courses, plant forage crops, and improve livestock. Whatever the ultimate cost to the smaller landholder, enclosure was certainly part of an agricultural revolution that made it possible to support a growing urban population. Without this spurt in agricultural productivity, England could not have sustained the rapid industrialization that followed.

Source: *House of Commons Reports, First Series* (1774–1802), vol. IX, pp. 211–212.

Appendix C. Extracts from the Reports,
Printed by the Board of Agriculture; Pointing Out the Advantages
of a General Inclosing Bill

THE ARGUMENTS for the continuance of Commons in their present state, are, in general, fallacious; and, though specious, are grounded on mistaken principles of humanity. The advantages they would be of to society, if properly cultivated, would be very great; and the attention of the new Board will, I trust, soon be fixed upon this important object, so as to find the means of removing the impediments which prevent their inclosure, upon which I shall have to observe under the head of Commons Fields.

If we properly consider the benefits resulting to population from inclosing (though that, as well as the advantages which might be derived from inclosing Commons, has been superficially questioned) it will strike us with astonishment. Let the population of England be compared with what it was fifty years since, and I presume it will be found increased nearly a third. If I were asked the cause, I should say, that I believe it is chiefly from inclosing; and my reasons for it are, that in all places where my observation has come, it carries full proof. I have seen many effects in many parts of England; but I shall subjoin one striking instance in this county. The parish of Felbrigg, belonging to Mr. *Windham*, consists of about 1,300 acres of land, and till the year 1771 remained, time out of mind, in the following state; 400 acres of Inclosed, 100 of Wood Land, 400 of Common Field, and 400 of Common or Heath. By authentic registers at different periods it appeared, that the number of souls had never been known to exceed 124, which was the number in 1745; in 1777 they were only 121; at this time they amount to 174. This rapid increase I attribute chiefly to the recent improvements made in the parish, by inclosing all the Common Field Land, and by converting most of the Common into arable land and plantations. The parish has no particular connection with any other, and therefore its own increase of labour and produce must be the principal cause at least of this striking alteration. The parish of Wyburn, which remains uninclosed in this neighbourhood, belonging to Lord *Walpole*, who possesses in a very eminent degree the three great characteristics of a country gentleman, a good magistrate, a good neighbour, and a good landlord, is the most like what Felbrigg was before its inclosure, consisting of about the same quantity of Common and Common Fields; but I do not find that the population there has increased of late, which is a corroborating proof of inclosures being in favour of population.

If then inclosing be found so beneficial, every obstruction to it ought to be removed. In the first place, were there one general Act of Parliament formed, under which any parish that could agree in itself should be able to take shelter, or even any two or more persons agreeing upon any exchange of land, or a separation of a mixed interest, whereby the inclosing of such land was the result, should, upon the payment of a small consideration, receive the sanction of a short summary law to bind their agreement—this would insensibly lead to a vast field of improvement.

No person who has reflected seriously on the state of the soil of England, but must be well convinced, that there want few instigations to cultivate Wastes, but the power to do it, without those very expensive applications to Parliament, which are at present necessary even for the smallest objects. If the Board of Agriculture be able to accomplish this desideratum, it will merit greatly, and the national interests find themselves advanced in a degree which no other event whatever could secure.

Hardly any thing farther seems material to add to the observations already made on the improvement of the Waste Lands. To that great object the attention of the Board of Agriculture will naturally be directed; and a happy circumstance it will be, if, under their auspices, every acre in this, and every other county in Great Britain, is brought under some useful and profitable mode of occupation. On this head, however, it is impossible to omit mentioning the very important observation made by Dr. *Wilkinson*, of Enfield, who thinks a general mandatory Inclosure Bill absolutely necessary.

Indeed it seems an opinion almost unanimous among those who have thought upon this subject, that one general Act of Parliament to empower the division and inclosure of all the Waste and Commonable Lands in the kingdom would be thankfully received by every individual, and prove an equal benefit to them and to the public.

A well-digested general Bill for the inclosure of Commons,

Common Fields, and Waste Lands, would wonderfully operate towards the success of inclosures, as it would be a means of saving a very considerable expence in the outset of the business.

In these cases, if a general exchange were to take place, and each individual were to be accommodated with his allotment of land equivalent to the value of his Common right, laid together as much as situation and circumstances would admit, the Commonable land inclosed, and each man's right specifically divided, the most must then be necessarily made of the property in each person's possession, and the number of small occupiers of land would still continue, which would be a great advantage to population, and the community at large. To effect this separation or division of the rights of individuals in a parish, something is wanting less expensive than an Act of Parliament for an inclosure, which oftentimes defeats the improvements, by the heavy charge incurred, seldom less than £300 or £400 besides the risk of not succeeding. In parishes where all parties are agreed, if this sort of business were to be done by Commissioners, composed of intelligent farmers, or gentlemen's stewards, under good regulations, many improvements would take place, which are now not objects of sufficient consequence to apply to Parliament for.

Our Waste Lands, including the Forests, may be estimated at full fifteen thousand acres; the greater part of which is as capable of producing Corn, after a certain time for necessary improvements, as the adjoining lands, and would in most instances, it is presumed, be made profitable to the community, could some method, such for instance as passing a general Act of Parliament to ascertain the rights of the lords of the manors, tythe owners, and the several tenants, which it is thought might be done by proportioning the tenant's claim to the nature and extent, or annual value of his tenements, held of the manor to which the Wastes belong, and then enable the lord, who is most frequently more enlightened, and better able to advance the various expences of inclosing and other necessary improvements, to purchase these rights as a jury should value them, and thus make it worth his while to erect farm houses and other conveniences; as without some such power of purchasing, the Wastes would be found in most places too small to admit of as many divisions as there would be claims given in, or the ground would be allotted to people unable, from want of experience or property, to render their little portions of much service to the public or to themselves.

And that brings us to consider the impediments that are thrown in the way of inclosures of Common Field Land, and indeed it may apply to inclosures in general. It is a known fact, that no Common Field Land, or Commonable Land, can be inclosed without an express Act of Parliament, unless indeed by the consent of all persons interested; but from the nature and disposition of mankind, such a consent is difficult to be obtained, and particularly where some of the parties are minors, abroad, or labour under any legal disqualification. It is indeed almost impossible to procure such consent. With interests so clashing, and difficulties so various, Parliament becomes the only resource; but what with the expence in carrying the Bills through both Houses of Parliament (and which, for aught we know, may be extremely proper) together with the much greater expence of bringing the parties to London, there to wait the unavoidable delays occasioned by other more important concerns of Parliament, until decision shall take place upon the subject, operate in many cases as a powerful discouragement to undertakings of this nature, and not unfrequently to an entire exclusion from the attempt.

With all due submission, therefore, something like the following plan may be adopted: To pass a general Act of Parliament for inclosures of every description, empowering the Magistrates at their Quarter Sessions to receive proposals from the parties interested in any inclosure to have power to appoint two or more Commissioners, and two able and respectable Land Surveyors, who should on oath make a plan of the intended inclosure, and take a view of the soil and situation thereof, to have full authority to make all exchanges of land, and to settle every difference that may arise from the present admixture of property. These Commissioners, having local knowledge of the premisses, and acting under the eye of the Magistrates, would proceed with that caution and circumspection so essential to the due administration of justice, and their decision or award might be legalized either by the Board of Agriculture, or by the Magistrates at a subsequent Sessions, as to the wisdom of Parliament shall seem meet. It is presumed that from some such plan very important benefits to the country would arise; it would awaken a laudable emulation among the gentlemen and farmers, by rendering that secure which in its present state is exposed and insecure; and, that emulation once set afloat, who can calculate the advantages?

The advantage resulting from inclosing, or at least severalling, Common Fields, is so obvious, and has of late years proved so beneficial, that it requires no observation from me to record its good effects. Some sound and well-digested measures are however much wanting, to accelerate this great benefit to the community. The difficulty and expence of procuring legal authority to effect this desirable improvement, act at present very materially against its extension.

The expence of an application to Parliament, and obtaining Acts for apportioning and dividing the Commons belonging to 47 parishes, and the after division of such apportionments, amongst the Commoners of each respective parish, might probably involve the proprietors of the whole in the enormous expence of 47 Acts of Parliament—a very sufficient reason for the proprietors dreading the expence of the measure of inclosing the fens, and no indifferent proof of the necessity for a general Act to promote the inclosure of all Commons, Common Fields, Common Meadows, and Waste Lands in the United Kingdoms, under such regulations and restrictions as the wisdom of Parliament may devise.

N.B.—The general Act for dividing 47 Commons, by the usage of the House, would be charged as 47 Acts, and pay the sum accordingly.

When the inclosing system is appreciated by its obvious tendency to increase the produce of land and the demand for labour, to augment the rate of wages to the husbandman, and to lessen the amount of the poor's rate, it is a subject of regret and astonishment that so few means have been devised by the Legislature either to facilitate or extend its progress. How much is to be done this way, a general Inclosure Act unfettered by tedious and expensive formalities, would speedily manifest. From the very great number of private Acts which have passed within the last twenty years, such general principles might be selected for its basis, as to implicate almost every possible variety of claim, interest, and property. An Act thus instituted might, without hazard or injury, be entrusted to a given number of Justices at the Quarter Sessions, to dispense its powers and controul its execution, and such Justices I should conceive perfectly competent to determine on the propriety or impropriety of any proposed inclosure.

Thus a total extinction of Parliamentary expence would encourage inclosing on the smallest scale, and, with advantages not
to be despised, would accommodate the most extensive.

This measure, however consonant to the principles of individual benefit and national policy, would notwithstanding have a
host of adversaries to encounter.

16. Agriculture in France

THE SUCCESSFUL Parliamentary campaign for enclosure is a stark contrast to the universal resistance to it in France. Communal rights
remained strong even in regions where royal edicts had authorized division of common lands and the abolition of communal rights of pasturage. Arthur Young asserted regretfully that without consent of the
local courts of law (*parlements*) no royal enclosure act could be executed. Nor could much be expected from the new National Assembly,
since the "people" were universally opposed to enclosure. Thus the
French protected the small owner, but at the cost of a more modern
agriculture.

The second selection from Young is one of the best brief compari-
sons of contemporary French and English agriculture found anywhere.
Young attributed the relatively high returns on land in France not
primarily to lower costs, but to the competition for land among all
Frenchmen, which he ascribed ultimately to the "excessive population
of the kingdom." This too was the cause of the "miserable state of the
labouring poor."

Turning to productivity, Young observed not only that the English
farmer produced a third more wheat and rye per acre but also that
English grains were better dressed and cleaned. He then described the
difference between the English and French tenant farmers. Saddled
with paying the taxes, the French tenants were "at the landlord's
mercy" and, lacking any capital of their own, they were "content
merely to live." Thus, half of the gross produce went to the landlord
in France, while in England he received only a fourth to a sixth. No
major capital improvements could be expected from such poor sharecroppers, and no country gentleman was inclined to "spend one penny
beyond the most pressing necessity." Yet it is the comparison of rotation systems that best demonstrates the English superiority in agriculture. Here is the crucial contrast between a modern and a traditional
agriculture. For the suppression of the fallow field and the introduction of artificial meadows mark the key breakthroughs of the agricultural revolution.

Source: Arthur Young, *Travels in France During the Years 1787, 1788, and 1789*, pp. 339–340, 353–358, 454.

Inclosures

THE OPEN arable fields of Picardy, Artois, part of Normandy, the Isle of France, Brie, and the Pays de Beauce, are cursed with all the mischievous circumstances known in similar cases in England, such as rights of common pasturage, commencing on given days, when under corn, and throughout the fallow year; as well as that miserable phantastical division of property which seems to have been contrived, for giving an occupier as much trouble and expence as possible in the culture of his scraps of fields. In England we have been making, for forty or fifty years past, a considerable progress in the allotment and inclosure of open fields; and through tythes, folly, obstinacy, prejudice, and heavy expences in parliament, operate powerfully in preventing great numbers of inclosures, yet we have enough to preserve the habit, mode, and system of doing the business; it goes on; and, from the progress of good sense and experience, we may hope to have the whole kingdom inclosed in another century. In France, on the contrary, they have not taken the first step; they have not devised a method of proceeding; they know not, nor have any idea of giving full powers to commissioners to go through the Herculean labour, as the French would esteem it, of making a fair division, without appeal. There was a royal edict for this purpose in 1764, or 1765, I think, which had a particular reference to Loraine; but, in passing through that province, I made enquiries into its effect, and found little or nothing had resulted from it. Nay, I was assured at Metz, Pont à Mousson, Nancy, and Luneville, that rights of common pasture were universal in the province, and that every thing was eaten which was sown contrary to the established routine. I asked, at Luneville, why they had not more lucerne? The answer was, the *droit de parcours* prevents it. But under the old government of France, no permission, or regulation of this sort, could be carried into execution, because there was in reality no legislature in France. I shall elsewhere shew this more distinctly: no law could be effectual, unless consented to *willingly* by the parliaments, and then vigorously executed by them; for, by means of the vicious constitution of their courts of justice, there was no executive government to carry the law into execution; so that if all parties were not fully united in executing, as well as enacting in any measure, nothing could ever be done—the King being really impotent in this respect, with all his despotism. Under the new government, which is establishing in France, I have great doubts whether any progress can ever be made in this great and leading step to all useful improvements in agriculture: as far as the present constitution can be understood, it is the will of *the people* that is to govern; and I know of no country where the people are not against inclosures. The Tiers Etat, and clergy of Metz expressly demand, that the edict of inclosure shall be revoked: that of Troyes, and Nismes, and Anjou, make the same request; another, that the right of commonage in forests shall be granted to the neighbouring parishes.—The nobility of Cambray declare, that commons ought not to be broken up. Nay, some of the *cahiers* go so far as to say, that the commons which have already been divided, ought to be thrown open again. Hence we may judge what probability there can be, of any new and effective laws to promote and *enforce* such a measure.

To enter largely into the advantages of inclosures, in such a work as this, and at this time of day, would be superfluous; it is sufficient to remark, that without a regular system of inclosures no cattle can be kept. . . .

Produce—Rent—Price

And now, drawing the whole into one view, we may say,

That the average price of all the cultivated land in the kingdom is, per English acre, 20l.
That the rent of such part as is let is 15s. 7d.
That the average produce of wheat and rye is 18 bushels.
That the seed yields return 6 for 1.
That land pays per cent 3 ¾.

Observations

I must, in the first place, caution the reader against supposing that these proportions are applicable to the whole territory of France; vines, and wastes, and gardens, and spots of extraordinary fertility are excluded; and the price of 20l. per acre, and the rent of 15s. 7d. are those of the cultivated lands commonly found throughout the kingdom. No waste, no sheep-walk, nor any tracks neglected, and not in profitable produce, are included. But whenever rent is mentioned, we must recollect, that much the greater part of the lands of France are not let at a money-rent, but at one-half or one-third produce, and that in those places, in the central and southern provinces, and in several of the northern ones, where rent occurs in the notes, it is probable that for one acre so let, there are twenty at half produce. This will serve in a good measure to explain the height of the rent here minuted, on comparison with the husbandry.—Such management in England would not afford any such rent; but as the landlord in France is obliged to stock his farms at his own expence, the greatness of this rent is more apparent than real; for it must not only pay him for the use of his land, but also for that of the capital, which he is obliged, through the poverty of the farmers, to invest upon it. Another circumstance, which raises rent beyond all comparison with it in England, is the freedom from poor rates; to which may be added, the very moderate demands made for tythes. By combining the preceding tables, there appears some reason to believe, that the persons who, in different parts of the kingdom, gave me intelligence of the interest per cent accruing from land, had in contemplation rather the *gross receipt*, than the *net profit*. The two accounts of rental and price give 3l. 18s. per cent gross receipt;—if the two vingtièmes, and 4s. per livre, being the landlord's tax, are deducted, there will remain about 3½ per cent —from which there must be a further deduction for incidental losses; and for the interest of the capital invested in live stock; which will certainly demand some deduction. It should therefore seem, that 3, or 3¼ per cent absolutely net, is as much as can be reckoned by this account; whereas the direct intelligence was 3¾. These little variations will for ever arise in such inquiries, when founded, as they must be, on the intelligence received from such a variety of persons, who have different degrees of knowledge and accuracy.

In order to judge the better of these particulars, so interesting to the political arithmetician, it will be necessary to contrast them with the similar circumstances of England; by which method their merit or deficency may be more clearly discriminated. In respect to England, may be remarked, in the first place, a very singular circumstance, which is the near approximation of the

two kingdoms, in the two articles of *price* and *rent*. The rent of
cultivated land in England, exclusive of sheep-walks, warrens,
and wastes, if it could be known accurately, would be probably
found not much to exceed 15s. 7d. per acre; at least I am inclined
to think so, for several reasons, too complex to give here. I have
indeed none for fixing on that *exact* sum; but I should calculate it
somewhere between 15s. and 16s. Now 15s. 7d. at twenty-six
years purchase, which I take to be the present average price of
land in this kingdom (1790 and 1791), is 20l. 5s. 2d. The two
kingdoms are, therefore, on a foot of equality in this respect. The
interest paid by land 3¾ in France, is higher than in England,
where it cannot be calculated at more than three, perhaps not
more than 2¾. If it be thought extraordinary, that land should sell
for as high a price in France as in England, there are not wanted
circumstances to explain the reason. In the first place, the net
profit received from estates is greater. There are no poor rates in
that kingdom; and tythes were much more moderately exacted, as
it has been observed above. Repairs, which form a considerable
deduction with us, are a very trifling one with them. But what
operates as much, or perhaps more than these circumstances, is
the number of small properties. I have touched several times on
this point in the course of the notes, and its influence pervades
every part of the kingdom; all the savings which are made by the
lower classes in France, are invested in land; but this practice is
scarcely known in England, where such savings are usually lent
on bond or mortgage, or invested in the public funds. This causes
a competition for land in France, which, very fortunately for the
prosperity of our agriculture, does not obtain here.

As to the next article, namely, the acreable produce of corn
land, the difference will be found very great indeed; for in England, the average produce of wheat and rye (nineteen-
twentieths the former) is twenty-four bushels, which form a vast
superiority to eighteen, the produce of France; amounting to
twelve for one of the seed, instead of six for one. But the superiority is greater than is apparent in the proportion of those two
numbers; for the corn of England, as far as respects *dressing*, that
is cleaning from dirt, chaff, seeds of weeds, &c. is as much better
than that of France, as would make the difference at least twenty-
five (instead of twenty-four) to eighteen; and I am inclined to

think even more. There is not a plank threshing-floor in France; and no miller can grind corn as he receives it from the farmer, without further cleaning. Another point, yet more important, is, that English wheat, in much the greater part of our kingdom, succeeds other preparatory crops; whereas the wheat of France follows almost universally a dead fallow, on which is spread all the dung of the farm. A circumstance, which ought to give a considerable superiority to the French crops, is that of climate, which in France is abundantly better for this production than in England; and, what is still of greater moment, the spring corn of France, compared with that of England, is absolutely contemptible, and indeed unworthy of any idea of comparison. While, therefore, in France, the wheat and rye are relied on for the almost total support of the farm and farmer, reason tells us, that the wheat ought to be much superior to the produce of a country, in which it does not bear an equally important part. Lastly, let me observe, that the soil of France is, for the most part, better than that of England. Under these various circumstances, for the average produce of the former, to be so much inferior, is truly remarkable. But eighteen bushels of wheat and rye, and miserable spring corn, afford as high a rent in France, as twenty-four in England, with the addition of our excellent spring corn: this forms a striking contrast, and leads to the explanation of the difference. It arises very much from the poverty of the French tenantry; for the political institutions and spirit of the government having, for a long series of ages, tended strongly to depress the lower classes, and favour the higher ones, the farmers, in the greater part of France, are blended with the peasantry; and, in point of wealth, are hardly superior to the common labourers; these poor farmers are *metayers*, who find nothing towards stocking a farm but labour and implements; and being exceedingly miserable, there is rarely a sufficiency of the latter. The landlord is better able to provide live stock; but, engaged in a dissipated scene of life, probably at a distance from the farm, and being poor, like country gentlemen in many other parts of Europe, he stocks the farm not one penny beyond the most pressing necessity:—from which system a wretched produce must unavoidably result. That the tenantry should generally be poor, will not be thought strange, when the taxes laid upon them are considered; their tailles and capitation are heavy in themselves; and the weight being increased by being laid arbitrarily, prosperity and good management are little more than signals for a higher assessment. Under such a system, a wealthy tenantry, on arable land, can hardly arise. With these farmers, and this management, it is not much to be wondered at that the lands yield no more than eighteen bushels. Such a tenantry, contributing so little beyond the labour of their hands, are much more at the landlord's mercy than would be the case of wealthier farmers, who, possessing a capital proper for their undertakings, are not content with a profit less than sufficient to return them a due interest for their money; and the consequence is, that the proprietor cannot have so high a rent as he has from *metayers,* who, possessing nothing, are content merely to live. Thus, in the division of the gross produce, the landlord in France gets half; but in England, in the shape of rent only, from a fourth to a tenth; commonly from a fourth to a sixth. On some lands he gets a third, but that is uncommon. Nothing can be simpler than the principles upon which this is founded. The English tenant must not only be able to support himself and his family, but must be paid for his capital also,—upon which the future produce of the farm depends, as much as on the land itself.

The importance of a country producing twenty-five bushels per acre instead of eighteen, is prodigious; but it is an idle deception to speak of twenty-five, for the superiority of English spring corn (barley and oats) is doubly greater than that of wheat and rye, and would justify me in proportioning the corn products of England, in general, compared with those of France, as twenty-eight to eighteen; and I am well persuaded, that such a ratio would be no exaggeration. Ten millions of acres produce more corn than fifteen millions; consequently a territory of one hundred millions of acres more than equals another of one hundred and fifty millions. It is from such facts that we must seek for an explanation of the power of England, which has ventured to measure itself with that of a country so much more populous, extensive, and more favoured by nature as France really is; and it is a lesson to all governments whatever, that if they would be powerful, they must encourage the only real and permanent basis of power, AGRICULTURE. By enlarging the quantity of the products of land in a nation, all those advantages flow which have been attributed to a great population, but which ought, with much more truth, to have been assigned to a great consumption; since it is not the mere number of people, but their ease and welfare, which constitute national prosperity. The difference between the corn products of France and England is so great, that it would justify some degree of surprise, how any political writer could ever express any degree of amazement, that a territory, naturally so inconsiderable as the British isles, on comparison with France, should ever become equally powerful; yet this sentiment, founded in mere ignorance, has been very common. With such an immense superiority in the produce of corn, the more obvious surprise should have been, that the resources of England, compared with those of France, were not yet more decisive. But it is to be observed, that there are other articles of culture to which recourse must be had for an explanation: vines are an immense object in the cultivation of the latter kingdom, and yield all the advantages, and even superior ones to those afforded by the assiduous culture of corn in England. Maiz is also an article of great consequence in the French husbandry; olives, silk, and lucerne are not to be forgotten; nor should we omit mentioning the fine pastures of Normandy, and every article of culture in the rich acquisitions of Flanders, Alsace, and part of Artois, as well as on the banks of the Garonne. In all this extent, and it is not small, France possesses a husbandry equal to our own; and it is from well seconding the fertility of nature in these districts, and from a proper attention to the plants adapted to the soil, that there has arisen any equality in the resources of the two kingdoms; for, without this, France, with all the ample advantages she otherwise derives from nature, would be but a petty power on comparison with Great Britain. In order the better to understand how the great difference of product between the French and English crops may affect the agriculture of the two kingdoms, it will be proper to observe, that the farmer in England will reap as much from his course of crops, in which wheat and rye occur but seldom, as the Frenchman can from his, in which they return often.

An English Course	A French Course	
1, Turnips	1, Fallow	
2, Barley	2, Wheat	18
3, Clover	3, Barley, or oats	
4, Wheat 25	4, Fallow	

5, Turnips		5, Wheat	18
6, Barley		6, Barley, or oats	
7, Clover		7, Fallow	
8, Wheat	25	8, Wheat	18
9, Tares, or beans		9, Barley, or oats	
10, Wheat	25	10, Fallow	
11, Turnips		11, Wheat	18
	——		——
	75		72

The Englishman, in eleven years, gets three bushels more of wheat than the Frenchman. He gets three crops of barley, tares, or beans, which produce nearly twice as many bushels per acre, as what the three French crops of spring corn produce. And he farther gets, at the same time, three crops of turnips and two of clover, the turnips worth 40s. the acre, and the clover 60s. that is 12l. for both. What an enormous superiority! More wheat; almost double of the spring corn; and above 20s. per acre per annum in turnips and clover. But farther; the Englishman's land, by means of the manure arising from the consumption of the turnips and clover is in a constant state of improvement, while the Frenchman's farm is stationary. Throw the whole into a cash-account, and it will stand thus:

English System	£. s. d.	*French System*	£. s. d.
Wheat 75 bushels,		Wheat 72 bushels,	
at 5s.	18 15 0	at 5s.	18 0 0
Spring corn three		Spring corn three	
crops, at 32 bushels,		crops, at 20 bushels,	
96 bushels, at 2s 6d.	12 0 0	60 bushels, at 2s. 6d.	7 10 0
Clover two crops	6 0 0		25 10 0
Turnips three crops	6 0 0	Per acre per annum	2 6 4
	42 15 0		
Per acre per annum	3 17 8		

In allowing the French system to produce twenty bushels of spring corn, while I assign thirty-two only to the English, I am confident that I favour the former considerably; for I believe the English produce is the double of that of France: but stating it as above, here are the proportions of forty-two on an improving farm to twenty-five on a stationary one; that is to say, a country containing 100,000,000 acres produces as much as another, whose area contains 168,000,000, which are in the same ratio as thirty-six and twenty-five.

Rise of Prices

OBSERVATIONS

THERE IS scarcely any circumstance in the political economy of France which makes so respectable a figure as that of the general rise of prices, which has taken place in the last twenty years. This is a sure sign that the mass of currency has considerably increased, which, in the case of that kingdom, must necessarily have arisen from an increase of industry. We know that taxes cannot have been the cause, as they have not in the same period been increased; or, at least, to so small an amount as to be irrelative to the question. The most remarkable circumstance attending this *apparent* prosperity (for this circumstance is usually concomitant with prosperity, though not of necessity flowing from it) is the still miserable state of the labouring poor; it is rather a matter of surprize, that the price of labour has not risen equally, or in some degree of proportion, with other things; this must probably be attributed to the too great populousness of the kingdom, of which I shall speak more particularly in another chapter. Certain it is, that the misery which we see amongst the lower classes in France seems quite inconsistent with a great rise in the price of commodities, occasioned by an increase of industry and wealth; and as the price of labour continues so low as not to enable the people to support themselves tolerably, notwithstanding the rise of other prices, it affords a clear proof, as it has been just observed, that there is too great a competition for employment, arising from the excess of population in the kingdom.

17. A Noble's Declaration for the Vingtième *(Twentieth Tax)*[1]

THE TAX declaration of the Marquis de Fourquevaux provides useful details on many aspects of agriculture and estate management. It has, however, two cardinal faults: the yields of wheat and maize are greatly underestimated and the market price of wheat is too low for 1750. By reworking this tax roll with wheat yields of 5 to 1 on the seed (instead of 3 to 1) and maize at 10 to 1 (instead of 4 to 1), and by calculating the market price of wheat at 10 livres rather than 7 livres and that of maize at 5 livres rather than 4 livres, and then making adjustments for the yields and prices of wine, wood, and hay, one arrives at a gross revenue of 4,833 livres instead of 2,543 livres, and at a net revenue of 3,654 livres instead of 1,215 livres. Applying this method to a sampling of noble tax declarations helps us determine the income of an average country nobleman in this region.[2] Unfortunately, the *vingtième* rolls are much less informative for other regions of France, often giving only a summary estimate of net revenues.

What else does the tax declaration tell us about the provincial French nobility? It suggests that some nobles, at least, were directly concerned with agriculture. The Marquis de Fourquevaux worked three of his four farms directly with wage labor. Second, it indicates that nobles in the province of Languedoc paid a *taille;*[3] in this case it represented over 10 per cent of the gross revenue. The declaration also indicates that seigneurial dues were less important as sources of reve-

---

[1] The Bourbon monarchy levied three principal direct taxes: the *taille*, the *capitation*, and the *vingtième*. The *taille* was the basic land tax paid by the nonprivileged social groups, that is, the peasants and noninfluential townsmen. In principle, the *capitation* and the *vingtième* were income taxes paid by all social groups. In practice, however, the privileged orders—nobility and Church—paid less than their share of these direct taxes.

[2] Robert Forster, *The Nobility of Toulouse in the Eighteenth Century* (Baltimore, 1960), Appendix I, which explains in detail the method of reworking tax declarations.

[3] In the province of Languedoc nobles paid a *taille* on "common" or non-noble land. Actually, most nobles around Toulouse owned "noble" land and paid no *taille*. The most important land tax on the French nobles was the *vingtième*. Given the falsification of noble declarations, Fourquevaux was not unique but typical—this tax was much less than 5 per cent, ranging from 2 to 3 per cent of the actual net revenue. Contrast the taxes of the English gentry which ranged from 10 to 20 per cent (see the Purefoys in the section on The Family, Document 50).

nue than the domain farms, though this does not necessarily mean that the burden of the dues on the peasant was negligible or that seigneurial dues were unimportant.

Source: *Archives Départementales, Haute-Garonne, C-1318* (Fourquevaux)

[1750]

M. FRANÇOIS-DENIS DE PAVIE BECCARIE, Marquis of the said place [a seigneur], having full justice, high, middle, and lower, landed and feudal [*foncière et directe*] declares to possess:

I   One large chateau and 10 *arpents* [13.9 acres] consisting of gardens, park, avenues, promenades, and other nonprofitable land. They include, however, 2½ *arpents* of vineyard, ½ *arpent* of meadow, and 2 *arpents* of woodland, to be declared below.

II Seigneurial rights:
Cens [ground rents]
  52 *setiers* [1] of wheat at 7# [2] per *setier*   364#
  8 *setiers* of oats at 4# per *setier*   32#
  in coin   45#
Right of *lods et ventes* [mutation fee]   40#
Cens in chickens combined with what I collect on the right of *fouage* brings 90 chickens at 15 sous a pair   33# 15s.

I enjoy one right called *siva dion,* for which each sharecropper must pay me 2 *pugnères* [1.32 bushels] of oats, but this right has now almost entirely disappeared. Since most of these sharecroppers have their land worked by day laborers, this right brings me only 6 *setiers* at 4# per *setier*   24#
The right of *corvée.* Each laborer owes me one day's work per year, but this right brings me very little because I am obliged to feed them, which costs me 4 sous a day. Hence this right nets me only   6#
Rights on the market hall of the village built by my ancestors. The merchants must pay for the use of the stalls and the slaughterhouse. Deducting repairs   35#

[1] 1 *setier* = 2.64 bushels.
[2] The "#" stands for livres.

III Utilities
     Three windmills.
          Two of these are on 4-year leases for
          40 *setiers* of wheat at 7#   280#
          5 *setiers* of maize at 4#   20#
          A third mill is leased verbally, yielding
          10 *setiers* of wheat at 7#   70#
          10 *setiers* of maize at 4#   40#
     One forge yields 10 *setiers* of wheat at 7#   70#

IV   Domain
     Four farms [*métairies*] totaling 128 *arpents* [178
     acres]. Three of these are worked by wage labor
     [*maîtres-valets*] and one by a sharecropper.
     On the three farms worked by wage labor, 33 of the
     86 *arpents* are sown in wheat at 1 *setier* per *arpent*.
     The 33 *setiers* yield 3 to 1 on the seed, or 99
     setiers. Deducting one eighth for the seasonal har-
     vest hands (12 *setiers*) and one third for the seed
     (33 *setiers*), this leaves 54 *setiers* at 7#   378#
     Another 33 of the 86 *arpents* are in fallow.
     The remaining 20 *arpents* are divided as follows:

          10 *arpents* in maize, yielding 4 to 1 on the seed,
          or 40 *setiers*. Deducting one half for the culti-
          vator, or 20 *setiers*, this leaves 20 *setiers* at 4#   80#
          10 *arpents* are sown in beans and subsidiary
          grains, yielding 4 to 1 on the seed, or 40
          setiers. Deducting 10 *setiers* for seed and one
          half for the cultivator (15 *setiers*), this leaves
          15 *setiers* at 4½#   67#

     The fourth farm, worked by sharecropping, consists
     of 42 *arpents*, including the land I have recently
     acquired from Sieur Clerc.
     21 *arpents* are sown in wheat at 1 *setier* per *arpent*
     and yield 3 to 1 on the seed, or 63 *setiers*. De-
     ducting 21 *setiers* for the seed leaves 42 *setiers*,
     and then one half for the sharecroppers (21
     setiers), leaves 21 *setiers* at 7#   147#
     On this farm there are also 2 *arpents* in maize,

yielding 8 *setiers*. Deducting one half to the sharecropper, this leaves 4 *setiers* of maize at 4#   16#

Two *arpents* of this farm are in beans, yielding 8 *setiers*. Deducting one half to the sharecropper, this leaves 4 *setiers* at 3#   12#

The lease of the said four farms has been negotiated by verbal agreement [and no lease can be submitted]. As for the dues that the *maîtres-valets* and the sharecroppers owe me, they consist only of fowl: 73 pairs (one third hens, one third capons, and one third chickens) at 15 sous a pair   54# 15s.

There are also 8 *arpents* of land with buildings for housing those who cultivate the land at equal shares.

Four *arpents* of this land are in wheat, yielding 3 to 1 on the seed, or 12 *setiers*. Deducting one half for the laborers leaves 6 *setiers*, and then one half for the seed, which I furnish, this leaves 4 *setiers* at 7#   28#

The remaining 4 *arpents* are in maize, yielding 16 *setiers*. Deducting one half for the laborers, this leaves 8 *setiers* at 4#   32#

Also 8 *arpents* worked by the millers at half fruits on land adjoining the mills. These are half in wheat and half in maize, yielding after deductions   45#

The laborers and millers pay me dues in fowl: 45 pairs at 15s. a pair   33# 15s.

These two pieces of land are also leased verbally, except the portions leased to the millers.

Also 16 *arpents* of vineyards, planted on bad soil. I work 6 *arpents* of this by shares, producing for my share only one cask per *arpent*, at 12# per cask   72#

The other 10 *arpents* of vineyard I work directly, producing 20 casks at 12# per cask   240#

I also obtain from the said vineyards 500 bundles of vine branch, which sells at 5# per 100   25#

I have 22 *arpents* of woods, which yield 1,000# every 20 years, or per year   50#

I have 17 *arpents* of meadow, 10 of which are used for

pasture. The remaining 7 produce 10 cartloads or
112 *quintaux* [3] of hay. At 1# per *quintal*   112#
There is very little profit on livestock because of the
shortage of pasture.

The brick factory produces   20#
50 or 60 mulberry trees   20#
I have 8# of rent on a recently acquired piece of land,
which is now abandoned by the peasants who owe
me this sum. I am deprived of the payment of this
sum, without hope of ever being paid, not to mention the arrears.

Gross Total Revenue	2,543#	2s. 6d.

[199 *arpents* or 276.6 acres]

Deductions
Tailles	524#	9s. 1d.

Wages of 5 *maîtres-valets:* 25 *setiers* of
wheat at 7#	175#	
25 *setiers* of maize at 4#	100#	
in coin	75#	
	350#	
Mill repairs	99#	
Upkeep on the tools of the forge [4]	28#	15s.

Upkeep on the farm tools, including five
plows at 8# per plow	40#	
Upkeep on 4 carts at 10# per cart	40#	
Labor in the vineyards	200#	
Upkeep on the market hall	15#	
Labor for cutting 7 *arpents* of meadow	30#	
Total Deductions	1,327#	6s.
Net Revenue	1,215#	16s. 6d.
Twentieth Tax for 1750	76#	6s. 3d.

[3] One quintal = 100 pounds.
[4] The accompanying lease for the forge states that the blacksmith and
not the seigneur is responsible for the upkeep of the tools.

18. The Estate Agent

In England the estate agent, along with the substantial tenant farmer, represented the spearhead of progressive farming and agricultural change. On the Continent west of the Elbe, tenant farmers (*fermiers*) were either near-subsistence peasant cultivators or rent collectors from subtenants. Estate agents also served as rent collectors rather than agricultural entrepreneurs. Their skills as accountants and local fiscal agents were more important than their imagination as improvers of the soil.

The instructions to the land agents of the Bartolommei family in Tuscany clearly reinforce our image of the accountant with his duplicate registers, bundles of receipts, and accounts for each peasant debtor. Every scrap of revenue from fish to fowl is tracked down. Strict penalties await negligent peasants or agents who extend credit or shelter the poor in the villa. On the other hand, unlike the French *régisseur*, the Bartolommei agents were permitted some room for speculation and even innovation. Directed to sell farm produce at the highest possible market price, the agents decided when that moment arrived. Moreover, the agent at Paggio was permitted to decide on his own what crops were most advantageous to cultivate—a liberty of action almost unheard of in France, where the leases consistently required peasants to follow traditional crop courses. Finally, the agents here had a duty to provide at least a minimum livelihood to the needy on the farms. Indeed, the Bartolommei estate with its walls, ditches, and guards keeping "strangers" out and peasants within and the final injunction to the agent to treat all "subordinates" impartially suggest a kind of paternalism that the Marquis de Mirabeau said was disappearing in France.

Source: *Archivio di Stato, Firenze, Carte Bartolommei, F-483.*

Instructions to Land Agents, 1775

Instructions and regulations to be observed by the land agent of the Illustrissimo Signore Marchese Girolamo Bartolommei at the estate of Monte Vettolini. *Ihus Maria,* 1775.

On workdays the agent will go early to the estate, where he will attend . . . to the peasants and others who for interest or business need to see him. Then he will spend the remainder of the day attending to current business, keeping the accounts, and treating other pressing matters. In the evening he will return to Monte Vettolini where he must reside, since it has been concluded that the permission given to the previous agent to live outside Monte Vettolini was of great prejudice to the owner and the primary reason for his dismissal.

It will be his duty to go in person to all the cattle markets and fairs to observe the purchase and sale of cattle by the peasants, and to make receipt and payment for cattle at the time of sale.

As much as possible, he will keep the accounting up to date and will register accounts day by day when money comes in or goes out, so that the account books will correspond with the receipts. He will collect the receipts into two bundles, one for the purchase or sale of cattle and the other for other payments, and will exhibit these when he makes his accounting.

From time to time he will review the book of estate debtors where the debts of peasants and others are registered in order to pursue debtors who are able to pay. When a debtor pays a sum, his account will be credited in the book and a similar entry will be made in the entry account of the estate as in the past.

He will also concern himself with the book of debtors for pasturing and fishing rights and will collect as much as possible from these.

He will look after the account of the purchase and sale of cattle and will not put off the collection of these accounts. If cattle have been entrusted to people suspected of debts, he will solicit them frequently and even threaten them to be sure to collect the necessary payment.

He will supervise the assistant agent at the Piano farm who has the special task of visiting the peasants daily. He is to observe how these peasants take care of the cattle, one of the largest sources of revenue of the estate, whether they are kept too much in their stalls or are of poor quality. He will observe how they work and keep the farms and see to it that they sow the proper crops. If he learns that any peasant is neglecting his duty, he will first go to him personally and warn him; but if he does not mend his ways, he will report the case to the owner, who will take whatever action seems necessary.

He will not allow the peasants to keep goats, either on shares with the owner or on their own account. An exception will be made for a single goat to lead the other animals, as long as it is kept penned up. It has been found that the keeping of goats by the peasants is of considerable damage to the farms.

He will make sure that the peasants keep a certain number of chickens in proportion to the size of the farms and he will collect rentals for the chicken yards. But he will see that they do not keep guinea fowl of any kind. As for large pigeons, the peasants shall be permitted to keep as many as four pairs and no more, since these birds for the most part eat at the expense of the owner.[1]

He will be careful to consider the best moment for the most advantageous sale of grain, wine, oil, and other products, and when the best moment comes, he will take advantage of it without waiting for the consent of the owner, unless he is instructed to the contrary. He will pay special attention to the sale of cattle, especially to those to be slaughtered, so that they are sent to reputable butchers. He will collect from them regularly and not extend credit for more than 200 *scudi*.[2] If one of these clients should fail, the agent will be responsible for any sums owed.

In selling other products the agent will extend credit to no one unless he receives particular instructions to do so, and, failing this, he will be responsible for the loss.

He will see that the assistant agents do their work in accordance with instructions sent to each of them and will visit the farm at Poggio to see that it is kept as it should be. He will not permit the assistant agents to shelter people at the villa except in a case of extreme need, and he will not permit them to use the horses of the estate for their errands except in cases of long trips of four or five miles.

He will see that his wife [the *fattoressa*] does her duty in keeping the villa and its outbuildings in good order. She will not keep people in the house when it is not necessary to do so and will manage in the most economical way.[3] She will not give the peasants who work in the house from time to time in the service

---

[1] Pigeon raising was also considered an aristocratic vocation and not to be encouraged among peasants.

[2] The *scudo* is equivalent to 5.86 *livres tournois*, or about $5.80 (1968).

[3] Apparently there was always a danger of inflating the number of servants and other hangers-on. Italian aristocrats were known for their large household staffs.

of the owner more than the wages fixed by the schedule kept in the study at Monte Vettolini.

He will see that the guard does his duty making the rounds of the estate and the marsh, permitting no one to enter who is not known to the estate. The guard will see that the peasants do no harm to one another and that they are not harmed by outsiders. He will see that strangers do not enter beyond the ditch bounding the estate without permission as specified in the Regulation of 1649 concerning the marshes of Fucecchio. To be sure that the guard does his duty toward the peasants, he is to receive from them no more than his due, that is, a *staio* of grain and a barrel of wine from each one taken from the total harvest.

From time to time, and especially at seasons when work can be done, he [the agent] will take note of all the dikes in the marsh and the walls around the farms and will maintain them at their correct height and thickness. If he should find some trace of a break or erosion, he will remedy this immediately, since from small beginnings large breaks may easily develop to the great damage of the estate. The conservation of the estate depends on the good repair of the dikes. For this reason the agents will see to it that the guard does not permit the peasants' cattle to walk on the dikes, since this is the principal cause of damage.

Finally, he will treat everyone, and especially the peasants and his other subordinates, with the greatest impartiality and fairness, without ever taking the part of anyone or showing a particular affection for anyone. This is the truest and safest way to behave in the best interests of the owner. By doing this he will win for himself the affection and esteem of his superiors.

Instructions and regulations to be observed by the assistant agent of Poggio.

He will superintend the seven farms of Poggio, that is, two at Roncone, two at Vaiano, the cabin at Roncone-Buondi', the rented holding at S. Donnini, the farm at Brancona worked by the Zari family, and the farm at Caliano worked by Giovanni Santi Pucci.

His care of the said farms will consist of going often to inspect them, looking after the upkeep of the lands and ordering that the peasants cultivate those crops that seem profitable and advantageous at that particular time.

He will see that the peasants take good care of the olive trees and other plantings.

He will see that they take diligent care of the cattle in order to make possible the largest profits. He will inquire into the economic situation of each family and ask the agent [4] to give a minimum livelihood to those who are really in need and who by their good behavior merit such assistance.

He will obtain from the agent at the time of sowing the seed he thinks absolutely necessary for the peasants' farms.

He will consign the harvest of grain, wine, and oil to the agent, who alone is responsible for it.

He will see that the chestnut grove at Roncone is well kept and that the necessary plantings are made for its maintenance. He will look after the woodland.

He will also have in his care the olive groves that are cultivated directly by the landlord and he will consign all the harvest of these to the agent.

Likewise, along with the head agent's wife, he will be charged with the garden and orchard of the villa and will keep an account of the expenses and revenue of them. Only when it is necessary to plow, reap, or sow the said garden, will he be permitted to call upon extra help. At all other times, this work will be done by himself. Any hired help in the gardens will be paid for in cash from the account of payments made by the peasants. Payment in bread or wine must be avoided since such payment would reduce the returns from the said gardens, which the owner wishes to know precisely and without error.

He will receive from the peasants under his supervision all the cheese and wool that is the owner's share. He will keep this on hand at the disposition of the agent, who will give him instructions as to its use.

He will be given wine, oil, and grain for use in the house and will keep a register of the grain that he receives from time to time from the agent: wheat for use of the family and rye for the peasants and for alms. And he will keep an account of the wine and oil used by the family and of all that is consumed in wine, oil, wheat, and other provisions when the owners are in residence. He will give an accounting of this to the agent and will keep a separate

[4] That is, the head agent of previous "Instructions."

account in his own registers so that the owners can at any time be entirely satisfied.

The wine from Poggio bottled at the villa will be in his care and should be placed at the disposition of the agent, who will tell him what to do with it.

When the sale of grain to the merchants of Pescia and Borgo begins, he will go twice a week to the markets to deliver the produce which the agent will have placed in our storehouses in these towns. He will keep an account with the estate, take care to sell at the largest profit to the owner, and never extend credit. He is responsible for all the losses if he does so.

Finally, when necessary, he will perform tasks requiring attention because of the incompetence of others, if he can perform them without prejudice to his other duties.

19. Rent Contracts or Leases

THE ITALIAN rent contract (Document A) is extremely short—too short for the agrarian historian who wants to know a great deal more about the land and tenure relations. Although the lease refers to "two small fields," one would like to know the exact area of the leased land in order to determine the rental value per acre. The fact that the lessor can sign his name and agrees to pay his rent in coin rather than in kind suggests a man a cut above the dirt farmer. He probably leased other land as well and might have sublet these two fields on shares. The lease does not specify any particular crop course. After the first year, the contract could be renounced by the landlord, hardly an encouragement to the tenant to make any capital investment or improvement. Since Serafini pays Mannelli's agent, it is probable that Mannelli had a number of scattered fields and farms leased in this manner.

The French sharecrop contract (Document B) is much more explicit, though scarcely more conducive to agricultural innovation. But unlike Serafini, who was probably a middleman, the French sharecropper cannot write his name. The terms of the contract suggest a near-subsistence dirt farmer, little more than an agricultural laborer with regular employment.

Sources: Document A: Rent contract, October 10, 1777. *Archivio di Stato, Firenze, Archivio Riccardi-Mannelli-Galilei, F-134.*

Document B: Robert Forster, *The Nobility of Toulouse in the Eighteenth Century: A Social and Economic Study* (Baltimore, 1960) pp. 193–195.*

A. Italian Rent Contract

BY THE present agreement which, although private, will be kept and held as if it were a publicly sworn and guaranteed instrument, it is declared and confessed that the Illustrissimo Signore Jacopo Mannelli-Galilei and the Illustrissimi Signori Pier France and Guido Mannelli, with the aforesaid Signore Jacopo acting in their names, give and concede for rent to Valente Serafini two pieces of land, that is, two small fields composed of arable land with vines in the parish of Santa Maria at Fibbiana, at the place called Lastre, under the following terms and conditions, to wit:

1. That the said rental year will begin on November 1, 1777, and be paid until the end of the month of October, 1778, inclusively, and continue from year to year until the agreement is renounced by one of the parties at least six months before the end of the year.

2. That the said Valente Serafini will pay annually as rent 8 ducats and 4 *lire*, money of 7 *lire* per ducat, at the end of the year into the hand of the agent of the said Signori Mannelli at the *fattoria* of Fibbiana.[1]

3. That all the expense of maintaining the said two fields will rest with the said renter as has been agreed.

4. And, since the said Serafini will receive the said fields unsown, at the termination of the rental year he will restore them in the same state. . . .

5. It is agreed that the said Serafini will care for the said two fields as a good husbandman and rather improve than deteriorate them, with the agreement that whatever expense he may incur, however large or excessive, he will expect no recompense, unless the expenses have been made with the agreement and permission in writing of the owners, that is, by agreement recognized by both parties.

* Reprinted by permission of Johns Hopkins University Press.
[1] *Fattoria*, estate or administrative center of the property. Presumably the agent lived there all year to collect rents and supervise the individual farms and several fields.

For the observation of the above, the said Valente Serafini pledges his person, heirs, and goods, present and future, and the goods of his heirs, and, in witness thereof, the present agreement is signed by him in the presence of the following witnesses this day and year at Fibbiana.

B.   A French Sharecropping Contract [Bail à demy fruits]

IN THE year one thousand seven hundred and seventy nine, the first day of August in the afternoon, at Villefranche de Lauragais was present before us, royal notary of the said town, Jaques Maurel, living at Seyres, agent of high and powerful seigneur Marquis d'Hautpoul, administrator of the said land of Seyres, who, by his free will, has leased and hereby leases for work and cultivation at half fruits to Pierre Reynes and Mathieu Reynes, father and son, *laboureurs,* living at the farm of Gérie, consulat of Reneville, both present and accepting jointly [*l'un pour l'autre et l'un d'eux seul pour le tout*] without division or discrimination, unless expressly renounced: the farm called la Grave and the lands in dependence, situated in the consulat of Seyres, diocese of Toulouse, with the exception of one meadow situated in the jurisdiction of Lagarde, which was attached to the said farm, and which the said Maurel expressly reserves as not being part of the present lease. This present lease is established for the time and term of one year, beginning the first of November of this year, during which time the said lessees will act on the said lands as good husbandmen [*bons ménagers et bons péres de famille*]. The said lease is also established on the following conditions:

1) The said lessees will furnish all kinds of seed, and the yield will be divided to the *sol* and the *pugnère,* after the said Maurel will have taken twenty setiers of wheat from the harvest, which the said lessees will give to him in advance. The remaining wheat will be divided as it is said. The portion of the said Maurel is to be delivered after cutting and flailing, as well as all the other kinds of grain which will be brought to the château of Seyres without costs for the said Maurel.

2) As the cultivated land is in "three fields" [*trois labours*], the lessees will be held to maintain it in this state, without being authorized to alter the system or to interchange its order, under

punishment of being held responsible for all major damages and interests. The land will be cultivated in such a way that one part will be planted in wheat, the second part will be in fallow [*guéret pur*], and the third will be planted with maize, beans, or other vegetables and grains, and if they do not want to plant it entirely, they will notify the said Maurel, so that he can lease the land which they do not want to some other party whom he chooses. In this case, they will not have any right to this portion.

3) As the lessees are not permitted to plant anything on the fallow, in case they do, they will not receive any portion of this harvest, unless the said Maurel gives them his permission.

4) All kinds of livestock and sheep will be held in common, and all profits and losses will be shared equally.

5) They will have charge of the hay and straw, and in case there is a shortage of these forages, they will have to buy half of it themselves.

6) They will dig the ditches, cut the brush, and will make drains for the water, in short, do everything necessary on the said lands; they will have charge of the vines which they will work and prune at the proper time and season, and their fruits will be shared as well as the vine-branches; they will furnish the carts, harnesses, plows, iron-tools and other instruments necessary for cultivation, without the said Maurel being held to furnish anything; yet, if there is some tree on the said land which is convenient for repairing work tools, it will be furnished by the said Maurel.

7) They will pay as rent: Thirty six chickens on St. John the Baptist's Day, thirty six capons on All Saint's Day, thirty six chickens on Christmas; the said fowl and six hundred eggs during the course of the year.

8) They alone will buy the young pigs, which will be later divided and of which the said Maurel will have the choice; they will raise geese and ducks and turkeys which will also be divided by the choice of the said Maurel, and in case that he does not wish any of this fowl, they will be held to give six fat geese to the said Maurel, to be delivered on the first of December, and in this case only and not otherwise the said Maurel will pay them the sum of six livres for the said six geese, fat or not.

9) The said lessees will be held to make the plows which are

ordered by the said Maurel, and they will have to pay the order
to the blacksmith themselves. Comprised in the lease is a vineyard which is north of the farm and of a surface of about two
arpents.

The parties declare that the said fruits do not exceed the value
of two hundred and fifty livres, and in order to observe the above
stipulations, the parties pledge their possessions to Justice: The
said Maurel those of the said Seigneur Marquis d'Hautpoul and
the said Reynes theirs, present and future.

Made and sealed in our study in the presence of the Sirs Jean
Paul Pujol and Louis Antoine Majoret, practitioners living in this
town, signing below as witnesses. The parties declare not to know
how to sign.

Signed: PUJOL FILS, MAJORET, PUJOL.

Editors' Comment:

Notice that a natural meadow is reserved for Hautpoul's agent,
that he takes 20 setiers of wheat before any division takes place,
and that his share is transported to the château without cost.
Notice also that the three field system is absolutely obligatory
(wheat, maize, fallow), and that the sharecroppers must pay half
the cost of any extra forage that is needed. All drainage and
upkeep must be done by the sharecroppers; they must furnish all
the tools and pay the blacksmith for any repairs. They must pay a
substantial rent in fowl and pigs. An estimate of the value of the
harvest is made to prevent "errors" in the division of the fruits.
Finally, notice that the sharecroppers cannot write. Since the rent
in fowl is 36 pairs, the farm is about 75 *arpents*. If the land was
worked in three equal fields or "labors," the seigneur received
three-fourths of the net harvest of wheat.

In the Lauragais a farm of 75 *arpents* had about 20% of its
surface in meadow and wood. Hence, about 60 *arpents* were cul-
tivable. If the "three labors" were equal (20 *arpents* wheat, 20
arpents fallow, 20 *arpents* maize), customary practice at Seyres in
1750, the yield of wheat at 5 *setiers* per *arpent* would be 100
setiers. Following Article I of the contract above, one can calculate as follows:

    100 *setiers* yield of wheat
    — 20 *setiers* "taken in advance" by the seigneur
    ————
    80

(80)

— 10 *setiers* cost of cutting and flailing

  70 *setiers*

— 35 *setiers* "half-fruits" to the seigneur

  35

— 20 *setiers* seed furnished by the lessees

  15 *setiers* net for the lessees

Hence, the Marquis d'Hautpoul would receive a total of 55 *setiers* of wheat and the lessees 15 *setiers*. A family of five would require about 20 *setiers* of wheat per year for minimum subsistence.

20. The Day Laborer in Brittany

DESPITE THE efforts of some later writers to idealize the countryside, the poor agricultural laborers of Brittany were certainly no better off than the industrial workers of the new English factory towns. Moreover, there was no regular poor relief in France as there was in England. Apparently the French Revolution had passed the day laborer by. Though sympathetic, M. de Coniac sees no hope of changing these conditions, which he ascribes to "the law of Nature which requires that the excess of population be reduced by misery."

Source: *Archives Départementales, Ille - et - Vilaine, Fonds Coniac-65.*

*Replies to Different Articles
of the Questionnaire
of the Imperial Society of Agriculture,
Written by M. de Coniac, 1804*

FARM LABOR

ON SMALL farms in the arrondissement leases vary between 400 and 500 francs. These farms are worked by the head of a family and his children. Even on the very largest farms, that is, those renting for 2,000 francs and above, the tenant farmer is always at his plow and cart in person. He has a hired man [*valet-char-retier*] under him who also takes care of the farmyard. His wages vary with his reliability. On the land I cultivated directly, I paid a hired man 72 livres in 1789 and 75 livres in 1804. My tenant farmer in another commune paid a hired man 90 livres in 1789 and 108 livres in 1804. In still another commune the wages were 100 and 108 livres per year respectively.

Sheep are not kept if there is no wasteland. Fallow land is reserved for pasturing livestock since the meadows are not used for pasture. Meadows produce the best hay, too good for sheep. Where there is wasteland, the sheep roam about without a shepherd or watchdog. They are watched by children seven or eight years old, or by a little girl from one of the poor families. These children receive their food (worth 4 sous a day) and 3 to 6 livres a year. This wage was the same in 1789 as it is now [1804].

The hired man takes care of the horses, oxen, carts, and plows, and makes all necessary repairs in the afternoon. If there is too much work for the tenant farmer and the hired man, the rest is done by day labor. . . .

In poor communes I gave to those who cut my grains 15 sous per day for the men and 12 sous for the women, without food. The threshers received the seventeenth bushel threshed, or 15 sous per day and several meals, in 1789. Where five meals were customary, the men worked until sunset.

Hay is cut by the sickle. The position of the harvest hand seems to be much more awkward than when a scythe is used, but the tenant farmers here claim that in this way the grass is cut closer to the ground, so that the complaints of fatigue are compensated by an increase in the product. In the last fifty years I have seen this practice continue, and, despite its awkwardness, a mower good with the sickle cuts as much grass as one using a scythe. A man can cut ½ *journal* [0.6 acres] per day. The harvest hands gather in the village square for tools and instructions. In the busy season, the farmers compete for hands. If the weather is good, the wage may reach 30 sous a day. On bad days it may be only 5 or 6 sous.[1]

Day laborers are the most numerous class and also the most miserable. Slavery in the colonies was much less oppressive, at least by comparison with our departments. In the colonies the master took some care of his slaves as part of his plantation capi-

[1] The subsistence wage was about 200 livres per annum in 1780. Even assuming a hand made 1 livre per day, he would need 200 days' employment throughout the year to feed himself and his family.

tal, giving them minimum housing and taking care of them when
they were ill and old. But in our departments look at the day
laborer! Born into an indigent family, he has no chance of obtaining an education, which might give him a way out of his
misery. He does not have a penny with which to begin any kind
of business; he has only his arms, their strength, and a certain
dexterity. If a day laborer is ill for three or four days because of
bad weather or an epidemic, the tenant farmer easily finds a re-
placement and the poor day laborer loses his precious work. His
wage is scarcely sufficient to feed and clothe him. He is much
worse off than the hired man who at least has food and lodging.
Nature and need make him their slave and require the most painful work in the manner of the severest of masters. All his time is
given to a person who pays him a small wage and does not even
feed him. His children are a heavy burden to him and many die
before working age. Most of the day laborers have a small plot of
land, but no livestock and no tools. They borrow plows from the
tenant farmers in return for labor time (one day's labor for each
day with the plow team). But unable to keep the weeds down,
with no time and energy left for their own plots, they see their
seed smothered. It is a disaster when a cow dies. It costs 75
livres—a fortune for a day laborer.

If Brittany has 2 million inhabitants, there must be about
100,000 day laborers such as these. Before the division of the
large properties there was some help for these poor, but it was
only a temporary relief, prolonging their lives for a few mo-
ments.[2] Few reach the age of fifty. These men received 5 sous
and their food, or 10 sous without food, per day in 1789; women
and children received 4 sous and food, or 8 sous without food.
Now [1804] the men receive 6 sous and food, or 12 sous without
food.

The day laborers eat three meals a day. For breakfast they have
a bowl of oatmeal soup with a little rancid butter. In this soup
they may cook cabbage or dried peas, and all this is poured over
rye bread which has been softened and passed through a sieve.
For dinner they eat buckwheat cakes soaked in a bowl of skim
milk or cider, if there is any. At supper there is oatmeal porridge

[2] The writer is probably referring to "division" under the new inheritance
law. The Breton nobility did not lose much of its domain lands by revolutionary confiscation.

with a piece of butter in the middle. Everyone eats out of the same kettle, touching the butter with a spoonful of porridge before every mouthful. This food costs about 5 or 6 sous a day. The day laborer is undernourished and therefore feels the need to drink; it is only by losing his senses that he forgets his awful misery. He even spends money he should bring home to his family on drink.

21. *The Russian Serf*

BETWEEN THE life of the French day laborer described by Coniac and that of the Russian serf described by Radishchev there seems little choice. As in France, the introduction of a managerial class in the form of a tight-fisted tenantry made conditions even more arduous for the serfs. But just as there was more than one kind of French peasant, there were many kinds of Russian serfs. Russian peasants who paid a commutation tax to the lord instead of working his land had some opportunity to escape a hopeless dependence. But the vast majority of manorial peasants were obliged to pay in kind and services almost anything the "master" demanded. Recognized by the czarist government only if they were criminals, serfs had no legal protection against forced labor or increased dues, and by the late eighteenth century they worked six days a week in the master's fields. In absolute physical and legal terms the mass of Russian serfs were much more oppressed and deprived than the small peasant owners of western Europe. Yet the very hopelessness and isolation of the Russian serfs made revolt, or even reform efforts from below, most unlikely. "It appears that the spirit of freedom is so dried up in the slaves that they . . . have no desire to end their sufferings," observed Radishchev.

Source: Aleksandr Nikolaevitch Radishchev, *A Journey from St. Petersburg to Moskow*, trans. Leo Wiener, ed., introduction, and notes by Roderick Page Thaler (Cambridge, Mass., 1958), pp. 46–47.

Lyubani

I SUPPOSE it is all the same to you whether I traveled in winter or in summer. Maybe both in winter and in summer. It is not unusual

* Reprinted by permission of the Harvard University Press. (Published originally in Russian in 1790.)

for travelers to set out in sleighs and to return in carriages. In summer. The corduroy road tortured my body; I climbed out of the carriage and went on foot. While I had been lying back in the carriage, my thoughts had turned to the immeasurable vastness of the world. By spiritually leaving the earth I thought I might more easily bear the jolting of the carriage. But spiritual exercises do not always distract us from our physical selves; and so, to save my body, I got out and walked. A few steps from the road I saw a peasant ploughing a field. The weather was hot. I looked at my watch. It was twenty minutes before one. I had set out on Saturday. It was now Sunday. The ploughing peasant, of course, belonged to a landed proprietor, who would not let him pay a commutation tax. The peasant was ploughing very carefully. The field, of course, was not part of his master's land. He turned the plough with astonishing ease.

"God help you," I said, walking up to the ploughman, who, without stopping, was finishing the furrow he had started. "God help you," I repeated.

"Thank you, sir," the ploughman said to me, shaking the earth off the ploughshare and transferring it to a new furrow.

"You must be a Dissenter, since you plough on a Sunday."

"No, sir, I make the true sign of the cross," he said, showing me the three fingers together. "And God is merciful and does not bid us starve to death, so long as we have strength and a family."

"Have you no time to work during the week, then, and can you not have any rest on Sundays, in the hottest part of the day, at that?"

"In a week, sir, there are six days, and we go six times a week to work on the master's fields; in the evening, if the weather is good, we haul to the master's house the hay that is left in the woods; and on holidays the women and girls go walking in the woods, looking for mushrooms and berries. God grant," he continued, making the sign of the cross, "that it rains this evening. If you have peasants of your own, sir, they are praying to God for the same thing."

"My friend, I have no peasants, and so nobody curses me. Do you have a large family?"

"Three sons and three daughters. The eldest is nine years old."

"But how do you manage to get food enough, if you have only the holidays free?"

"Not only the holidays: the nights are ours, too. If a fellow isn't lazy, he won't starve to death. You see, one horse is resting; and when this one gets tired, I'll take the other; so the work gets done."

"Do you work the same way for your master?"

"No, sir, it would be a sin to work the same way. On his fields there are a hundred hands for one mouth, while I have two for seven mouths: you can figure it out for yourself. No matter how hard you work for the master, no one will thank you for it. The master will not pay our head tax; but, though he doesn't pay it, he doesn't demand one sheep, one hen, or any linen or butter the less. The peasants are much better off where the landlord lets them pay a commutation tax without the interference of the steward. It is true that sometimes even good masters take more than three rubles a man; but even that's better than having to work on the master's fields. Nowadays it's getting to be the custom to let villages to tenants, as they call it. But we call it putting our heads in a noose. A landless tenant skins us peasants alive; even the best ones don't leave us any time for ourselves. In the winter he won't let us do any carting of goods and won't let us go into town to work; all our work has to be for him, because he pays our head tax. It is an invention of the Devil to turn your peasants over to work for a stranger. You can make a complaint against a bad steward, but to whom can you complain against a bad tenant?"

"My friend, you are mistaken; the laws forbid them to torture people."

"Torture? That's true; but all the same, sir, you would not want to be in my hide." Meanwhile the ploughman hitched up the other horse to the plough and bade me good-bye as he began a new furrow.

The words of this peasant awakened in me a multitude of thoughts. I thought especially of the inequality of treatment within the peasant class. I compared the crown peasants with the manorial peasants. They both live in villages; but the former pay a fixed sum, while the latter must be prepared to pay whatever their master demands. The former are judged by their equals; the latter are dead to the law, except, perhaps, in criminal cases. A member of society becomes known to the government protecting him, only when he breaks the social bonds, when he becomes a criminal! This thought made my blood boil.

Tremble, cruelhearted landlord! on the brow of each of your peasants I see your condemnation written.

While absorbed in these thoughts I happened to notice my servant, who was sitting up on the box in front of me, swaying from side to side. Suddenly I felt a chill coursing through my veins, sending the blood to my head and mantling my cheeks with a blush. I felt so ashamed of myself that I could scarcely keep from bursting into tears. "In your anger," I said to myself, "you denounce the proud master who wears out his peasants in the field; but are you not doing the same or even worse yourself? What crime has your poor Petrushka committed that you should deny him sleep, the consolation for our miseries, and nature's greatest gift to the unfortunate? He gets pay, food, and clothing, and you never beat him with a whip or cudgel. (O moderate man!) And you think that a piece of bread and a scrap of cloth give you the right to treat your fellow human being as though he were a top, and you merely boast that you do not often whip it up while it is whirling. Do you know what is written in the fundamental law, in the heart of every man? He whom I strike has the right to strike me. Remember the day when Petrushka was drunk and did not come in time to dress you. Remember how you boxed his ear. If only he had then, although intoxicated, come to his senses and answered you as your question deserved! And who gave you power over him? The law. The law? And you dare to defile that sacred name? Miserable one!"—Tears gushed from my eyes, and while I was in this state the post nags brought me to the next station.

IV

Trade and Commerce

SOCIAL HISTORIANS have become skeptical, and rightly so, about such vague clichés as "the rise of the middle classes." It would be no less an error, however, to underestimate the importance of the most dynamic social group in eighteenth-century Europe—the wholesale traders, merchant bankers, and a sprinkling of manufacturers. Varying in number, wealth, initiative, and respectability, European merchants and manufacturers were creating new forms of business and financial organization, committing energy and capital to wider areas, and acquiring an ever greater sense of self-confidence and social importance.

Alongside the traditional, even routine, commercial activities—ranging from the grain trade of Angoulême to the fairs of Leipzig—was the rapidly increasing overseas commerce of the Atlantic ports of London, Liverpool, Nantes, Bordeaux, and Cadiz. Handsome profits were made on exports of textiles, hardware, glass, and paper, and imports of salt fish, sugar, indigo, and tobacco. This American trade was closely associated with the slave trade, which transferred over 2 million Negroes from West Africa to the British American colonies alone. Prodigious accumulation of capital created not only a larger number of wealthy and educated merchant families but also new sources of income for their respective governments. Although the wealthy merchant communities, even in the larger cities of England or France, were always minorities, governments had to recognize their importance. Moreover, such economic dynamism was bound to affect other institutions. The search for public office or direct pressure for legislation was one aspect of this; the lure of a mercantile dowry was another. Moreover, with a clientele of lawyers, agents, and employees, not to mention dependent middlemen and associated retail tradesmen, the merchant community possessed impressive political and social weight.

In general the size, wealth, and influence of the merchant community was directly related to its proximity to the Atlantic seaboard. The German and Italian merchants were falling further and further behind their western competitors, becoming increasingly dependent on English and Dutch carriers. The Baltic was no longer the preserve of the German Hanse, and the Mediterranean from Livorno to Smyrna was dominated by the English, Dutch, and French. As for Poland,

Russia, or southeast Europe, aside from a noble-operated grain trade, interior trade was in the hands of the mule-packing peddler, Jewish, Greek, and Armenian. Inland commerce everywhere contrasted sharply with the dynamism of seaborne commerce. Customs barriers, miserable roads, and too few canals made the transport cost of heavy goods prohibitive. Thus, as seaborne trade expanded, overland trade decreased, evidenced by the steady decline of the once thriving commercial towns of south and west Germany.

It was in England that commercial growth was most dramatic. Favored less by natural advantage than by superior technology, organization, and maritime victories, England increased her merchant marine almost sixfold in the course of the century. Moreover, she developed the most advanced and flexible banking system in the world, capable of financing long-term commercial ventures and providing sufficient capital to sustain continuous growth. And in the English hinterland was a hardware and textile industry already developing the Sheffield cutlery and Lancashire cottons that would undersell all competitors.

Organization and technique were not the only factors deciding commercial advantage. The respectability of trade was not easy to establish. Not only in Catholic countries, but everywhere, landownership carried more prestige, and an income drawn unobtrusively from rents and annuities was always more socially acceptable than "merchandizing." On the Continent, even wholesale trade failed to escape the plebeian stain of "handling money." Here, ennoblement by purchase of a royal office was still the accepted road to higher social status, and to enter trade was to "derogate" from nobility. Although in England this prohibition was not written into law, a writer like Defoe, or Beauwes in his English commercial dictionary, still felt it necessary to insist on the gentility of trade and commerce.

Of course, even in mercantile England the small, self-financed partnerships and single-family enterprises far outnumbered the large joint-stock companies. Conservatism of business operation existed side by side with entrepreneurial imagination, risk, and an inevitable number of business failures. The same Daniel Defoe who lauded the success and respectability of English trade was opposed to lending money at interest. While such an attitude was unusual in England by the end of the century, commercial expansion on the Continent was greatly hindered by the popular prejudice against usury and finance. Retailers were especially conservative, counting more on high unit profits than on a large turnover, honoring thrift and economy more than expansion and risk. As for the average consumer, Mercier probably expressed his views when he candidly assumed that all retailers and shopkeepers were frauds. "Customer beware!" was the normal attitude.

22. *The Dignity of Trade*

DANIEL DEFOE's Letter XXII is something of a classic. A panegyric on
English commercial prowess, it is above all an assertion of the respectability of trade. "By trade and learning have our gentlemen built
their fortunes and ascended to a prodigious height." According to
Defoe, not only did most of the English gentry and nobility "derive
from trade," but trade was the "readiest way for men to raise their
fortune"—a veritable open road to success. Defoe exaggerated the opportunities trade offered "even to mere shopkeepers," as well as the
openness of the English aristocracy to men of business origins in the
eighteenth century. But he was certainly correct when he insisted on
the *relative* dignity of trade in England compared to the Continent.

Source: Daniel Defoe, *The Complete English Tradesman in Familiar Letters* (London, 1727), pp. 304–311.

Letter XXII.
Of the Dignity of Trade in England
More Than in Other Countries

SIR,

IT IS said of *England* by way of distinction, and we all value our
selves upon it, that it is a trading country; and King *Charles* II
who was perhaps the Prince of all the Kings that ever reign'd in
England, that best understood the country and the people that he
govern'd, us'd to say, *That the Tradesmen were the only Gentry
in* England: His Majesty spoke it merrily, but it had a happy
signification in it, such as was peculiar to the best Genius of that
Prince, who, tho' he was not the bright governour, was the best
acquainted with the world, of all the Princes of his age, if not
of all the men in it; and tho' it be a digression give me leave, after
having quoted the King, to add three short observations of my
own, in favour of *England,* and of the people and trade of it, and
yet without the least partiality to our own country.

I We are not only a trading country, but the greatest trading
country in the world.

II Our climate is the most agreeable climate in the world to live in.

III Our *Englishmen* are the stoutest and best men (I mean what we call men of their hands) in the world.

These are great things to advance in our own favour, and yet to pretend not to be partial too; and therefore I shall give my reasons, which I think support my opinion, and they shall be as short as the heads themselves, that I may not go too much off from my subject.

1. We are the greatest trading country in the world, because we have the greatest exportation of the growth and product of our land, and of the manufacture and labour of our people; and the greatest importation and consumption of the growth, product, and manufactures of other countries from abroad, of any nation in the world.

2. Our climate is the best and most agreeable, because a man can be more out of doors in *England* than in other countries. This was King *Charles* the second's reason for it; and I cannot name it, without doing justice to his Majesty in it.

3. Our men are the *stoutest* and *best*, because strip them naked from the wast upwards, and give them no weapons at all but their Hands and Heels, and turn them into a room, or stage, and lock them in with the like number of other men of any nation, man for man, and they shall beat the best men you shall find in the world.

From this digression, which I hope will not be disagreeable, as it is not very tedious, I come back to my first observation, that *England* is a trading country; and two things I offer from that head.

First, Our tradesmen are not, as in other countries, the meanest of our people.

Secondly, Some of the greatest and best, and most flourishing families among not the gentry only, but even the nobility, have been rais'd from trade, owe their beginning, their wealth, and their estates to trade; and I may add,

Thirdly, Those families are not at all ashamed of their original, and indeed have no occasion to be ashamed of it.

It is true, that in *England* we have a numerous and an illustrious Nobility and Gentry; and it is true also, that not so many of the those families have rais'd themselves by the sword as in other nations, though we have not been without men of fame in the field too.

But *Trade* and *Learning* has been the two chief steps, by which our gentlemen have rais'd their relations, and have built their fortunes; and from which they have ascended up to the prodigious height, both in wealth and number, which we see them now risen to.

As so many of our noble and wealthy families are rais'd by, and derive from trade, so it is true, and indeed it cannot well be otherwise, that many of the younger branches of our gentry, and even of the nobility it self, have descended again into the spring from whence they flow'd, and have become trademen; and thence it is, that, as I said above, our tradesmen in *England* are not, *as it generally is in other countries*, always of the meanest of our people.

Indeed I might have added here, that trade it self in *England* is not, as it generally is in other countries, the meanest thing the men can turn their hand to; but on the contrary trade is the readiest way for men to raise their fortunes and families; and therefore it is a field for men of figure and of good families to enter upon.

N.B. By trade we must be understood to include Navigation, and foreign discoveries, because they are generally speaking all promoted and carried on by trade, and even by tradesmen, as well as merchants; and the tradesmen are at this time as much concern'd in shipping (as Owners) as the merchants, only the latter may be said to be the chief employers of the shipping.

Having thus done a particular piece of justice to ourselves, in the value we put upon trade and tradesmen in *England*, it reflects very much upon the understandings of those refin'd heads, who *pretend* to depreciate that part of the nation, which is so infinitely superior in number and in wealth to the families who call themselves gentry, and so infinitely more numerous.

As to the wealth of the nation, that undoubtedly lies chiefly among the trading part of the people; and tho' there are a great

many families rais'd within few years, in the late war by great
employments, and by great actions abroad, to the honour of the
English Gentry; yet how many more families among the tradesmen have been rais'd to immense estates, even during the same
time, by the attending circumstances of the war? Such as the
cloathing, the paying, the victualling and furnishing, &c. both
army and navy? And by whom have the prodigious taxes been
paid, the loans supplied, and money advanced upon all occasions?
By whom are the Banks and Companies carried on? And on
whom are the Customs and Excises levied? Has not the trade and
tradesmen born the burthen of the war? And do they not still pay
four millions a year interest for the publick debts? On whom are
the funds levied, and by whom the publick credit supported? Is
not trade the inexhausted fund of all funds, and upon which all
the rest depend?

As is the trade, so in proportion are the tradesmen; and how
wealthy are tradesmen in almost all the several parts of *England*
as well as in *London*? How ordinary is it to see a tradesman go off
of the stage, even but from mere shop-keeping, with, from ten to
forty thousand pounds estate, to divide among his family? when,
on the contrary, take the gentry in *England* from one end to the
other, except a few here and there, what with excessive high
living, which is of late grown so much into a disease, and the
other ordinary circumstances of families, we find few families of
the lower gentry, that is to say, from six or seven hundred a year
downwards, but they are in debt and in necessitous circumstances,
and a great many of greater estates also.

On the other hand, let any one who is acquainted with *England*, look but abroad into the several countries, especially near
London, or within fifty miles of it: How are the antient families
worn out by time and family misfortunes, and the estates possess'd by a new race of tradesmen, grown up into families of
gentry, and establish'd by the immense wealth, gain'd, as I may
say, behind the counter; that is, in the shop, the warehouse, and
the compting-house? How are the sons of tradesmen rank'd
among the prime of the gentry? How are the daughters of tradesmen at this time adorn'd with the ducal coronets, and seen riding
in the coaches of the best of the nobility? Nay, many of our trading gentlemen at this time refuse to be Ennobled, scorn being

knighted, and content themselves with being known to be rated among the richest Commoners in the nation: And it must be acknowledg'd, that whatever they be as to court-breeding, and to manners, they, generally speaking, come behind none of the gentry in knowledge of the world.

At this very day we see the son of Sir *Thomas Scawen* match'd into the ducal family of *Bedford*, and the son of Sir *James Bateman* into the princely house of *Marlborough*, both whose ancestors, within the memory of the writers of these sheets, were tradesmen in *London;* the first Sir *William Scawen's* apprentice, and the latter's grandfather a P——upon, or near, *London-Bridge.*

How many noble seats, superior to the palaces of sovereign Princes (in some countries) do we see erected within few miles of this city by tradesmen, or the sons of tradesmen, while the seats and castles of the ancient gentry, like their families, look *worn out*, and fallen into *decay!* witness the noble house of Sir *John Eyles*, himself a Merchant, at *Giddy-hall* near *Rumford;* Sir *Gregory Page* on *Black-heath*, the son of a *Brewer;* Sir *Nathanael Mead* near *Weal-green*, his father a *Linen-Draper*, with many others, too long to repeat; and to crown all, the Lord *Castlemain's* at *Wanstead*, his father Sir *Josiah Child* originally a Tradesman.

It was a smart, but just repartee of a *London* Tradesman, when a gentleman *who had a good estate too*, rudely reproach'd him in company and bad him hold his tongue, for he was no gentleman; *No, Sir*, says he, *but I can buy a gentleman*, and therefore I claim a liberty to speak among gentlemen.

Again, in how superior a port or figure (as we now call it) do our tradesmen live to what the middling gentry either do or can support? An ordinary Tradesman now, not in the city only, but in the country, shall spend more money by the year, than a gentleman of four or five hundred pounds a Year can do; and shall encrease and lay up every year too; whereas the gentleman shall at the best stand stock still, just where he began, nay, perhaps decline; and as for the lower gentry, from an hundred pounds a year to three hundred, or thereabouts, *though they are often as proud and high in their appearance as the other;* as to them, I say, a *Shoemaker* in *London* shall keep a better house, spend more money, cloath his family better, and yet grow rich too: It is evident where the difference lies, *an Estate's a pond*, but a Trade's a *spring;* The first, if it keeps full, and the water wholesom, by the ordinarry supplies and dreins from the neighbouring grounds, 'tis well, and 'tis all that is expected; but the other is an inexhausted current, which not only fills the pond, and keeps it full, but is continually running over, and fills all the lower ponds and places about it.

This being the case in *England*, and our trade being so vastly great, it is no wonder that the tradesmen in *England* fill the lists of our nobility and gentry; no wonder that the gentlemen of the best familes marry tradesmen's daughters, and put their younger sons apprentices to tradesmen; and how often do these younger sons come to buy the elder sons estates, and restore the family, when the elder, and head of the house, proving rakish and extravagant, has wasted his patrimony, and is obliged to make out the blessing of *Israel's* family, where the younger son bought the birth-right, and the elder was doomed to serve him?

Trade is so far *here* from being inconsistent with a Gentleman, that *in short* trade in *England* makes Gentlemen, and has peopled this nation with Gentlemen; for after a generation or two the tradesmen's children, or at least their grand-children, come to be as good Gentlemen, Statesmen, Parliament-men, Privy-Counsellors, Judges, Bishops, and Noblemen, as those of the highest birth and the most ancient families; and nothing too high for them: Thus the late Earl of *Haversham* was originally a Merchant, the late Secretary *Craggs* was the son of a *Barber*, the present Lord *Castlemain's* father was a Tradesman; the great grandfather of the present Duke of *Bedford* the same, and so of several others: Nor do we find any defect either in the genius or capacities of the posterity of tradesmen, arising from any remains of mechanick blood, which 'tis pretended should influence them; but all the gallantry of spirit, greatness of soul, and all the generous principles that can be found in any of the ancient families, whose blood is the most untainted, as they call it, with the low mixtures of a mechanick race, are found in these; and, as is said before, they generally go beyond them in knowledge of the world, which is the best education.

We see the tradesmen of *England*, as they grow wealthy, coming every day to the Herald's office, to search for the Coats of Arms of their ancestors, in order to paint them upon their coaches, and engrave them upon their plate, embroider them upon their furniture, or carve them upon the pediments of their

new houses; and how often do we see them trace the registers of
their families up to the prime nobility, or the most ancient gentry
of the kingdom?

23.   Restriction of Moneylending in France

TURGOT, WHO was to become controller-general of France in 1774, was
without doubt one of the most conscientious and enlightened provincial administrators in eighteenth-century France. As intendant of
Limoges in the 1760's, Turgot made Herculean efforts to increase local
production, stimulate trade and industry, and assure the population just
treatment within the bounds of a privileged and hierarchical society.

The selection here describes the modest commerce of Angoulême,
typical of the greater part of provincial France. Among the many
retardative influences on commercial growth, the usury laws struck
Turgot as especially nefarious. The second part of the selection is a
lucid, well-argued indictment of the pernicious effects of the usury
laws and their application in France. The situation was in striking
contrast to England where, despite the moral apprehensions of someone like Defoe, loans at interest were legal, open, and respectable.

Source: A. R. J. Turgot, *Oeuvres*, ed. Eugène Daire and Hippo-
lythe Dussard (Paris, 1844), vol. I, pp. 106ff., 114–116.

Memoir on Moneylending

I. OCCASION OF THE PRESENT MEMOIR

SOME MONTHS ago,[1] a complaint was lodged with the seneschal of
Angoulême[2] against an individual who was said to have demanded usurious interest in his financial transactions. This
caused considerable agitation among the merchants of this town.
This agitation has steadily increased because the initial complaint
was recognized. New complaints followed, and moneylenders are

---

[1] In early 1769.
[2] The "seneschal of Angoulême" was the presiding officer at the court of
first instance, which had the right of appeal.

now threatened from all sides. All these developments have produced the results to be expected: anxiety and discredit in the merchant community, an absolute lack of money in the economy, a complete standstill of all commercial speculation, disparagement of the Angoulême market elsewhere, suspension of all payments, and nonacceptance of a mass of bills of exchange. These developments appear to merit the most serious attention of the government. It seems most important to halt this evil at its inception, for if the kind of jurisprudence the court is trying to establish at Angoulême became general, every commercial market would soon be exposed to the same troubles, and credit, already badly shaken by the frequent occurrence of bankruptcies, would cease to exist altogether. . . .

III. General View of the Commerce of Angoulême

In order to give a fair view of the maneuvers of those individuals who reported the incidents of usury, to show where they originated and provide a full understanding of their results, it is necessary to give some detailed information about the nature of commerce in Angoulême and the transactions that have taken place here in the last few years.

Since the town of Angoulême is situated on the Charente at the point where the river becomes navigable, one would think that the town would be greatly interested in commerce. Yet it is not. Probably one of the principal obstacles to commercial progress is the easy access to nobility, which all the well-to-do families attain via the office of *maire*. The result is that as soon as a man has amassed a fortune in commerce, he hastens to leave trade in order to become a noble. The capital he had acquired is soon squandered in an idle life attending his new estate, or at least it is lost to commerce. Therefore, what little commerce exists is in the hands of people of modest fortune who can form only limited enterprises since they are short of capital and who are almost always obliged to work with borrowed money. They can only borrow at very high interest rates, partly because the actual supply of money is limited and partly because they can offer little security to creditors.

By and large, the commerce of Angoulême consists of only

three main types: papermaking, brandy export, and iron manufacture. The last has become very important since the king has
recently ordered large quantities of cannon from the forges of
Angoumois and Périgord, not far from Angoulême.

In general, the commerce in paper goods follows a rather
steady course. The same is not true for the trade in brandy. This
commodity is subject to extreme price fluctuations and gives rise
to very uncertain speculation. Such fluctuations can bring immense profits or ruinous losses. The enterprises of the ironmakers,
who supply the navy, demand very large and long-term advances
on their part, and profits are dependent on the time limit of these
advances. In order not to miss the opportunity of obtaining a
large contract, the ironmakers are obliged to find money at any
price. This is particularly important since they can obtain their
raw material at a considerable discount if they pay cash for their
wood and iron ore.

IV. Origin of the High Interest Rate in Angoulême

It is easy to understand that the circumstances of the town of
Angoulême, where commerce is potentially risky as well as profitable and where money is in short supply, have resulted in a rather
high interest rate, higher than rates in other markets. It is notorious that in the last forty years most financial transactions in
Angoulême were negotiated at an annual interest rate of 8 or 9
per cent, and sometimes even 10 per cent, depending on the risks
incurred. . . .

XIV. Faultiness of Our Laws in Matters of Interest Rates, Impossibility of Rigorously Enforcing Them, Disadvantages of the Arbitrary Toleration That Must Be Observed in Practice

I shall have to speak frankly. The laws on interest recognized by
the courts are bad. Our legislation is based on strong prejudices
concerning usury, which originated with theologians of ignorant
ages who did not understand the sense of the Scripture any better
than the principles of natural law. Strict enforcement of these
laws would destroy all commerce, and that is why they are not
strictly enforced. They prohibit any stipulation of interest as long

as the capital is not alienated and brand as illicit any interest beyond the rate fixed by royal ordinance. And yet it is a notorious fact that there is not one business community in the world where most enterprises do not operate on borrowed money without alienation of capital and where the rate of interest is not determined by the circumstances alone, depending on the supply of money and the degree of solvency of the borrower. The rigidity of our laws has had to give way before the necessities. Jurisprudence has had to moderate its speculative principles in actual practice, and it has openly come to tolerate promissory notes, discounting bills, and all other kinds of monetary transactions among merchants. It will always be so whenever the law prohibits anything that is necessary by the very nature of things.

However, this situation, where the laws are not enforced and yet continue to exist instead of being repealed and where they are even enforced in certain cases, is extremely unwholesome. On the one hand, the open disregard for the law diminishes the respect all citizens should have for everything bearing that stamp; on the other hand, the continued existence of the law keeps an unfortunate prejudice alive, stigmatizing an action which is quite legitimate in itself, without which society cannot exist, and in which, consequently, a large class of citizens must engage. This class of citizens is considered degraded because of it, and once it is thus lowered in the opinion of the public, its own sense of honor, an important factor in maintaining honesty, will also weaken. The author of the *Esprit des Lois* [Montesquieu] has aptly said that, regarding these very usury laws, they prohibit a necessary function and only succeed in making dishonest people of those who engage in it. Aside from that, since the cases where the law is enforced and those where their infraction is tolerated are not specified by the law itself, the fate of the individual citizen is left to an arbitrary jurisprudence which changes with public opinion. That which is practiced by a vast number of citizens with the approval, as it were, of public opinion will be punished as a crime when practiced by others, so that it takes only one judge of little experience or one blinded by an uninformed zeal to stigmatize and ruin a citizen who confidently counted on the customary toleration.

The municipal courts permit interest to be stipulated when the capital is not alienated,[3] while the royal courts reprove it or apply the interest to the capital. Penalties for usury are on the books. They are, for the first offense, the formal confession of guilt [*amende honorable*], banishment, and imposition of a high fine; and for the second offense, confiscation of all property and imprisonment, i.e., a penalty which amounts to legal death, just as imprisonment or banishment for life does. The Ordinance of Blois, which stipulates these penalties, makes no distinction among the various cases brought together under the heading of usury by the theologians and legalists. Thus, as far as the letter of the law is concerned, any man who lends money without the alienation of capital, any man who accepts securities in a business transaction, any man who lends at an interest rate higher than that fixed by the ordiance merits these penalties. There is no doubt that there is not one merchant, not one banker, not one financial agent of the king who is not exposed to these penalties. Yet it is a notorious fact that almost all the day-to-day operations of the entire commercial world are based on these kinds of transactions.

It will no doubt be argued, and this objection is even found in otherwise perfectly respectable authors on the subject, that the tribunals only prosecute exorbitant usury. But this very objection shows how arbitrary any attempted enforcement of this law must be; for by what rule could we distinguish exorbitant and punishable from middling and tolerable usury? There probably is no greater usury than that which is practiced in Paris under the name of "weekly loans." Sometimes the interest has been as high as 2 sous per week for a loan of 1 *écu* of 30 sous—a rate of 173⅓ per cent. And yet this truly exorbitant usury is the basis of the retail trade in the commodities that are sold in the central market and retailed in the neighborhood markets of Paris. The borrowers do not complain about the conditions of this loan without which they could not engage in the trade they live by, and the lenders do not become very rich since the exorbitant interest hardly does

[3] Turgot's note: "I know, of course, that the municipal courts never state expressly that interest must be paid because it is stipulated in a simple loan contract in which the capital is not alienated; but in actual practice they do the equivalent to authorizing interest. The loan contracts which they declare valid usually include the interest with the capital, and the municipal judges do not heed the borrowers who protest that their contract comprises interest as well as the capital.

more than compensate them for the risks they take. In fact, the insolvency of only one borrower uses up all the profit a lender can make on thirty, so that, if the risk of defaulting or insolvency among the borrowers were one to thirty, the lender would not make any profit on his interest, and if [the risk ratio] were higher, he would lose money.

Now, if the public official is obliged to overlook such usury, what kind of usury will he be able to prosecute without being unjust? Will it be decided that it is best to remain silent and wait for a borrower who believes himself injured to lodge a complaint or a denunciation, before the law is made to speak? In that case the law would become but the instrument of the bad faith of knaves who want to break a freely contracted agreement. It would protect only those who are unworthy of its protection. These people would find themselves in a better position than honorable men who are faithful to their engagements and would be ashamed to break them by the means offered by the law.

24. A Scottish Banking House [1]

THE BANKING house of Sir William Forbes was not a large, well-known establishment comparable to the latter-day Lloyds of London or Barclay's Ltd. Four to five partners closely connected, often by marriage and blood, directed a countinghouse that relied more on "prudence, care, and diligence" than on "needless risks." The following selections from Forbes's account of his own firm reveal all the trademarks of a tight family enterprise. Sir William's opening letter exhorting his son to learn to love the business, his touching comments on the death of his lifelong partner, and his constant effort to find places in the firm for the sons of his associates—all deepen the impression of a business house cemented by strong sentimental ties.

In the 1760's Forbes and his partner, Hunter, disengaged from grain speculation and other ventures in "merchandising" and directed the firm toward its "proper and natural business of exchange and banking," a policy the partners believed had saved them from the wave of Scottish bankruptcies in 1772. Prudence did not prevent them from realiz-

[1] The family papers and accounts of eighteenth-century merchants and bankers are extremely hard to come by.

ing handsome profits in the "public funds," however, and the repeated warnings of Sir William against "speculations" must not be taken too literally. In fact, it appears that the Forbes banking house issued its own notes by the 1760's, an imaginative and successful venture, supplementing inadequate supplies of hard money in the economy as a whole.

Source: *Memoirs of a Banking-House by the Late Sir William Forbes of Pitsligo, Bart., Author of the "Life of Dr. Beattle"* (Edinburgh: printed for private circulation, 1859), pp. vii–ix, 12–15, 38–41, 65–67. According to the editor, the manuscript was completed in 1803.

Address of the Author to His Son

EDINBURGH, *1st January* 1803

MY DEAREST WILLIAM,

You have often heard me express an intention of writing some account of our house of business in Edinburgh, from its first establishment by the Messrs Coutts.

The history of a society in which I have passed the whole of my time, from my boyish days to this present hour, during the long period of almost half a century, cannot but be very interesting to me, especially since by means of my connection with it, I have arrived, through the blessing of Providence, to a degree of opulence and respectability of position, which I had very little reason to look for on my first entrance into the world. I have often thought that such a narrative might not be without its advantage to you, as calculated to teach you the necessity of prudence and caution in business of every kind, but most particularly in that of a banker, in whose possession not only his own property, but that of hundreds of others, is at stake; and as shewing you how, by a steady, well-concerted plan, with a strict adherence to integrity in all your transactions, aided by civility, yet without meanness, you can scarcely fail, by the blessing of Heaven, to arrive at success.

From such a history, too, some general knowledge may be gained of the progressive improvement of Scotland. For, although it is no doubt true that, even where things remain in a good measure stationary in a country, the business of a banking-house, the longer it exists, has a natural tendency to increase, when it has been conducted with prudence and ability, yet it is certainly to the rapid progress of the prosperity of this country, that the very great extension of the business of our house during the last twenty years must, in a great measure, be attributed. To illustrate this part of my proposed subject, I have subjoined to my narrative a short and, I must acknowledge, a very imperfect sketch, collected from the best authorities I could meet with; to some of which, my situation as a man of business has given me peculiar access. The subject is curious, and to me extremely interesting; as I have lived in the very period when this improvement of our native country has assumed some form, and seems still to be making daily advances to yet greater prosperity—a reflection highly grateful to me as a Scotsman.

To my own memory this narrative will recall many scenes on which I cannot look back without the most heartfelt gratitude to that Almighty Being, who has been graciously pleased to shower down upon me so large a share of prosperity. Nor can I contemplate the many years I have spent in business, and the number of friends of whom death has in that interval deprived me, without the most serious reflections on the rapidity with which this life is wearing away, and the propriety of my bending my thoughts towards another—a subject of meditation at all times proper for a rational being; but peculiarly so for one who has lived so long as I have done in the hurry and tumult of a constant intercourse with the busy world—a state extremely unfavourable to sober thought and reflection.

I cannot conclude this address to you, my dearest William, in a better manner than by expressing my hope that this narrative will confirm you in a love for that profession which you probably adopted at first on my suggestion. My wish certainly was to insure your succession to the fruits of my labours, as far as I have had any merit in helping to raise the house to its present flourishing state. If you continue to pay the same attention to business that I have done (I trust I may speak it in this place without vanity), I have no doubt that, by the blessing of Heaven on your endeavours, you may preserve the house in credit and respectability long after I shall have paid my debt to nature. But I never can too often nor too earnestly inculcate that the continuance of that credit and prosperity, under Providence, must entirely depend on yourself. If you prove yourself worthy of the notice of your father's friends (of which I must do you the justice to say, I have at this moment the fairest hope), you may expect their most cordial support, as well as a continuance of that favour and preference with which they have so long and so steadily honoured me. But if your own endeavours be wanting—if negligence take the place of attention to business, and economy be abandoned for profusion of expense—you may be assured that the concerns of the house will go speedily into decay, until at last that decline shall terminate in absolute ruin. For, in the course of a long experience, I can safely say that I have never known a single instance in which relaxed management and unbounded expense did not end in total bankruptcy.

That the providence of the Almighty may ever watch over you to shield you from harm, is the earnest and daily prayer of,

My dearest William,

Your fond and affectionate father,

WILLIAM FORBES

. . . Mr. Farquharson had been my father's most intimate friend and companion from a very early period, and although not in the nomination of my guardians, his high regard for my father had attached him strongly to my mother and her infant children, to whom he proved himself a steady and most useful friend to his dying hour. The slender provision which my father had left me—although he had by great attention to business and frugality been enabled in the course of his short life to double the pittance which originally fell to him out of the wreck of our family estate, when sold by his grandfather—having rendered it absolutely necessary that I should attach myself to some profession for my future support, Mr Farquharson suggested to my mother the propriety of breeding me to commercial business, in preference to any of the learned professions, as a surer road to independence. In prosecution of this plan, after my education in the usual branches of school learning was completed, he prevailed on his young friends, the Messrs Coutts, to receive me as an apprentice into their counting-house, the circumstance to which, by the blessing of Heaven, I owe that respectable situation in life to which I have attained.

At this period, as I have already said, Messrs Coutts carried on business both at Edinburgh and London—at Edinburgh, under the firm of Coutts Brothers & Co., conducted by John and James Coutts and Mr Stephen; at London, under the firm of Coutts, Stephen, Coutts, & Co., conducted by Patrick and Thomas Coutts. The business at Edinburgh [1] comprised extensive transactions in corn on their own account. They also did business on commission, in the sale of wines and other consignments, and in shipping lead, salmon, and other articles; and, lastly, they acted as exchange dealers and bankers by receiving deposits of money, for which they allowed interest. The house in London was the correspondent of the house in Edinburgh, which conducted through them all their exchange operations, and they also transacted business both in buying and selling goods on commission.

In the month of August 1754, Mr James Coutts, who had never been out of Scotland, went to London on a visit to his brothers. There he very soon afterwards married Miss Polly Peagrim, the niece of George Campbell, an eminent banker in the Strand, by whom he was immediately received into partnership, under the firm of Campbell and Coutts, and he in consequence withdrew from the partnerships with his brothers in London and Edinburgh.

Some short time afterwards, Mr William Dalrymple, merchant in Cadiz—brother of Sir Hew Dalrymple of North Berwick—was assumed as an acting partner in the house at London, the firm of which was then changed to Coutts Brothers and Dalrymple. In a very short time, however, Messrs Coutts, disliking Mr Dalrymple's too great love of speculation, the partnership between them was dissolved by mutual consent, and the firm was again changed to Coutts Brothers & Co., being the same with that of the Edinburgh house.

About the year 1760, Mr George Campbell, the banker, dying, Mr James Coutts assumed his youngest brother, Thomas, as a

[1] The whole office staff, besides the partners, then comprised only four clerks and two apprentices including myself. I cannot omit mentioning, that, the year after myself, we were joined by Mr. Lewis Hay, and the year following by Mr. Hunter, afterwards Sir James Hunter Blair, who both became partners and my most intimate friends. In the same manner Mr. Bartlet came into the house as a clerk in 177–, and my brother-in-law, Mr. John Hay, in 1778, and you, my dear William, became an apprentice in 1788, and have since all been partners in the house. All footnotes are Forbes's—Eds.

partner in that banking-house, the firm of which then became James and Thomas Coutts. In consequence, Thomas also withdrew from the two houses of Edinburgh and London, the last of which was thereafter managed by Mr Patrick Coutts, with the assistance of Mr Thomas Walker, their principal and confidential clerk, who had been originally bred in the counting-house at Edinburgh. Some difference having arisen between Mr Walker and them, he quitted their service; and a procuration was then given to Mr George Keith, who had been bred with Mr A. Gregory of Dunkirk, and had been recommended to Messrs Coutts as a clerk in their London establishment. Mr John Coutts and Mr Stephen continued to conduct the business of the house at Edinburgh.

While those changes were so rapidly succeeding each other, my apprenticeship of five years was completed on the 14th May 1759. Mr Francis Farquharson, my much esteemed friend, having it greatly at heart to procure for me an interest in the house at Edinburgh, advised me to continue to serve the company in the capacity of a clerk after my apprenticeship was finished, which I did for very nearly two years, without receiving any emolument, in the expectation of being at some convenient opportunity, through his means, admitted a partner.[2] On the 6th of August 1760, I was intrusted with a power of attorney, by which I was enabled to take an active part in the conducting of the business of the house; and Mr John Coutts with much kindness took every opportunity of bringing me into notice, by inviting me to dinner occasionally when he had parties of friends at his house. I take pleasure in mentioning this circumstance, though trivial in itself, as a grateful testimony of his goodness to me on every occasion. At length, a new contract for ten years having been executed by Mr Patrick Coutts, Mr John Coutts, and Mr Stephen, commencing 1st January 1761, an agreement was entered into between them and me on the 13th March 1761, by which I was to be concerned to the extent of one-eighth share of the house at Edinburgh. But so jealous were they of the effects of this concession in

---

[2] So strict was Mr. John Coutts in the discipline of the counting-house, that I slept but one night out of Edinburgh from the commencement of my apprenticeship in May 1754 till the month of September 1760, when I obtained leave to go to Aberdeenshire with my mother, to pay a visit to our relations.

my favour, that the agreement was only to last for three years, with a power to any of them to put an end to it at the end of one year, if they should judge it expedient, and without permitting me to appear to the world in the character of a partner; so that I still continued to act by virtue of the power of attorney. These prudential restrictions on the part of Messrs Coutts might perhaps be deemed a little hard, as they had had a seven years' experience of my close application to business and zeal for their interest; yet they were cheerfully submitted to by me, with the hope of one day becoming an ostensible partner.

A few months after the execution of this agreement, Mr Patrick Coutts was laid aside from business by bad health, which ended in a deprivation of reason; and in the course of that summer, Mr John Coutts was seized at London with a painful disease, which brought him to the gates of death, and so broke his constitution, that, being ordered by his physicians to drink the waters of Bath, he died there in August 1761, deeply lamented by all who knew him, but by none more than by myself, who lost in him an able guide and a steady friend. By this unlooked-for stroke, the two houses of London and Edinburgh were left in a most destitute situation. The business of the house at London was of itself noway considerable; but it became of importance to the general interest by their being the correspondents of the house at Edinburgh, who drew their bills on them, and transacted through them their exchange business. The London house had not a person in it who was entitled to sign the firm, and although the business was very well attended to by Mr Keith, who held the company's power of attorney, it was impossible that he could have the weight of a partner, and it is wonderful that things went on so well as they did. At Edinburgh, matters were, if possible, still worse; as there was no ostensible partner but Mr Stephen, whose slender abilities were altogether inadequate to the task of conducting the houses, and for which my youth and inexperience rendered me extremely ill qualified. It was therefore a singular instance of the goodness of Providence to us, that, under such feeble management, the houses still supported their credit and reputation. Indeed, I must chiefly attribute it, under Heaven, to the popularity of Provost Coutts and his family in Edinburgh, and the established reputation of their firm, by which the friends and correspondents of the house were induced to continue their business there as formerly. Yet even that advantage would not have been sufficient, had I not been strongly supported and assisted by my intimate friend and companion, Mr Hunter, whom I have mentioned as my fellow-apprentice in the house. Although he was nearly two years younger than me, yet such were his superior abilities, that, through him alone, I may say, it was owing that Mr Stephen and I did not sink under the load of conducting a banking-house such as ours, inconsiderable as the business then was compared with what it has since become. Even then, however, the house was one of the first reputation in Edinburgh, for, of course, everything must be estimated by comparison. The first resolution which Mr Hunter and I formed, on finding ourselves practically the sole conductors of the house, was to wind up the corn-speculations then existing, and to relinquish that trade entirely, so as in future to confine the house to its proper and natural business of exchange and banking, by which prudent resolution, and by unremitting assiduity and attention, we were enabled to go on without any apparent diminution of business. . . .

The other speculation I alluded to, as entered upon by Mr Hunter and me, was, if possible, still more indefensible, because more of a precarious nature; but fortunately it happened that the loss did not prove to be very extensive. It took place thus. When Mr Hunter was married to a niece of the Earl of Cassillis, he became, of course, much connected in friendship with that nobleman, on whose estate there was believed to be a lead-mine, which had been wrought, though with no success, a good many years before. Mr Hunter, wishing to oblige Lord Cassillis, who was anxious that a further trial of his mine should be made, mentioned the matter to Mr Alexander Sheriff, merchant in Leith, who had a concern in the lease of the Earl of Hopetoun's mines at Leadhills, and was supposed to be master of the subject. Mr Sheriff, a man of a speculative genius and sanguine temper, grasped at the idea of undertaking to work Lord Cassillis's mine, and it was agreed that the earl himself, Mr Hunter, Mr Herries, Mr Sheriff, and I, should enter into a copartnery for the purpose, but limiting the concern so strictly, that we were each of us to contribute only £30 to a joint-stock, for the purpose of making the trial, and an overseer, named Barker, was engaged to carry it on so far as to ascertain whether we might reasonably expect to hit upon a productive vein of lead-ore or not. After working about a twelvemonth, Mr Sheriff became bankrupt in the disastrous year 1772, and this event, fortunately, put a stop to the undertaking, before any more than the original subscribed sum was expended, which, therefore, was all the loss that each of us sustained. I say fortunately, not in allusion to the bankruptcy of poor Mr Sheriff, who was a very industrious, honest man, but for us, as there is no saying to what lengths we might have been led, for I regard mining as a very deep species of gambling, whereby there has probably been more lost upon the whole than gained.

The year 1772 will long be remembered in Scotland for the numerous bankruptcies which took place at Edinburgh in the month of June, and which may be said to have entirely changed the current of the business in our northern capital. I have formerly noticed the extensive speculations which were entered into by some Scotchmen for the purchase and cultivation of lands in the newly acquired West India Islands; as well as the spirit which took place about this time for improvements in agriculture at home. Some of the houses which carried on the banking business in Edinburgh, having embarked in these speculations, required a larger capital than their own resources could command. To this must be added, the rage which then began to take place for building larger and more expensive houses, than had been customary in Edinburgh before the plan of the New Town was set on foot; and larger houses necessarily led to more extensive establishments, as to furniture, servants, and equipages. At the same time those projectors and improvers, flattering themselves with the prospect of the immense advantage to be derived from their speculations, launched out into a style of living up to their expected profits, as if they had already realised them. Such causes combined had induced those gentlemen to have recourse to the ruinous mode of raising money by a chain of bills on London; and when the established banks declined to continue a system of which they began to be suspicious, the bank of Douglas, Heron, & Co., commonly known as the "Ayr Bank," was erected. But, instead of proving a cure to the evil, they, by their improvident and injudicious management, found themselves compelled to plunge into this kind of circulation still deeper than the others, although

with a more solid foundation. The fictitious paper in the circle
between Edinburgh and London had thus arisen to an astonishing height, and was falling into great and general disrepute in
London, when the first check was given to it by the failure of the
London banking-house of Neale, James, Fordyce, and Downe,
which had been but recently established. Alexander Fordyce, a
native of Aberdeen, had gone to London, and become a clerk in a
banking-house. Having acquired some knowledge of that business, he persuaded Mr Roffey, a brewer, and a man of some property, as well as Mr James and Mr Neale, to establish a banking-
house, of which he was to be the principal acting partner. Not
contented, however, with the regular profits of their trade, he
indulged in speculative tendencies, by embarking deeply in the
public funds, in which he was at first successful, and was believed
to have acquired a large fortune. In consequence, he assumed a
splendid style of living; had an elegant country-house at Roch-
ampton, in the neighbourhood of London; went into parliament;
and affected a profuse generosity in presents to his relations and
connections in Scotland. To crown his good-fortune, he had the
address to marry Lady Margaret Lindsay, a daughter of the Earl
of Balcarras, a lady of great beauty and accomplishments, doubt-
less captivated by the splendour of his appearance and the reputation of his wealth. His speculations in Change Alley, however,
were not always equally fortunate; and having large differences
to pay, he unwarrantably employed for that purpose, without the
knowledge of his partners, the funds deposited in the house by
their customers. The moment that this became known to the
other partners, they very honourably stopped payment, in order
that they might do such justice to their creditors as was still in
their power; but this bankruptcy set fire to the mine, which at
once blew up the whole traffic of circulation that had been carrying on for a number of years. All those houses in London who had
largely accepted bills drawn on them from Scotland—of which
the sum total was to an astonishing amount—finding it no longer
possible to discount the remittances that had been made to them
for their reimbursement, were instantly compelled to stop payment, and, by unavoidable consequence, the drawers in Edinburgh were compelled to do the same. It was on Monday the——
of June—emphatically called the *Black Monday*—that Fordyce's

house stopped payment. Another banking-house in London, of older standing and greater eminence, which, induced by the idea of perfect safety, and the temptation of a lucrative commission, had become the correspondent of the Ayr Bank, and had been drawn in to go under acceptance for that company to a very great extent, also found themselves under the necessity of suspending their payments for a time; but they soon resumed, and are still a banking-house of eminence. So great was the alarm in London that day,[3] and such the discredit into which every Scotch house was thrown, that there was a violent run even on Mr Drummond's and Mr Coutts's banking-houses, although they were no way engaged in or connected with the chain of circulation from Scotland. The resources of these two capital houses, however, were so great, and they answered all demands with such readiness, that the run on them lasted only during that single day. . . .

The loss of Sir James Hunter Blair was a most severe misfortune to his family, to his partners, and to the city of Edinburgh. His family, consisting of three sons and three daughters, were all young, his eldest son being only fifteen years of age; a fourth son was added after his death. We, his partners, were deprived of a most able associate in business. Edinburgh lost by his death a most active magistrate, who had projected and carried on public works equally conducive to the ornament and advantage of the city. I, in particular, was deprived by his death of a friend whom

[3] ["Every day was ushered in with the disagreeable accounts of new failures, and by the 19th no fewer than ten capital houses had stopped. Words cannot describe the general consternation of the metropolis on the 22d. A universal bankruptcy was expected. The whole city was in an uproar, and many of the first families in tears. Every countenance appeared clouded, occasioned either by real distress, or by what they feared for their friends. * * The Messrs. Adam, of the Adelphi Buildings in the Strand, being unfortunately involved by the failure of some capital houses, upwards of two thousand valuable artificers and workmen, supported by their undertakings in different parts of the kingdom, were thrown out of employment, and their families deprived of subsistence. The poor men had begun their work in the morning, before the melancholy news of their masters' misfortunes was communicated to them: when informed of it, they came down from the walls in silence, and stood for some time in the street in a body; and at last went off one by one, with every mark of regret for the fate of their masters, whose business had supported them and their families for several years. However, to the great joy of every good man, the Messrs. Adam resumed their works on the 26th"—*Scots Magazine*, June 1772.]

I can never replace, with whom I had lived in a degree of intimacy which few brothers can boast of during one-and-thirty years, in which long period we never had a difference nor a separation of interest. It has been stated how we went on together from the time of our apprenticeship, till we gradually arrived, after a variety of changes, to be at the head of the house. But I should do great injustice to his superior talents, did I not declare that to him it was chiefly owing that the house rose to such a pitch of unlooked-for prosperity and reputation. He possessed a sound and manly understanding and an excellent heart. In his friendships he was warm, steady, and sincere, and ever ready to promote the interest of those to whom he formed an attachment. In his disposition he was cheerful and fond of society, and his house was at all times distinguished for hospitality. As a magistrate, he was active and zealous in the discharge of his duty; as a senator, he was honestly independent, supporting the measures of the ministers of the crown when he thought them consistent with the principles of the constitution and the good of the people. Too early and too deeply immersed in business, he had little or no leisure for study, and was therefore but little acquainted with books or literature; but he possessed, in an eminent degree, a species of knowledge of the utmost importance to him as a man of business—great knowledge of the world, and an almost intuitive discernment of the characters of men. In business, both of a public and private nature, he was skilful and active, and capable of the most unwearied application, and his plans in general were contrived with prudence and executed with steadiness. Of this a memorable proof was afforded by the magnificent idea, which he formed on his being elected Lord Provost of Edinburgh, of a communication between the High Street and the south side of the city, by a bridge over the Cowgate. In the prosecution of which extensive and important improvement, notwithstanding he met with no inconsiderable degree of opposition from ignorant and interested individuals, he was not to be discouraged, but kept on the even tenor of his way, combating the prejudices of some and the influence of others, till at last he accomplished his purpose. In his temper there was a degree of warmth, which, in the pursuit of a favourite object, or in the heat of an argument, occasionally bordered on vehemence and impetuosity, and which sometimes, in the intercourse of society, led him to forget or overlook what Lord Chesterfield calls the graces. In his notions of right and wrong, he was rigid and even stern, and he had no allowance to make where he perceived in others any departure from the standard he had formed of propriety of conduct. But his virtues will be remembered and the utility of his public conduct felt and applauded long after those slight imperfections are consigned to oblivion.

A few days before I received the account of Sir James's illness, and when, God knows! I had little notion which of us was first to pay the debt of nature, I had written to him about a plan that had occurred to me for continuing an interest in our house to the eldest son of any of the partners who should happen to die. It had often been a subject of conversation between him and me, how hard it would be, were either of us to die, that our family should entirely lose the benefit of their father's exertions in having brought the house into such a respectable position, and we had several years before entered into a mutual agreement, that whichever of us should survive the other, should pay to the son of the deceased an annuity of £500 a year during eight years. But even this I did not think enough, and therefore proposed that the son should be entitled, if he chose, to an interest in the house of one-third of his father's share, which the surviving partners were to hold for his account until the termination of the contract, but without the son being permitted to interfere in the management of the business. This letter Sir James had received, but had not had time to answer before he was seized with his last illness. It was found among his papers after his death, and as it contained the strongest proof I could give of my belief in the utility of the proposal, I was anxious that it should still be acted on; and therefore, with the concurrence of the other partners, I proposed to the tutors to whom Sir James had left the care of his family, that a new contract should be entered into on that footing. Of this plan the tutors gave their most cordial approbation; but a difficulty occurred which seemed to present an insuperable bar to its taking effect. Had Sir James lived to execute our new contract, he could of course have bound his son and successor to any conditions he pleased. But his eldest son, being left a minor, could not engage in any contract or become bound to the world for his proportional share of the engagements of the house. In order to get the better of this difficulty, the tutors,[4] being impressed with the importance of preserving an interest in the house to their young ward, were pleased to carry their approbation so far as, with an unexampled confidence in us, the other partners, to take upon themselves the responsibility, and to become personally bound for young Sir John Blair until he should come of age and confirm the contract himself—a measure which reflected the highest honour as well on them who conferred, as on us who received, such a proof of their confidence. In conformity with this arrangement, a new contract was executed for twelve years from 1st January 1788, the shares being thus divided—Sir William Forbes, 16; James Bartlet, 7; John Hay, 7; Lewis Hay, 2; Sir John Blair, 5⅓; the remaining of Sir James's shares, 10⅔, being kept unappropriated, in case any desirable partner should come in our way. In the meantime, the profit belonging to those shares undisposed of went to the other partners in proportion to their respective interests in the house.

25. The Formation of a Commercial Company

"COMMERCIAL COMPANY" suggests exotic cargoes, hundreds of stockholders, and profits of six digits. Not all commercial companies were like this. In fact, the typical commercial organization in west Europe was the small partnership. This document is a contractual agreement establishing a commercial company of three associates in Florence with a capitalization of 18,000 *scudi*, a modest sum by English standards. The active administration consists of a director and two permanent clerks. The agreement is for six years, though renewal is possible and even presumed. Profits are divided in proportion to the capital subscribed. Typical of small commercial companies, most of the contract is concerned with defining the responsibilities of the director, who is given a share of the profits. The partners are encouraged to reinvest at least one third of their profits in the company at 5 per cent and their liability is limited to the amount of their investment. Maritime insurance is mandatory for all distant voyages.

[4] They were Lady Blair, the Earl of Cassillis, Mr. Kennedy of Dunure, Dr. Gregory, Mr. John Buchan, writer to the Signet, and myself.

Source: *Archivio di Stato, Firenze, Carte Bartolommei, F-174* (*accomandita*).

FLORENCE, SEPTEMBER 27, 1782. In the name of God

By the present private agreement, as binding as a public instrument notarized by a public Florentine notary, let it be known that the Signore Abate Stefano Rossi, son of Girolamo, a Genoese who has lived for many years in this town, wishes to retire from the business that he has actively conducted until now in his own name and for his own interest, and, specifically, the business managed for many years by Signore Francesco Artz of this town. Wishing to give to this man, his agent, a sincere proof of esteem and gratitude for faithful service, he has resolved to form a commercial company [*accomandita*] with the participation of the following gentlemen, his good friends and clients: the Signore Marchese Girolamo Bartolommei of this city and the Signore Marchese Giovanni Maria Belmonte Stivivi of Rimini. These men, wishing to enjoy all the benefits and privileges accorded to those investing money in business companies by the statutes and ordinances of the Commune of Florence and the Court of Mercanzia and any other law, statute, or provision affecting such matters, have agreed among themselves to create with the aforesaid Signore Francesco Artz a true business company to do business in the city of Florence under the following conditions, that is:

1. That the capital of the said company shall be 18,000 *scudi* [1] of 7 *lire*, Florentine money, to be subscribed as follows:

13,000 *scudi* from the said Abate Stefano Rossi.

3,000 *scudi* from the said Marchese Girolamo Bartolommei.

2,000 *scudi* from the said Marchese Giovanni Maria Belmonte Stivivi.

2. That the said business is to be conducted in this city of Florence in the trade of buying and selling merchandise, following those beginnings and that same kind of business that has been the principal activity of the said Abate Stefano Rossi and his agent. And since for just and reasonable ends, the said Abate

---

[1] By the rate of exchange in 1760, the *scudo* was worth 5.68 livres. This, then, is a modest capitalization, roughly equivalent to 90,000 French livres or 4,500 English pounds. The gross *profits* of the Forbes Banking-House reached this figure in the 1770's.

Stefano Rossi has never engaged in the trade of foodstuffs for his own account, such trade will be prohibited to the director of the company and will be carried out only on commission for others under the usual provisions.

3. That the company director will be Signore Francesco Artz, that the company will carry the name of Signore Francesco Artz and Company, and that it will last for six years. At the end of this time it can be renewed for a similar period, and thus sucessively every six years unless notice to dissolve the company is given one year before the end of the six-year period. The company will begin operations on the first of January of next year, 1783, and will continue on the condition that an honest and appropriate return be made to the investor partners and that the director observe the conditions established in the present agreement, with the further provision that in any year that the company is more to the disadvantage than to the advantage of the investors, or when the director does not observe the conditions of the present agreement, the interested partners may at any time dissolve the company as a body in a manner most to their advantage, especially in the case of negligence of the said director. The liquidation of the company will take place with all the precautions necessary to protect the interests of the director and the investors.

4. The director will have the particular responsibility for the ready cash of the firm, which he will continue to have until it shall please the investors to provide otherwise. The papers and account books related to this shall be kept by a young clerk to be selected by common agreement, preference being given, if possible, to Signore Giovanni Rinieri, the present clerk of the said director. His salary will be increased to 6 *scudi* a month, with the intention of awarding him a further increase if his attention, diligence, and exactitude in the fulfillment of his duties should so merit; his service in the company serving otherwise for his instruction. The accounts will be kept daily and the clerk will also undertake, insofar as he is able, the remaining tasks of the bank and the market place, as he does at present.

5. For sending goods through the customs, paying for them in the markets, and other banking business, the said director will have the services of a second clerk, in whose choice he will give precedence to Signore Filippo Pinzauti, who is now paid 8 *scudi* a month. Signore Artz is authorized to make him a small increase immediately, [bringing his salary] to the sum of 100 *scudi* a year.

Furthermore, if the said director thinks it necessary to take on a boy to carry out the more trivial banking affairs, he will be free to do so, but if he wishes to take on one of his own sons, it would be best to do this when his son is of an age and disposition to profit from the experience.

6. Should it become necessary to make any new selection of assistants or clerks, or any increase in salaries, the director will be authorized to do so, always, however, with the approval of the investors, or at least of Signore Abate Rossi, the principal investor.

7. For his services and to encourage him in his work and in the good management of the business, the said director will receive a monthly salary of 15 *scudi* and 15 per cent of the profits. He will have the right to take this from the ready cash of the firm in the same way and under the same limitations as the other investors exercise in taking their respective profits year by year.

8. It will be the duty of the said director to make a true, real, and exact accounting, as he promises and obliges himself to do, in January of each year of the duration of the company, showing what profits have been made so that they may be divided by shares. And, since the investing partners do not wish to increase their profits at the expense of capital existing as merchandise and other effects, or as bad creditors or uncertain and perilous consignments, if these should exist (God forbid!), an estimate will be made both of funds in merchandise or other effects and in ready cash. The example of other similar companies where the directors give a large account of profits to the investors by reducing their own capital to an imaginary amount or to a bare minimum will thus be avoided.

9. The director will give an exact copy of his accounting to Signore Abate Rossi, the principal investor, and to the other investors, who, like the director, will be permitted to dispose of two thirds of their share of the profits, the other third to remain [with the firm] as a safeguard against such misfortunes as may occur and to increase the capital of the company. This will be done every year.

10. The investors and the director may leave as a deposit in the cash account of the company a part or all of their share of the profits, and by doing this they will be paid 5 per cent yearly.

11. Signore Francesco Artz, as director of the said company, will have the permission and authority to make such purchases and sales of merchandise as he thinks most advantageous and

generally do everything necessary and useful for the good conduct of the business. Nonetheless, insofar as circumstances permit, he will do nothing substantial without consulting the said
Signore Abate Stefano Rossi, who in wisdom and experience enjoys the entire trust of the other investors.[2] The director will keep
him informed daily of current transactions. When the said Signore Abate is away from Florence, the director will send him a
weekly accounting or report of his actions and will act in accordance with the instructions he receives.

12. The director will be prohibited from irresponsible acts
such as lending money, speculating on the exchange, or standing
security for the convenience or interest of individuals. If he fails
in this, it will be understood that he has relinquished the benefits
of the present agreement. Moreover, for the duration of this
agreement, the director will not undertake or conduct any other
business of any kind in his own interest, under his name or under
the name of others, directly or indirectly. Failing in this, besides
losing the benefits of the present agreement, the entire liability of
such business will be his and all the profits will belong to the
company.

13. Considering that the larger part of the merchandise to be
brought to the market of this city will be purchased in foreign
lands or markets, involving goods that must arrive by sea at Livorno if the purchases have been made in Amsterdam, London, or
other such ports, the director must insure these shipments for
their entire value. When shipments come from Genoa or Marseilles, he may take risks in the name of the company, but he
should not take risks on a shipment worth more than 1,000 *scudi*.
When France is at war and there are sea reprisals, shipments
from Marseilles must also be insured. When circumstances require different actions, the director will consult with the said
Signore Abate Rossi and regulate matters entirely according to
his pleasure.

14. No investor shall sell his share in the company for the
duration of this agreement without consulting the other investors,
and, should one of the other investors wish to participate in the
purchase of the share being sold, it is agreed that he should acquire it at the original price and under the original conditions.
This is understood to be an agreement between living persons.

---

[2] Presumably, the partner investors would determine when this occurred.

The investors will be free to dispose of their shares to whomever they might wish by testament or other last act of will.

15. The profits of the company will be understood to be only those profits remaining after calculation of loss or expense, including both the interest of the investors and the interest of the director.

16. In the case, if God so wills, of the death of one of the said investors during the term of this agreement, the company will not be ended or dissolved; the heirs of the deceased will continue in his place, despite any law or statute to the contrary, which the said parties expressly renounce and disallow. But in the case, may God keep it distant, of the death of the director during the course of the agreement, the company will be dissolved at once and measures will be taken immediately to secure the best interests of all.

17. The said investors intend to avail themselves at all times of whatever benefits, exemptions, and privileges are usually accorded to investors in business companies by the statutes and ordinances of the Commune of Florence and the Court of Mercanzia or by any other law, statute, or provision affecting such matters. Consequently, the said Signore Francesco Artz agrees that he will be held and obligated to make formal registration of the present commercial-company contract [accomandita], in the public registers for commercial companies existing in the Supreme Magistrates Bureau within the specified time and to do whatever may be necessary to ensure that the the investing partners may enjoy the said privileges.

18. In confirmation of the above agreement all the profits that have been made at the end of each six-year period will be registered at the Supreme Magistrates Bureau and the profits of each of the investors or the increase of their capital indicated.

19. Should there be any disagreement among the investors, or between them and the director, this should be settled among themselves in a friendly way or be judged by common friends without the formalities of law. A penalty of 200 scudi will be paid by the party that has acted against the interest of the others.

20. In order to terminate the company, the investors are authorized to liquidate the company in whatever way they think best, observing the conditions described in paragraph three of the agreement.

21. Since the company will begin on the first of January of next

year, 1783, it is agreed that the investors will pay into the hands
of Signore Artz the entire sum of capital for which they are
obliged by the first of November coming, so that he may make
those purchases and orders necessary to sustain the business and
provide for his stock.

22. It being known to the investors that the furnishings of the
business office belong to the director, they think it appropriate to
make a declaration of this fact. Since these furnishings have been
provided for the use of the company without any recompense, the
director declares himself content with this condition. When the
company is terminated, these furnishings will be at the director's
disposal.

And, in observation of the terms of this agreement, the interested parties oblige their persons, heirs, goods, and the goods of
their present and future heirs, in faith of which the present is
countersigned by each of the interested parties by their own hand.

26. The Growth of Liverpool

NOWHERE WAS commercial growth more dramatic than in the port
cities of the Atlantic seaboard. Liverpool, like Bordeaux or Nantes,
experienced a rapid expansion of population and wealth, based largely
on profits from trade in slaves and sugar.

After a brief allusion to the protests of humanitarians against slave
trade, John Aikin concentrates on the beneficial "commercial effect"
of the trade for the city of Liverpool. Having only 12,000 people in
1730, the port city's population more than doubled by 1760 and tripled
by 1773. Equally as important as the increasing number of slavers and
merchantmen bound for Africa and the West Indies was the Duke of
Bridgewater's new canal system, intended to link Leeds to Liverpool
and greatly to facilitate the exportation of coal and textiles from the
hinterland. Urban construction kept pace with new docks, churches,
theaters, hospitals, and poorhouses. Here were all the aspects of a city
"ardent in the pursuit of individual and national wealth."

Source: John Aikin, *Description of the Country from Thirty to
Forty Miles Round Manchester* (London, 1795), pp. 338–344.

Liverpool

IN THE year 1703 the number of people exceeded 12,000. This is the first year in which we find an account of ships sailing to Africa, the single sloop in 1703 excepted. Concerning the slave trade, for which Liverpool has since became so peculiarly distinguished, it is difficult to speak with the coolness of discussion that belongs to commercial topics in general. On the one hand, it has been warmly arraigned by the friends of justice and humanity, and, indeed, by the common feelings of the uninterested part of mankind; on the other hand, it has been as warmly defended by those who are ardent in the pursuit of every extension of individual and national wealth. To consider only its *commercial* effects upon this place, we may say, that it has coincided with that spirit of bold adventure which has characterised the trade of Liverpool, and rapidly carried it to its present state of prosperity; has occasioned vast employment for shipping and sailors, and greatly augmented the demand for the manufactures of the country. Some, however, are of opinion that it has pushed this adventurous spirit beyond all due bounds; has introduced pernicious maxims and customs of transacting business; has diverted to itself the capital and attention which might have been better employed on other objects, and has occasioned a great waste of lives among the seamen. Meantime, its being still an object in which the town regards its interests as deeply involved, seems a sufficient proof that its benefits, in a commercial view, have at this port apparently exceeded its mischiefs.

An act had passed in 1717 for enlarging the time granted by the first dock act, which contained powers for making an additional dock and building a pier in the open harbour, and for enlightening [illuminating] the said dock; and in 1738 another act passed for enlarging the time of the last act; whence it may be concluded, that its purposes as to the making of the second dock were not yet completed. It was probably for the want of these conveniences, that the tonnage of ships entering inwards was no greater in the year 1737 than it had been in 1716; but after this period, the increase became rapid. The augmentation of inhabitants was proportional; for in 1740, they were by computation more than 18,000.

About the year 1745, a subscription was opened at Liverpool for the establishment of one of those excellent charities, an infirmary. The work was begun the same year; but owing to the national disturbances at that period, its completion was retarded, so that the house did not open for the reception of patients till 1749. This, however, was earlier than the date of the greater part of those institutions of the like kind, with which so many of our provincial towns are now honoured.

At the same period (that of the last rebellion) the town of Liverpool displayed its consequence, and its attachment to the present royal family, in a very spirited manner. A regiment of foot, called the Liverpool Blues, was raised in the town, consisting of eight companies of seventy men each, with proper officers, &c. They continued in pay about fifteen weeks, during eight of which they were under marching orders, and were at the taking of Carlisle, where they were reviewed by the duke of Cumberland. The whole expence of this armament amounted to £4859, of which the corporation contributed £2000, and the town raised the rest. Besides this regiment, five companies of volunteers, consisting of sixty men each, exclusive of officers, were raised in the town, and instructed in the military exercise: one of which kept guard nightly while the disturbances of the kingdom lasted. Though Liverpool was then only in its early youth, few towns in England were probably capable of a similar exertion.

In 1749 an act passed for building another church in Liverpool, and for lighting and cleaning the streets. The church was St. Thomas's, consecrated the next year, and distinguished by the simple beauty of a lofty and elegant spire.

An institution of peculiar use, the design of which was formed in 1747, was carried into execution in 1752. This was an hospital for decayed seamen, their widows and children, supported by a monthly contribution of sixpence, which every seaman from this port is obliged to pay out of his wages. The building forms the wings of the infirmary; it cost £1500. The business of the institution is conducted by a committee chosen annually.

An act for the more speedy recovery of small debts in the town and its liberties, similar to what has been found necessary in all populous and trading towns, passed in 1753.

The internal water-communications of Liverpool were increased by the Sankey canal, the act for which passed in 1755, and which for many years after continued to improve in the facility and extent of its navigation. It afforded from the first a new supply of coals to Liverpool, and by the works since established upon it, has in various ways added to the business of this port.

By the year 1760, the population of Liverpool had reached, by computation, 25,787 souls, and the tonnage of the shipping belonging to its port was above four times that of the year 1709. It was provided with a convenient custom-house, a large and handsome exchange, a neat playhouse, and all the other useful and ornamental structures belonging to a wealthy commercial town. In 1762, such was the present state and future prospects of the town, that an act was obtained for building two new churches at once, and also for making an additional dock and pier, and erecting lighthouses in or near the port. The taste for show and expence, however, caused more than all the money destined for the two churches to be consumed in building one, which was St. Paul's, consecrated in 1769. This is a magnificent structure, upon a plan in some measure imitative of that of the first religious edifice in England, which bears the same name. Like that, it has a grand portico at the west end, two inferior projections in the north and south fronts, and a dome. This last, though favourable to its architectural effect, has been found greatly to injure its utility as a place for speaking in. It is to be observed, that the erection of places of worship for the various classes of separatists had been keeping pace during these periods, in number and elegance, with that of the churches of the establishment.

The new dock, more spacious than either of the former, was a vast addition to the accommodation of the port, and its piers and quays greatly improved its beauty and grandeur. It was not finished till about 1771.

The duke of Bridgewater's canals had by this time begun to operate in adding to the business of Liverpool. The Grand Trunk communication between the Trent and the Mersey, so important to the trade of both rivers, was carrying on with vigour. The vast design of a communication between Liverpool and Leeds, crossing one large county, and penetrating into another, was begun to be executed in 1770, and it was not long before that part of it which extends from Liverpool to Wigan was completed, affording such plentiful supplies of coal as greatly to add to the exportation of that commodity from this port.

The increasing number of poor in Liverpool had caused several successive changes in the management of them. At length it was determined to erect a large and commodious poor-house in an airy situation adjoining to this town, and money for this purpose was borrowed under the corporation seal. The building was begun in March 1770, and finished for the reception of the poor in August 1771, at an expence of near £8000. It was calculated to contain 600 inhabitants, and few institutions of the kind have been better managed.

A new and spacious theatre, by royal patent, built by subscription at the expence of £6000, was opened in June 1772. It is probably the largest in England out of London, and is elegantly finished both on the outside and within. Its passages and communications are particularly well managed, and were much superior to those of the London theatres at the time of its erection. The inhabitants of Liverpool have at all times been liberal encouragers of dramatic entertainments.

In the beginning of the year 1773 a plan was executed which ought never to be long neglected in a large town—that of an actual enumeration of its inhabitants. The result was as follows:

Inhabited houses	5,928
Untenanted do.	412
Families	8,002
Inhabitants	34,407

Persons to a house, 5 4/5; to a family, 4 1/3.

In this statement, the poor-house, infirmary, and other buildings, where large numbers live together, were included. With respect to the seafaring men employed in the Liverpool ships, they were found to be about 6000. Of these, about two-thirds were reckoned to be usually absent from Liverpool, and therefore not to be accounted among the stated inhabitants. The annual deaths in Liverpool were estimated upon an average of three years, at 1240, or one in 27 7/10 of the inhabitants; the annual births on the same average were computed at 1290. It is imagined by many, that this enumeration was considerably short of the real number; the poor, it is said, frequently giving in a defective list, through fear of a tax. This may in some instances have been the case; but, on the other hand, we should be on our guard against that spirit of exaggeration, which, in *every* town, disposes its inhabitants to aggrandize all its claims to superiority. The proportion of people to families and houses as stated, agrees very well with the best authorities in other places. We shall further remark, that enumerations of this kind should not be left, as this was, to the exertions of individuals, but should be undertaken by authority, whence all suspicion of inaccuracy might be obviated.

Having thus carried our historical sketch of the rise and progress of Liverpool to a period in which it takes its fair station as the *second* sea-port, and one of the largest and most important towns, of the kingdom, we shall compose the rest of the article of papers and documents respecting its subsequent events and present state, with various detached particulars of its commerce and other circumstances belonging to it.

27. The African Slave Trade

THOSE WHO see the eighteenth century as an unmitigated period of human betterment would do well to remember the African slave trade. Clearly related to a good European market for cane sugar and the use of slave labor in the West Indies, the slave trade required large outlays of capital that were only partially refunded by the notoriously slow-paying planters. By 1770 it was even possible for French critics to add an economic argument to the moral one. Document A describes both the commercial and the human aspects of the trade, while Document B is a classic defense of slave labor from the English-planter point of view. Slavery was abolished in France and the French colonies in 1793, and the slave trade ended in the British Empire in 1807. With due respect to such dogged single-causers as William Wilberforce and the *Société des Amis des Noirs*, it was probably uncertain profits and soil exhaustion as much as humanitarian feelings that finally removed one of the worst blemishes from western civilization.

Sources: Document A: *Ephémérides du Citoyen ou bibliothèque raisonnée des sciences morales et politiques*, XI (1771), part 2, 51–56. Document B: G. Francklyn, Esq., *Observations occasioned by the Attempts made in England to effect the Abolition of the Slave Trade* (London, 1789), pp. 10–15.

A. Letter from a Traveler
to the Author of the Ephémérides
Concerning the Observations on Negro Slavery
That Appeared in Volume VI in the Year 1771

[The author of this letter claims to have made several voyages to
Guinea and to have spent a number of years in the Antilles. He
argues that the slave trade is not only immoral but also far less
profitable than generally realized. He establishes the following
calculation:]

IT IS an established fact that a vessel can carry only as many
Negroes as the tons it contains. I shall make a calculation for a
vessel of 300 tons, which is supposed to carry 300 slaves, and by
the profits of their sale in the Antilles it will be seen whether or
not the profits are much larger than the expenses. . . .

Résumé of the costs:

Outfitting of vessel	20,000	livres
Food for the crew [60 at 20 sous per day for 20 months]	36,000	
Salary for captain	3,000	
Salary for second in command	2,000	
Salary for first mate	1,600	
Salary for 2 second mates	2,400	
Salary for logkeeper	1,200	
Salary for 2 surgeons	2,000	
Wages for the rest of the crew	30,000	
Purchase of Negroes	90,000	
Food for Negroes	10,750	
Presents [to obtain permission to trade]	300	
[in French money]	201,050	livres

In money of the Islands, this amounts to 301,575 livres

Assuming that not one of the Negroes perishes
(which is never the case) and that they are sold
in the Antilles at 1,100 livres each, their sale will
bring   330,000 livres

The receipt, therefore, exceeds the expenses by the
sum of 28,425 livres in money of the islands, or,
in French money by   18,951 livres

This profit and more would be absorbed if I included in my calculation the loss of Negroes, insurance, interest on money, and several other expenses I do not mention.

Where then, you will ask, is the profit encouraging the merchants to continue to engage in this trade? It comes solely from the return cargoes of sugar and other colonial products.

But if, as you propose, these colonies were cultivated by free men, sugar, coffee, and indigo would be more plentiful and less expensive, so that their consumption would be much greater. Consequently, the merchants would have more opportunities for gain, while they now make profits only on the return voyage. They could engage in their trade with a much smaller capital outlay if the slave trade were abandoned.

In this manner their profits would be just as great, yet they would not have to pay for them by the remorse that no European can avoid feeling when he buys slaves on the coast of Africa, knowing that he engages in injustice and cruelty.

As soon as the ships have lowered their anchors off the coast of Guinea, the price at which the captains have decided to buy the captives is announced to the Negroes who buy prisoners from various princes and sell them to the Europeans. Presents are sent to the sovereign who rules over that particular part of the coast, and permission to trade is given. Immediately the slaves are brought by inhuman brokers like so many victims dragged to a sacrifice. White men who covet that portion of the human race receive them in a little house they have erected on the shore, where they have entrenched themselves with two pieces of cannon and twenty guards. As soon as the bargain is concluded, the Negro is put in chains and led aboard the vessel, where he meets his fellow sufferers. Here sinister reflections come to his mind; everything shocks and frightens him and his uncertain destiny gives rise to the greatest anxiety. At first he is convinced that he is to serve as a repast to the white men, and the wine which the sailors drink confirms him in this cruel thought, for he imagines that this liquid is the blood of his fellows.

The vessel sets sail for the Antilles, and the Negroes are chained in a hold of the ship, a kind of lugubrious prison where the light of day does not penetrate, but into which air is introduced by means of a pump. Twice a day some disgusting food is distributed to them. Their consuming sorrow and the sad state to

which they are reduced would make them commit suicide if they
were not deprived of all the means for an attempt upon their
lives. Without any kind of clothing it would be difficult to conceal
from the watchful eyes of the sailors in charge any instrument apt
to alleviate their despair. The fear of a revolt,[1] such as sometimes
happens on the voyage from Guinea, is the basis of a common
concern and produces as many guards as there are men in the
crew. The slightest noise or a secret conversation among two
Negroes is punished with utmost severity. All in all, the voyage is
made in a continuous state of alarm on the part of the white men,
who fear a revolt, and in a cruel state of uncertainty on the part
of the Negroes, who do not know the fate awaiting them.

When the vessel arrives at a port in the Antilles, they are taken
to a warehouse where they are displayed, like any merchandise, to
the eyes of buyers. The plantation owner pays according to the
age, strength, and health of the Negro he is buying. He has him
taken to his plantation, and there he is delivered to an overseer
who then and there becomes his tormentor. In order to domesti-
cate him, the Negro is granted a few days of rest in his new place,
but soon he is given a hoe and a sickle and made to join a work
gang. Then he ceases to wonder about his fate; he understands
that only labor is demanded of him. But he does not know yet
how excessive this labor will be. As a matter of fact, his work
begins at dawn and does not end before nightfall;[2] it is interrupted for only two hours at dinnertime. The food a full-grown
Negro is given each week consists of two pounds of salt beef or
cod and two pots of tapioca meal, amounting to about two pints
of Paris.[3] A Negro of twelve or thirteen years or under is given
only one pot of meal and one pound of beef or cod. In place of
food some planters give their Negroes the liberty of working for
themselves every Saturday; others are even less generous and
grant them this liberty only on Sundays and holidays. Therefore,
since the nourishment of the Negroes is insufficient, their ten-

[1] In 1750, a La Rochelle vessel coming from Guinea arrived at Santo
Domingo with only six men left of the crew; the others had perished in a
slave revolt as had the 300 Negroes aboard—author's note.
[2] On sugar-cane plantations the Negroes must stay awake until midnight,
and, when the mills are running, half the Negroes work day and night—
author's note.
[3] A capacity measure equal to 18 litres or 15.84 quarts—editors' note.

dency to cheat must be attributed to the necessity of finding the food they lack.

The Guinea trade which makes these poor Negroes so miserable also contributes to the depopulation of Europe. It is certain that the vessels which engage in slave trade have crews twice as large as those sufficient for the ordinary voyages to America. It is estimated that half of them perish either from excessive heat, scurvy, or bad water. This then, is another reason to abolish the slave trade.

[The author admits that it is not practicable to have Europeans cultivate the land in the islands, partly because the climate is not suitable, partly because European states would not like to see their populations emigrate. But he feels that, since there is now a sufficient supply of Negro workers, these must be encouraged to marry and to have children and also be given the means to raise these children properly. Also, he feels that some of the farming could be done by animals and that fertilizers should be used before the soil is completely exhausted. In addition, crops other than sugar and coffee should be planted. Nutmeg, for example, would grow well in certain regions of the islands, demand little labor, and bring large profits. He even suggests that the colonists plant food for their own consumption so as not to be totally dependent on trade with Europe, which becomes problematical in times of war.]

B. A Classic Defense of Slave Labor
from the English-Planter Point of View

How STRANGE and inconsistent is the conduct of mankind! It is not to be doubted, but amongst these petitioners for abolishing the Slave Trade, may be found men who have commanded troops against those who never injured them; nay, who may even now be soliciting their friends, or expending their money in procuring means or license, for themselves, their sons or relations, to be impowered to lead a battalion of Seapoys, or a company of Europeans, (enslaved, for that purpose) against the sage and religious inhabitants of Benares, who, actuated by real humanity, reject, with horror, the idea of shedding blood, even the blood of animals.

Shall I be answered, that what I complain of are evils which must be borne, because the welfare and prosperity of the nation require it! And may not the West Indians avail themselves of the same plea, against the present clamour?

Fully am I convinced, in the present state of the world, of the impracticability of a nation existing without soldiers and sailors; but, I insist upon it, they are in a state of slavery. Well I know, that "the rich ruleth over the poor, and the borrower is the servant of the lender." Sure I am, that the labourer in England, who is the *slave* of *necessity*, serves a harder task-master than the African finds in the West-Indies. No severities, there exercised, are equal to the cruelty of enticing poor people, by a small addition of wages, to work in lead, quick-silver, or other metals, or deleterious manufactories, which in a very few months, or years, render the life of the poor victim an unremitting scene of torture and misery, which death alone can relieve him from. Is purchasing negroes in Africa, and keeping them in slavery, so great an act of cruelty as the declaring them free, and then suffering them to perish with cold, hunger, and disease, in the streets of the metropolis? Such is too frequently the lot of the poor of Great Britain, to be regarded; the members of the society met in the Old Jewry profess their abhorrence of West Indian cruelty, while they seem not to be shocked at the scenes of misery which are daily before their eyes. Although, I allow that many of the evils which exist in England, cannot be totally eradicated, yet I hope I may be permitted to say, to the gentlemen who are members of the society abovementioned, and the other petitioners for procuring the abolition of the Slave Trade, that we have a right to expect, if they are actuated by the true spirit of Christianity, they will begin by alleviating the fate of their own poor, as far as may be possible, before they trouble themselves about us. When we have the satisfaction to know that the brave and undaunted seaman is secure from being torn from the arms of the partner of his soul, and from the children of his love, whose happiness, certainly, and whose existence, probably, depends upon the exertion of his industry and skill: When we see that the man, who has been, perhaps, forced to enlist as a soldier, but whose nerves are so unstrung, as to render him incapable of facing his enemy, can with facility, procure his release from a slavery he is incapable of supporting—when for the sale, or loss, of a pair of spatterdashes, or trifling accoutrement, he shall not be subjected to a punishment at the halberts, severer than those which negroes in the West Indies undergo, for burglaries and other felonies of equal enormity?—When we know that the industrious peasant in England shall be allowed to work for his living, wherever he can find employment, without fear of being seized on by an unfeeling parish officer, and passed back to his native parish.—When we learn that the young people of both sexes are encouraged, or even permitted, to avow their mutual inclinations for each other, and suffered to marry, without fear or threats of being dismissed from their employments, under the apprehension they may encrease the number of honest and industrious poor; we may acknowledge their right to censure, and regulate our conduct. Those who act from religious motives, are entitled to have great allowances made for them, however they may be mistaken; but can the prelates, and other dignified clergymen, or even the pious and humane Mr. Ramsey, think it possible, we should be persuaded that their present outcry is occasioned by a zeal for the Christian religion, and a regard for its precepts? We know *that* establishes a perfect equality among its professors, even in point of rank. Matth. 20 and 27, Mark 6 and 27,—and the disciples of our blessed Master are enjoined to sell all they have and give to the poor. Christians, when the influence of the gospel had a proper effect on their lives and conversations, had all possessions in common. Mark 10, v. 21, Acts, c. 4, 32, 34, 35.

Perhaps it is not possible a nation can exist as such, if the people, in every circumstance, conformed strictly to the laws of Christianity. But those who particularly devote themselves to the service of God and his Church, might obey the positive precepts, and follow the examples above cited. There is nothing therein which is impossible; nothing which will disturb, or be injurious to society; on the contrary, nothing would contribute so much to influence the laity, as such bright examples of forbearance and charity; and therefore have we not a right to say to these reformers, shew us, gentlemen, that you act from principle, by obeying the laws of that religion, which alone can give you a right to consider that species of servitude, you call slavery, unlawful; or, entitle you to endeavour to put a stop to a commerce which has existed throughout the whole world, from the remotest antiquity,

and which is authorized and encouraged, not only by the municipal laws of your own country, but by those of every other commercial nation in Europe. When you have shewn, gentlemen,
your sincerity, by the unequivocal proof of giving up your own
fortunes, to be divided among the poor, and distressed, you may
expect we shall not so strongly oppose your disposing of ours; we
may then think it worth our while to read the sermons and pamphlets with which we hear the pulpit and the press have been
groaning for some months past; until then, gentlemen, you must
excuse us, if we think the best excuse which can be made for you,
is *"ye know not what ye do."* . . .

28. The Plight of German Overseas Trade

JUSTUS MÖSER (1720–1794) came from a conservative, professional,
Protestant family of teachers and clergymen. After studying law at the
Universities of Jena and Göttingen, he became *advocatus patriae* or
attorney general of the state of Osnabrück in northwestern Germany.
Möser passed most of his life in this official post and eventually became
the *de facto* regent during the minority of the prince-bishop, the son
of George II of England. In addition to his official duties, Möser edited
the *Osnabrückische Intelligenzblätter*, and his articles were later collected under the title of *Patriotische Phantasien*, from which the selection below is taken.

From his writings Möser appears widely read in law, history, and
economics, his observations keen, and his interests extremely varied.
Although his concerns are chiefly utilitarian and public-spirited,
Möser will have no truck with the philosophers of his day, whom he
regarded as naïve and impractical.[1] Far better to rely on the stolid
virtues of his "German forefathers," who understood the importance
of the traditional order of things. Möser's preoccupation with thrift
and sobriety led Goethe to compare him to Benjamin Franklin; but the
similarity stops there.

In dealing with the plight of German overseas trade, Möser combines nostalgia for the heyday of the Hanseatic League with skepticism
toward middlemen in general and international merchant bankers in
particular. But the days when the Hanse merchants dominated North
European trade from Stralsund to the Steelyard had long since passed.

[1] See also his comments on guild regulations, Document 33.

Herring fisheries had moved, harbors like Bruges atrophied in silt, and the proud Hanse ports of Bremen, Hamburg, and Lübeck were now havens of numerous, aggressive English and Dutch carriers. Möser calls for a renewal of German entrepreneurship and a change in the pattern of international trade requiring a minimum of political power the German inland towns could not hope to muster. Hard work and will power were simply not enough.

Source: Justus Möser, *"Patriotische Phantasien"* in *Sämtliche Werke, historisch-kritische Ausgabe* (Oldenburg and Berlin, 1944), vol. IV, pp. 15ff.*

Some Thoughts About the Decline of Commerce in Inland Towns

WE SHOULD be ashamed when we think of our forefathers of the German Company [*Hanse*]. All we do now in the inland towns is entrust our manufactured goods to a man in Hamburg or Bremen and let ourselves be led by him. Many a man is so short-sighted or in such need of money that he sells directly to Hamburg and Bremen, accepting the prices set by the assembled buyers at the exchange. The whim of a port merchant, a mistake on mail day because of contacts with so many commercial centers, a temporary change in the money market, an advantageous freight charge, an expiration date for which he cannot wait, the distress of a seller—these and other contingencies decide the advantage of the man who should reap the entire benefit; but the middleman makes off with his bride. The merchants in our inland towns hardly know when their goods will sell best. They sell their grain right after the harvest and their linen around Whitsuntide, and they do not care when the fleets leave England and Spain for the East and the West, nor that the agent on the spot fleeces the hard-pressed shipowner, or at least earns 30 per cent more on merchandise that was sold at a price hardly sufficient to keep the first seller alive. Everything, everything is for the port merchant, and, with a hanging lip and a frown, he will gleefully humiliate the inland merchant impatient to exchange his goods for money or other merchandise.

How far-sighted, how fortunate, how strong, by contrast, were

* Translated by permission of Gerhard Stalling, A.G. (Oldenburg and Berlin).

the views of our forefathers of the German Company! It is true that they used the ship bottoms of the port merchants. But they did not sell their goods on the Bremen market; they did not hand themselves over, body and soul, to the good faith of some Hamburg merchant. Their merchandise was shipped on their own account. At its destination, at Bergen, London, Novgorod, Bruges, and elsewhere, they had their own factors, their own warehouses, their own markets. Their factors, found in all the corners of the earth, faithfully reported to them. They did not see only through the spectacles of the middlemen in the ports. They did not permit themselves to be undercut by competitors, but knew immediately when and why an article was no longer attractive, how tastes and needs were changing, who offered better prices, and what could make up for them, what colors and what kinds of stripes were preferred, what fashions were the most in vogue, and which articles had to be of good quality and which had to be merely pretty. They were informed early, thoroughly, and faithfully of every change, every rise in price. Every folly was immediately taken advantage of, every prospect was promptly seized, and enterprises were conducted accordingly. Every payment was made directly, and the ports were obliged to buy their bills of exchange from the Hanse in the inland towns.

Today it is easy for a port merchant to ruin the commerce of an entire country. He imitates the trademarks of another country with impunity and affixes them to inferior merchandise, thus giving a bad name to the man and the town who had honestly striven to live up to this trademark. He alters the weight, shortens the foot, and sells Polish goods for Prussian goods until the buyers, finally disgusted with such inferior merchandise, are led to other sources and are served better with merchandise from elsewhere. Where, nowadays, is the inland merchant who can boast of receiving any information from the centers of commerce, of becoming aware in time of the causes of a rising or falling market, of making his plans on certain knowledge, of knowing the needs of every colony and every country, and of acting accordingly? On the contrary, he is scarcely able to meet small payments with his own bill of exchange. But this does not apply to Moses and Abraham. They, of course, can draw any number of bills of exchange; but may we ask how? And can we consider that without shame?

They buy up bills of exchange in Hamburg, Bremen, or Amsterdam, send them to their friends in England and Spain to be redeemed, and these men finally present us the bills for the money owed. The man in Hamburg, Bremen, or Holland thus earns 50 per cent on the sum, the man in England or Spain makes as much, and Abraham and Moses surely earn 100 per cent. But what is this money? Does it not represent the payments that were owed us in England and Spain? Was it not due for goods that were sent from the inland towns to the ports? And do they not sell us our own money? First, the port merchants cheat us out of our merchandise, then they pilfer our purses as well. Can we imagine anything more shameful, and would not every child of the old Hanse say that we are completely out of our minds?

But this is to consider the matter only from one side, namely, from the side on which we are trying to sell our goods only through middlemen in the ports. But if we also add the other side, namely, how we receive our needs and the so-called superfluities from foreign countries, the disadvantage of the inland towns will appear all the greater, since imports are now exceeding exports. Our forebears of the Hanseatic League necessarily received everything directly, without middlemen. They did not buy herrings from the Dutch, their factors in Bergen had them caught. They did not buy linseed in Bremen around Eastertime, but in the fall from a producer at the place where it grows, or at least in the market of Riga or in the Libau. Every merchant living in a Hanse town had his blubber boiled at his branch establishment in Bergen, where he also had his fish dried and salted. The town of Soest was involved in so many enterprises connected with the sea that it was worth its while to take out special letters of franchise from the Danish monarch. But where do we now find such spirit of enterprise? How many are there who so much as go to England for their rice? And that despite the fact that the English send it to Bremen without payment and are glad to wait a year for their money. Almost everyone buys his tobacco in quantities of five or six barrels in Bremen and will often take for good merchandise those lots discarded during the repacking in England. And who pays any attention to the arrival in England of the tobacco ships from the colony of Maryland? Who knows the difference between the good prices of Glasgow and Liverpool and those of London? Who knows about the various duties in the different ports and their influence on the price of merchandise? All this is left to the attention of the man in Hamburg or Bremen, and he alone draws his profit from it. At the last sale of the East India Company in Amsterdam spice merchants from Italy and France were present, but not a single German one appeared in person. And yet a new kind of auctioning, whereby the merchandise is adjudicated to the highest bidder, was introduced at that occasion, so that spices will become considerably more expensive and brokerage fees will become even more burdensome in the future. All that could be detected of German business acumen was the fact that the finest cinnamon was bought for Italy, the medium grade for France, and the poorest quality for Germany.

What a distance separates such principles from those of the old Hanse! To the Hanse the ports were merely depots. In the interest of the ports it was held that every town belonging to the League could only export its own goods, and in the interest of the inland towns it was held that all manufactured goods had to be finished at the place of their origin. This meant that the inhabitants of the ports were not allowed to make any profits by dyeing a piece of cloth or by finishing a piece of linen not made there. It was understood [by the Hanse] that ports would not have sufficient cheap labor to undertake spinning, and that, on the contrary, it would be easier for them to dye and finish raw material. It was also recognized that, once the ports were permitted to do this, the inland towns would soon work only for them, and they would in the end take over commerce altogether and reap all the profits.

What would the men who had these insights think if they learned that the full significance of these two fundamental rules are hardly understood any longer? If they learned that there are now all kinds of factories and manufactories in the ports, and that hats and stockings can be sent from there to the inland towns? They would think that the world has been turned upside down and that labor is now cheaper in a port than in an inland town. Our historians describe the wars of the Hanse, but not the spirit of commerce in those days. The life and the deeds of a mayor of Lübeck are so important to them that they do not even censor those commercial companies which established a system of conquest. When they did this, the ports were already sacrificing German inland commerce to a chimera.

But, then, is the way to other regions barred to inland towns? Have they never heard about the Scottish factories and ports? Are Oporto and Lisbon closed to them any more than to the port merchants? Cannot inland merchants have factors in Lisbon and Cadiz as well? Could they not, as well as an Englishman or a Dutchman, trade with all Spanish and Portuguese colonies if they had a depot in Lisbon and used the name of a Spaniard or Portuguese? Does a citizen of London lend his name to no one but a German port merchant? Or is it impossible to find an agent who, for a share in the profits, will analyze the market, find new prospects, and serve as a faithful steward? And could not our idle diplomatic envoys serve the state in other ways?

It will be objected that in this kind of commerce it is necessary to entrust one's goods to the sea and to strangers, to wait for returns for three years, and to take in exchange merchandise from the Spanish and Portuguese Indies demanding a wide market. It will be argued that an inland town cannot make a profit on a cargo of oil, lemons, raisins, wines, domingo, indigo, and other merchandise sent from Spain, but that a port can, and this is the real reason for its domination of commerce. But risks, after all, are the very soul of commerce; and the longer one has to wait for his money, the larger the profit will be, since small operators and interlopers must have their few pennies back immediately and dare not participate, and therefore cannot spoil the enterprise. The last-mentioned difficulty would be serious only if the markets of Hamburg and Bremen were restricted to the citizens of these ports and if other merchants were not free to sell wholesale there. An inland merchant could unload his Spanish return cargo there, sell it, and expedite it to all corners of the earth. If he has customers inland and if he can offer better prices than the Bremen merchant, the latter will have no advantages over him. And he will be able to offer better prices if he sends goods, such as linen, directly to Spain, while the Bremen merchant has them sent there in payment, or to the Indies under the name of a Spaniard.

If Hamburg and Bremen refuse this, Harburg and Emden are open, and they need nothing as much as return freights for foreign parts.

29. The Great Commercial Fairs

IN THE eighteenth century, the great commercial fairs were already venerable institutions. In times when communication was difficult, they served to maintain contact among the merchants of different regions who assembled at prescribed times to transact business. Although the fairs at Leipzig, Frankfurt, and Nizhni-Novgorod were the most famous international ones, almost all the large towns of Europe had their own fairs.

Paul Jakob Marperger (1656–1730), an extremely prolific German economist, whose observations fill ninety-four published volumes, knew these fairs from personal experience. The following selection from his *Beschreibung der Messen und Jahrmärckte* (1710) presents a lively picture of the excitement created by the market fair. Besides merchants and traders, we hear about animal trainers, comedians, funambulists, quacks, charlatans, freak shows, prostitutes, and the inevitable brawls, gambling, crowded inns, and exorbitant prices.

The varied types encountered at such a fair are as much a part of social history as the precise measure of business transacted. Marperger, of course, was a serious German economist. He intended his book as a practical guide for the merchant, treating such matters as the trade routes, international currency, double-entry bookkeeping, and the optimum quantity of goods to be hauled to a fair. Here he is concerned with the most advantageous organization of a fair, trying to strike a balance between propriety and health on one side and good business on the other. Marperger was also a strict Sabbatarian, a self-appointed moralist, tidy, fearful, suspicious, and anti-Semitic—in short, a rather cramped provincial, worlds apart from Diderot or Samuel Johnson.

Source: Paul Jakob Marperger, *Beschreibung der Messen und Jahrmärckte* (Leipzig, 1710), pp. 203ff.

Chapter XII.
Of the Various Ordinances Passed and Published
by the High Authorities of Towns and Countries
for the Benefit of Fairs and Marts,
Which Must be Observed by the Merchants Attending the Fairs
and Other Persons Connected with Them

THE FEAR OF GOD is necessary in all things and it is this sentiment which has inspired the most important and necessary ordinance, according to which fairs and marts must no longer begin on Sundays and other High Holidays, so that the Sabbath can be kept; and more important still, that such fairs will not be planned for, or held on, such days—and if they should fall on such a day they will be prohibited and put off until the following Monday or another day. In this manner, GOD, whose Sabbath we should keep holy, since He who has instituted it is Holy will have no cause to complain about us as He complained through Ezekiel (22:8) about the apostate people of Israel: "Thou hast despised mine holy things, and hast profaned my sabbaths." Upon which complaint, in that selfsame chapter, the thundering voice of the Lord's wrath is heard: "And I will scatter thee among the heathen, and disperse thee in the countries, and will consume thy filthiness out of thee." Likewise: "Yea, I will gather you, and blow upon you in the fire of my wrath, and ye shall be melted in the midst thereof."

[Two more lengthy biblical quotations about the Lord's wrath follow.]

And no doubt it was this most important consideration that caused the otherwise not very commendable Emperor Wenceslas to send the following missive concerning the Frankfurt fair to the town council and citizens of Frankfurt, which document can be found in Limnäus . . . [The document from Emperor Wenceslas follows.]

Similarly, it was deemed necessary by the diet held at Trier in 1512 to examine how the Frankfurt fair might be changed, for the greater glory of GOD, from the weeks of Lent to a more appropriate time. (See *Reichs-Abschied de anno 1512*.)

Even today we still hear frequently of princes who are making commendable efforts to exterminate this sinful abuse of holding fairs on Sundays and holidays by severe mandates and strict orders. Thus there are especially the mandates concerning an exact keeping of the Sabbath by H. M. the King of Prussia, mandates which, under high penalties, seek to abolish all buying and selling, all opening of stands and drinking in beer halls—in short, everything that can profane the Lord's Sabbath. To a large extent, these ugly abuses of fairs and marts falling on a Sunday date back to the days of Papism with its feast days of the patron saints. At that time, as we said at the beginning of the first chapter, the people who had assembled for purposes of devotion retreated to

public houses and beer halls after the end of the service in order
to refresh themselves after their long journey, or perhaps after their
devotions; and, as it might happen, they profited from the occasion to buy things they needed while they were in town. All of
this would not be objectionable in itself had it not led to the
abuse of curtailing the divine service, which was reduced to a
short mass or, in Protestant terms, to a short, early sermon—
whereupon everyone spends the rest of the day in worldly pursuit, in gorging and feasting, as if this were the way to keep the
Sabbath and as if GOD had not ordained the other days of the
week for the pursuit of worldly business and the Sabbath for
sanctification.

The second beneficial ordinance which the authorities must
pass in this connection should do away with the useless rabble
who always converge at such fairs and marts, or at least curtail
their sinful and distasteful actions. These are the comedians,
funambulists, keepers of Fortune's urns, players of marionettes,
quacks, and people who show forbidden, scandalous and suspicious things for money, such as deformed children, horrible and
grotesque figures, and miraculous horses. As far as these last are
concerned, it is quite obvious that having such a dumb beast
perform supernatural feats which not even an intelligent man's
senses and sympathetic or antipathetic impulses would be able to
follow and penetrate can only be done by witchcraft, demonic
illusion, and with the help of a *familiar spirit* (which must be
hidden under the mane, in the reins, or in another part of the innocent beast's body and which will some day bring great sorrow to
the miserable apostate whom it serves). Once in a well-known
free town of the Empire such a sorcerer, becoming aware that the
local authorities were beginning to suspect his dangerous activities and were considering a closer investigation of the matter,
managed to escape under the cover of night, and nothing was
heard from him thereafter.

As for the comedians, they will have to be tolerated at the great
fairs so long as a town or a country, and also our other fellow
Christians, are not suffering from any public calamities such as
war, famine, or pestilence, but it must be under the proviso that
all ribaldry and obscene buffoonery apt to offend modest ears be
banished from their theaters. This injunction should also be given

to the funambulists and the marionette players. The keepers of Fortune's urns, whose doings usually aim at swindle, are also unwelcome guests at fairs. And the quacks, dentists, hernial surgeons, and patent-medicine mongers will also have to be permitted to sell their remedies for the duration of the fairs, since it is a public affair and since the world, after all, wants to be deceived. So they will have to be permitted to sell mouse droppings for pepper, crushed tobacco pipes for powdered crab eyes, and brandy made from fish gall for *elixir proprietatis*. (I am speaking here only of the rabble, not of honest *chymicis, destillatoribus, operatoribus, opthalmicis*, and those who have good experience in surgical procedures, or those who have honestly learned their craft and have invented or dispose of *arcana* useful to human health.) The above-mentioned patent-medicine mongers will have to be admitted to the fairs to the extent of only selling their wares and foregoing all ribaldry and buffoonery, which offends the Holy Ghost, corrupts the youth, and puts many scandalous things before the eyes and into the hearts of idle spectators. But above all, the public gambling tables, where all manner of low rabble come to gamble with a few groschen and kreutzer, must be prohibited under high penalties, because there certainly is no other place where there is so much swearing and cursing and damning of the souls that have been bought so dearly with Christ's blood than at these gambling tables. If the passers-by should suddenly have their eyes opened, they would see as many devils standing close to these miserable and God-forsaken people, waiting for their souls—since they had been wantonly invited to do so by frequent and repeated swearing—as Elisha's servant saw fiery horses and chariots for the protection of his master near Dothan (more of which may be read in chapter 6 of Kings II).

The Dutch are dealing with this matter in the most commendable manner, for frequently, when a fair is to be held in some place, the magistrate of that place posts printed announcements stating that he will not permit comedians, funambulists, jugglers, gambling tables, and Fortune's urns, but that, if anyone should wish to bring exotic animals or other rare curiosities for exhibit, he should have permission to do so.

Whether Jews should be admitted to public fairs and marts is a question about which many are still doubtful, given that this stubborn nation is seeking gain only by deceit and by duping the Christians. However, since public fairs are called "public" because everyone in Frankfurt-am-Main (even those proscribed by the Empire) is admitted to them, these people must be permitted to enter and depart without hindrance if the privilege of the fair is to be upheld. Such rights cannot be denied to the Jews who are from time to time admitted to the Empire. This is especially true if they do not come from suspect and infected places and if they are not the lowest type of beggars and peddlers but are known as merchants of some importance, provided with good passes and references, and, for the rest, conform in all things to the ordinances concerning the Jews, such as the commendable Leipzig Ordinance, which we shall append *in extenso* to this chapter.[1]

Above all, the authorities must see to it that, if there is any danger of contagion, no infected wares and persons be brought to the location of the fair, and this applies particularly to the cloth, bedding, feathers, wool, and clothing which the peddling Jews usually carry. At the gates as well as at the frontier every traveler should be thoroughly examined and every foreigner should be warned beforehand by published edicts and by the newspapers that, if he is not completely sure of his wares or if he cannot pass a rigorous examination, he should stay away or expect exemplary punishment for his person and the burning of his wares. At such times of contagion, nobody should set out without proper and authoritative certification. However, in this matter caution should be used in the interest of the fair not to continue to declare a town or a country infected after the last vestiges of contagion have disappeared. It is only fitting to count among the infected persons the ignominious public whores who usually travel to such great fairs with their infected bodies and minds, finding there more than enough buyers for their stinking and rotten wares, so that many a man has had reason to repent sooner than he hoped.

The third ordinance should be passed with respect to inns, lodgings in private houses, and places to be used for stores, stands, cellars, and warehouses, as well as to the victuals of food and drink. All this should be available at reasonable prices and in sufficient quantities to attract strangers, since, if it is lacking or

[1] See Document 74, *Ordinance Concerning the Jews*, in the section on An Age of Reform?.

too costly, strangers will either stay away from the fair altogether or at least leave it as soon as possible. They may also bring such a quantity of victuals from their homes that inns or private guest-houses will not be able to count upon their patronage to any great extent. Measure, then, is good in all things, and a moderate price is the best for all victuals and meals. But it is also important at such times to open privileged and well-run eating places where the ordinary man can get something for his money and be properly served.

Concerning the opening of stands, the authorities would have to see to it that the available space be well distributed, that everyone be assigned a measured area, and especially that the various kinds of wares, such as those of the linen-, cloth,- lace-, and cottonmongers, those of the hatters, furriers, and those of the lower craftsmen, be arranged together in their own particular location. In this manner, the buyers would not have to search around and would be able to find and choose from what they need, since everything would be close together, without wasting their time milling about and looking for things.

Concerning the householders and farmers of the surrounding countryside who usually come once a week to the town where the fair is held with the fruits of their fields and gardens, victuals, and forage, they would have to be assigned to another quarter of the town for the duration of the fair, making room for the stands of the foreign merchants who are dealing in more important wares. For this purpose, printed posters stating to what location every one of these produce stands has been moved could be affixed to the most important corner buildings. The authorities of the towns could also make use of the principal country roads, where the travelers could find good inns and stables for their horses as well as some food at reasonable prices at such times and all year round. In these places they should always be able to hire hackney horses and coaches, relay horses and carts for money. As far as comfortable inns and quick transportation of passengers—and I should like to add good and well-kept roads—are concerned, no country, except perhaps Holland, measures up to Sweden and Austria, where even the prices of meals and change and relay horses are posted. The traveler, therefore, since the innkeeper must stay within the price set down by the local prince, cannot be cheated in any way. But in many places our merchants traveling to the fairs at Frankfurt, Leipzig, Braunschweig [Brunswick], and other places are not as fortunate. They are poorly lodged, since ancient Germanic barbarism as described by Erasmus in his *Colloquia* is still evident, at least in the village inns, so that they cannot find much except stinking straw, sour beer, and coarse bread. The roads also are so bottomless and so wretched that the carters' first reply to any complaint about unreasonable charges always refers to the bad roads and the high price of forage. For this reason the high cost of transportation must be added to the price of the goods, which, in turn, has lowered the profits of many a merchant.

The fourth ordinance should make adequate arrangements for diligent supervision, inspection, and good service to the merchants at fair time. It is part of that supervision that the gentlemen and citizens in charge of fire fighting remind everyone, and particularly the innkeepers, who at such times keep great quantities of hay and straw as well as many foreign carters and horse drivers in their houses, to be most careful with light and fire. They should also be reminded to have fire hoses in readiness against all danger and especially to watch out for bad and suspicious characters. To that end, the nightly patrols should be doubled, and in the daytime, too, good sentries should often be seen in order to avert such mischief as brawls and thievery. Even before the beginning of the fair, certain honest and well-known but indigent citizens could be enrolled as sentries and placed under the command of a captain chosen from among the citizens. The latter could then hire them out for a fee to such merchants as requested their services, and he could also send them to the busiest quarters of the town *ex officio*. After the fair he could exact a certain modest fee from each store or stand in that quarter.

Persons necessary for the service of the merchants, from the brokers, customs officials, toll collectors, and weighers down to the ordinary porters, should be available in such a way that, given the short duration of the fair and the great amount of business to be transacted, everything can be taken care of immediately upon arrival and without delay at departure. Those whom a merchant chooses for his helpers and workers during the fair should serve him faithfully.

30. Retail Tradesmen

DANIEL DEFOE was much more the spokesman for the retail shopkeeper than for the wholesale merchant or large entrepreneur. To Defoe, the business virtues consisted of economy, thrift, and prudent planning rather than a spirit of adventure and risk-taking. It followed from this that shop display was a dangerous extravagance, threatening the solvency of the tradesman by reducing the capital available for stock. "Gay appearance and fine gilding" did not attract customers; a sober shop and good value were the surest way to success.

Perhaps Defoe's views were more fitted to English than French customers. In any case, Mercier viewed the Parisian grocer-druggists as inveterate frauds, demanding maximum consumer vigilance regardless of the shop's décor. The two documents make a curious contrast. Defoe, from the inside, was basically confident that proper (and honorable) management would ultimately bring business success; Mercier, from the outside, was less concerned about the tradesman's solvency than his business practices at the expense of the defenseless consumer, especially the poor one.

Sources: Document A: Daniel Defoe, *The Complete English Tradesman in Familiar Letters*, pp. 257ff. Document B: Helen Simpson, ed. and trans., *The Waiting City: Paris, 1728–88, Being an Abridgement of Louis-Sebastian Mercier's "Le tableau de Paris*," pp. 160–162.

A. Letter XIX
Of Fine Shops, and Fine Shews

SIR,

IT is a modern custom, and wholly unknown to our ancestors, who yet understood trade, in proportion to the Business they carried on, as well as we do, to have tradesmen lay out two thirds of their fortune in fitting up their shops.

By fitting up, I do not mean furnishing their shops with wares and goods to sell; for in that they came up to us in every particular, and perhaps went beyond us too; but in painting and gilding, in fine shelves, shutters, boxes, glass-doors, sashes and the like, in which they tell us now, 'tis a small matter to lay out two or three hundred pounds, nay five hundred pounds to fit up a Pastry-Cook's, or a Toy-shop.

The first inference to be drawn from this must necessarily be, that this age must have more fools than the last, for certainly fools only are most taken with shews and outsides.

It is true, that a fine shew of goods will bring customers; and it is not a new custom, but a very old one, that a new shop very well furnished goes a great way to bringing a trade; for the proverb was, and still is, very true, *that every body has a penny for a new shop;* but that a fine shew of shelves and glass windows should bring customers, that was never made a rule in trade till now.

And yet even now, I should not except so much against it, if it was not carried on to such an excess, as is too much for a middling Tradesman to bear the expence of; in this therefore it is made not a grievance only, but really scandalous to trade, for now a young beginner has such a tax upon him before he begins, that he must sink perhaps a third part, nay, a half part of his stock, in painting and gilding, wainscoting and glazing, before he begins to trade, nay, before he can open his shop; as they say of building a water-mill, two thirds of the expence lies under the water; and when the poor Tradesman comes to furnish his shop, and lay in his stock of goods, he finds a great hole made in his cash to the workmen, and his shew of goods, on which the life of his trade depends, is fain to be lessen'd to make up his shew of boards, and glass to lay them in.

Nor is this heavy article to be abated upon any account; for if he does not make a good shew, he comes abroad like a mean ordinary fellow, and no body of fashion comes to his shop; the customers are drawn away by the pictures and painted shelves, tho' when they come there, they are not half so well fill'd, as in other places, with goods fit for a trade; and how indeed should it be otherwise? the Joiners and Painters, Glasiers and Carvers, must have all ready money; the Weavers and Merchants may give credit, their goods are of so much less moment to the shop-keeper, that they must trust, but the more important shew must be finish'd first; and paid first; and when that has made a deep hole in the Tradesman's stock, then the remainder may be spar'd to furnish the shop with goods, and the merchant must trust for the rest.

It will hardly be believ'd in ages to come, when our posterity shall be grown wiser by our loss, and, as I may truly say, at our expence, that a Pastry-Cook's shop, which twenty pounds would effectually furnish at a time, with all needful things for sale; nay, except on an extraordinary shew, as on Twelfth-day at night for cakes, or upon some great Feast, twenty pounds can hardly be laid out at one time in goods for sale, yet that fitting up one of these shops should cost upwards of 300 *l. Anno Domini*, 1710. Let the year be recorded: The fitting up of a shop for Pastry ware in *London* to consist of the following particulars;

1. Sash windows, all of looking-glass plates, 12 inches by 16 inches in measure.
2. All the walks of the shop lin'd up with galley-tiles, and the Back-shop with galley-tiles in pannels, finely painted in forest-work and figures.
3. Two Large Peir looking-glasses and one chimney glass in the shop, and one very large Peir-glass seven foot high in the Back-shop.
4. Two large branches of Candlesticks, one in the shop and one in the back-room.
5. Three great glass lanthorns in the shop, and eight small ones.
6. Twenty five sconces against the wall, with a large pair of silver standing candlesticks in the back room, value 25 l.
7. Six fine large silver salvers to serve sweet-meats.
8. Twelve large high stands of rings, whereof three silver, to place small dishes for tarts, jelleys, &c. at a Feast.
9. Painting the cieling, and gilding the lanthorns, the sashes, and the carv'd work, 55 l.

These with some odd things to set forth the shop and make a shew, besides small plate, and besides China basons and cups, amounted to, as I am well inform'd, above 300l.

Add to this the more necessary part, which was,

1. Building two ovens, about twenty five pounds.
2. Twenty pounds in stock for pies, and cheesecakes, &c.

So that in short here was a trade, which might be carried on for about 30 or 40 l. stock, requir'd 300 l. expence to fit up the shop, and make a shew to invite customers. . . .

B. Grocer-Druggists

THEY SELL cinnamon, and poisons like *aqua fortis*, together with oil, cheese, emetics, brandy and paint, sugar and arsenic, senna and jam; statutes exist to confirm them in their rivalry with the apothecaries. When drugs and salts of somewhat similar appearance are mistaken for each other, so much the worse for medical science, and so much more the worse for the unwary purchaser of the packet. The perpetual danger of such a transfer ruffles no single sheet of foolscap in the bureaux of our rulers.

Drugs and spices, both are retailed by the same individual; his assistant doles out now a handful of raisins, now a lump of Glauber's salt; soap or emetics, prunes or treacle, the same scales serve for all, to weigh out food and nostrums alike. If the assistant fails to interpret the chemical characters on a box, if he cannot read at all, if he is entirely unfamiliar even with the look of the different drugs and so by mistake hands out something deadly, nobody cares, nobody protests, and the victim of error is quietly buried next day. But the statutes of his mystery are peremptory; the druggist has a right to purge his quarter, and sell groceries into the bargain.

These grocers sell ground pepper, done up in a twist of paper; and the dishonest ones make it go further by mixing in a little dog-dung, which being blackened and powdered blends perfectly with the pepper; so that the innocent Parisian savours his food, not with the spices of Malacca, but a product very different from what he supposes, and what he pays for. The only precaution against this kind of trickery—they pound up horse-beans from Auvergne, too—is to have the pepper ground under your own eyes; otherwise the grocer will continue to put this revolting indignity upon your palate.

Watching these shops, they seem perpetually busy, always someone in and out. The Parisian poor have no store of provisions, they buy in fractions, two ounces of this, one ounce of that, at a time; they never have a good piece of cheese in the house, nor a whole pound of sugar, nor a pint of oil. They never have in hand more money than will see them through the day, and so they go on buying in tiny portions for their dinner in the morning, for their supper at night. They buy their wood, too, very dear,

faggots and drift-wood about double what it costs the *bourgeois;*
they are for ever obliged to be carrying it, and having the logs
split, and the kindling chopped small.

For a purgative, in the same way, they go to their grocer, who
is cheaper than the apothecary, and think they have made a good
bargain; the grocer may be dangerous, but he costs far less.

Hence this eternal procession of servants and boys, carrying
their tiny packets of groceries or drugs, wrapped in paper, of
which these tradesmen are great users, always buying up spoiled
sheets from the printers, so that the despair of authors and book-
sellers is their delight. Without the grocer and the butter-women
we should be crowded out of our houses by the ever-congesting
mass of paper.

The Chevalier Blondeau, going about among these shops, and
examining with care all such papers, bought by them by the
pound, has rescued a perfect treasure of charters and deeds that
otherwise must have perished as envelopes, wrappers, and screws.
Among these lost deeds he recovered the actual marriage contract
of Louis XIV. Time, mice and the worms attack and destroy these
proud parchments on which human genealogies depend. Such
and such a famous house goes down in ruin because an old paper
has been twisted up to cork an apothecary's flask; or some poem
at which Europe might have wondered, humbly holds an ounce
of snuff for the nose of an undertaker's mute. A nation's genius, a
family's origin are alike unprovable when the documents are
gone; when through ignorance, or fire, or some extraordinary
chance precious papers have been destroyed or sold for what
their weight will fetch.

In four hundred years, time will have dealt so with all our
books, except such as have the luck to be reprinted. Book of mine!
Will this be your fate? Or will you set up a bold front, brazen,
diamond-hard, to resist the destroyer, together with the viable
labours of our Forty Immortals? [1]

[1] The Forty Immortals are the members of the French Academy (founded
in 1635 by Richelieu), which constantly strives to uphold the purity of the
French language.

V

The Guilds

A NUMBER of questions must be raised about the guilds. Apparently disappearing during the eighteenth century as an economic and even social institution in England, they remained strong on the Continent. Why was this so? Was it because most of the textile industry was still employing the "putting-out" system, and merchants found in the guilds a guarantee of quality workmanship they could not otherwise enforce? On the other hand, it appears that the town guilds often persuaded the public authorities to limit the number of artisans working in the countryside. Was it because local governments, influenced perhaps by mercantilist considerations, wanted to use the mechanism of the guild to regulate production over a larger area? Or was it simply that, as local bureaucracies developed, they found it convenient to reinforce the guild regulations on labor discipline in the interest of public order? Were local public authorities tempted to draw guild fines into state coffers? Whatever the reasons, it seems clear that public power had infused new life and vigor into the continental guilds in the eighteenth century.

What were the results of this development? First, the trend to increase the number of master artisans was reversed. Second, the renewed vitality of the guilds probably reinforced traditional hierarchies, especially in Germany (see Document 33). This was related to the role of the guild as a local social institution with many of the overtones of the modern fraternity—secrecy, ceremonialism, exclusiveness (see the selection from Frisius, Document 34). Finally, although legislation such as the Imperial Letter Patent of 1731 was intended to liberalize admissions and end the most obvious, irrational discrimination in the guilds, its total effect was to reinforce scarcity by prolonging the stages of apprenticeship and upholding quality specifications, thus hindering quantity production. The low prices of English cloth were a striking contrast to the high unit cost of continental producers. But the implications of social conservatism are perhaps equally noteworthy. Were the small German principalities and free towns better able to enforce these regulations than the larger states of Prussia and France?

31. The Cahiers of Rouen Artisans

THE CAHIERS—notebooks of grievances—form one of the most fruitful series of documents for a study of the Old Régime in France. Drawn up in every village and town in France in the spring of 1789, the cahiers reflect opinions from almost all social groups.

Until recently, emphasis has been placed on the village or parish cahiers as a source of rural conditions and peasant grievances. Although the parish cahiers continue to deserve exploration, the cahiers of the towns are less known. For this reason, the sample below is taken from the guild cahiers of Rouen. Here we find not the demand to abolish various seigneurial rights so typical of parish cahiers but grievances of a different kind. To be sure, the appeals for a uniform land tax and the abolition of internal customs, *aides*, and *gabelles* are no different from most parish cahiers. But the main emphasis seems directed against grain hoarders, the exorbitant profits of tax farmers, the threat of technological unemployment, and foreign competition. Although these grievances may not constitute anticapitalism, they clearly demonstrate divisions within the amorphous "middle class." At the same time, the cahier appeals for unity of action between artisan and *capitaliste* in order to create a new, representative local government, where individual merit will take precedence over traditional hierarchies. It is quite clear where the modest author of the following cahier believes this merit to reside—in the "first classes of the Third Estate."

Source: Marc Bouloiseau, ed., *Cahiers de doléances du Tiers Etat du bailliage de Rouen pour les Etats Généraux de 1789* (Paris, 1957), vol. I, pp. 106–116, in *Collection de documents inédits sur l'histoire économique de la Révolution française.**

Cahier of the Hatmakers, Fur-skin Dealers, and Furriers of Rouen

THIS GUILD assembly having honored me with its vote to set forth its grievances, I have endeavored, as much as it is in me, to state clearly the diverse demands of the guild, to which I am proud to belong because of the fortunate intelligence which guides it and forms the principal rule in all the duties it performs

---

* Translated with permission of Marc Bouloiseau and Presses Universitaires de France.

in order to satisfy the will of the monarch. If, from a lack of knowledge, which is not given to every practitioner of a craft, I do not render all their ideas in the terms usually applied to the particular grievance, I ask the indulgence of the respectable assembly to which I shall present them, for the great and appropriate terms are an object of study which is not always within the reach of the craftsman—his work is that object, but unfortunately it has too long been the only one he has studied systematically. Believing that the needs of general welfare, which are the motive of all our assemblies, should not be limited to the point where every *corps* includes only the grievances that concern it directly, I have decided to set forth all the demands which tend to relieve the most highly taxed class of people and the poorest class, as well as those demands which would check the spreading of an evil that results from the circumstances.

1. The land tax on all property, without distinction, has been unanimously accepted and recommended, since there should be a single tax applicable to all property, both in town and country or whether belonging to clergy, nobility, or the Third Estate. This tax appears all the more legitimate since the social contract recognizes in a great kingdom devoted to its king only one great family, wherein the oldest son owes his younger brothers the example of paying taxes for the support of the state.

2. Commerce free from tariffs and extending over all of France is also among our demands. It is painful to see that this great family —since I have used this term, which I believe to be to the honor of humanity—is obliged, if it wants to obtain the things it needs, even clothes, to pay enormous duties on goods entering and leaving conquered regions such as French Flanders or other regions such as Brittany, when they are all governed by one and the same monarch. The painstaking inquests into customs declarations are so annoying that it takes only a very small mistake—such as forgetting to declare an unimportant item that is discovered at the examination—and everything is immediately confiscated by a company that is judge and party to its own cause. Therefore, in order to give commerce the liberty to flourish again, we demand the abolition of all tariffs and tolls in the interior of the kingdom.

3. The abolition of *aides* [indirect taxes] is also among our demands because of the vexation they cause. A man will not give a

neighbor in distress a bottle of wine if he has paid an enormous duty on it when it entered [town]. There was the example of an unfortunate man who was prevented from helping another because of a bottle of wine. A third man from kindness went to much trouble in order to spare him the penalties stipulated by the regulations and finally paid 536 livres for the bottle. It is therefore for the entire kingdom that we demand the abolition of the *aides*, so that it will be possible to take care of unfortunate people and also bring all the wines and spirits one produces into town. Then, the only [extra] price one would pay would be cartage. This would also stop the abuse of officials at the toll gates . . . who put the unfortunate carter . . . at the mercy of the tax farmer who confiscates his horse and cart and condemns him to a fine besides.

4. The *gabelles* [salt tax] also are revolting in themselves and by their consequences. Salt, the manna of Providence, is bought by the tax farmer at 1 sou 6 deniers per pound and sold at 13 sous per pound. Is this price proportionate to its original cost? Does the cost of transportation cause the increase? It is about 1 denier per pound. Is it the cost of storage, since salt must remain unused for a certain time before it is good for consumption? This again can be calculated at about 1 denier per pound. Is it the interest on the loans they [the tax farmers] had to make before purchase? If one looks closely, one will see that a *muid* [1] of salt costing the tax farmer 360 or 400 livres will produce 3,000 livres—an enormous and revolting profit. What results from the fact that this precious provision is kept in the hands of the tax farmer? He pays underlings drawn from the same unfortunate class of people and makes them live in open war with men equally unfortunate who are trying to lighten the burden of their misery by lowering the price of this basic necessity. The interest of the tax farmers has made it all the more basic since, under a law obtained by ruse from the monarch, every householder is obliged to consume a quart of salt per head under penalty of a fine, if he has not done his duty by the *gabelle;* and he is ruined if he is found with a handful of salt which is not judged *gabelle* salt.

5. Condemnation to the galleys is an insult to humanity. We demand that it no longer be the punishment of the unfortunate

[1] A dry measure equivalent to 51.48 bushels of winter wheat. Like all French measures, the *muid* varied from region to region, and from commodity to commodity.

whose misery has led them to smuggling and often forced them to revolt against petty officials whose low salaries lead them to graft. These officials are so little respected by their superiors that they are often disavowed if a protective hand defends the unfortunate smugglers, or if the smuggler himself is a man who is in a position to take his case to court so that his voice reaches the ear of the prince. We demand, therefore, that this penalty be imposed only on those convicted of theft or knavery.

6. We also demand free trade in tobacco for the entire kingdom, since the same inconveniences attending salt, mentioned above, are connected with the transport of tobacco from one town to another or from one house to another. The result is a search at the toll gate if an official suddenly decides to suspect you, and during such a search there is always a danger that some dishonest individual will place some smuggled item in your baggage.

7. The bad year we have just passed provokes another grievance, and this respectable assembly should present it to the monarch as the most dangerous calamity that can befall a kingdom which is supposed to be a law unto all and to set an example by its wise laws and precautions against all disastrous events: it is the permission to export grain.

Grain, it is said, is scarce in all the provinces of the kingdom, the reason being either a misfortune sent from Heaven or the abuses resulting from it. Let us see if the misfortune sent from Heaven is as terrible as it seemed to be at first. Selfish persons have been able to create enough terror to intimidate people and thus to bring about a steady increase in the price of a basic commodity; for if we closely consider events, it appears that the disastrous hailstorm which ravaged several cantons was not sufficiently general to bring such a calamity to almost the entire kingdom. If we also realize that the disaster area is to the kingdom what one dot is to this sheet of paper, how can we believe that the immense area unaffected by the disaster would not compensate the needs of the smaller area? If that were true, we could not claim that the soil under cultivation is sufficient for the subjects of the kingdom.

The present calamity, therefore, is even more terrible because it is revolting to humanity. The individuals who are interested in the price rise are men who store grain for export and in this way force a rise substantial enough to satisfy their greed for gold. It is not exceptional to see immense storehouses of wheat covered with mites. These people always wait for the highest price before they sell, holding on to the very last moment, when the quality is deteriorating. This often leads to diseases, whose causes are ignored; but this grain cannot possibly be healthy since the insect that eats it appears only in hot weather. Some time ago, grain hoarding was favored by the export regulations, which were [subsequently] interpreted in terms of quintals.[2] At the time it was stipulated that wheat could be exported provided the price of the *mine* did not exceed 12 livres, but it was not made clear that the *mine* weighed from 145 to 155 pounds, as it still does. Thus, the export regulations may present no hardship to those engaged in export, but they are clearly causing the present evil.

In a kingdom such as France, a two years' food supply should be stocked to prevent accidents. Formal law should enforce this and previous decisions by the Court [Royal Council] be replaced. . . . Also, in the future, export must be permitted only if the *mine* of wheat weighing 145 to 150 pounds does not exceed 12 livres. At that price everyone can live, from the independent farmer to the poor workman.

8. [Demand for reform of the bankruptcy law, especially with regard to exposing "fraudulent bankruptcy."]

9. [Special appeal for aid to the hatmakers' guild, including a regulation to reduce the cost of raw materials. This appeal is justified by the fact that the hatmakers' guild employs over 300 workers in Rouen and in the surrounding countryside.]

10. Almost unconsciously, these demands have led us to the great bond which once united all parts of the kingdom in the interior as well as with the exterior—and by exterior I mean the colonies. But this tie has now been broken by a commercial treaty which, far from tightening the bond, has completely shattered it.[3] The result has been that the specious attraction of a lower price for a considerable amount of semifinished goods has threatened the livelihood of people necessary to the state, namely, the poorer class. The situation cannot be denied. Every day this poor man is

[2] One quintal = 100 pounds.
[3] The Treaty of Eden (1786) reduced the duties on English textiles, which then entered the French market and undersold domestic producers. French advantages in the English wine market hardly compensated for her competitive shortcomings in cottons and woolen cloth.

clearly useful by his work, the mainstay of commerce. Moreover, this poor man is useful in the service of our monarch, for who among us, gentlemen, sacrifices himself so readily, enlisting under the colors for some eight years in order to defend his fatherland? It must be granted that hardly one in a hundred like him could be found among the well-to-do. Well then, gentlemen, this class which is already half destroyed by ever-present misery will be completely annihilated if the use of machines continues to spread in France.

Certainly, it would be convenient if we could imitate our neighbors and even surpass them in everything that favors the arts and crafts. But there are special considerations holding our society together, namely, the subsistence of all the individuals composing it, who, forming but one family under our good monarch, must mutually provide bread for each other. It is therefore an undeniable fact that machines are not suitable to a great kingdom where surplus hands would be obliged to leave the body [the social *corps*] in order to beg bread abroad in countries that would be only too happy to weaken a nation inexhaustible in men and resources, a nation that has already expanded throughout the entire world but that would find itself exhausted by the desertion of its lower classes, who would, perhaps in the near future, become Germans, Prussians, Englishmen, or Russians. Already there are many unfortunate examples of this. They had another cause, which we dare not recall without apprehension.[4]

Depopulation, gentlemen, always has dreadful consequences, but I shall not labor this point. Everyone is well aware of this fact. Let us return to the main issue, which makes us view machinery with skepticism. A small number of men can handle the principal operations of a machine and, even there, must form a "special company." It is perfectly true that these "companies" will be able to lower the prices of manufactured goods. But [as a result] they witness unfortunate people at their doorsteps who reproach them for having taken away their work and who hide in

[4] The author of the cahier refers to the revocation of the Edict of Nantes (1685), which resulted in the emigration of a substantial number of Huguenot artisans. It was widely believed, with some exaggeration, that this emigration had seriously weakened French industry. See Warren C. Scoville, *The Persecution of the Huguenots and French Economic Development, 1680–1720* (Berkeley, Calif., 1960).

the woods in despair, perhaps devastating the countryside, making the highways unsafe, and laying waste the entire kingdom. Would it not be better to leave things as they are and to let this great family take care of itself as it did before the commercial treaty was concluded? Once this treaty is repealed, there will be no more competition for our manufactured goods in this kingdom, and they will be sold here as well as in our colonies. It would be imperative to prohibit importation of all foreign manufactured goods and to keep matters in hand by extremely severe penalties. Then we shall see contentment reappear in every heart, contentment which today is manifest only in a small number of wealthy people, who are in a position to resist the terrible things that are happening every day. And yet we should not accuse these rich capitalists of egoism; they are our brothers. Let us, on the contrary, convince ourselves that they will unite with us for the general welfare, the source from which all individual welfare flows.

Louis XV, gentlemen, has given a great example of this feeling for the people. The question of machinery was raised in his reign, and it was M. d'Aristois who introduced it in France. He obtained a privilege for this new industry, but later the King said that his kingdom was too heavily populated to permit a manner of manufacture which would threaten the livelihood of his people. For a great king, this was truly the way to show the kindness of his heart, to take to his bosom all his subjects, all his children. Nevertheless, gentlemen, we must admire the industry of our great capitalists, whose views are only directed toward the good they thought they pursued and toward which their inclination leads them. Let us believe their pure intentions. It is unfortunate that, if the machines are done away with, French goods will be somewhat more expensive than foreign ones; but, as I pointed out, gentlemen, if there is no competition, then there will be no worry about a home market.

The use of machinery must have suited our English neighbors, but let us see what caused them to adopt it. It is the immense volume of their trade coming from their colonies and North America added to the scarcity of goods to carry on that trade; this can be proven by a three-to-one comparison. Besides, that nation is too wise politically to have adopted a harmful system. There are all kinds of ways, gentlemen, of obtaining beneficial results. I had wanted to be brief, and I see myself engaged in a labyrinth of details that lie behind France's misfortunes, a labyrinth which your penetrating eyes, so much better than mine, will make more intelligible and more conducive to the general welfare.

11. Now I shall state the wishes of the city. I use this term because the individuals who compose it seem to be voicing a grievance. The provincial administration, respectable though it be by its origin, respectable also by its membership, does not correspond to the general wishes. Without entering into all the individual reasons for this, [I must state that] the creation of Provincial Estates by His Majesty seems generally desirable. These Estates should establish an administration whose members should be named by the assembled city, uninfluenced by protection or rank, which too often brings together only a small group of people frequently devoid of merit. For they come from a group [corps] whose breadth of vision is not as wide as that of the first classes of the Third Estate....

32. Attempt at Abolition of the Guilds in France

BARON TURGOT became controller-general of France in 1774, the climax to a brilliant career in government service. Greatly influenced by physiocratic ideas on increasing production by policies of laissez faire in agriculture, commerce, and industry, Turgot was especially anxious to abolish the merchant and craft guilds. In this memorandum to the new king, Louis XVI, he argued his case against the still powerful "corporations" of merchants, master artisans, and manufacturers. Once the guild restrictions had been broken by royal edict, Turgot anticipated not only lower prices for the consumer but also an influx of skilled labor from England to help modernize French manufactures. However, French textile merchants, who most often operated through the putting-out system, probably preferred the guilds as a guarantee of quality they could not otherwise enforce.

Turgot was dismissed four months after this memorandum was written, and his edicts were rescinded.

Source: A. R. J. Turgot, *Oeuvres*, ed. Gustave Schelle (Paris, 1923), vol. V, pp. 158ff. [From a memoir to Louis XVI concerning plans for various edicts, January, 1776.]

YOUR MAJESTY has known my views on guilds for some time. I dare say that this way of thinking is shared by all those who have any notion about the nature of commerce. I believe that it is impossible to maintain seriously and in good faith that these corporations, their exclusive privileges, the barriers they erect against work, competition, and the progress of industry are of any usefulness whatsoever.

Yet there are many people who have a strong interest in their continued existence, namely, the heads of these communities or those who profit from them, for the suits brought about by these institutions are one of the most abundant sources of profit for the profession of law. It therefore would not surprise me to find a great deal of sophistry expended in their favor, especially if it is done by vague reasoning and not supported by the facts. If Your Majesty would deign read the memoir concerning the abuses of these communities which M. Albert [1] had drawn up and verified for the guilds of Paris, Your Majesty would easily be in a position to recognize that only hopeless excuses are employed to cover up the harm done by these institutions.

Again, Your Majesty will find the preface to this edict rather long, but I feel that it is necessary to demonstrate the injustice inherent in the establishment of the guilds and to see how harmful they are to commerce. I believe that it is only by stating clearly the reasons for such a measure [abolition of guilds] that one will be able to silence the sophisms advanced by the special interests.

Sire, I regard the destruction of the guilds and the complete abolition of the hindrances imposed by these establishments upon industry and the poor but hard-working class of your subjects as one of the most beneficial deeds Your Majesty could perform for his people. After the freeing of the grain trade, it is one of the greatest steps the administration can take toward the amelioration, nay, the restoration, of the kingdom. This measure will do for industry what [free grain trade] will do for agriculture.

Since the suppression of useless expenditures will enable these communities to repay their debts, in a very few years Your Majesty will enjoy a considerable revenue, which he can employ in better ways or restore in part to his people.

[1] *Lieutenant de police* of Paris.

It is all the more necessary to suppress these communities since they constitute an almost insurmountable obstacle to lowering the price of foodstuffs needed for the subsistence of the people. If grain costs between 20 and 26 livres per *setier* today, and most good wheat 24 livres, the people should have excellent bread at 2 sous 2 deniers.[2] It is still 2 sous 9 deniers. The same obstacles exist with respect to the price of meat, and as long as there are bakers' and butchers' guilds it will be impossible to overcome their maneuvers to raise the cost of food beyond its real price.[3] Only by completely free competition can one hope to achieve this. As long as the needs of the population are satisfied by a small number of persons linked together in exclusive association, they will always conspire to force the authorities to accept their inflated prices by threatening to cease sales altogether.

It will be necessary to take precautions against this aspect of their uncooperative attitude at the time the change is made. These precautions have been provided for, and on this point Your Majesty can rely upon the wisdom and activity of M. Albert.

One particular circumstance furnishes an additional reason for abolishing the guilds at this very instant. It relates to the situation of English industry after commerce with the American colonies has ceased. If there is one moment when we might hope to attract many English workers to France, and with them a great number of useful procedures unknown to our manufacturers, it is now. The existence of guilds that are closed to any worker who has not gone through a long period of trial and to all foreigners in general would prevent the kingdom from taking advantage of this unique opportunity. It seems to me that this consideration should carry a great deal of weight.

33. Guilds and Social Hierarchy

JUSTUS MÖSER, the prolific political economist who deplored the decline of German inland trade, also deplored almost any change in social mores and customs. The precise provisions of the ruling of the Diet of

[2] That is, per loaf of approximately 4 pounds, the daily family ration.
[3] Turgot meant the cost of food if supply alone governed price.

1731 are not important here, but Möser's defense of the long-standing guild restrictions is. It is obvious from Möser's comments that the guilds performed the function of upholding traditional social mores, above all, the hallowed respect for hierarchy. Möser was not prepared to apply what he called "the principles of a philosopher or a Christian" to practical living. To each class its own honor in the seven tiers of the Germanic *Heerschild!*

Source: Justus Möser, *"Patriotische Phantasien"* in *Sämtliche Werke, historisch-kritische Ausgabe,* vol. IV, pp. 240ff.*

Whether the Authors of the Ruling of the Diet of *1731* Were Right in Declaring Many People Honorable Who Were Not Previously

FURTHERMORE, IT is certain that the trades and guilds suffered greatly from the recent ruling of the Diet requiring them to accept all bastards legitimatized by any palatinate count and, for that matter, almost any creature with two legs and no feathers. Following humanitarian feelings which have lately come into fashion and perhaps even following our religion, whereby God makes no distinctions among men born from the womb, this ruling may be well-intentioned enough. However, no good political reason can be found for it, unless we accept the order of a certain prince of the realm which began as follows:

> We, by the Grace of God, etc., herewith proclaim, having exempted Ourselves with our Princely family and Our Councillors from the common lot of human society, that the latter consists of nothing but rabble: We thus order most graciously that all bastards to whom we have conferred the privileges of legitimate birth under Our Princely seal must be accepted in that state, under penalty of one hundred gold Gulden.

"Is it the fault of the innocent babe? Why should it suffer because its mother gave birth?" it is commonly asked. On the other hand, a certain abbess exclaimed, "Out with the changeling!" when a princely bastard was to be brought into her noble convent. An Imperial act of legitimation was proposed. Everyone felt sorry for the poor innocent child, but to no avail. The changeling had to go, for the abbess would have none but those

* Translated by permission of Gerhard Stalling (Oldenburg and Berlin).

begotten in a pure, noble, German marriage bed. And she was right. Why deprive the guilds of these principles which are essential to German honor? Why was common national honor violated more than the high-titled honor? Why did the large, productive part of the nation deserve less consideration than the smaller, unproductive part? Surely the reason was none other than that given by the aforementioned most gracious prince. The authors of the ruling were standing on a mountain peak and those at the foot of the hill seemed like so many mosquitoes.

The principle of the newer legislators that fornication must be made less shameful in order to prevent infanticide is wrong and insufficient. The old principle that extreme shame must be attached to it in order to promote matrimony is far stronger and conceived in accordance with the best philosophical principles.

The ruling of the Diet makes *honorable* a great many people who hitherto had been considered *dishonorable*. I wager that the authors missed the meaning of the word *dishonor* and again considered the matter from the unpolitical, humanitarian point of view. To the [old] Germans, all those who did not fight in the *arrière-ban*[1] or in the militia [*Bürgerbann*] were dishonorable, and under this principle they would, in our time, deny honor to all those who are not soldiers. This seems a strange way of thinking. Even now, does not every captain forbid his men to drink to brotherhood with other people who are not in his company or to be on a thou-to-thou footing with them? And did the *arrière-ban* have less cause not to drink from the same mug with everyone? Those who did not belong with the company did not belong with the mug either. Thus our forebears would say: "We don't drink with shepherds and such because they do not fight for the fatherland but stay home to watch the flocks." They did not deny the Christian and moral probity [of the shepherds]. But just as the camp follower lacked the honor of a soldier, so the shepherd lacked the honor of a warrior. This kind of dishonor would have pertained to all tenant farmers (except the lifetime fief holders) had our forebears had tenant farmers in the countryside.

The reasoning whereby shepherds, herdsmen, and such people are, after all, indispensable members of society and therefore should be fairly given all honor may seem right in the mouth of

[1] *Arrière-ban:* a feudal troop levy.

the philosopher and the Christian, but it is not the language of good policy. The second class may feel insulted by exclusion from the first, and the third class can be just as touchy about exclusion from the second. But, for all that, it is no shame to belong to the third. The dishonorable class in civil society is nothing but the lowest or eighth class. Honor was divided into seven classes in the *Heerschild.*[2] The common feudal levies belonged to the seventh class. Hence, if the eighth rank cannot be counted with the seventh, should it not bear this status with the same patience that the seventh bears its position below the sixth?

Thus the ruling of the Diet, which found Christian and moral honorability in people who belong in a class without honor, was unjustified in moving them from the eighth to the sixth class. Even now, tenant farmers, *Markkötter,*[3] and others who only pay rents in kind should not be counted in the seventh class along with *Vollerben, Halberben,* or *Erbköttern,*[4] who purchase their honor from the state with monthly rents in money or cartage services. This keeps better householders on the farms and gives the tenants an incentive to prepare the way to civil honor by assuming a greater [financial] burden. In our present confusion, we risk changing all [landholders] into tenant farmers.

The results of the ruling of the Diet have been especially bad for the guilds. For the removal of their honorable status will soon make it less respectable to join a guild. Only in England [even] the king does not disdain the guilds. The rich man prefers to become a so-called manufacturer, and those who have some wealth buy patents of nobility in order to rise from the seventh class to a higher one. The policy of our forebears was infinitely more subtle. According to their principles, "low honor" was to be protected as carefully as "high honor," because the estate of low honor carries all the burden so that the state has an interest in its constant increase. Surely this will not happen if the estate is to be despised. The emperor cannot qualify a person from the seventh class for a canonship; nor should he have qualified anybody from the "class without honor" for admission into a guild.

But those who wrote the ruling of the Diet were not of the

---

[2] The military hierarchy of feudal society.
[3] Grimm's *Wörterbuch:* peasants who own nothing but a cottage and a small garden.
[4] All freeholders.

seventh class. They spoke only for themselves and not for others. They thought as the aforementioned prince of the realm, without saying so in public. Indeed, it was a poor way of lawmaking, where one estate sat in judgment over another in this manner. The common soldier cannot be judged unless two of his comrades are present at the judgment. And, according to German law, the ruling should not have been issued without special deputies from the seventh class. This class loses both freedom and property if it is subjected to arbitrary laws without consent. The Empress of Russia deals less harshly with her subjects than the Diet has dealt with . . . the guilds.

34. Customs and Regulations of a German Guild

THE CEREMONIAL book of the Tailors' Guild gives us an excellent picture of the requirements of the trade, the steps from apprentice to journeyman and finally to master, and the ceremonies that punctuate the long, tedious process. Equally interesting is the didactic form in which this manual is presented—questions and answers interspersed with banal quotations from the classics or the Bible and supplemented with the aphorisms of the author. Curious as the ceremonial details may seem, the dominant theme is one of hierarchy, paternalism, deference, and sobriety, where hard work, patience, and docility earn their eventual reward, while initiative, impatience, or pretension are doomed to failure. Reading this, one sees the guild as the very center of the artisan's professional and social life.

Source: Fredericus Frisius, *Der vornehmsten Künstler und Handwercker Ceremonial-Politica* (Leipzig, 1708–16).

THE CEREMONIAL BOOK
OF THE TAILORS
IN WHICH NOT ONLY THEIR LONG-STANDING OBSERVANCES PERTAINING TO
INDENTURE AND FREEING OF APPRENTICES
AND THE MAKING OF MASTERS ARE PRESENTED
ACCORDING TO THE STATUTE BOOKS OF THE GUILDS OF DIFFERENT PARTS
BUT IN WHICH IT IS ALSO PROPOSED TO PRESENT
THE RIDICULOUS AND AT TIMES QUESTIONABLE
ACTS AND EXAMINATIONS
PERTAINING TO THE MAKING OF JOURNEYMEN
BY QUESTIONS AND ANSWERS.
WITH THE ADDITION OF USEFUL
REFLECTIONS AND INCIDENTAL THOUGHTS
BY
M. FREDERICUS FRISIUS, SCHOL. ALTENB. CONR.
LEIPZIG
TO BE FOUND IN GROSCHUFS BOOKSTORE, 1708.

The Tailoring Trade

INTRODUCTION

I

What preliminary remark can be made about this trade? That,
just as it requires few instruments and tools, it is not bound to
many ceremonies. From this, one can to some extent prove the
antiquity of this trade, since it is known that our forebears dis-
liked the superfluous in all things. Thus, it is rightly said: *Quo id
antiquius, eo simplicius*, the older a thing, the simpler. This also
appears on the escutcheons of our forebears, which were quite
simple and not ornamented with as many pictures as those of today.

II

How shall the ceremonies be presented?
We shall see what happens with

I. Apprentices
II. Journeymen, and
III. Masters.

III

What happens with apprentices?
Here we can observe what happens at the ceremonies of

I. Indenture and
II. Freeing.

IV

What happens with journeymen?
Here a curious mind might ask

I. How one is made a journeyman?
II. How many years a journeyman must travel?
III. How one journeyman is to act toward another?

V

What happens with masters?
Here it is well to remember the things one who wants to become a master

I. Must do in order to gain the right to make a master-piece,
II. What this master-piece consists of, and
III. What happens while it is being made and afterward.

DISCOURSE

I. ABOUT APPRENTICES

1

What must be done if a boy is to be indentured into this trade?

The boy must appear with his father or relative before the master as well as four other masters, and two more, if this be the
regulation, to be inscribed before the open chest of the Guild,
which is placed on the table. In large places, the eight Aldermen
of the Guild are present.

Which incidental thoughts does this bring to mind?

That GOD is a GOD of order, and that all estates and all actions
should be conducted in an orderly manner.

What other thoughts did this bring to mind?

The well-known verse:
  Ordine fac discas, & bene doctus eris
  Do your studying in good order,
  And you will soon be well-learned.

II

Who is speaking for the apprentice?

The master whom the apprentice has chosen.

What good thoughts come to mind here?

That the teaching masters also come under the Fourth Commandment, since they are made to speak as *patres cura*, foster fathers of their apprentices, who are as children under their care.

III

What must the apprentice do at this point?

He must put a certain sum of money, viz., 7 groschen, 4 pfennig, into the chest [of the Guild] and also make a firm promise to be upright, diligent, and discreet; and present his birth certificate, if he be from out of town.

What good thoughts come to mind here?

That discretion is a very good virtue, to be highly recommended to all young people.

What else do we think of?

The beautiful saying of Quintus Lucianus, Chap. 4, v. 6:
> *Non magna res sustineri potest ab eo, cui tacere grave est;*
> *quod homini facillimum voluit esse natura.*
> One is unfit for great things if he cannot keep silent:
> yet the nature of man does not make this easy.

Item, the exhortation of Syrach, chap. 23, v. 7:
> Dear children, learn to keep your mouths shut.

IV

For how many years does an apprentice usually have to learn?

He cannot be freed before two years, but before he begins, he must be tried out for two weeks. The patent of apprenticeship is then made out for three years, so that he might be better able to make his way in the land.

What reflection came to mind here?

That all things must have their time and that nobody can learn anything *per habitum infusum*, or, as it were, in his sleep.

Item, that, as the saying goes: *Natura non amat saltum*, Nature does not like jumps. This might also be applied to Art, which is, as it were, a sister to Nature.

V

What is the custom for freeing an apprentice?

Only two masters and the Alderman of the Guild, as well as two others if such be the regulation, are required, and the teaching master has the final word.

VI

Who answers him?

The Alderman of the Guild, who seriously admonishes the boy to be true, upright, and honest with everyone. Thereupon he wishes him and the other masters present, who also give the boy good advice, the best of luck.

What reflection did this bring to mind?

That a young man who is learning needs nothing more than admonition and that nothing profits him more than the blessing of those who have taught him.

VII

What else is to be observed here?

That the boy is now an apprentice journeyman, i.e., that he receives wages until he is made a regular journeyman.

II. ABOUT JOURNEYMEN

I

What happens when an apprentice journeyman is declared a regular journeyman?

When a master recognizes him as a journeyman by his work, he must go to the journeymen and let himself be inscribed at a so-called public meeting.

What did this bring to mind?

The meditation that a young soul should not be made great

before his time, but rather be kept in meekness and respect before his superiors.

II

When and where is the meeting held?

Every two weeks, and at the residence of whomever is in charge of the meeting. Since this is not always a master, an inn is often rented for the occasion.

III

What are the ceremonies of the journeymen on this occasion?

Two masters sit at the table next to the open chest, as well as two senior journeymen and two "table journeymen," who are in charge. Thereupon the apprentice journeyman steps forth and asks for the "Honest Welcome" [1]

What reflection did this bring to mind?

That one has to seek after honors, and that nobody will gain anything without searching and asking, according to the well-known saying:

> *Non venit in buccas assa columba tibi.*
> Roast pigeons will not fly into thy mouth.

IV

Who answers him?

The senior journeyman does and speaks thus: Behold, since you have not pretended to be a journeyman in this town of NN, masters and journeymen offer the Honest Welcome to you. You shall drink it down in two quaffs, being free to give the third one away. You must drink it with your shoulder covered and your head uncovered, your feet standing still, without moving or shifting or wiping your beard. If you can do it thus, your name shall be honored and praised and inscribed with white chalk on the black beam; if not, you shall be fined by masters and journeymen.

What reflection did this bring to mind?

That this way of drinking no doubt comes from the old Germans, to whom this was very important. Hence the well-known saying,

[1] Drinking vessel.

Canto meos Francos, qui se cervice supinant.
I praise my Francs, who wiggle their heads.[2]

What other reflection is to be retained here?

That the Welcome or drinking vessel decorated with pictures and emblems, from which everyone drinks, is somewhat comparable to those of the ancients. Thus we read in Vergil:

. . . pocula ponam
Fagina, Caelatum divini opus Alcimedonta.
Here I put the vessel, it was made by Alcimedon.

What else does it make us think of?

That our forebears had three kinds of drinks: 1) the drink of praise, with which they praised their gods and the deeds of their heroes; 2) the drink of refreshment, with which they quenched their thirst; and 3) the drink of love with which they sealed friendship and brotherhood.

V

What is the answer of the boy who is to be made a journeyman?

It is the following: I thank masters and journeymen for the Honest Welcome, and not only for [the cup] but also for the beer that was in it. The beer is too strong for me, and I am too weak for the beer; so I will duly pay the fine for it.

What reflection came to mind here?

That gratitude must always be shown and that nothing must be done against Nature.

What else is to be retained?

That excessive drinking is exceedingly harmful and sinful and comparable to the magic vessel of Circe, which bears this inscription:

Qui bibit inde; procul discedite queis est,
Cura bonae mentis; qui bibit inde, furit.
He who drinks of this will lose his senses;
If you have sense, flee from this place.

XVIII

What is the custom if a journeyman becomes ill?

[2] This makes no more sense in Latin or German than in English translation!

He is helped with the funds from the chest, and after he is well he repays or expresses his gratitude.

What is to be retained here?

That Christian charity requires us to assist our suffering neighbor with our fortune.

III. ABOUT MASTERS

I

How many years does one who wants to become a master have to travel?

One who is not a master's son has to travel for six years, but a master's son only four years.

What reflection did this bring to mind?

That traveling is a way to gather good experience in various things.[3]

II

What does he have to do when he applies for mastership?

In the Christmas quarter of the year he must go to the Alderman of the Guild and deposit his application fee, saying: Having spent my traveling years honorably, I now wish to settle down with an honorable Guild. According to custom, I herewith apply for admission. What other honorable people have done before me I also wish to do.

What reflection did this bring to mind?

That no one can come to his future trade with, as it were, unwashed hands, but that one must agree to and suffer what is the custom of the trade.

What else did it remind us of?

The well-known verse:

Multa tulit fecitque puer, sudavit et alsit.
The boy has borne much,
He has sweated and shivered.

III

What happens thereupon?

[3] It also suggests that masters' sons had privileges.

When he applies for the third time, he is asked to forego the company of the journeymen so that the master-piece will not become public. He is given the space of one month to bring it to perfection.

What reflection did this bring to mind?

That one who aims to attain a higher estate must leave certain things in his way of life, always remembering this:

> *Haec vita alios mores postulat.*
> This kind of life requires different ways.

IV

What, and how many, pieces is the young master required to make?

They are seven and twenty pieces, the most important being a priest's coat and a gusseted coat. In Nürnberg they make almost a hundred pieces.

V

How is this done?

Besides four masters and the Alderman of the Guild, two other masters are present. The above-named Alderman speaks thus to the prospective master: Hear now how you are to prove your master-piece by the material.

VI

What else happens?

Then he must declare how much [material] was used for every piece. This declaration is entered in a certain ledger which has three rubrics: namely, 1) good, 2) fair, and 3) ruined.

VII

What happens thereafter?

Now the so-called material man must draw the contour of each piece with a sharp piece of chalk and then withdraw. Then one master usually measures the length and one the width.

VIII

What else happens?

The Alderman asks the two who have measured whether they have found the work good, fair, or ruined. The answers are entered into the above-mentioned ledger.

IX

What else happens?

The material man must remove the chalk drawings with his sponge [and go on to the next group] until he has done all the pieces.

X

How long does this take him?

At least one day, from four o'clock in the morning until five in the afternoon.

XI

Are there exemptions for anybody?

Not for the master-piece.

XII

What happens after the master-piece is finished?

The prospective master will be refused [admission to the Guild] the first time, but asks [the masters] to be patient with him. On the third day, after he has already become a *Bürger* [full citizen], he again applies for admission to the Guild.

What reflection did this bring to mind?

That, in all things, we must show respect for our superiors, showing modesty in our dealings with them.

XIII

What happens thereupon?

The Alderman as well as the other four masters and scribes rise with their ceremonial coats on, and the Alderman says: Since you have proven your master-piece by the materials, I shall pronounce you a master by virtue of my office, conferred to me by the council of the town, in the name of GOD the Father, the Son, and the Holy Ghost.

Hereupon he proffers his Christian good wishes and the proceedings are ended with a banquet, to which the youngest [last-received] master must invite [the others].

35. Reforming the German Guilds?

THE LEGISLATION below clearly indicates the desire of public authorities, that is, the German principalities and municipal governments, to gain greater control over the guilds. The local authorities must confirm all new statutes or usages instituted by the guilds. Control of masters over their journeymen and apprentices is reinforced, including the granting of permission for a journeyman to move from one locality to another. Under the pretext of relaxing the severity of guild regulations toward journeymen, public officials shall have authority to review cases previously under exclusive guild control. The succeeding provisions for punishing wayward journeymen suggest that severity was not the exclusive province of the guild master. In fact, it would appear that the public authorities were responding to an appeal by the masters to discipline rebellious journeymen.

True, the ordinance condemns certain blatant examples of vocational discrimination (blatant at least to the modern eye). It also outlaws price fixing by the masters and favoritism shown to masters' sons and sons-in-law. But the main purpose of the ordinance is to strengthen, not weaken, the guild as an instrument of labor and production control.

Source: Hans Proesler, *Das gesamt-deutsche Handwerk im Spiegel der Reichgesetzgebung von 1530–1806* (Berlin, 1954), *Nürnberger Abhandlungen zu den Wirtschaft-und Sozialwissenschaften*, vol. 5, pp. 54ff.*

Opinion of the Imperial Diet
Concerning the Abuses of the Guilds,
Regensburg, August 14, 1731 [1]

IN VIEW of the fact that several rulings of the Diet concerning abuses in the guilds, especially those of the reform measures of

---

* Translated by permission of Dunker & Humblot Verlag, Berlin.
[1] The English version of this text is a paraphrase rather than a word-for-word translation of the original German, which is so redundant, complex, and stilted as to require considerable study even on the part of a modern German reader.

1530—title 39, item 1548, titles 36 and 37, item 1577, titles 37 and 38—dealing more particularly with servants, sons of masters, journeymen, and apprentices, have not been followed and since, moreover, new and different abuses have crept into the said guilds, it has been deemed necessary to renew, amend, and augment the regulations concerning the guilds of the latest ruling of the Diet *de anno* 1654 . . . as follows:

I

In the Holy Roman Empire the artisans shall not meet together without the knowledge of their public authorities, who may, if they see fit, send an observer to such meetings. No articles, customs, and usages shall be instituted anywhere without being confirmed by the regional, or at least local, authorities. All new statues instituted or to be instituted by the masters' or journeymen's guilds without the knowledge of the authorities shall be null and void.

Those who disregard his regulation, wherever it may be in the Holy Roman Empire, and introduce their own customs, also those who do not desist after having been punished by their authorities . . . shall not be admitted to any guild in the Holy Roman Empire, but shall be considered unfit for their trade by everyone and be publicly denounced proscribed *ad valvas curiarum* [at the doors of all city halls] and other public places until such time when, having served their sentence for this transgression, they are reinstated *publica autoritate* into their guild. This shall also apply to masters and journeymen who have disregarded this regulation, even if they have not been punished by the authorities in the above-mentioned manner.

. . . The masters shall retain a certain salutary control over journeymen and apprentices. In all guilds every apprentice who is indentured must deposit his birth certificate and other proofs of his origins in the chest of the guild. He must also deposit his certificate of apprenticeship when he is freed, leaving the originals of both in the said chest until such a time as he has decided to settle in a certain locality and become a master there. In this case he must produce a certified statement under the seal of the guild authorities of that locality. The guild [in which he has served his apprenticeship], on the other hand, must give him certified copies of these originals when he begins his travels in search of work in other localities . . . or else a letter concerning his conduct, . . . with which the journeyman can travel to other localities, where masters who need a journeyman are under firm obligation to aid him if he produces such a letter.

As soon as he begins work in the new locality, the journeyman must deposit the said documents in the chest of the local guild, leaving them there until he continues his travels. If a journeyman wishes to leave a locality where he has been working, he must so advise his master at least eight days prior to his departure, unless it is the custom to give more advance notice [the delays are as much as three to six months in the barbers' and printers' guilds]. Thereupon he must fulfill his obligations to the authorities and any other obligations he may have. The masters must be careful to find out whether the journeyman had to leave because of any undetected misdemeanor. They are under obligation to report any such misdemeanor to the authorities, being liable to prosecution for collusion if they fail. In such a case, the journeyman shall not be given his certificates, and must therefore remain in place until his case is settled.

Since it has happened all too frequently that the guilds, which were hitherto entitled to punish an accused journeyman, were excessively severe, the masters' guilds, and even more the journeymen's associations, shall henceforth no longer be permitted to withhold a journeyman's certificates or to punish him on their own authority. Such a case must be brought before the heads and officials of the guilds as well as before the public officials in charge of guild matters, and they shall examine the case quickly and without unnecessary pomp and circumstance and decide such matters free of charge. Unless it is a case that can be fairly settled by a minor penalty of one to two Rhenish florins and does not otherwise involve any dire consequences, the guilds are earnestly warned not to judge it on their own authority, but to consult with their regular local authorities. If, on the other hand, a journeyman has acted properly in all particulars and wants to continue his travels after having asked for leave within the appointed delays, he must be handed the certificates he had deposited on his arrival and be given a certificate of good conduct. . . .

Furthermore, if, after the publication of the present prohibition, a journeyman fails to receive the certificates he had deposited because of bad conduct and then dares proscribe and defame the guild which has refused to give him the said certificates, he shall be . . . apprehended, wherever he be in the Holy Roman Empire, as a mutinous criminal, be made to revoke his defamation at the locality it concerns, and be punished by more-or-less severe imprisonment, according to the circumstances. Should he flee abroad, and should extradition prove impossible, . . . any possessions and expected inheritances in his place of birth shall be lost to him. Should he be a foreigner, . . . he shall be declared an outlaw. . . .

IV

The public ordinance *de anno* 1548, title 37, and 1577, title 38, stating that the children of men in certain occupations shall not be excluded from guild offices, guilds, corporations, and trades shall remain in vigor, and shall henceforth be rigorously observed everywhere. Likewise the children of constables, wardens, gravediggers, night watchmen, jailers, cleaners of streets and waterways, shepherds, and, in short, the children of people in all occupations shall be comprised in this ordinance and be admitted to the guilds without fail, except for the children of flayers,[1] who must wait until the second generation, with the condition that the first generation has chosen an honorable occupation and continued in it as a family for thirty years. . . .[2]

X

In some guilds an abuse against all reason is beginning to spread: it is the custom of the journeymen, after an arrogant decision of their own, to summon the masters and order them to adhere to all manner of senseless rules. If the masters refuse to observe these, the journeymen defame and criticize them or even refuse to work. Another, related abuse consists of defaming and dishonoring those journeymen who work for such a master afterwards. Such disorder and insolence shall herewith . . . be absolutely abolished. . . .

Since a number of guilds have contracted the bad habit of

---

[1] The flayer, whose occupation consisted of removing the skins from animals deceased from natural causes, was as sinister a figure as the executioner in the public imagination.

[2] One might detect here an effort by the government to look after its own civil servants.

swearing future masters to secrecy concerning the hidden practices of their guild, they are herewith absolved from their oath, and the authorities shall henceforth no longer tolerate any secret organizations, under severe penalties.

XI

Since it has frequently happened that the guilds . . . discriminate against illegitimately begotten children born before and after the ecclesiastic ceremony, as well as against those who were legitimized by us as the Imperial Majesty or otherwise by Imperial Authority, and that certain guilds also refuse to admit into their ranks those who marry a woman who was impregnated by another man while still unmarried and those who were forced as a punishment to marry the person with whom they have fornicated, the above-mentioned difference [between "legitimately" and "illegitimately begotten"] shall be abolished. . . .

XIII

Beyond this, the following disorders and abuses have crept into the guilds.

1. The tanners defame each other in several places over working with dog hides and other unnecessary quibbles. Those who do not work with these materials wish to declare the others dishonorable and also wish to impose penalties on those who have worked in places where it is done. Likewise, some guilds want to declare dishonorable any artisan who has killed a dog or a cat either with a stone or by throwing or drowning it, or if he has so much as touched a dead animal. . . . They go so far as to enable a gravedigger to exact a fee of release from any artisan whom he has dishonored by poking him with a knife or other weapon; moreover, it is often made a cause of dishonor to have eaten, driven, or walked with a gravedigger, to have been one of his pallbearers, or to have attended his funeral or that of a member of his family, even if it has happened unintentionally. Also, it is often considered a cause for dishonor to have cut down, removed, or helped to bury a "suicide from melancholy," declared such by the authorities; item, if in times of war and pestilence there is no gravedigger to remove the dead animals from the stables and to help bury them. Also, some guilds have often caused great difficulties to the

clothmakers, and even their children, who have worked with wool taken from dead animals.

2. The following practices are henceforth declared abuses: The custom of certain guilds prohibiting any master from finishing what another has begun, especially with respect to the surgeons and barbers, who refuse to open the bandages or continue the treatment of an injured person started by another, even upon the patient's request. It is an abuse to defame barbers and surgeons for treating criminals who have been subjected to torture. Certain guilds want to hamper a son in the exercise of his trade because of a crime committed by his parents. If a customer wishes to change artisans, [it is an abuse] if the second master refuses to finish the work of the first, even though the first master has been paid. Likewise, it is an abuse for a master not to take over, or otherwise handle, a piece of work that has been made by and bought from . . . another master.

3. It is an abuse if, as sometimes happens, the artisans make a pact among themselves, agreeing that none of them will sell for a lower price or work for a lower daily wage than the others; also to agree among themselves about the prices they intend to ask, so that the buyer or the person who commissions work at a daily wage is obliged to pay whatever they ask.

4. It is an abuse not to accept artisans who have been imprisoned and examined because of a suspected crime but proven innocent by the test of torture or other legal means and exonerated by the authorities.

5. It is an abuse to exclude a master who has committed a crime after he has served his penalty, or to exclude a master whose wife has committed a crime, if he takes her back after she has served her penalty and is given a *restitutio famae*, or to exclude a person who has only been suspected in either of these cases, for such a person either was never disqualified at all, or at least he was rehabilitated. An even more irresponsible abuse is committed if the entire guild is declared dishonorable and if, as a result, the journeymen leave their masters, defame each other, and impose penalties upon each other for these reasons.

6. In several places no one may become a master if he is already married. In other places, an unmarried journeyman who has qualified as a master is not permitted to exercise his trade and establish

himself until he has married, and he must marry into the guild
[e.g., a master's widow or daughter].

7. In certain places a young master, even though he has traveled
for many years as a journeyman, may not exercise his trade unless
he has lived in that place for a certain number of years, having
visited the so-called confraternity for some years, or unless he has
paid a certain sum in order to become a member of the guild. In
other places, on the contrary, the sons of the local masters, and
also those who marry the widows and daughters of the local masters, are given certain advantages, such as a shorter traveling
period and, later, an easier master-piece—all to the detriment of
the community, which is thereby burdened with inferior artisans.
In other places, no more than a certain number of masters, fixed
once and for all time, will be admitted to the guild; also, a particularly industrious and skillful master who has more work than his
colleagues will not be permitted to have more journeymen than
his fellow masters. . . . [All these practices are declared "abuses."]

XIV

In view of the above ordinances, as well as those proscribing
irresponsible journeymen from leaving, striking against, or ridiculing and defaming their masters—the true sources of the deplorable state into which the guilds have fallen—it is hoped that
in their own interest, masters and journeymen will henceforth be
more sedate in their ways, showing due obedience to their appointed [civil] authorities. Nonetheless, it has proven absolutely
necessary to abandon our former patience and to point out in all
seriousness to masters and journeymen that, if they continue in
their irresponsible, evil, and stubborn ways, the Emperor and the
Diet might easily be moved, following the examples of other
countries, and in the interest of the public, which is hurt by such
criminal, private quarrels, to suppress and abolish the guilds altogether.[3]

[Instructions follow as to the publication and enforcement of
these ordinances.]

[3] It is doubtful whether the public authorities in Germany wanted to do
this. Properly controlled, the guilds could serve as an instrument of police
power, labor discipline, and public order. The regulations here prohibit
price fixing but they make no breach in guild regulations on quality, probably the greatest impediment to increased production.

36. Journeymen's Associations in Marseilles, 1787

JOURNEYMEN'S ASSOCIATIONS (*compagnonnages*) dated from the late Middle Ages and were divided into several sects or *devoirs*. These organized the journeymen not only against the masters but also against other *devoirs*. While masters frequently faced strikes, public authorities were disturbed by fighting between different journeymen's associations. The Marseilles documents concern the *garçons du devoir* and the *gavots*, who precipitated street fights, causing authorities to close the various public houses, cafés, and *guinguettes* where the journeymen met and to impose a curfew. While the motives for resistance to the masters and master's guilds are clear enough, historians have been more curious about the fighting among the various *devoirs*. These rivalries probably arose from the fact that there was not enough work for all journeymen, so that the members of one *devoir* tried to prevent the members of another *devoir* from finding work with the masters of the town. This was often done by making newcomers pay a fee to the *compagnonnage* of three livres, or about four days' wages. A refusal by the newcomer to pay this fee could easily lead to fighting. Some features of the modern "closed shop" are clearly recognizable here.

A particularly spectacular series of brawls in Marseilles in the summer of 1787 prompted the Parlement of Provence to investigate the statutes of the *garçons du devoir*. The results of this inquest were published as a preface to a ruling of the Parlement against the association of journeymen hatmakers, known formally as the "Luminary of Saint Catherine." These statutes suggest a rather tightly organized, permanent association, complete with emblems, liturgy, and dues.

Public authorities throughout Europe, including England, were increasingly hostile to such embryonic unionism. The French revolutionary leadership outlawed all such journeymen's guilds in the Le Chapelier Law of 1791, later incorporated into the Napoleonic Code. In England the same objectives were achieved by a whole series of statues, climaxing in the Combination Acts of 1799. Journeymen's associations were considered subversive, as the passage below makes clear. They were in a class apart from the craft and masters' guilds, which public authorities were more inclined to manage than destroy.

Source: E. Isnard, ed., "*Documents inédits sur l'histoire du compagnonnage à Marseilles au XVIIIme siècle*" in J. Hayem, ed., *Mémoires et documents pour servir à l'histoire du commerce et de l'industrie en France* (Paris, 1916), vol. IV, pp. 208–209.

THE DIFFERENT workers or journeymen meet in various convents, and, with the excuse of having masses performed and paying for them out of the common fund, they keep their money chests in the said convents. They make the newcomers pay in order to have access to these funds and then chase them out if they refuse to pay the arbitrary sums imposed upon them. When there is a certain sum of money in the said chests, they band together and riot, leaving the masters without assistance and trying to force them [the masters] to pay what they demand. They also leave their shops for several days, filling the public houses to celebrate, and are armed with sticks decorated with ribbons and little flags. They also pit association against association and engage in the most ferocious fighting. They have statutes providing for regular meetings, specifying fines, and authorizing their members to prevent those who have not paid the dues they have arbitrarily imposed from working and to pursue them as rebels. Article II of the statute book of the hatmakers of the same town [Marseilles] carries license so far as to forbid workers to make more than two hats per day or be fined 6 livres, while those who have learned of such a case and fail to report it [to the organization] shall be fined 3 livres. All these rules, it is said, apply to the whole association [of garçons du devoir].

They claim they are authorized to assemble as a venerable pious institution known as the Luminary of St. Catherine. In principle this authorization had been given, since the association originally seemed to be of some value, but it has now led to the most serious abuses. . . .

The tanners also have statute books. These two associations have been the initiators of the last riot in Marseilles. Both have chests in the convents of Les Recollets, La Palud, and Les Picpus, and both have very frequent assemblies. Last Sunday, they assembled again, two hundred of them, and deliberated about a new contribution.

Everything about such acts is illicit, clandestine, and contrary to every law and regulation, old or new. We must completely destroy these unruly and abusive associations. It is time to safeguard those who do not want to become involved in daily disturbances, and it is time to bridle the leaders by all possible means.

37. *An Apprenticeship Contract*

DESPITE the renewed vitality of the guilds, not all artisans belonged to them. Here we have an example of a contract of apprenticeship coming under no apparent guild regulation. It is likely that this was more frequently the case in France than in the smaller towns and principalities of the Empire.

Source: *"Archives de la Corrèze, E-947"* in J. Hayem, ed., *Mémoires et documents pour servir à l'histoire du commerce et de l'industrie en France* (Paris, 1916), vol. III, p. 86.

Contract of Apprenticeship for the Gunsmithing Trade, 1704

DONE AT Tulle, Bas-Limousin, the twenty-first of November, 1704, in the afternoon, before the undersigned Royal Notary . . .

Were present Antoinette Faugeyron, widow of Jean Haste, master glovemaker, who of her own will has apprenticed her son, Jean Haste, present here, to Claude Serre, gunsmith of this town, also present here, who accepts him in order to teach him well and conscientiously, as much as is in his power, the art of gunsmithing, which consists in the filing and forging of gunplates. [The said Serre] promises to teach him the secrets necessary to that effect. The said apprenticeship has been contracted for two years, beginning today and to be finished on the same day at the end of the said two years, during which time the said Serre shall feed and lodge the said apprentice and furnish him all the tools necessary to the said trade, and the said Faugeyron shall furnish his clothes and do his laundry, and all the work done by the said apprentice during the said time shall belong to the said Serre. The said apprentice shall not leave without a legitimate excuse, in which case the said Serre can take another [apprentice] at the expense of the said Faugeyron; conversely, the said Serre cannot dismiss the said apprentice without a legitimate excuse, and in this case the latter can learn another trade at the expense of the said Serre. Also, the present apprenticeship has been contracted at the price of 30 livres, half to be paid in cash now and half after the end of one year [by the widow Haste]. . . .

VI

The Poor

"ENGLAND, BAD as she is, is yet a Reforming Nation." [1] Defoe's statement is confirmed more in the efforts of reformers than in the social legislation obtained. The historian is immediately struck by the prodigious amount of pamphlets, brochures, and books devoted to this and that particular social problem. The roster of English single-causers begins with such dedicated men as Child, Davenant, Burn, Gee, the two Fieldings, Gilbert, Hanway, Howard, and Eden, ably seconded by a regiment of more neutral fact finders led by Gregory King, John Massie, John Aikin, and Patrick Colquhoun. There seems little doubt that these individuals made a major contribution to social "improvement" by widely publicizing the precise measure of human suffering. Their empirical approach, conveyed by an already advanced free press, awakened a social conscience that precedes the Victorians by a full century. As Henry Fielding put it in 1753: "But if we were to make a Progress through the Outskirts of this Town, and look into the Habitations of the Poor, we should there behold such Pictures of human Misery as must move the Compassion of every Heart that deserves the Name of Human." [2]

In England much of the debate centered on the Elizabethan Poor Law, its cost, effectiveness, and improvability. And although few of these pamphleteers failed to allude to the necessity of self-help and the "culpable causes of indigence," almost all agreed that there were innocent and accidental reasons for poverty that no civilized nation could ignore. They focused attention on improving the local administration of poor relief, eliminating callous labor contractors and greedy overseers, exhorting the gentry to do more than pay their poor rates, and improving the workhouses. Indeed, the workhouse need not be uni-

---

[1] Daniel Defoe, *Review* (December 26, 1706), quoted in Dorothy George, *London Life in the Eighteenth Century* (London, 1925), p. 1.
[2] Henry Fielding, *A Proposal for Making an Effective Provision for the Poor* (Dublin, 1753), p. 10. Fielding notes that some members of Parliament made this "progress" and were struck by the poverty. Here was a first step toward action.

versally regarded as a kind of Bastille, but rather as a potential refuge for the indigent, ill, aged, and helpless. To read Eden's cold statistics on the workhouse diet is to realize that a pauper consumed meat and even beer at least twice a week in England. This is not to suggest that the workhouse was a country hostelry, but such a diet should be contrasted with the almost pure carbohydrate consumption of continental peasants, not to mention the meager fare served in European prisons and *hôpitaux*. To be sure, we have more to learn about local justice and poor relief in such places as Hungary or Poland, but the firm hold of serfdom in these areas suggests conditions only slightly better than in Russia.

Reactions to the problem of poverty in France were different than those in England. Few of the great names of the Enlightenment made poverty their primary or even secondary concern, and a French Eden or Fielding is hard to find. Administrative statistical studies of local conditions there were, but with little of the moral dedication and purpose one discerns in the English improvers. Of course, the lack of a developed free press and the absence of a national legislature limited the scope of action for any single-causer. But there were other, perhaps deeper, differences. There was no regular poor relief and no interest on the part of the local aristocracy to provide it in France. Seigneurial justice was more often employed to enforce collection of dues than to relieve misery. True, the royal administration made efforts to alleviate the worst effects of a bad harvest, but on an *ad hoc* basis and primarily to maintain public order and assure the collection of royal taxes. The Church, of course, had its charities and bore the greatest burden of poor relief, but this effort could not compare with the comprehensive and well-financed English system. French observers of poverty were more likely to be strict "Malthusians," arguing that chronic epidemic and disease were the inevitable consequences of over-population. Contrast the pessimism—indeed alarm—of Restif de la Bretonne, the "nocturnal spectator" of the Parisian scene, with the cautious optimism of Defoe or Fielding:

> Among all our men of letters, I am perhaps the only one who knows the common people and mingles with them. I want to describe them; I want to be the sentinel of orderly conditions. I have gone down into the lowest classes in order to see everything that is vile. Beware, philosophers! Love for humanity may lead you astray! What you call the best may be the worst! The people must not earn too much; they are like stomachs swollen and rendered sluggish by too much food. In the belief that you do good—listen to the words of experience—you may bring on total ruin . . .[3]

[3] Restif de la Bretonne, *Les Nuits de Paris or Nocturnal Spectator: A Selection*, trans., L. Asher and E. Fertig (New York, 1964), p. 68. Reprinted by permission of Alfred A. Knopf, Inc.

38. English Social Structure, 1688 and 1803

AMONG THE predecessors of our contemporary statistically oriented historians are a number of English "calculators" of exceptional merit. Gregory King and Patrick Colquhoun were persistent tablemakers, concerned with establishing the taxable income of each social group in the England of their time. True, Colquhoun's table was not really an estimate of national income, since none of the eighteenth-century calculators were able to measure savings, increases in capital or stock, or revenues from trusts or colleges. The tax and census data with which they worked yielded only consumed family income.

This has been disappointing to the economist anxious to determine per capita and national income or to the demographer needing information on age composition or birth and death rates. Fortunately, social historians are less demanding of their sources. Despite the problems of overlapping and changing categories and a certain imprecision in statistics based on hearth taxes or poor rates, the tables of King and Colquhoun tell a great deal about the structure of English society. Between 1688 and 1803 the population of England and Wales almost doubled, and consumed income increased fivefold. The relative portion of income from agriculture fell from 38 to 22 per cent, while the income from trade and manufacturing rose from 17 to 46 per cent of the total—a dramatic change in the income structure of the nation. Equally interesting, the upper-income groups—peers, gentry, manufacturers, merchants—seemed to have increased their wealth more rapidly than other social groups. The gentry retained about 15 per cent of the national income in both years, which means a fivefold increase in their actual incomes over the century. The absolute number of paupers and vagrants remained almost constant at 1.3 million. Needless to add, these observations do not signify uniform changes; two points over 115 years cannot tell us what an annual census can. But the historian would gladly settle for similar data for each of the European countries in 1688 and 1803.[1]

Source: Patrick Colquhoun, *Treatise on Indigence Exhibiting a General View of the National Resources for Productive Labour With Propositions for Ameliorating the Conditions of the Poor* (London, 1806), p. 23. (Tables)

[1] See Peter Mathias, "The Social Structure in the Eighteenth Century: A Calculation by Joseph Massie," *Economic History Review*, second series, X (1957), 30–45.

A General View of the National Income and State of Society,
in England and Wales,
According to Mr. Gregory King's Estimate, Anno 1688

Number of Heads of Families	Ranks, Degrees, Titles, and Descriptions	Persons in each Family	Aggregate Number of Persons in the Family of each Rank	Yearly Income £.	Aggregate Income of each Rank £. Sterling
160	Temporal peers	40	6,400	3,200	512,000
26	Spiritual lords	20	520	1,300	33,800
800	Baronets	16	12,800	880	704,000
600	Knights	13	7,800	650	390,000
3,000	Esquires	10	30,000	450	1,200,000
12,000	Gentlemen	8	96,000	280	2,380,000
5,000	Persons in greater offices and places	8	40,000	240	1,200,000
5,000	Persons in lesser ditto	6	30,000	120	600,000
2,000	Eminent merchants by sea	8	16,000	400	800,000
8,000	Lesser merchants by sea	6	48,000	198	1,600,000
10,000	Persons of the law	7	70,000	154	1,540,000
2,000	Eminent clergymen	6	12,000	72	144,000
8,000	Lesser clergymen	5	40,000	50	400,000
40,000	Freeholders of the better sort	7	280,000	91	3,640,000

A General View of the National Income and State of Society, in England and Wales,
According to Mr. Gregory King's Estimate, Anno 1688 (Cont'd)

Number of Heads of Families	Ranks, Degrees, Titles, and Descriptions	Persons in each Family	Aggregate Number of Persons in the Family of each Rank	Yearly Income	Aggregate Income of each Rank
120,000	Lesser freeholders	5½	660,000	55	6,600,000
150,000	Farmers	5	750,000	42½	6,375,000
15,000	Persons of the liberal arts and sciences	5	75,000	60	300,000
50,000	Shopkeepers and tradesmen	4⅓	225,000	45	2,250,000
60,000	Artisans and handicrafts	4	240,000	38	2,280,000
5,000	Naval officers	4	20,000	80	400,000
4,000	Military officers	4	16,000	60	240,000
35,000	Common soldiers	2	70,000	14	490,000
50,000	Common seamen	3	150,000	20	1,000,000
364,000	Labouring people	3⅓	1,275,000	15	5,460,000
400,000	Cottagers and paupers	3⅓	1,300,000	6½	2,000,000
	Vagrants, beggars, gipsies, thieves, and prostitutes	—	30,000	—	60,000
1,349,586 Net Totals		4⅓	5,500,520	4⅓	£43,491,800

SUMMARY RECAPITULATION OF THE TABLE, 1803

Description of Classes	Single Persons	Families	Aggregate Number of Persons	Aggregate Incomes £.
1. The Sovereign, for himself, his Queen, and resident family	—	1	50	200,000
2. Peers, country gentlemen, and freeholders of lands and houses, &c. mines, minerals, funds, and public incomes	—	167,177	898,775	32,241,000
3. Persons having colonial and East India property, funds, and jointures, &c. including foreign incomes	—	20,000	160,000	14,000,000
4. Merchants and bankers, deriving income from trade, funds, lands, &c.	—	15,000	111,000	15,600,000
5. Ship-owners, deriving income from freights and other property	—	5,000	25,000	2,500,000
6. Manufacturers of all descriptions, including ships, houses, works, &c. &c.	—	55,300	301,800	24,960,000
7. Inland traders and shopkeepers of all descriptions, trading on capitals, including publicans	—	125,000	625,500	16,575,000
8. Agriculturists or farmers, graziers, and dealers in cattle, &c.	—	160,000	960,000	19,200,000
9. Established clergy, and dissenters from the church duly ordained	—	13,526	68,890	2,104,000
10. Liberal professions—law, *physic, literary*, and the *fine arts*	—	27,300	136,500	8,088,000
11. Persons employed in the education of youth, including universities	—	20,500	122,000	3,300,000

Summary Recapitulation of the Table, 1803 (Cont'd)

Description of Classes	Single Persons	Families	Aggregate Number of Persons	Aggregate Incomes
12. Persons employed in theatrical and musical exhibitions	—	500	2,000	400,000
13. Civil and military labourers for the state, and in its defence, &c.	387,079	110,675	466,500	17,494,575
14. Labourers in agriculture, manufactures, commerce, navigation, and fisheries, &c. exclusive of menial servants	—	1,183,004	5,226,646	53,511,720
15. Hawkers and pedlars, with and without licenses	2,500	800	4,000	100,000
16. Persons employing capitals in asylums for lunatics and deranged persons	—	40	400	20,000
17. Lunatics supported in asylums	2,500	—	2,500	75,000
18. Persons confined in prisons for debt	3,510	2,000	10,000	87,750
19. Vagrants, gipsies, common prostitutes, and criminal offenders in prisons and at large	222,000	—	222,000	2,220,000
20. Paupers included among the class of labourers who only earn part of their subsistence, the deficiency made up by parishes to the amount of	1,040,716	—	—	4,267,000
21. Persons, included in all the above description of families, who have money in the funds or otherwise, either as trustees for orphans, minors, and charitable institutions, or on their own account	—	—	—	5,055,955
		1,905,823	9,343,561	222,000,000

39. *Eden's* State of the Poor

SIR FREDERICK EDEN wrote only one major work. It made him famous, and rightly so, for his voluminous *State of the Poor* represents perhaps the most complete compilation of the material conditions of England's poorer classes at the end of the eighteenth century available any-where.[1] Eden was a statistician and "calculator" more than a single-causer. As for poor relief, he was a firm believer in self-help and, like Patrick Colquhoun, he was certain that there were "culpable" as well as "innocent" causes of indigence. Among the former were want of industry, frugality, and economy. Wise legislation, therefore, would do well to emulate the Quakers, who had prevented beggary from arising among their brethren.

Eden's second volume contains parochial reports, veritable store-houses of information on construction, housing, population, rents, taxes, workhouses, employment, grain prices, wages, and expenses of day laborers.[2] By selecting Liverpool and Walton-upon-Thames, the editors hope to demonstrate a difference of the treatment of the poor in the large city and the small village parish. The Liverpool poor appear to have been well cared for, with semi-private rooms, regular employment for the able-bodied, and a diet which included beef, but-ter, ale, and beer—all at modest cost. In Walton, where the land tax was three times as high (6.5 per cent), it seems to have been much more difficult to employ the poor, and apparently there was less will-ingness to spend money on them. City resources and organization, unavailable to a village like Walton, were not without their benefits to the indigent.

Source: Sir Frederick M. Eden, *The State of the Poor* (London, 1797), vol. I, part II, pp. 585–588; vol. II, pp. 327–330; vol. III, 723–724.

Relief and Employment of the Poor

HAD RELIEF of the able-bodied Poor been in the contemplation of the framers of the 43d Eliz. or had it been expected that the Rates would have been that enormous tax on the landed property which

---

[1] It is not surprising that Marx found Eden's work very interesting.
[2] Summaries of baptisms and burials, so important to historical demography, can be found in the section on The Family.

they now are, the clause, which directs the assessment to be made by the overseers, would not have been so loosely worded as to leave it a matter of doubt whether personal property should or should not be rated.

The Poor Laws, as delivered by the Statute 43 Eliz. c. 2. and the preceding Statutes, appear to have had two objects in view, 1. the relief of the impotent Poor; and, 2. the employment of the able-bodied and idle. In considering the first division of the system, we enter on an investigation connected with the nicest principles of jurisprudence. Whether compulsive charity can be justified; or whether the refinements of morality can be enforced by the sanction of positive law, are questions which admit of considerable doubt. A distinction is justly made by Montesquieu, between the duties of religion, the infringements of which are punishable only in a future world, and the moral duties, which are (if I may use the expression,) more tangible in this, or more amenable to human laws. But, whatever may have been the intention of the Legislature with respect to the enforcement of that moral, and (as described in the New Testament) that divine charity, the overt act, which consists in the giving alms, was the only part of it that could be enforced. The impracticability of compelling this charity according to every man's ability, is the only reason why personal property is not assessed: the presumption of the Law is, that it should be assessed. This impracticability is a material argument against the whole of the system; but the wealth and the humanity of this nation would never have suffered this question to have been agitated, if the execution of this part of the Poor Laws had been as confined as its design. It is not precisely known how soon after the promulgation of the Poor Laws the two parts of the system were blended; but it may be suspected that the evil had grown to some enormity when it became necessary that the settlement of Paupers should be ascertained with accuracy and precision. But if the first part was objectionable on grounds of more recondite law, the second part proceeded upon the supposed existence of facts in political economy, which was doubtful at the time, but which experience has since proved to be mistaken. The framers of the Poor Laws conceived that the capital of individuals was inadequate to the employment of the labouring Poor of the kingdom, and that it was necessary to provide a public stock for their employment. This

mistake was then more excusable, because, since that time, and
even to the present, most of the theoretic systems for the employment and maintenance of the Poor have proceeded on the
same, or similar, principles. It is a most satisfactory circumstance,
however irreconcilable with the deductions of visionary spec-
ulatists, to have the proofs of this mistake in our possession; to
shew that the capital stock of the Public cannot enter into competition with the capital, and well-exerted industry, of individuals; and that the Poor, even when working in public establishments for little or no wages, cannot earn sufficient for their own
support. In gaols, every thing is in favour of public capital with
respect to health and strength, in comparison with the infirm Poor
of a work-house: but, (as it is justly observed by Sir George
Paul, in his Address to the Magistrates of the county of Glou-
cester) "the working by machine in almost every branch of hard
labour, that requires no skill, has so completely undervalued such
work by hand," (and the same remark will apply to various kinds
of work which require considerable skill) "that the public expectation should not be raised too high, relative to the *productive*
consequences of forced labour."

By the blending these two systems in practice, a kind of glare,
which obscures the truth, has been thrown upon work-houses and
houses of industry, where, I am induced to believe, from experience and actual observation, the saving arises from the decreased
expence, in accommodations, which takes place in consequence of
a number of Poor being collected together. The advantages,
therefore, are only negative; and so far, and no farther, have they
merit. This is the merit of the public kitchen of Munich, and of
the much-vaunted work-house of Shrewsbury.

If a system of national maintenance of the infirm and impotent
has failed, or been perverted, we have surely some reason to hesitate on the adoption of a system of national education, which is
founded on one of the principles of the Poor Law. Mr. Pitt is too
good a political economist, not to know that the waste of capital
is a national, as well as an individual, loss; and he must look
forward to this national loss, when national education is made a
part of the law of the land. The maxim "pas trop gouverner," was
never more fully illustrated than in the review of the system of
the Poor Laws. A small attention to the practice of ministerial
powers will convince us of the caution with which they should be

delegated; and of the difficulty (I had almost said the impracticability) of laying down any regulations of positive law, for the relief and instruction of the Poor, which shall not degenerate into abuse.

The Poor should not be deceived: the best relief they can receive must come from themselves. Were the Rates once limited, the price of labour would necessarily advance. To expend what labour actually produces, in the most beneficial manner for the labourer, depends entirely on good management and economy.

This economy in all cases is the more to be urged, because the difference in comforts of the same families, at the same expence, well or ill conducted, is greater often than that of different families at different expences. There is more difference, comparatively, in the mode of living from economy, than from income; the deficiency in income may possibly be made up by increase of work or wages; but the want of economy is irremediable, and the least income in question *with it*, will do more than the greatest *without it*. No master can in the first place afford wages; next, no overseer can make allowance; lastly, no magistrate can order relief, enough, on any calculation but that of their being severally well managed. If the Poor do not prudently serve themselves, none can effectually assist them; if they are not their own friends, none can sufficiently befriend them: the idle in procuring, or the wasteful in using, the means of subsistence, have neither merit in themselves to deserve, nor have others power to grant them, that supply, which is alone due, and can be alone afforded, to the honest, industrious, and prudent. It highly then interests all conversant with the Poor, who ought to be literally all, and it is hoped are most, to consult and co-operate with them in the practice of economy; it is far more useful to teach them to spend less, or to save a little, than to give them much more.

The above [from the *Annals of Agriculture*] is certainly a very striking passage, and well deserves that attention and consideration which it seems to solicit. It is to be regretted, that this pleasing writer did not see fit to give his Readers some detail of that polity which he appears so justly to admire, and which it is so much the interest of all orders and classes to emulate. Much as it falls within the scope of this Work to go into the discussion, *data* seem to be wanting for it to all but the immediate members of the society in question. Quakers only can know, or inform others with accuracy, how far it is, or is not, true, that there neither are, nor have been, any Quaker beggars; nor, what is neither less extraordinary nor less commendable, any Parochial Poor, of their sect. They, however, will forgive one, who, far from entertaining any ill-will towards their society, has a very sincere respect for it; yet doubts, whether there may not be something like a fallacy in the foregoing extract. There is reason to believe that the people of this society advert, with great care and strictness, to the moral conduct, as well as to the religious faith, of their members: and considering, with great propriety, the want of industry, frugality, and economy, (those instances of misconduct which most generally lead to poverty,) as the least pardonable moral delinquencies, they rarely fail to check their weaker brethren in their first deviations into idleness and extravagance, by admonitions of singular earnestness and weight. If, after such warning, the delinquents are incorrigible, and, continuing to be profligate, become also poor, they are then looked upon as irreclaimable offenders, unworthy of being any longer regarded as *Friends;* and so, in the phraseology of the Society, are *read out,* i.e. are expelled. Hence, there is reason to believe, that, though it may be true, that there *are* no Quaker beggars, nor any Quakers who receive parochial aid, there may be, and no doubt are, many under both these descriptions, who *have been* Quakers. As, however, neither the members of the National Church, nor the people of the nation at large, have any such coercive authority over disorderly persons, to check them in their progress to ruin, they are forced, in ten thousand instances, to see them first become spendthrifts, and then Paupers. And, having no power of rejection, any more than they have of restraint, like the net thrown into the sea, they must needs receive all who offer; and, among others, no doubt, sometimes reprobate Quakers.

Still, however, the case does not cease to be extraordinary; and, as such, it still merits consideration. For, admitting the fact to be as it is here suggested, that the Quakers really have not, strictly speaking, any Poor among them, the means they take to prevent it, shew very clearly, that they consider the want of industry, and the want of frugality, not only as the natural fore-runners, but as the general causes, of poverty. The instruction, therefore, conveyed to us by this striking fact, is, that, instead of exerting ourselves, as hitherto has been the case, only to relieve indigence and distress, however produced, it might not be beneath legislative wisdom to emulate the better policy of this prudent sect, and, if possible, fall on ways and means to prevent them.

The singular economy and good management which are to be found among Quakers, are highly deserving of general imitation: it may, however, be doubted, whether the accounts which are usually given respecting the Poor, that are to be found among this respectable order, are altogether correct. Dr. Lettsom, in his Memoirs of Dr. Fothergill, observes, that "what is familiar and near us excites little scrutiny or investigation; but the time may come, when a wise Legislator may descend to enquire, by what medium a whole society, in both the old and new world, is made to think and act with uniformity for upwards of a century;—by what polity, without emolument from Government, they have become the only people on earth free from poverty:—by what economy they have thus prevented beggary and want among any of their members, whilst the nation groans under taxes for the Poor." . . .

Liverpool

The parish of Liverpool contains, by admeasurement, 2102 acres. Mr. Simmons, the general overseer, took the number of houses and population in 1790, of which the following is an account:

Number of Front houses 6540,	containing 39188	inhabitants
Back houses 1608,	7955	inhabitants
Cellars 1728,	6780	inhabitants
In the work-house	1220	
Charity school	300	
Infirmary	150	
Seamen's hospital	83	
Alms-houses	126	
Total	55732	
Houses inhabited,		
exclusive of cellars	8148	
Empty houses	717	
Total number of houses	8865	

Since that period, it is supposed that 300 or 400 houses have been built. Dr. Aikin mentions an enumeration having been made in 1773, the result of which is as follows:—

Inhabited houses	5928
Untenanted houses	412
Families	8002
Inhabitants	34407
Number of persons to a house	5 4/5
Number to a family	4 1/3

It appears from the subjoined bills of mortality, that 1397, the number of christenings in 1773, was to 34407, the number of the then existing inhabitants, as 1 to 24¾ nearly; and that 1109, the number of burials in 1773, was to the number of inhabitants as 1 to 31. From these proportions, we are, in some degree, enabled to calculate the population of Liverpool, at the two succeeding periods of 1790, and 1794.

2244 christenings in 1790 × by 24¾ = 55539 inhabitants
1763 burials   in 1790 × by 31   = 54653 inhabitants
2527 christenings in 1794 × by 24¾ = 62544 inhabitants
2009 burials   in 1794 × by 31   = 62279 inhabitants

These proportions tally very well with Mr. Simmons's enumeration, and are, probably, near the truth.

75 seamen were raised by the town of Liverpool, in pursuance of the late Act for manning the Navy; so that reckoning one man for 68 rateable houses, (the proportion which has been observed in most parts of England,) we may estimate the number of houses subject to the window-tax at 5100; and the number of houses exempted at about 4000. The number of inns and ale-houses is 917; so that every tenth house, at least, is a public-house. The magistrates, however, are certainly extremely attentive to this branch of police, and reduce the number of unnecessary public-houses, whenever a fair opportunity offers. It is said that a few years ago, there were 1500.

The subjoined tables exhibit the growth of population in Liverpool; the great progress of its commerce; and the still more rapid increase of its Poor's Rates. It is, however, consoling to reflect, that, notwithstanding this apparent disproportion, the resources of wealth are more than adequate to the calls of charity; and that the Poor of Liverpool, although more numerous, and proportionably more expensive than they were 30 years ago, are yet less

burthensome to the town, than when its trade was less flourishing, and its parochial expenditure more contracted.

It is hardly necessary to add, that every branch of employment,
connected with foreign commerce, is here carried on with great
exertion, and great success. The neighbourhood of Manchester is,
perhaps, more congenial to manufactures; but some, very important ones, that are not peculiar to a sea-port, may be found at
Liverpool. The most considerable are glass-houses, salt-works,
copperas-works, copper and iron-works, sugar-houses, rasping
and other mills, breweries, roperies, watch-movements, and stocking manufactories.

The rent of land, in the neighbourhood of the town, is from £4
to £6 the statute acre. The land-tax is very low, and is supposed to
amount to about 6d. in the pound [2½ per cent] on the net rental.

No correct information could be obtained relative to Friendly
Societies in Liverpool: their number is about 12; and the members, in each, are from 80 to 100. In one of the Societies, the
members meet once a fortnight, spend 3d. and pay 1s. into the
box: members of 2 years standing are allowed, when sick, 15s. a
week; superannuated members, 8s. a week during life. From £10
to £20 according to the time a man has been a member, are paid,
on his decease, to his widow, if there is one; or to his children; or,
in default of children, to his legal representatives. The Society is
governed by a president and stewards, with the assistance of a
committee of four members; bye-laws are made by a majority of
the whole body.

The Poor are partly maintained in the work-house, and partly
relieved at home. The work-house is well situated, on a rising
ground, in a detached situation; and is, in many respects, constructed upon an eligible plan. The old people, in particular, are
provided with lodging, in a most judicious manner: each apartment consists of three small rooms, in which are 1 fire-place and 4
beds, and is inhabited by 8 or 10 persons. These habitations are
furnished with beds, chairs, and other little articles of domestic
use, that the inmates may possess; who, being thus detached from
the rest of the Poor, may consider themselves as comfortably
lodged as in a secluded cottage; and thus enjoy, in some degree,
(even in a work-house,) the comforts of a private fire-side. The
most infirm live on the ground floors: others are distributed

through two upper stories. They all dine together in a large room, which serves occasionally for a chapel.

The children are, principally, employed in picking cotton, but are too much crowded together: 70 or 80 work in a small room. About 50 girls are bound apprentices to a person who attends in the house, and employs them in sprigging muslin. The house receives a small weekly sum for their work during their apprenticeship. The sum is from 1s. to 2s. 6d. a week, according to their proficiency in tambour-work. They are bound for 3 years, and provided with victuals by the parish. A few old men are employed in boat-building: tailors', and other trades, are carried on in the house. The women pick and spin cotton, for household use: linen, and most other articles of domestic consumption, are manufactured within. . . .

Weekly Bill of Fare in the Work-house

	Breakfast	Dinner	Supper
Mon.	Burgo and Milk [1]	Milk pottage, & bread	Milk pottage, & bread
Tue.	Ditto	Lobscouse [2]	Milk pottage, & bread
Wed.	Ditto	Broth, beef, & bread	Broth, beef, & bread
Thu.	Ditto	Lobscouse	Milk & bread
Fri.	Ditto	Milk pottage, & bread	Milk & bread
Sat.	Ditto	Lobscouse	Milk pottage, & bread
Sun.	Ditto	Broth, beef, & bread	Broth, beef, & bread

Diet used in Liverpool Work-house in one week

		lbs.	d.	£.	s.	d.	£.	s.	d.
	Oatmeal	118 at	2½	1	4	7			
40	Loaves, household bread, at 2s.	1040	—	4	0	0			
	Beef, 570 lbs. paupers— beef, 17 lbs. governor, &c.	587	3	7	6	9			
	Ale and beer	142½	1	0	11	10½			
		1887½					13	3	2½
	Oatmeal	118	2½	1	4	7			
41	Loaves, household bread, at 2 s.	1066	—	4	2	0			

[1] Burgo is oatmeal hasty-pudding.
[2] Lobscouse is beef cut in small pieces, and boiled with potatoes.

	Beef, governor, sick, &c.	60	3	0	15	0	
99	Gallons sweet milk	792	2¾	1	2	8¼	
61¼	Gallons butter ditto	490	1⅓	0	6	2	
	Ale and beer	142½	1	0	11	10½	
		2668½			8	2	11¼

Carried over　£ 21　6　2¼

Walton-upon-Thames

THE PARISH of Walton contains 280 houses; of which, 158 are rated to the window-tax, and 122 are exempted. The inhabitants are chiefly employed in agriculture. Before the war, labourers received 8s. a week, in winter; and 9s. a week, in summer: at present, they are paid 9s. a week, in winter; and from 10s. to 12s. a week, in summer. In hay and corn harvest, wages, by the day, are from 2s. to 3s.; reaping an acre of wheat, 10s., and mowing an acre of grass, 3s. 6d.; women, employed as weeders, earn 1s. a day.

The rent of land is about £2 an acre, for meadow land; £1. 10s. for inclosed arable land; and £1 for common-field land. The land-tax is 1s. 3½d. in the pound [6½ per cent] on the net rental, and produces £547. 2s. 2½d. Tithes are mostly taken in composition. There are a few Methodists in the parish. Farms vary from £10 to £275 a year; but are generally from £50 to £100 a year. There are about 4000 acres of common. The extent of the parish is about 5 miles by 2, or 6400 acres. In consequence of encroachments on the common, about 40 or 50 acres have been enclosed within the last 40 years.

There are 9 ale-houses in the parish; and two Friendly Societies; of which, one contains 56; and the other, 71 members. The former has had its rules confirmed by the magistrates: the other has been established only half a year.

The Poor are maintained by a contractor, who receives £500 a year. The parish pays county-rates, militia-men's families, and expence of raising men for the Navy. The contractor keeps the Poor in a poor-house: there are usually about 70 or 75 inmates in winter, and about 45 in summer. They generally have meat for dinner, and bread and broth for supper and breakfast.

12 poor widows, above 70 years old, have an out-allowance of 1s. a week, each.

The following particulars respecting Parochial concerns are

taken from the Returns made to Parliament in the years 1776 and 1783:

	£.	s.	d.
In 1776, the net expences for the Poor amounted to	282	16	0
In 1783, the money raised by assessment amounted to	592	0	3
In 1784,	502	9	6
In 1785,	681	13	0
Medium of those three years	£ 592	0	11
Medium of money applied for county purposes, including vagrants, militia, county bridges, gaols, houses of correction, &c.	51	2	3
Medium of expences not concerning the Poor; viz. repairing churches, roads, &c. salaries to ministers, &c.	9	8	9
Medium of net money annually paid for the Poor	531	9	11
Medium expences of overseers in journies, and attendances on magistrates, &c.	14	5	8
Medium expences of entertainments, at meetings relative to the Poor	3	6	8
Medium expences of law-business, orders, examinations, and other proceedings, relative to the Poor	13	9	10

There have been great disputes in this parish, relative to the administration of parochial concerns. A very respectable committee, appointed by the parishioners, about four years ago, to manage the affairs of the parish, stated, in a printed paper, that, in the course of a few years, the expenditure in the article of Poor's Rate, only, had increased from £400 to £836 a year. In order to find employment for the Poor, who are very numerous, they distributed spinning wheels among the women and children; but spinning is now wholly laid aside, and the management of the parish is now in the hands of the opposite party.

According to a new valuation, which the committee caused to be made, of all the houses and lands in the parish, the rental was found to be £8276. I subjoin their comparative view of the old and new valuation [not shown]: it clearly demonstrates, that land-taxes, whatever their merit in other respects may be, must ever, in the progress of improvement, become very unequal and partial.

40. Gentlemen to Be "Men of Feeling"

IN 1750, Jonas Hanway left a promising business career to devote the remaining thirty-six years of his life to "improvement" and philanthropy. A man of unbelievable energy, Hanway found time amid various campaigns for the poor, the apprentices, the prostitutes, the foundlings, charity schools, and "practical religion" to write some seventy-four tracts and books. The following selection is an appeal to the "gentry of the kingdom" to concern themselves more actively with the misery of the poor. Here is the paternalistic urge at its best: "The philanthropy of an *English gentleman* cannot reject his [the poor man's] request."

Source: Jonas Hanway, *The Defects of Police: The Cause of Immorality* (London, 1775), pp. 142–147.

Letter XVI

THIS GENERAL remark must be allowed: The nobility and gentry of this kingdom, where the poors law constitutes so considerable a part of our police, have in process of time fallen-off, and compared with the custom of ancient times, totally neglected the poor. The reason of this is obvious; they suppose the indigent are amply provided for by means of the *parochial tax;* but they do not consider that the administration of this kind of justice, and the proper expenditure of such tax, is as essential a duty as the paying of it. In the mean while the increase of wealth has opened the portals of amusement so very wide, both in town and country, every hour may be filled up in a round of dissipation. At length there is some reason to hope they will grow tired of the vanity of such pursuits, carried to such an excess, and vary their object. Many, at least in the country, *begin* to consider what satisfaction they may derive from entering into the concerns of the poor; by endeavouring to make the parochial taxes produce the happy effects for which they were intended. Frequent occasions point out That which dignifies human nature, and expresses the most cordial *patriotism*. Religion co-operates, and the grand object of life, *immortality*, turns the balance, and influences many whose hearts are not estranged from the great truths contained in the New Testament, to act with consistency. Hence we find them forming themselves into societies for the better government of the *indigent*: and whilst these constitute so large a portion of mankind, in all ages, and in all countries, the office must be honourable: in spite of the depravity of the heart, or the tyranny of custom, it must afford a solid satisfaction.

The county houses of industry, so warmly recommended by the ingenious author of the pamphlet which I have quoted, is a proof of what I advance. When this kind of humanity has had its reign, it will be a higher degree of improvement in moral excellency, for men of fortune and sentiment, in conjunction with the *clergy*, to take care of the indigent in the ordinary method of domestic life; that the virtues of filial duty may be more exercised; fraternal love be less a stranger to the hearts of the labouring poor; and maternal tenderness operate as the God of Nature intended it should do. It would be romantic to expect the golden age to be so far restored, that no misery should be found among *infants, aged, sickly, maimed,* or *insane* persons, without seeking succour, by availing ourselves of such asylums, as the houses of industry now in question so amply supply. The happy regulation of them, especially if they extend to vagrants, without refining on their possible evil consequences, deserves the attention of the ablest politician. In whatever we are defective, in these vast cities, which are so much the *fairs of vanity*, we may learn from country gentlemen, without any great mortification to our pride. Indeed we have but few country gentlemen who are not town gentlemen also: but the *field*, which the country affords, is so vastly superior to the town, for *space, air, occupation* and *health;* if a true principle were adopted, *all paupers* would be removed into the country, where the same work may be carried on within doors as in town; whilst the culture of the earth, the common parent of us all, might by the hands of *paupers*, contribute towards the furnishing of food as well as raiment. He who should produce a bushel of turnips, might deserve as much as he who has two pair of stockings knit by his own hand.

This general argument may suffice to remove those objections which are urged against the *county houses of industry*, and to give them a preference to the *workhouses* of the respective parishes in the county. According to the gradations of moral improvements among the nobility and gentry, this practice of taking care of *paupers*, will bend their thoughts to the indigent in general, till by precept and example, benevolence and charity, they shall establish a more consistent conduct in their respective towns and villages: and thus they will check the growth of that immorality, which at this time wears so formidable an aspect.

Before we proceed to the proposal of any *resolutions*, with regard to the remedy of evils in these cities in particular, let us hear the evidence of the worthy author, with regard to what is passing in the kingdom in general. We usually take the *lead*, but we have often occasion to *follow*: and those who have the most leisure, may have the best ability to teach us. In tracing the sentiments and observations of the ingenious country clergyman, who mixes the *gentleman* and the *man of feeling* with his sacerdotal duty, we find many reflections and informations of importance to our subject. In his capacity as a *moralist*, he chastises us for our ingratitude to Heaven! He says,

"Whilst we are rolling thro' the kingdom in our post-coaches, post-chaises, chairs, whiskies, and a variety of whirligigs of a whimsical construction, the high culture of our lands gives us the idea of a *Ferme bien orné;* our nobility live in *palaces*, our gentry in *villas*, commerce has made us a nation of *gentry*, every farmhouse is a *grange*, and the whole is one delightful scene of convenience, plenty, elegance, splendor, and magnificence. Mean time our *interior police* is disgrac'd with the number of our starving, naked, unshelter'd, miserable poor; this is an ulcer in our vitals, that spreads, and rankles, and diffuses its corruption thro' every part; some remedy, some timely remedy is necessary!" The *evil*, for so we must call it, he adds, "hath long been observ'd, and engag'd the attention of very able men, who have propos'd their several plans of regulation to the public. The first was the great and good Lord Chief Justice *Hale*. The strong and comprehensive genius of Sir *Josiah Child* form'd a bolder and a larger scheme: these have been follow'd by Dr. *Davenant*, Mr. *Hay*, Lord *Hillsborough*, Sir *Richard Lloyd*, Mr. *Fielding*, Dr. *Burn*, and many other writers of great sensibility, and penetration. These have all look'd up to Sir *Matthew Hale* as their great pattern, except Mr.

Gee, who computed the poor at a *million*, and upon that supposition was for sending them to the colonies; but whether his bad policy or his inhumanity is most to be execrated, may be a question. None of these plans have been adopted; and the Legislature hath gone on from time to time making fresh provisions, till "the laws concerning the poor," as Dr. *Burn* complains, "may not improperly be compar'd to their apparel. Where a flaw is observed, a patch is provided for it. Upon that another. And so on, till the original coat is lost amidst a variety of patch-work. And more labour and materials are expended (besides the clumsiness and motley figure) than would have made an entire new suit."

Our author observes, that no society can subsist without some restraint; and speaking of the *Norfolk* and *Suffolk* houses of industry, informs us, "no restraint is there established, but what is necessary to good order.—The old sailors in *Greenwich Hospital*, the maimed veteran at *Chelsea*, the children in *Christ's*, and the *Foundling-Hospitals*, are all, and must be, under restraint and rule. The inhabitants of these houses are children, or infirm and aged persons: that children ought to be under a proper restraint is acknowledged; here they are allowed two hours in the day for *play*; and more, when their industry deserves it.—Infirmity and age are of themselves a confinement; but such as are able to walk out are *never* denied a proper liberty. The *governor* is not constituted the judge of such propriety, but the weekly Committee."

As to letting out *paupers* to be maintained by *contract*, it is, with some exceptions, a barbarous practice. "The statute which empowers the overseer to cram them into a narrow, nasty workhouse, and to contract with any person to lodge, keep, and maintain them, is often abused. The fund of such house is not sufficient to redeem them from their filthy rags; nor the capacity of it to furnish them with convenient, decent, and distinct apartments. The young, the old, the virtuous, the profligate, the sick, the healthy, the clean, the unclean, are huddled together, and inhaling a stagnated and putrid air, deplore their miserable situation: this receives the higher aggravation from their irremediable servitude to the *contractor*, some low-born, selfish, surly ruffian, from whose sordid tyranny there is no appeal, no redress, till the unhappy sufferers repose in the grave."

This is a striking description of this gentleman's abhorrence of contracting out the poor, which is sometimes done in *London:* but where the *contractor* is well paid, as in the case of a number of small parishes within the walls of *London*, he finds it his interest to act with humanity: the poor here will not bear severity.—The author in question wishes the Directors of these *houses of industry*, should not be "vested with the power of farming out their poor, but that a preventive clause should be inserted in every future bill, were it only to vindicate the integrity of their intentions, and to satisfy the public:" adding, that "on the same principle it were to be wished the clause, which empowers them to contract with any person for employing all the poor within the house, were omitted; and That also, whereby they may bind the children apprentices to the *Governor* of the house; one end of the institution being to make such children useful to the *community* as soon as may be; and such unnecessary detention, tho' it has nothing oppressive in it, little answering that salutary purpose."

He then takes up again the consideration of *aged paupers*, by observing, "it may sometimes happen that the honest, industrious cottager, now incapable of labour and reduced to ask for support, by a long continued residence, an association of ideas, a partial affection to one particular spot, is wedded to his little habitation; to divorce him from it would be *cruel:* he raised That *hedge;* he planted That *tree;* some unaccountable attachment hangs upon his mind; in the church-yard of his village lies his wife, a son, or a darling daughter. All this is ideal: but many of our acutest pains and sublimest pleasures exist only in idea. It is a prejudice: but it is founded in human nature; and from this prejudice the noblest of our passions, *the love of our country*, arises. Might not this rural veteran be favoured with a little relief in his favorite cottage? It cannot be expected that the *act* can provide for *his case;* but the Guardians and Directors can; they are his neighbours; they know him and his merit; he never can want some friendly voice to plead his cause; the circumstance will seldom happen; an indulgence to it can be attended with no ill consequence; he surely will not be refused; the philanthropy of an *English gentleman* cannot reject his request."

41. The Intendant and Relief of the Poor

IT WAS with a mixture of surprise, shock, and envy that Englishmen, ranging from Samuel Johnson to Arthur Young, learned that the French government provided no regular public-supported poor relief. There seems little doubt that whatever their reservation about proper "police" of the poor, Englishmen accepted care of the poor as a community responsibility. In France, as we have seen, the government's response to poverty was intermittent and *ad hoc*, taking place only when local or national conditions became acute—during a year of very bad harvest, for example.

Here we have an intendant's report to the Controller-General at Paris during one of the worst winters of the eighteenth century. The report reiterates the classic governmental response to grain shortage— lowering of taxes for one year, construction of state grain magazines, and temporary establishment of workhouses (*ateliers de charité*). This was essentially the same relief program pursued by the famous minister Turgot seventy years later.[1] Notice that the appropriations are only for temporary relief and that the intendant emphasizes his sense of economy. This is not to say that he was callous toward the poor. Indeed, he was the one man most aware of their problems, as the letter shows. Yet it must have appeared to him that poverty was a chronic problem, ultimately insoluble. As an administrator, his chief concern was to prevent public disorder, though his means, fortunately, went beyond reinforcement of the mounted police.

The intendants' reports are a very valuable source for social history, since they come closer to an objective appraisal of local conditions than almost any other source. The printed collections by Depping for the seventeenth century and by Boislisle for the early eighteenth century form an excellent introduction to local social conditions as well as to the workings of the most modern and complex royal administration of the time.

[1] Turgot's charity workshops were to serve only as temporary relief while the French consumer "adjusted" to his long-run policy of free trade in grain. It has been cogently argued that this well-intentioned policy actually worsened the plight of the poor by raising grain prices even higher because of transportation costs from province to province. Cf. A. R. J. Turgot, *Oeuvres*, ed. E. Daire (Paris, 1844) vol. II, pp. 454ff.

Source: A. M. Boislisle, ed., *Correspondance des Contrôleurs-Généraux avec les Intendants des Provinces, 1683–1715* (Paris, 1874), vol. III, pp. 57–58.

M. de la Bourdonnaye, Intendant of Bordeaux,
to the Controller-General,
September 30, 1708

HAVING SEARCHED for the means of helping the people of Agen in this cruel situation and having conferred with His Eminence, the Bishop, it seems to us that three things are absolutely necessary if the people are not to starve during the winter.

Most of the inhabitants do not have seed to plant their fields. However, we decided that we would be going too far if we furnished it, because those who have seed would also apply [for more]. Moreover, we are persuaded that all the inhabitants will make strenuous efforts to find some seed, since they have every reason to expect prices to remain high next year. If some of the inhabitants fail to cultivate their fields, the consuls and the tax collectors will see that they are planted in order to raise enough to pay the *taille*, which is based on the land here.[1] I decided to issue an ordinance authorizing them to do this. For these reasons, we are hopeful that all the land will be planted.

But this project will come to nothing if the collectors of the *taille* continue to be as strict in the exercise of their functions as they have been of late and continue to employ troops [to force collection]. Those inhabitants who have seed grain would sell it to be freed from an oppressive garrison, while those who must buy seed, since they had none left from their harvest and have scraped together a little money for this purchase, would prefer to give up that money [for taxes] when put under police constraint. To avoid this, I feel it is absolutely necessary that you order the receivers-general to reduce their operations during this winter, at least with respect to the poor. This does not mean that the *taille* cannot be collected from those who are in a position to pay.

We are planning to import wheat for this region from Languedoc and Quercy, and we are confident that there will be enough. But there are two things to be feared: one is the greed of

[1] In most of France the *taille* was assessed on "persons," not on land.

the merchants. When they see that general misery has put them in control of prices, they will raise them to the point where the calamity is almost as great as if there were no provisions at all. The other fear is that the artisans and the lowest classes, when they find themselves at the mercy of the merchants, will cause disorders and riots. As a protective measure, it would seem wise to establish two small storehouses, one at Agen for the Garonne region and one at Villeneuve for the Lot region. Ten thousand *écus* [30,000 livres] would be sufficient for each. This measure would enable us to work in secret [2] against an excessive rise of prices [of grain] and also deal with accidents that might occasionally occur because of the impatience of the people.

A third point demanding our attention is the support of beggars among the poor, as well as of those who have no other resources than their wages.[3] Since there will be very little work, these people will soon be reduced to starvation. We should establish public workshops to provide work as was done in 1693 and 1694. I should choose the most useful kind of work, located where there are the greatest number of poor. In this manner, we should rid ourselves of those who do not want to work and assure the others of a moderate subsistence. For these workshops, we would need about 40,000 livres, or altogether 100,000 livres. The receiver-general of the *taille* of Agen could advance this sum. The 60,000 livres for the storehouses he would get back very soon. I shall await your orders on all of the above.

Marginal Comments by the Controller-General

Operations for the collection of the *taille* are to be suspended. The two storehouses are to be established; great care must be taken to put them to good use. The interest on the advances will be paid by the king. His Majesty has agreed to the establishment of the public workshops for the able-bodied poor and is willing to spend up to 40,000 livres on them this winter.

[2] That is, without the consumers' knowing. The very knowledge of government stocking could cause a panic.
[3] I.e., landless.

42. "Improvers" and Single-Causers in France

WHERE WERE the French single-causers? Not among the *philosophes*
who, if they were concerned with the poor at all, almost always included them in the broadest schemes of institutional change.[1] Perhaps
single-causers require the opportunity of a hearing in Parliament, a
free press, and a public attuned to empirical investigations like those of
Eden or Howard. Restif de la Bretonne saw himself as the common
man's *philosophe*, but he was hardly a single-causer on behalf of the
poor of Paris. Flower girls were not objects of pity or reform but the
reflection of a wasteful luxury trade. For Restif, they were no different from that band of petty hucksters and peddlers who overcharged
foolish buyers and drew labor away from more productive pursuits.
The Parisian wage earner, according to Restif, was overpaid, lived
only for the present, and squandered his wages on drink.[2] Lower the
price of labor, he said, and the masses will work six days instead of
three. How typical were these attitudes of the lower middle class of
France?

Source: Restif de la Bretonne, *Les Nuits de Paris or Nocturnal
Spectator: A Selection*, trans. L. Asher and E. Fertig, (New
York, 1964), pp. 108–111.*

The Flower Girls

ONE SAINT John's Eve, after watching the vicar of Saint-Nicholas
burn the ceremonial faggot, I set out by rue Saint-Victor and
arrived at the Faubourg Saint-Marcel. Along the way I saw and
heard nothing but flower girls, who adorned the street corners or
strolled along shouting: "Bouquets for Jeannot-Jeannette!" Others, who wished to play the purists, were calling: "For Jean and
Jeanne!"

[1] This is not to imply that the *philosophes* were unrealistic Utopians, but
that those like Mably, Morellet, and Linguet who were concerned about
the poor were not inclined to reform institutions piecemeal, and so hardly
meet the definition of single-causer.
[2] One wonders what kind of labor could earn 18 livres in three days as
Restif claimed. All sources from Young to Coniac set the wages of day
labor at 12 sous to 1 livre in 1789.
* Reprinted by permission of Alfred A. Knopf, Inc. (The original French
edition was published in 1788.)

Observing them, I reflected on the extent of luxury, which reaches its murderous hand even to the lowest class. And then I proceeded to define luxury: that which gives rise to occupations which bring the worker a profit for sterile labor. Thus, gambling —where one often wins immense sums—is a sterile occupation. Two gamblers or a hundred, who ceaselessly compete against each other, will end in ruin and die of hunger. Actually such labors of luxury as gilding, painting, embroidery and the manufacture of artificial flowers are not as worthless as gambling, for these products can be sold abroad—the first-mentioned especially. But I maintain in fact that such occupations, confined within the State, are deadly and destructive, that a country which employs a great number of hands in the building of vainglorious edifices must become impoverished—like a farmer or a vine-grower who spends his time erecting fences about his field or vineyard instead of tilling, sowing or planting. According to the lights of common sense, I claim that luxury and its manufactures should be tolerated by the government only insofar as they keep the population from procuring them abroad; that the prohibition on Indian calicoes, which went to the point of seizing them on women's backs, was a fine law and a just one, and that the punishment ought to have been still harsher than the fine. Luxury products are advantageous in a highly populated country only when there is a superabundance of food—and when I say advantageous, I only mean favorable to the augmentation of wealth and to the perpetuation of the inequality of riches, for luxury is always antithetical to sound morals and to the true happiness of the human race. It remains to be seen if in the state of affairs in Europe today a country with sound morals and an abundance of food, but little money, can be safe against outside enemies. But these are things I cannot know, since I have never been employed in public administration. Let us return to the flower girls.

I felt within myself that it was an evil for the women of the populace to be employed solely in uselessly peddling worthless things like flowers, which involve gardens and gardeners in pure loss. I felt sure that any individual who wished to purchase flowers would find them easily enough without the existence of flower girls. I felt, furthermore, that since there are fruit markets in every quarter, it would be wise and useful to gradually abolish all fruit peddlers, who are but idlers; that all peddlers of Paris make bad citizens whose children are but spies, thieves, and prostitutes; that we have everything at hand without such people. I thought further that a whole segment of the population is occupied in the vain, purposeless trafficking of light nourishments and petty wares; that to dispose of the poorest pieces of fruit whose greenness causes illness and degenerates the human species they sell them to children; that if such peddling were abolished little by little, and worthwhile occupations indicated to the populace, it would result in great benefit to the labor force engaged in useful manufactures; that in order to gain the greatest advantage from the populace, and turn it to good use, the export of grain abroad should be prohibited, and instead, the harvest should be devoted to easing the workers' subsistence; that instead of exporting grain, the low-cost products of silk and wool manufacturing should be exported; that the duty on wine should be lifted in Paris, and the cost of labor lowered in all trades, thus earning for ourselves—from the increased sales of our manufactures—the benefit previously derived from the export of grain. I have no doubt that crops would be more abundant then and the people better nourished, above all if useless private parks were abolished and all large landowners rigorously taxed at a louis per acre for untilled land. Then there would be a surplus of grain, and after the whole realm had been supplied, the surplus could be disposed of at whatever price one wished, because everyone would have been provided for.

I reflected on the terrible drawbacks of the high cost of labor; thought of this in terms of the noxious effects on the masses, who, like savage tribes, think only of the present. If they earn enough in three days for necessities, they work for three days only and spend the other four in debauchery. Then they can no longer afford their essentials, are miserable, borrow, neglect to pay up, ruin the baker, the cobbler, the wine merchant (although the latter poisons them so he can retire). Everything is in disorder. But, lower the price of labor, and the masses would automatically work for six days because they would need to work in order to meet their expenses; they would be less disorderly and less in debt earning nine livres a week than earning eighteen in three days. I know what I am saying, and I proclaim to the public and to the government that this is the exact truth, the result of observations made a thousand times over and which, given my position, I am perhaps alone in being able to make.

I strolled throughout the faubourg, and everywhere I saw men, women, girls, even children in rags, buying bouquets. Then I took a turn through the better sections. Flower girls were not so abundant there and they sold very little, because there were fewer *Jeans* and *Jeannes* (they have finer names there); and also because in those sections more people have done away with the custom of giving flowers.

VII

The Family

UNTIL RECENTLY, historical study of the family as a separate institution has been neglected.[1] It was customary to regard the family as an immobile institution, a fixed point, when all other institutions were in flux. We now recognize that the family has undergone considerable change over the centuries. Nor can these changes be reduced to the progressive decline of family cohesion before the onslaught of individualism, urbanization, and the modern mobile society. Actually, the family has undergone successive periods of contraction and growth in size and solidarity.

Perhaps the best way to examine this is to contrast the small "conjugal family" with the larger clan or "patriarchal family." In France, where the process is best known, the conjugal family, permitting its individual members great freedom of action, seemed dominant when the state offered reasonable security. This was true, for example, in the tenth century. But when the state failed to provide this security, the closely knit patriarchal family asserted itself. For example, after the year 1000 an estate was kept undivided as long as possible, two or three generations lived under one roof, and wives surrendered their property to their husbands. Again in the thirteenth century, greater economic security and political efficiency revived the conjugal family, but this time without a return to the complete individualism of the tenth century. Primogeniture, the right of the eldest son to inherit the paternal property, gained ground; paternal authority held on; and women failed to regain their earlier status.

By the sixteenth century—and here the relation to political security seems less clear—the husband reigned supreme, discipline of all children became increasingly severe, marriages were strictly arranged, and cadets were deprived of landed property and placed in the army or Church. At the same time, the child gained more recognition in other ways. No longer depicted as a miniature man, by the seventeenth century he was treated as an individual in his own right—at first sen-

[1] Since 1960, French scholars, led by Georges Duby, Robert Mandrou, and Philippe Ariès, have initiated a new interest in the history of the family. See Joan Thirsk, "The Family," *Past and Present*, XXVII (1964), 116–122. Much of our commentary here is based on this review article.

timentalized, then more carefully surveyed, trained, and even studied psychologically. This development, apparently beginning before the Enlightenment, eventually weakened primogeniture by placing all children on the same level of affection and attention. The French Revolution marks a culmination of this process, and efforts to restore primogeniture in the early nineteenth century failed, despite cogent economic arguments in its favor. Curiously, the status of French women did not undergo a comparable change. In fact, the property rights of wives and widows in some regions of France were greater in the eighteenth century than under the Napoleonic Code. Women remained legal minors well into the nineteenth century.

All that has been said, however, applies to the upper classes—nobility and well-to-do townsmen. In France, at least, the peasants have had a different family history. When the state failed them in the eleventh century, they turned not to the patriarchal family or clan, but to the village community for security and cooperative farming.[2] Hence, the near-absence of primogeniture in the transmission of peasant property.

We know less, of course, about the more personal aspects of family life among the lower classes. The iconographic and literary sources employed with such skill by Philippe Ariès largely reflect upper-class mores.[3] Differences of wealth and social status can mean differences in educational opportunities for the child as well as in the amount of leisure and energy available to parents for the care of their offspring. Similarly, the independence of the wife of a shopkeeper or artisan working beside her husband might well have been greater than that of the delicate, ornamental upper-middle-class spouse.

In addition to differences among social groups and between rich and poor, there seem to have been appreciable national and regional variations of family behavior. Roman-law areas of France retained greater paternal authority than customary-law areas. In England, the patriarchal family never attained the importance it did in France, nor did the status of English women deteriorate in the sixteenth and seventeenth centuries as in France. The freedom of English women, already a shock to continental Europeans in the sixteenth century, may have increased through the propagation of a doctrine of spiritual equality of the sexes by the separatist sects in the seventeenth century. It goes without saying that widows with land or wealthy heiresses everywhere were treated with considerable deference, though how long this lasted after the inheritance was settled is open to question.

Historical demographers have been able to uncover more evidence about the lower-class family through the study of parish registers. It is precisely the isolated village community that suits their purposes best,

---

[2] The relationship between village solidarity and the manorial lord in this period is not altogether clear. In England, however, heavily manorialized areas and village solidarity seem to be correlated.

[3] *Centuries of Childhood*, trans. Robert Baldick (London, 1962).

since immobility is essential to establishing a sufficiently complete series of baptisms, marriages, and burials. The results of this research go beyond general population trends revealed in line graphs of crude birth and death statistics. Family histories, reconstructed over considerable spans of time—two to three centuries—can suggest answers to the questions of population growth and stagnation by pointing to changes in marriage age, intervals of birth, and alterations in infant mortality rates. Parish registers can also yield information on the place of origin, abode, and sometimes occupation of people who are otherwise completely unknown to the historian. If peasants marry at twenty-eight years of age and there is no evidence of illegitimacy in the village, this tells us something about peasant mores. If a number of children are born in a cluster after each marriage, but none after the wife passes thirty, there is good reason to suspect birth control. It appears that upper-class families were already practicing birth control in the eighteenth century, implying that the mass of peasantry and the lower classes of the towns were responsible for the increase in population after 1750. Aggregate statistics and a fertile imagination can do a great deal to compensate for a shortage of more direct evidence about family life.

The parish register is not the only source of family history. Families in western society have kept records, letters, and accounts that are the best sources for the more personal, intimate aspects of family life. Furthermore, expanding bureaucracies, supported by the legal profession, required an increasing amount of legal registration of family transactions, such as marriage contracts, wills, gifts in life, and inventories after death. There is no doubt that the emergence of the lay state has been a great boon to the social historian.

Marriage contracts and wills should be examined together. They are the legal instruments for the transmission and preservation of property. They indicate the manner in which the family estate was divided, the efforts made to prevent fragmentation of wealth, the treatment of daughters and younger sons, as well as the kinds of provision made for widows and widowers. Besides the more obvious property clauses, the marriage contract and will can tell us something about the literacy, charitable inclinations, and even the education, attitudes, and tastes of the family concerned. Such notarial documents suggest more than the relative wealth of social groups or the growth of literacy (from signatures). Carefully used, they can help us re-create a whole style of life. The samples which follow should make this clear.

More rare and interesting are private family papers. Families have a habit of destroying correspondence they consider too intimate and personal for outsiders' eyes. Consequently, a continuous series of letters, so important to reconstructing individual attitudes and the whole pattern of family life, is very hard to come by. Moreover, surviving family papers are usually those of the upper classes, necessarily limiting our sample. The passages from Blundell and Purefoy (Documents 45 and 50) are, therefore, precious indicators of family attitudes. Both cases reveal the importance of family respectability and an ambivalence between parental love and family discipline. Finally, the family accounts of the Saulx-Tavanes (Document 51) tell us how a wealthy noble family could spend 200,000 livres (about $200,000) in a single year.

43. To Marry or Not to Marry

MONEY PLAYED a large role in the marriage policy of all classes. Peasants usually married late since a new family had to await a father's land. In the middle classes and the nobility, the size of the dowry determined the marriage prospects of a daughter, and an economizing family reduced dowries for younger daughters to a minimum. A girl with a small dowry or no dowry at all had no choice but to enter a religious order or become a spinster. Similarly, younger sons were often sacrificed to preserve the estate in the hands of the eldest. Consequently, a cadet often had to rely on a small annuity or enter the army or Church. Louis Sébastien Mercier believed that some of these young people actually enjoyed their freedom from the "heavy yoke" of marriage. He objects to this new attitude, partly because he considers it "unnatural," especially for women, and partly because it threatens the social balance. If the rich marry late or never, they will have few children, while the poor marry "early and rashly and have children in dozens."

Mercier's impressionistic observations here complement the suspicions of demographers that birth control was also reducing the number of nobles and the upper-middle class while the mass of the peasantry and artisans increased dramatically.[1]

Source: Helen Simpson, ed. and trans., *The Waiting City: Paris, 1728–88. Being an Abridgement of Louis-Sebastian Mercier's "Le tableau de Paris."* pp. 49–50.

Marriageable

UNCOUNTED NUMBERS of our women have not married. True, there are difficulties, not religious so much as civil; their diffidence, which would accept the eternal nature of the knot, baulks at the necessary couple of notaries and the payment of cash down. Plain

[1] See D. V. Glass and D. E. C. Eversley, eds., *Population in History* (New York, 1965), especially the article by Louis Henry.

women with only youth to offer have no chance of a husband, and even the beauties must do battle. It might be no bad thing to revive here in Paris the Babylonian custom, whereby all young women were assembled in the market-place for the bachelors of the city to choose from; naturally enough, the best-looking fetched the best prices, and this money went to provide dowries and thus husbands for their plainer sisters.

Marriage nowadays is a yoke, and a heavy one; people avoid it as long as they can. No wonder, for the appeal of the single state is strong, with its promise of security, tranquillity, and reasonable self-indulgence, and that men should prefer not to marry is understandable. The strange thing is, that nowadays women too reject all idea of it, at least in the middle classes, where girls join with sisters or friends to live together, and with the money that might have acquired them husbands, buy annuities. This voluntary refusal to adopt what is, after all, a woman's natural state, this anti-conjugal outlook, is surely one of the most curious comments on our time.

Each year in Lacedæmon unmarried persons were publicly whipped in the temple of Venus by women. I should like to hear Lycurgus's opinion of our younger generation, living singly from choice, and proud of it; living like men, in freedom such as no other nation in the world permits to their sex.

And the result of all this? The middle class, those with sufficient incomes, who either marry late or not at all, have hardly any children; the poor marry early and rashly and have children in dozens; so that money tends to become concentrated more and more in the hands of a few, while the largest class, and that which has most need of money, gets least.

Every social circle has its old maids, women who have refused the duties of their sex, and have no corner of a hearth they can call their own. Marriage with its pains and pleasures they have passed by, and therefore should be allowed to usurp none of the consideration and respect due to those who have accepted the responsibility of life. These women are barren vines, whom the sun has never warmed to fruitfulness; their rare and withered leaves make but poor showing. They are more malicious than their married neighbours, quarrelsome, with sharper tongues and quicker tempers; and they are apt to have an ugly passion for money.

These celibates, men and women alike, should be taxed. I would raise the age of consent for religious vows, which are taken sometimes under compulsion and sometimes too impulsively; the army should be allowed to marry, which would mean as many girls husbanded as there are soldiers; moreover a man with a family makes a better patriot, he has more to defend. Finally there should be a revival of our ancestors' custom of the left-handed marriage; this alone would solve many of our present difficulties. A mistress, in the old days, was not too different from an honest woman.

It does not do to attack man's social freedom; he finds his liberty elsewhere. Here is a case where it may truly be said that the law has made the crime.

44. Parish Registers

THE CRUDE summaries of baptisms, marriages, and burials presented here fall short of what historical demographers would like to know, especially about the age structure of a community. Moreover, Walton is too small for the best statistical results and Liverpool is too large for reconstructing family structure.[1] Nevertheless, some conclusions can be drawn. From the Walton-type summary one can quickly evaluate the population changes and also derive the birth and death rates.[2] The Liverpool figures give us the monthly variations, indicating that more marriages were contracted in the fall and more children born in the spring and summer. The ages at death are noteworthy; almost half of the deaths in this year are infants. Presumably, most Dissenters and Catholics were buried in Anglican graveyards.

Source: Sir Frederick M. Eden, *The State of the Poor*, Vol. II, pp. 726, 338.

[1] A large volume of migrations makes it impossible to trace a sufficient number of family histories over time.
[2] This can be done by an algebraic formula. The birth rate would be 24.5 per 1,000, a very low birth rate, but large enough to replace the losses from death and leave an excess.

Table of Baptisms, Burials, and Marriages,
in the Parish of Walton-upon-Thames

Years	BAPTISMS Males	Fem.	Total	BURIALS Males	Fem.	Total	MARRIAGES
1680			35			40	3
1685			27			28	2
1690			30			31	3
1691			31			26	4
1692	The Register		29			20	8
1693	in the years		26			17	9
1694	preceding		20			25	7
1695	1775 was so		29			19	3
1696	confused, that		33			22	2
1697	the sexes could		18			26	3
1698	not be		21			23	7
1699	distinguished.		40			17	5
1700			32			25	10
1720			37			38	5
1740			25			49	
1760			46			46	
1775	19	13	32	14	20	34	
1776	19	24	43	9	16	25	
1777	25	17	42	16	22	38	
1778	22	19	41	15	18	33	
1779	25	20	45	17	14	31	
1780	23	24	47	19	19	38	
1781	21	17	38	22	23	45	
1782	15	30	45	20	18	38	
1783	26	22	48	19	22	41	
1784	27	22	49	19	15	34	
1785	20	22	42	16	9	25	
1786	23	21	44	16	13	29	
1787	22	25	47	19	15	34	
1788	26	24	50	18	15	33	
1789	27	29	56	18	18	36	
1790	17	21	38	12	14	26	
1791	24	25	49	12	13	25	
1792	25	27	52	29	16	45	
1793	15	13	28	24	29	53	
1794	26	19	45	22	23	45	

July, 1795

General Bill of Mortality for the Town and Parish of Liverpool

Comprising an Annual and a Monthly Table of the Births, Burials, and Marriages, as enumerated from the several Registers of the Parish Church of St. Peter, the Parochial Chapel of St. Nicholas, St. George's, St. Thomas's, St. Paul's, St. Ann's, St. John's, Trinity, St. James's, and St. Stephen's Churches: including that likewise from the several Chapels of Dissenters, & c.

From the 25th of March 1795, to the 25th of March 1796

ANNUAL TABLE

	BIRTHS			BURIALS			MAR-RIAGES
	Males	Fem.	Total	Males	Fem.	Total	
At St. Peter's,	156	140	296	171	186	357	229
St. Nicholas's,	510	525	1035	127	159	286	250
St. George's,	7	9	16	2	3	5	8
St. Thomas's,	43	26	69	25	26	51	56
St. Paul's,	34	38	72	82	88	170	55
St. Ann's,	9	5	14	11	10	21	96
St. John's,	40	31	71	680	565	1245	40
Trinity,	21	16	37	11	11	22	31
St. Stephen's,	5	3	8	0	0	0	0
St. Catharine's,	0	0	0	0	0	0	0
St. James's,	86	46	132	72	105	177	33
Baptists, Byrom-street,	15	12	27	14	14	28	0
Ditto, Matthew-street,	0	0	0	0	0	0	0
Dissenters, Paradise-street,	22	11	33	0	0	0	0
Ditto, Benn's Garden,	13	19	32	0	0	0	0
Ditto, Toxteth Park,	8	6	14	7	9	16	0
Independents, Renshaw-street,	17	14	31	3	5	8	0
Methodists, Mount Pleasant,	22	19	41	0	0	0	0
Scotch Kirk, Oldham-street,	22	32	54	0	0	0	0
Roman Chapel, Lumber-street,	77	89	166	0	0	0	0
Ditto, Sir Thos. buildings,	13	20	33	0	0	0	0
Ditto, Seel-street,	33	30	63	0	0	0	0
Quakers' meeting, Hunter-street,	6	1	7	4	4	8	1
Total	1159	1092	2251	1209	1185	2394	799

MONTHLY TABLE

	BIRTHS			BURIALS			MAR-RIAGES
	Males	Fem.	Total	Males	Fem.	Total	
March	24	25	49	14	29	43	15
April	107	104	211	83	88	171	61
May	94	108	202	111	107	218	63
June	107	80	187	92	68	100	54
July	89	90	179	72	69	141	53
Aug.	107	105	212	98	63	161	69
Sept.	97	87	184	110	102	212	65
Oct.	88	90	178	116	123	239	88
Nov.	109	81	190	120	133	253	71
Dec.	94	63	157	128	140	274	87
Jan.	97	110	207	106	112	218	69
Feb.	84	90	174	93	82	175	71
March	62	59	121	66	63	129	28
Total	1159	1092	2251	1209	1185	2394	799

Decreased in Births,   276
Increased in Burials,   385
Increased in Marriages,   46

Of the Number of BURIALS, in the above list, there have died

Under 2 Years	1074	Between 60 and 70	108
Between 2 and 5	384	70 and 80	78
5 and 10	134	80 and 90	37
10 and 20	88	90 and 100	3
20 and 30	117	Above 100	1
30 and 40	137	Total	2394
40 and 50	122		
50 and 60	111		

45. Marriage Negotiations

THE FOLLOWING series of letters tells the story of a father's efforts to conclude an advantageous marriage for his daughter. As soon as the eighteen-year-old girl had returned from school, negotiations were opened in various quarters, with priests often acting as intermediaries. The Blundell case is somewhat special since the family was Catholic gentry. In this instance, it was particularly important to produce a direct heir to the family estate, since it would otherwise revert to the Crown.

Even though Nicholas Blundell was very anxious to see his eldest daughter married, he insists repeatedly that the final choice is hers. It is not position and money that will make a woman happy, but "parts and humour." It goes without saying, of course, that the man she weds will be "a Gentleman of a cumpotent Estate, one of a good caracture, and a Catholick." Nevertheless, as in other families of gentry and middling nobility, parents were probably giving more consideration to a child's own feelings than in the century before. In western Europe the conception of the "noble house" was gradually giving way to the more sentimental ties of family.[1]

Source: Margaret Blundell, ed., *Blundell's Diary and Letter Book* (*1702–1728*) (Liverpool, 1952), pp. 217–219, 222–225.*

To Mr Roydon[2]

Jan. 10th, 1724

SIR

. . . . The caracture you give of Mr Strickland is very good and I question not but he deserves it, and as to his estate and what I should have settled on my daughter, I question not but we could have adjusted matters so as to make all things easy and both sides and the young Cupple Happy. I did not think proper to acquaint my daughter with what I was about until I was resolved where to fix, but upon my arrivall home I told her, haveing severall in choyce (without nameing the person,) that I hoped I had heard of a gentleman with whom she might be happy, his caracture being without exception. But she told me she was not the least disposed to marry as yet, so beged I would not urge her to it, which I was really sorry for. I should have been truly glad of an Allyance to so worthy a Famoly and so deserving a Gentleman and do sincerely wish him well settled to his Content and Satisfaction. You may be assured that I shall never mention anything

---

[1] Cf. Ariès, *Centuries of Childhood.*

* Reprinted by permission of Liverpool University Press.

[2] Mr. Roydon, a secular priest, had made the first approach for the hand of Blundell's daughter Mally on behalf of Mr. Thomas Strickland of Sizargh. Mr. Blundell would have considered him a very desirable son-in-law.

that this affaire was ever in agitation, neather shall I ever forget your readiness in endeavouring to procure me a good husband for my daughter. Your letter was extreamely particular to all Poynts and very obleging.

To Brother Joseph [3]

May 16th, 1724

DEAR BROTHER

Yours of April 21st I received not till the 2nd inst. . . . I do not find my doughters are desirous to marry nor I to settle any of my estates upon them whilst there is the least prospect of a son, all I shall do is to settle conditionally and, in case I have a son, then such a portion certain, but as for a present fortune and the estate at last, 'tis what no one can reasonably expect. I have had severall proposed but will not fix of any only such as I am pretty well assured my doughters may live comfortably with, for I assure you they are deserving of good husbands and when I think I can light of such a one I shall not slip ye opportunity. But to tell me he is a Barronet's son and will have £1500 per annum will not tempt me, I have already refused a Barronet of a better estate. I vallew the persun, parts and humours of the man (for that must make a woman happy) more than quallity. When I know who the Barronet's son is, and have enquired sufficiently of his Person, Parts and Humour, I shall think of fixing upon Preliminaries if I find his caracture be to my licking, so have writ to Mr Busby to know who the person is, and have sent it enclosed that you may see what I write. This I suppose is sufficient for a Blinkered as now is

Your affectionate brother
NICHOLAS BLUNDELL

[August 20, 1724]

To Mr Eccleston in Answer to His Sent to Me by His Servant [4]

SIR

When I last had the favour of your company I told you what my Resolutions were, that I was not in haist to match my daughters till I had severall proposalls made, and then I would endeavour to choose the best . . . I have had some Persons of good

---

[3] Father Joseph Blundell, also a priest.
[4] The Reverend Thomas Eccleston, S.J., a distant relative of Blundell.

familys and others of good estates proposed, but none so well qualified in all respects as to think deserving of my daughters for I will do the part of a good and kind father as far as in me lyes to settle where I think they may be truly happy. But to give you a positive answer at so short a warning is what I hope you don't expect. I have so good an opinion of you that I will not give you now an absolute denyall, but in a few weeks you shall heare againe from

Sir

Your affectionate kinsman and humble servant

Ni. Blu.

To Mr Roydon

April the 6th, 1725

Sir

I am glad to find by yours of the 4th Ult my two got safe to hand and am beholding to my friends for the good caracture they are pleased to give my daughters . . . I do not find my daughter any more inclineable to marry than she was, yet am entirely of opinion that she is not so averse to it that an accomplished gentleman with whom she may be happy may obtain her favour. However I thought it would be rude to let any one come to court her, and then for her to declair she would not marry. That would look like an imposition upon a Gentleman and he might really take it as an affront put upon him. But if Mr Strickland or any other deserving gentleman think it worth while to try if he can gain her affections I am not against his coming. . . . I perceive there has been another gentleman proposed to my Doughter but she returned the same answer that she was not as yet disposed to marry. I long since told her I would not compel her to marry, much less to marry one she could not love and so to make her miserable as long as she lives, so leave her entirely to pleas herself, all I require is that he be a Gentleman of a cumpotent Estate, one of a good caracture, and a Catholick. I have never ceriously proposed marriage to Frances, my second doughter, so cannot tell how she stands affected, but my opinion is Mr Strickland would not dislike eather her person, parts or humour. But self praise is no praise so excuse me for giving a good Caracture of my own dear Child, which would seem much better of another hand. Though she has been long ill I hope she will in time recover for I can by no means say she is unhealthful.

To Mr Roydon

April 30th

. . . You are pleased to say I have a Full Purs, but if I can stretch so far as to pay £1000 in hand tis the utmost I can reach to, and £1000 more at my death if I have a Son (which tis 20 to 1 I have not), and if no son then £400 per annum and a very good Hous; this I hope, with a good wife, may make Mr Strickland or anyone elce happy who is not hard-pushed for Money; but as I have said before tis my chief aime to settle my daughters to lickeing and that they may make choyce of a man they can love, and I'll doe my endeavours to propose such to them whose Sarcomsteenses may make them happy, which is the reason I gave consent for Mr Strickland to come to Crosby to try if he could gain my daughter's affections, and since then, another being proposed, I also gave my consent for him to come to see which my daugher licked the better, and this I· was the more willing to do because I heard Mr Strickland was married to the daughter of Mr Higgens the Goldsmith, which, by yours I find is a Story. If my daughter approve of the Gentleman who makes his Addresses to her and that he is content with what I am at present able to do as for Jointure and provition for the younger children etc. those things may easily be settled. So think tis not necessary to give Mr Strickland the trouble of my company at Sizargh, however returne him thanks for his kind invitation and his Civility, to conduct me to his Hous, and Heartily wish Matters may be Adjusted to the Satisfaction of him, to the comfort of my Daughter and according to the real desire of

Sir
Your Humble Servant
NICHOLAS BLUNDELL

To Mr Strickland

June 29th, 1725

SIR

Finding by yours of June 17th that you are desirous of an Alliance, I shall endeavour to give you the opportunity of an Intervieu which I hope may be don without troble or much notice being taken. Tuesday and Wednesday the thirteenth and fourteenth of next Month there will be Hors-Raises at Ormschurch. The first day is likely to be the best diversion, and then my Doughter will be on the ground if it be a fit day to stir abroad on; if you find she answers your expectation we may adjourn to Crosby or elce where as may be then Agreed upon, to discource the Affair; and though I have already profered more than I can without inconvenience comply to, yet perhaps I may make you a further Proposall. If I can be assured you'l be on the Ground I shall most certainly be there, let the Weather be what it will.

46. Two Marriage Contracts

THE TWO marriage contracts that follow are quite different both in their purpose and the information they provide the social historian. The Toulousan example tells us a great deal about how a dowry was raised—the mobilization of a whole clan to attain a respectable round sum. It shows how payments were echeloned to lessen the burden on the estate. Precise arrangements were made for widow or widower as well as for the younger brother of the bridgegroom, who was given a small annuity and a furnished room in the family château. Finally, the couple pledged half of their property to the eldest son to be born of the marriage. This is a tight, sober contract, typical of the provincial nobility of Toulouse.

By contrast, the Florentine contract contains no provisions for a widow's jointure and is not intended as a vehicle for the settlement of an estate. This was left entirely to the will. The wife's legal position seems less advantageous than that of her French counterpart. The future Marquise de Fourquevaux was promised three fourths of her dowry in widowhood, while the future Signora Bartolommei was guaranteed less than 2 per cent as an annual allowance. On the other hand, the Bartolommei family was at the very top of Florentine society, and the Capponi probably had to make concessions. The Capponi dowry was about three times the Fourquevaux dowry and about half a "good" noble dowry in Paris.

Sources: Document A: Robert Forster, *The Nobility of Toulouse in the Eighteenth Century: A Social and Economic Study*, pp. 196–198.* Document B: *Archivio di Stato, Firenze, Carte Bartolommei, F-158.*

* Reprinted by permission of Johns Hopkins University Press.

A. *A Contract of Marriage, Toulouse, 1722*

(A.D., *Contrats de mariage séparés*, 11803, March 24, 1722)
This is not a sample document but a summary of the articles of
a marriage contract.
Prospective Husband: M. François-Denis de Pavie de Becarie, Marquis de *Fourquevaux* (military nobility)
Prospective Wife: Dlle Henriette de *Catellan* (daughter of a councilor of Parlement)

Attending:

For Groom:

1. Dame Marie de Prohenques de Fourquevaux, widow,
   mother of the prospective husband.
2. M. de Pavie de Fourquevaux, brother of the prospective
   husband.

For Bride:

1. Dame Marie de Boisset de Catellan, widow, mother of the
   prospective wife.
2. M. Jean-Baptiste de Catellan, Former Canon of the Church
   of Toulouse, great uncle.
3. Dlles. Jeanne et Françoise de Catellan, aunts.
4. M. Jean-Louis de Catellan, Councilor of the King at the
   Parlement of Toulouse, brother.
5. M. Aimable de Catellan, Canon of the Church of Toulouse,
   brother.

Articles of Marriage:

1. The marriage will be celebrated according to the rites and
usages of the Roman Catholic and Apostolic Church.
2. Dame de Catellan, mother, promises to "gild" [*dorer*] the
bride, that is, provide her trousseau.
3. For the charges of the marriage, Dame de Catellan constitutes 8000 livres for the amount of the paternal portion regulated
betweeen the future wife and her brother, Seigneur de Catellan.
The future wife renounces all claims to a paternal portion.
Seigneur de Catellan pays 2000 livres at present to the prospective
husband. The remaining 6000 livres will be paid by the brother of
the bride as follows:

4000 livres in three months

2000 livres in two years at 4% [*denier vingt-cinq*] (to be paid
in coin, not in any kind of paper)

4. Dame de Catellan, mother, constitutes 4000 livres, payable
by the Seigneur de Catellan, brother, on the same conditions as
above (in two years at 4%).

The future wife renounces all claims to a maternal portion,
unless the number of Catellan children diminishes before the death
of her mother, Dame de Catellan.

5. M. Jean-Baptiste de Catellan, canon, great uncle of the
bride, makes a donation to his grand niece of 2500 livres to be
paid as follows:

1500 livres already "ceded to the Seigneur de Fourquevaux on
M. le Comte de Miran."

1000 livres paid after his death without interest.

6. Dlles. de Catellan, aunts of the bride, constitute 8000 livres
payable by the Seigneur de Catellan after the death of the aunts.

If the prospective wife dies without children, this donation will
be returned to the aunts or to other heirs whom they may designate.

7. M. Aimable de Catellan, canon, brother of the bride, makes
a donation of 1000 livres payable after his death and under the
above conditions of "right of return."

8. All of these sums *total 23,500 livres*, of which only 12,000 are
"dotal." Following the Customs of Toulouse, if the prospective
wife dies first, her husband will gain the 12,000 livres. In the
contrary case, the prospective wife will gain the 12,000 livres and
the "increase" [*augment*] of 6000 livres.

9. Nevertheless, the prospective husband will enjoy the revenues on the entire sum of 23,500 livres.

10. The prospective husband will recognize on all his property
all of the sums he will receive and he does recognize the 2000
livres received at present.

11. If the prospective wife dies childless, the prospective husband will retain 12,000 livres of the sums received. The rest will
be restored to the family Catellan.

12. If the prospective husband dies first, the prospective wife
will have an apartment in the château of Fourquevaux and 1000
livres during the year of mourning.

13. M. de Fourquevaux, brother of the prospective husband,

cedes, remits, and transports all of his property, rights, and claims in his quality as heir or beneficiary of his father, Marquis de Fourquevaux (who died of wounds received at the Battle of Hochstädt in 1704) to his brother in return for a life annuity of 600 livres per year. He can claim no change in this annuity for whatever reason. He also reserves the use of a furnished room in the château of Fourquevaux.

14. "Finally, the prospective married couple has given to one of the male children to be born of this marriage half of all their property, present and future, preferring to elect and name him, . . . but if they fail to name him, they have named and elected the eldest son not engaged in Holy Orders."

Signed at Toulouse, March 24, 1722
by the Fourquevaux and Catellan
families before witnesses.

Notice that of the total dowry of 23,500 livres, only 12,000 livres represented the paternal and maternal portions for which Seigneur de Catellan, eldest brother, was responsible. The rest was payable by an array of relatives, generally· after their deaths. Of the 12,000, Catellan paid 8000 (4000 in claims on third parties) by August 15, 1772. (Account on cover of marriage contract)

B. *A Contract of Marriage, Florence, 1745*

In the name of God . . . January 10, 1745

With the help of God and in the presence of worthy gentlemen, mutual friends, it is agreed that the marriage to be contracted between the Illustrissimo Signore Marchese Mattias Maria, son of the late Illustrissimo Signore Marchese and Cavaliere Girolamo Bartolommei, Chamberlain of his Cesaric Majesty, on the one part, and the Illustrissima Signora Maria Francesca, daughter of the Clarissimo Signore Senatore and Cavaliere Lorenzo Maria Capponi, Lady of Honor to the late Serenissima Elettrice Palatina, on the other, will take place with the following conventions and declarations.

The Signore Marchese Mattias Maria Bartolommei appeared personally before me and promised to take for his legitimate wife the said Illustrissima Signora Maria Francesca Capponi, to bestow on her the matrimonial ring, and to perform the wedding according to the rites of Holy Mother Church and the Holy

Council of Trent. And, likewise, the Illustrissimo Clarissimo Signore Senatore Cavaliere Lorenzo Capponi promised and promises to give to the said Signore Marchese Mattias Maria Bartolommei for his legitimate wife and consort the said Signora Maria Francesca Capponi, his daughter, and that she will consent to this marriage, receive the matrimonial ring, and follow the rites of the Holy Mother Church and the Holy Council of Trent. And for dowry of the said bride the said parties agreed to the sum and quantity of 13,000 *scudi*, money of 7 *lire* per *scudo*, to give and pay before the bestowing of the ring, which the said Signore Senatore Cavaliere Lorenzo Capponi promised and promises to give and pay to the said Signore Marchese Bartolommei.[1] In this dowry will be included the bride's trousseau to the value of 800 *scudi* in accordance with dowries generally given to women of the court, with the agreement that, if the bride's own jewelry is appropriate and satisfactory to the Marchese bridegroom, it will be assessed by two assessors known to the two parties and included in the dowry to the value of 500 *scudi*, the remainder being kept as an extra-dotal possession by the said bride. As for the annual allowance usually given the bride, the two parties agree that the aforesaid Signore Marchese Bartolommei promises and obliges himself to give to the bride 180 *scudi* annually for her clothing and for incidentals as well as a gift of her own choosing for the celebration of Christmas every year, and the said Marchese bridegroom will be obliged to provide these sums to the said bride for her clothing and other expenses.

It is furthermore declared and agreed by the two parties that, should the said bride receive any gift or legacy from any persons known to her, however unrelated, after the giving of the ring, this will belong entirely to her, both in property and in revenue, notwithstanding any disposition that might appear from the statutes of the commune, common law, or other.

And in fulfillment of the above agreement, the aforesaid Signore Senatore Lorenzo Maria Capponi gives and consigns to the aforesaid Signore Marchese Mattias Maria Bartolommei, here present and agreeing, the sum and quantity of 11,700 *scudi* in coin, together with the aforesaid jewels and trousseau, assessed

---

[1] The *scudo* is equivalent to 5.86 *livres tournois*, or about $5.80 (1968). A dowry of 75,400 livres would be high for provincial France, though modest for Parisian nobility.

and valued by assessors mutually elected and consigned for the value of 13,000 *scudi*, with the understanding that any remaining jewelry or other that the bride might retain will be her extra-dotal possession, as agreed above.

And for all this aforesaid, Signore Marchese Mattias Maria Bartolommei gives spontaneously and entirely to the aforesaid Signore Senatore Lorenzo Capponi, here present, assurance and perpetual agreement to ask no more, or request no further payment in connection with the said dowry, and he furthermore promises and promised to acknowledge and maintain the said dowry and return it to the said bride and her family, along with the marriage gift, the marriage or widow's ring, the dotal agreement, and whatever else is needed by the bride and her family, in accordance with the usages of Florence, if the marriage is dissolved.

Which particular things mentioned above the said parties promised and promise to respectively hold and observe . . .

47. The Will of a Parisian Noble, 1763

THE TESSÉ family represented old, military nobility. The elder branch gravitated to the court during the reign of Louis XIV and held numerous honorific posts at Versailles until the Revolution. The Marquis de Tessé, however, avoided prolonged stays at court and spent much of his time on his Norman estate at Aunay. This no doubt helped him preserve his great wealth. His daughter, an heiress of great attraction, married the Marquis de Saulx-Tavanes, whose children became the heirs of the Tessé fortune.

Ten years before this will was made, the Marquis de Tessé owned substantial investments in overseas commerce operating from Cadiz, which he had probably acquired from his father-in-law, the Lyon banker, Castan. This would account for his large reserve of liquid capital. Instead of reinvesting in commercial ventures, however, the Marquis apparently lent part of the money to tax receivers and robe nobles [1] and kept the larger portion in strongboxes in his townhouse. At the same time, he appears to have spent very little money for personal consumption (note the small clothing bill), and his charitable bequests were meager indeed.

Tessé was a millionaire both by inheritance and personal economy,

[1] Magistrates, chancellors, judges, and other high officials.

but he could hardly be called a capitalist entrepreneur. His Tavanes grandchildren knew better how to stimulate the Parisian luxury trades by prodigious consumption of fine cloth, jewelry, furnishings, and all that goes with a magnificent style of Parisian living. (The Tessé will is part of the Saulx-Tavanes family papers.)

Source: *Archives Départementales, Côte d'Or, series E-1702.*

Testament of Marquis de Tessé, October 4, 1763

[In a short, almost perfunctory paragraph, Marquis de Tessé affirms his adherence to the Roman Catholic and Apostolic Church and recommends his soul to God]

I WISH to be buried in my parish of the Isle de Notre Dame [in Paris] without any pomp and heraldry and to have my body accompanied by fifty foundlings. I give 2,000 livres to the curé for my funeral expenses and for the poor, to be used at the discretion of the curé of St. Louis en l'Isle.

I institute as my principal heir my grandson, Marquis de Tavanes, with the following conditions: to give to his brothers and sister 150,000 livres each, which sum is to be taken from the gold and silver coin to be found in my strongboxes or in the desk of my study. . . . So that the land of Aunay will remain untouched and be given after the death of my wife, Madame de Tessé, to the Marquis de Tavanes . . .[1] I expressly forbid M. de Saulx, their father [son-in-law of the testator], to dispose of the inheritance in any manner, either to pay the debts of his family or to meet any other obligations, except with their written permission.[2]

Moreover, they will enjoy life annuities on the Hôtel de Ville [of Paris], and in the case of death of one or more of the children before their majority, their share will be equally divided among the surviving brothers or sister.

Since Sieur and Dame de Tessé were married according to the written [Roman] law and since all of her property is "acquired," she is absolutely free to dispose of it as she sees fit.[3] For this

[1] The estate of Aunay in Normandy was worth about 400,000 livres or about 15,000 livres income in 1763. The livre is about one American dollar (1968).
[2] The three grandchildren, two boys and one girl, who were the chief beneficiaries of the will.
[3] Under Roman law, the widow had disposition over the "*acquits.*"

purpose I give to my wife as a supplement to her jointure: all the movables, jewelry, and precious stones either in Paris or on the domain of Aunay, half of the silverware, and 30,000 livres in coin. I leave to her my clothes to be given to the poor of the parish.

I give a life annuity of 400 livres to Dame Lecomte for the education of the children, to be paid from the children's portions, and I give an annuity of 200 livres to her husband, if he survives her.

I give a life annuity of 400 livres to Dame Deautier, wet nurse of M. de Tavanes, to be paid quarterly.

I leave to Dominique, my cook, a life annunity of 150 livres.

I leave to my two lackeys 100 livres each, in one payment, and their old uniforms, in appreciation of the care they gave me during my illness.

I leave to the curé of Aunay 1,000 livres for his salary, and, if there is any left over, it is to be given to the poor.

I beg M. de Saulx to please accept two beautiful oval paintings by Carlo Maratti.[4]

The liquid capital amounts to about 500,000 livres; that is, about 180,000 livres in gold, to be found in the desk of my secretary, about 100,000 livres in silver *écus*, either in the desk or in the strongbox above my clothes closet, and 120,000 livres in the hands of M. de Murlan, tax receiver of the Generality of Paris, payable according to drafts to be found in my secretary, the keys to which are in the hands of Madame de Tessé. Madame de Tessé should not issue these drafts before they come due, which will be in the course of next year, 1764. . . .

In addition, 60,000 livres are owed to me by Sieur Richard, Receiver General of Finances at the Hôtel Montbazon, from a mortgage of an equal sum on the said house, which he [Richard] owes and promises to pay soon.

In addition, I urge and enjoin M. de Saulx to activate and pursue for the benefit of his children a claim of 200,000 livres on the inheritance of M. Bernaud, *Maître de Requêtes*.

Also, to pursue and terminate the law case pending against Abbé de Jean over the house on the Place Royale.

Note that, regarding my *rentes*, my intention is that they be divided equally among the children.

[4] Italian artist (1625–1713), painted mostly Madonnas and other religious subjects.

I name as my testamentary executor, M. de la Loire, former notary . . . whom I ask to accept a diamond of 3,000 livres.

Supplement to These Testamentary Dispositions, Made on October 5, 1763, on His Deathbed

The testator wishes that Mademoiselle de Tavanes remain with her grandmother and that 4,000 livres a year be given to Madame de Tessé from her inheritance for room and board until God has decided her future.

All the annuities are to be paid by the children out of their inheritance.

The testator has given Madame de Tessé 30,000 livres to avoid all discussion and embarrassment regarding the children.[5]

He gives Madame de Tessé, in addition to the household furnishings, the horses and carriages belonging to the house.

In addition, he begs Madame de Tessé not to leave the house until the money has been removed.

He leaves Madame de Tessé 2,000 livres for her mourning.

Marquis de Tessé owes Madame Maurice Bouchère 2,000 livres and establishes a pension of 100 livres while she is awaiting reimbursement.

Marquis de Tessé has a draft for about 800 livres in the hands of Sieur Bourgiot, draper, of which one half was due immediately and is already paid.

Bills for provisions are to be paid.

Madame de Tessé will find a drawer in his [her husband's] secretary filled with memoranda and also silver pieces, which he gives to his grandaughter for pocket money.

He also gives a gold box with a portrait to M. de Tavanes, his grandson, and another porcelain snuffbox to Madame de Tavanes, and a gold ring to M. l'abbé Marjean, tutor of the chevalier de Tavanes.

[The Marquis ends this codicil by reiterating his desire for a simple burial service]

From a note attached to the will:

The burial took place over three years later (December 18, 1766), at a cost of 1,462 livres. Despite the dispositions of the

---

[5] That is, regarding the children's claims to the estate.

Marquis, a wooden coffin "pleased neither the family nor the curé," and was replaced by a lead conveyance more befitting the rank of the deceased.

48.   The Will of a Florentine Patrician, 1744

THE BARTOLOMMEI will is an interesting contrast to the will of the Parisian Marquis de Tessé. The wealth of the Marchese Bartolommei seems much more uniform in composition. Land is the principal asset. Although like Tessé he possessed a certain amount of "movables," the Marchese, unmarried, was much more concerned with entailing his estate. Notice the strict family settlement, explicitly prohibiting alienation, or even mortgaging, of the entailed property. Since the entail includes cash, bonds, stock shares, plate, and books, as well as land, it would seem that younger children in future generations were to be sacrificed to the head of the family. Notice too that the will establishes a perpetual entail ("from male to male indefinitely"), a practice prohibited by law in France from 1744, though occasionally violated.

Bartolommei's religious convictions may be more formal than profound. His charitable bequests (30 *scudi*) do not seem excessive, considering that his silver plate alone exceeded 6,000 *scudi*. His interest in books and the opera, however, suggest a man of some refinement and taste.

Source: *Archivio di Stato, Firenze, Carte Bartolommei, F-188.*

IN THE name of God, amen, in the year of the incarnation of our Lord Jesus Christ one thousand seven hundred and forty-four, on the eleventh day of December, in the pontificate of Benedict XIV and in the glorious reign of His Royal Highness Ferdinand III, Duke of Lorraine and Bar, and Grand Duke of Tuscany, done in Florence in the house of usual habitation of the undersigned testator, in the parish of San Piero Maggiore, Via della Pergola, in the presence of witnesses asked and invited by the same, to wit:

The most reverend father Giovanni Maria of Florence
The most reverend father Giovanni Gualberto of Fiesole
The most reverend father Ferdinando of Florence

The most reverend father Giovanni Battista of San Oreste
Brother Francesco of Pelago
Brother Raffaello of Carmignano, and
Brother Giuliano of Ponte a Rignano, all members of the Reformed Order of Saint Francis.

Since there is nothing in the world more certain than death, nor more uncertain than the hour of its coming, *cum staium fit homini semel mori,* his excellency, Signore Marchese Ferdinando, son of the late Signore Marchese Mattias Maria Bartolommei, noble patrician of Florence, State Councilor of Her Majesty the Queen of Hungary, and one of the Councilors of State of His Royal Highness, sound, by God's grace, of mind, senses, vision, and intellect, although weak in body and confined to his bed, wishing to dispose of his affairs, made and makes his last testament in the following manner, to wit:

First, he recommends his soul to Omnipotent God and the Glorious Mother always Virgin Mary, to his guardian angel, and to all the celestial court of paradise, desiring that, after his soul be separated from his body, his body be exhibited in his house and buried in the Church of San Stefano in his family tomb with that funeral expense fitting to his station and that in supplication for his soul a thousand requiem masses, and as many more as possible, be said in the church of his funeral.

Being reminded of the needs of the poor of this city under the protection of San Giovanni Battista, he leaves to that almshouse 30 *scudi* [176 livres].

He leaves in legacy to the Opera of Santa Maria del Fiore of this city of Florence 3 *lire* and 10 *soldi,* in order to continue his usual contribution as a customary legacy.

He orders that all agreements signed by himself and notarized by a public notary be executed.

As for his other possessions, movable, immovable, cash, municipal bonds, business shares, and assets belonging to the said testator, he designates as his sole heir the Illustrissimo Signore Marchese Cavaliere Girolamo Bartolommei, his brother, and after his death he designates the first-born male child of the said heir and his children and male descendants from male to male indefinitely in order of primogeniture. And if the male line of the said firstborn son of the said heir should become extinct, he substitutes the second born with his male line, and then the third, fourth, and later born with their respective male lines, one after the other, always preserving the order of lineal primogeniture.

And should the male lines of the male children of the said Signore Marchese Mattias, the designated heir, become extinct, he substitutes the Illustrissima Signora Caterina Bartolommei, his niece by his brother, wife of the Signore Giovanni Baldovinetti, and, after her death, her first born son, and thereafter the male descendants in the same order of primogeniture. And should the male line of her first son become extinct, he substitutes the second, third, fourth, and later-born sons with their respective male lines one after the other in the order of lineal primogeniture so long as there is a male descendant of the said Signora Caterina, his niece.

And should the male lines of the Signore Marchese Mattias Bartolommei, his nephew, and of the Signora Caterina Bartolommei-Baldovinetti, his niece, fail, he substitutes all the persons, lines, and families substituted in the testament of the late Illustrissimo Signore Marchese Mattias Maria Bartolommei, his father, of December 13, 1695, notarized by Lorenzo Borghigiani, as if the said persons, lines, and families were described in the present testament, under the condition that the said persons, lines, and families succeed in order of lineal primogeniture, the first-born son always being preferred to the others.

And, since the said testator has used and alienated silver plate and jewelry included in the entail of the said Signore Marchese Mattias Maria Bartolommei, his father, in his aforementioned will, [the testator], in order to reintegrate the said entail, orders that the said executors take silver plate from his own estate comparable in value to the plate and jewelry alienated, reckoning from the inventory of his father's estate, and that this plate be assigned to the entail. And he desires that, from his remaining plate, anything exceeding the value of 6,000 *scudi* [35,160 livres] be sold, and that its value, along with the cash found in his house at the time of his death or employed in current affairs, be invested in landed property in Tuscany or in municipal bonds of Florence or another city, and that these investments be included in the entail. And, remembering in the above-mentioned will that he was left the entire library of his father under bond of entail and has enlarged it by the purchase of various books, he wishes that all the books bought by himself be included in the entail and be bound by all its restrictions and regulations.

And in order that the landed property and other possessions included in the said entail be preserved undivided in the hands of those who succeed to the entail, he prohibits alienation by any legal device, whether voluntary or necessary, so that the property shall not be alienated or transferred in any way. Failing to obey this stipulation, the guilty party *ipse jure et ipso facto* shall be deprived of the said entail, and another heir will replace him as specified above in the case of death.

He excludes from the said entail any person in cloistered religious orders, out of no disrespect for religion, which he venerates highly, but so that the revenue and profit of the estate should serve for the decorous maintenance of laymen, who may thus preserve the family.

And should any of those called to the enjoyment of the said entail commit any crime (God forbid!) that might lead to the confiscation of the property or contract debts or go bankrupt, in such case, the delinquent will be deprived of the benefit of the said entail for a year, and the next in line of inheritance will have the estate as if it were a case of death. [The testator] stipulates this not out of disrespect to fiscal officials or creditors, but so that those called to enjoy the entail refrain from contracting debts and live in the holy fear of God and in accordance with the law of their prince.

Furthermore, he prohibits to all the said heirs to give bond or security on the estate, and, in case of disobedience, he substitutes the next in line of succession, as established for the case of death.

Finally, he elects as executors of this his last will and testament, the Illustrissimo Signore Conte Vincenzio de Bardi, the Illustrissimo Signore Cavaliere Pietro Mannelli, the Illustrissimo Signore Cavaliere Ricovero Uguccioni, and the Illustrissimo Signore Giovanni Baldovinetti, giving to the same all the powers usually given to executors and begging them to exercise all vigilance so that the above-mentioned sales and investments be made.

And he declares that his last will and testament, which if it is not upheld as a last will, shall be observed in the form of its codicils. . . .

49. Raising Noble Children

PHILIPPE ARIÈS, in his provocative history of childhood, traces the
changes in parental attitude toward child raising from the Middle
Ages.[1] By the eighteenth century, he sees a more sentimentalized concern with the personality of the child as a child, not as a miniature
adult or a plaything for adults. With this new attitude came a change
in child rearing.

The anonymous reformer in the French periodical *Ephémérides du
Citoyen* suggests that this new attention to the child may have become
overprotective. In any case, he castigates the upper nobility for pam-
pering their children, making them physically unfit for the rigors of
adult life at court, in the army, or in the high councils of state. Child
raising, claims this observer, cannot be divorced from the future profession of the individual, and training must begin early.

Source: *Ephémérides du Citoyen ou bibliothèque raisonnée des
sciences morales et politiques,* V (1766), 163ff.

Child Raising in the Upper Nobility

To AN observer, it is an extraordinary experience to compare the
life led by the children of that class [the great nobility] with the
life their parents are obliged to lead, even if they are sober and
good patriots. The former are always put to bed as night falls, to
be taken up again late the next morning after a night of profound
sleep. They are regularly given wholesome, easily digested food
and are kept all day long in as perfect a temperature as possible,
without exposure to excessive heat or cold. From fear of exhaust-
ing them by immoderate fatigue, they are never permitted to run
or jump but are made to walk around in measured steps. Every
care is taken not to arouse any of their passions, and this is almost
the entire art of governesses, tutors, and governors, as well as the
mania of misled parents. They avoid making children angry, arousing any of their desires, or restricting them; they put them to
work in a very cautiously measured manner. These regular and

[1] *Centuries of Childhood.*

invariably moderate practices are considered the very best home education.

It is not necessary to describe the life of high society in any detail to make the reader understand that it is precisely and necessarily the contrary of such regularity: it entails going to bed at the crack of dawn, arising after the sun has run more than a third of its course, sustaining violent exercise under the guise of pastime or pleasure, and working mentally or physically as time or circumstance require—what a contrast! . . .

The excessive delicacy of their [the children of great nobles] physical education, especially in the early years of childhood and youth, has today made them the most wretched specimens of the human race; they hardly have a breath of life in them and often perish before maturity. The complacency or indifference of fathers, the blind tenderness, vanity, and inconsistency of mothers, the ineptitude and the adulation of governesses and other more-or-less titled valets, plus the quackery of physicians, who take hold of them as soon as they are born—all conspire to give them a weak constitution, making them unable to withstand the exertions imposed upon them by the duties and even pleasures of their station in life. This is all the more true since they are carefully locked up in hermetically sealed apartments three fourths of the time, where they are either lying down, sitting, or tenderly carried about. They are hardly permitted to spend a twentieth of their time on their own two feet and besides take nothing but light dishes and often useless, or even harmful, medications. When they reach maturity, you see them pale, spare, delicate, and infirm.

50. Family Discipline Among the Provincial Gentry

THE PUREFOYS—Elizabeth and her son Henry—were English country gentry. Their 1,500-acre estate near Stowe in Buckinghamshire yielded less than £400 per annum, a modest 2 per cent return. Taxes were a substantial burden—two shillings to the pound (10 per cent) before 1740 and 4 shillings to the pound (20 per cent) after. Economy was essential, and both Purefoys knew how to make do. Their correspondence demonstrates how well they grasped the pound value of everything—from servants' wages to the cost of yarn. Yet the Purefoys were not harsh landlords. Henry actually appealed for legal help for the poor of a neighboring parish who had lost their pasture rights. His rents remained unchanged for thirty-four years. Understandably, Elizabeth Purefoy had little sympathy for her spendthrift nephew, who loved "fine equipage" and "velvet silk" too much. Here family discipline was a function of a modest income. The habits and outlook of the Purefoy family seem little different from those of the provincial nobility throughout western Europe.

Source: G. Eland, ed., *Purefoy Letters, 1735–1753* (London, 1931) vol. II, pp. 142–143, 246–247.*

No. 379. E. P. to Mrs Porter

Shalstone [&c.]
Octob^r the 21st 1739

DEAR SISTER /

I received yours a considerable time ago and am glad to hear your son Porter & his spouse were to visit you. Wee should have been glad if it had been in our power to have done your younger son any acceptable service, but as it is now War Time I hope you will find it no difficulty to have your Expectations answered as to him, as he has been bred to sea affairs. All our ffriends who could have served him are either dead or who [sic] have no interest at Court. I have my health pretty well now, all but a sore Leg which has been very bad as I have been in health. It is a Scorbutick humour & I cannot learn when it is to be well. My son presents his Duty to you & wee both desire our love & service to your ffamily & shall be glad to hear of all your healths, which concludes mee

Your affect. sister
E. P.

ffor /

Mrs Porter
        at
            Scarborough
        in Yorkshire
By London /

* Reprinted by permission of Sidgwick & Jackson, Ltd.

No. 380. E. P. to Mrs Jane Cunnington

Shalstone [&c.]
December the 31st 1740

MADAM /

I reced yours of the 20th instant & in answer thereto I do assure you I have never given my nephew Ralph Porter one farthing of money since hee has been married nor some time before, nor never shall give him anything for I have a son of my own & if I had ten times what I have I would leave it him. My nephew lost my favour on account of some little Indiscretions here, & soon after I heard hee had bought chambers at Barnards Inne, or rather built them at a great expence & put himself in a garb of velvet silk, gold & silver, & a fine Diamond ring at a greater Expence, & after that I discarded him knowing that his circumstances could not bear anything of that kind, ffor I suppose my sister Porter has £40 a year in land at old Newton in Yorkshire for her life, & hee has it after her in ffee, & I suppose my sister may have to the vallue of £1.000 besides at her disposall, as hee told mee for I have not seen my sister Porter since the year 1716.

As to what Dr Trimnell said about my giving my nephew a great summe of money I heard it from severall of my neighbours that Dr Trimnell should say so, & when the Dr was at Astrop Wells last season I took care to send him word there was nothing in it. I look on the Doctor to be a very worthy gentleman & am sorry to hear my nephew has used him as hee has. I doubt my nephew takes his basenesse from the Porters, for I never knew any of my ffather or mother's kindred behave as hee has done. I think his father made a poor Improvement of the fortune hee had with my sister, for hee had £3.000 with her at my ffather's death besides what hee had with her before.

I once thought my nephew Porter as likely to get an Estate by his Businesse as any young fellow whatsoever, & if I could have prevailed on him to have been advised by mee & my son wee thought no otherwise than to have encouraged him & to have been kind to him.

I hope Mrs Porter as an Heiresse has kept her land to herself at least. Hee reported when hee came to Town & bought the Chariot

& fine equipage that hee had £400 a year in land left him by the
Conington family, exclusive of you & there was a report that hee
had got your money in his hands, wch came from a merchant in
the City & that hee had put £800 thereof in the late Alderman
Childs hands to take up to pay Tradesmen, and hee once gave out
hee had my will in his keeping wch is entirely false. I aver this for
Truth and wish it may be serviceable to you.

 I am, Madam,

Your humble servant
E. P.

ffor /

 Mrs Jane Conington
 To be left at Mrs Ruxtons
 in the ffishmarket below the
 Hill in Lincoln in Lincolnshire
 By London

No. 231. E. P. to Mrs Mary Sheppard

Shalstone [&c.]
ffebr^u 12th 1743

Mrs Sheperd/

 My maid Mary, her sister being dead & her mother very ill, she
is oblidged to go home to look after her; and I want a maid in her
place. She must be a thorough servant & capable of seeing the
sending in of 5 or 10 dishes of meat upon occasion. Tho' I keep a
cookmaid she must understand that part, and she is to wash the
small Linnen & clean part of the house & make some beds. Her
wages are to be £3 or £3. 10s. but she will meet with other
encouragements if she does well. Pray let mee have an answer by
the post as soon as may be if you are likely to succeed & charge
this letter to my account. Your son Joseph is very much grown,
hee gives his Duty & Love to you all. This will oblidge

Your freind to serve you
E. P.

ffor /

 Mrs Mary Sheppard at
 Cornwell near Chipping-norton
in
Oxfordshire
By way of London

No. 232. E. P. to Mrs Mary Sheppard

Shalstone
ffebᵛʳ 23ᵗʰ 1743

I reced Mʳˢ Sheppard's letter, I hope the maid will do if she can sow well, that is to work fine plain worke as mobs & rufles. If she comes she must bring a Character of her Honesty from the person she lived with last. My custom is to give the servants a shilling for horse hire & they come themselves, & I will give her half a crown because she comes so far. If she agrees to this she may come next Wensday or next Thursday. The horse & man who attend her shall be wellcome to stay here all night, & shall be glad to see you here when fine weather comes. If I don't see her here by Thursday next I shall conclude she will not come at all. I am

Your freind to serve you
E.P.

P.S. Your son presents his Duty to you. Hee has but 4 shirts to wear & desires you would send him two shirts when the maid comes. The sleeves must be very near half an Ell long.

ffor /
Mʳˢ Mary Sheppard . . .
This

51. The Accounts of the Duc de Saulx-Tavanes in 1788

FAMILY ACCOUNTS need not be dry registers of meaningless figures. On the revenue side of the ledger, they tell us about the composition of individual fortunes, the relative worth of land, offices, bonds, commercial investments, or royal pensions. On the expenditure side, they contain information about relative costs, types of loans, consumer tastes, and style of living. They also reveal the degree of sophistication of accounting techniques. Family accounts will vary from the small personal diary-style account book to the printed yearly statement kept by a professional accountant and estate manager.

The account below is of the latter type. The Saulx-Tavanes (cf. Document 47) were court nobility who lived on a grand scale at Paris and Versailles. About two thirds of their regular annual income came from the land and another third from royal pensions. Despite a rapid increase in landed income after 1750, it was not enough to cover increasing expenses. Notice that two new loans are listed under the "receipts" and that the interest due on loans and annuities stands at about 83,000 livres, not counting the interest on family obligations of 34,000. It is not surprising that this account was accompanied by a budget proposing that the duke reduce his household expenses to 56,000 livres. The budget plan also stated that receipts for 1790 "will increase" by about 20,000 livres, presumably by a policy of continuing to raise rents on the estates in Burgundy and selling more land in Normandy. Excluding new loans, the duke's regular income was 120,000 livres. In France this sum represented about twelve times the revenue of a provincial nobleman, one hundred times that of a solicitor or small merchant, and six hundred times the annual wage of a day laborer.

Source: *Archives Départementales, Côte d'Or, E-1715* (Saulx-Tavanes).

Receipts and Expenses from January 1, 1788, to December 31, 1788

Monsieur Jean Godard, advocate at *parlement*, declares that, although he is the intendant of Monseigneur le Duc de Saulx-Tavanes, he does not receive the revenues directly from the tenants, *rentiers*, and debitors, but from Monsieur le Duc himself, to whom he gives receipts for each item.

Receipts

Ch. I.	Lands in Burgundy (sent by M. Billard)	62,456#[1]
Ch. II.	Lands in Normandy (sent by M. Poignant)	15,227#
Ch. III.	*Dîmes* [tithes] of the Calaisis	7,900#
Ch. IV.	Appointments and pensions:	
	Pension on the royal treasury	15,000#
	Commander of the Order of the King	3,000#
	Chevalier d'Honneur of the Queen	10,460#
	Governor of Château Toureau	9,900#
	Lieutenant-General in Burgundy	820#
	Total pensions	39,180#
Ch. V.	*Rentes:*	
	On the *Hôtel de Ville*	6,276#
	On the Clergy of France	578#

[1] The "#" stands for livres.

	On Marquis de Mirepoix	1,167#
	Total *rentes*	8,021#
Ch. VI.	New loans:	
	From M. le Comte de Rieux at 5 per cent	18,500#
	By draft payable Oct. 21, 1789 for the	
	trousseau for M. le Comte de Tavanes,	
	son of M. le Duc	19,100#
Ch. VII.	Extraordinary receipts:	
	Surplus on the account of the inheritance of	
	M. le Comte de Saulx, father of M. le Duc	20,029#
	TOTAL RECEIPTS	190,413#

Expenses

Ch. I.	Due for 1787	4,814#
Ch. II.	Personal expenses of M. le Duc	76,475#
Ch. III.	Interest on 19 loans by drafts	21,341#
Ch. IV.	Life annuities to 20 individuals	12,275#
Ch. V.	Perpetual *rentes* to 33 individuals	49,422#
Ch. VI.	Rent for townhouse in Paris for 6 months	3,160#
Ch. VII.	Interest due on children's portions:	
	M. le Comte, 18,000# due, 9,000# paid	
	Vicomtesse de Castellane, 10,000#	
	Comtesse de Kercado, 6,000# due, 4,000# paid	
	Total interest on portions	23,000#
Ch. VIII.	Extraordinary expenses:	
	1. Estimation of silverware of M. le de	
	Saulx, father 60#	
	2. Capitation tax for servants [2] 124#	
	3. Spent because of marriage of son 36#	
	4. Price of a company of dragoons in	
	the Dauphiné regiment acquired	
	for M. le Comte de Tavanes, son,	
	vacant by the promotion of	
	Comte de La Roche to the rank	
	of major 5,250#	
	5. Deducted from appointments	
	of 900# 15#	

[2] In 1787 the duke paid a capitation tax for himself of 1,176 livres, about 1 per cent of his income. The twentieth tax on his land was paid in Burgundy and Normandy, and had already been deducted from the receipts. It represented 10 per cent of his rents in the 1780's.

6. Honorarium to M. Boursier,
   notary   200#
7. To M. Bro, notary   2,650#
8. To the administration (Godard):
   Bonus for extra work   2,400#
   Honorarium for 1788   800#
   Miscellaneous   48#
   Total   3,248#
   Total of Chapter VIII   11,583#
   TOTAL EXPENSES   202,070#
   Deficit for 1789   11,657#

Made in duplicate at Paris, January 31, 1789. Approved,

LE DUC DE SAULX
GODARD

VIII

Education

THE DISSEMINATION of new ideas and knowledge we associate with the Enlightenment took place largely outside the formal educational system. In fact, the quality of education in the schools may have declined. A growing population threatened a chronic shortage of money and teachers. In Catholic countries, the teaching orders—especially the Jesuits, Oratorians, and Christian Brothers—made this less of a problem, since they often taught free of charge. But the quality of education remained low almost everywhere.

Of course, few of the advanced reformers believed in universal free education. The mass of the peasantry should attain only bare literacy at most. Curriculum was the central interest of reformers. The selection below (Document 53) from an anonymous French reformer writing in the *Ephémérides du Citoyen* stresses the necessity for a more utilitarian education that would better prepare each "class" of citizens for its function in society. Both French reformers and such English educators as Campbell (Document 52) were ardently opposed to the amount of effort expended on Latin grammar and literature. They suggested that more time be spent on the living languages and on history and geography. Campbell was also opposed to the hazing of younger students by seniors and the rigid discipline of the masters in the English public schools, while the anonymous French reformer was more concerned with professional training, and even physical exercise, especially for the nation's elite.

The universities, as always, were slow to respond to curriculum reforms. Oxford and Cambridge do not seem to have undergone any radical changes since the Middle Ages, but continued to live on their illustrious reputations. The University of Paris seemed impervious to D'Alembert's charge that the young graduate emerged with a superficial knowledge of dead languages, rhetoric, philosophy, and even religion. The best universities were in Germany, though the quality varied from principality to principality. Göttingen was probably the most advanced university in Europe, and Gedicke's description of it is an interesting contrast to Forster's of the University of Vilna—in the academic "Siberia" of eighteenth-century Europe. The same sharp contrast could be made between Edinburgh and Alcalá. By all academic criteria—academic freedom, faculty, library, teaching methods, and fields of research—Edinburgh was first class, Alcalá pathetic.

There was no relation between university excellence and university accessibility. Oxford, Cambridge, Göttingen, and a number of German universities drew their students almost exclusively from the upper classes, the aristocracy in particular. The twenty-two French universities and the Italian ones, despite their conservatism in every other way, were relatively open to all social groups who could pay their board. Surprisingly perhaps, the University of Moscow was open to all regardless of social status.

Unfortunately, historians know less about secondary and grammar schools. French critics might rail against the local clergy for their rote learning and scholastic ineptitude, but the Church provided the only large teaching force available to inculcate the three R's. In England the charity-school and Sunday-school movements had some success with the lower classes, though distrust of state education, complicated by strong feelings between Anglicans and Dissenters, was a serious obstacle to educational reform. Without question the widest elementary education was found in Prussia after Frederick II made it compulsory in 1763 and in Scotland, where pressure from church and public opinion obtained the same result.[1]

52. Education in England

CAMPBELL's London Tradesman is a manual on education and training for the trades and professions. The document here presents his views on educational reform. Without displaying either the radicalism of Rousseau or the comprehensive programing of the authors writing in the Ephémérides (see Document 53 below), Campbell recommends a reduction of Latin studies from seven to three years and a firm foundation in English grammar, literature, history, and customs. This is to be followed by French, "the courtly language of Europe" and a "trading tongue" besides. Other living languages useful in commerce—Dutch, Spanish, Portuguese, and Italian—can be learned by the "Youth's own application." However, curriculum changes like these had more chance of adoption in German universities like Göttingen than in the public schools and private academies of England.

Source: R. Campbell, The London Tradesman (London, 1747), pp. 82–88.

[1] Cf. M. S. Anderson, Europe in the Eighteenth Century, 1713–1783, p. 285.

Remarks on Education

As I shall have frequent Occasion in the Course of this Treatise to mention the particular Education of Youth who are not designed for the Practice of any of the three Learned Professions, *viz.* Law, Physic, or Divinity, I have taken this Opportunity to point out the Errors of the present Schools, and the Manner I apprehend the Time employed in these Seminaries may be best improved.

At present, private Boarding-Schools, called Academies, are preferred to the Public Seminaries; and, perhaps, not without a great deal of Reason: The Public Schools entertain too many Scholars for the Masters to be able to do Justice to their Pupils; and, in general, those employed in them are mere Pedants, versed in nothing but mere Letters, without any Knowledge of useful Literature, and profoundly ignorant of Men and Things. Such an one has no Talent for discovering and humouring the Boy's Genius; but teaches him by some dogmatic Method, from whence he can no more be persuaded to swerve, than the *French* Nation to abrogate the Salique Law: He goes on in one continued dull beaten Track; his Brain too is baren, and perhaps he is too lazy to consider the Method of conveying Knowledge according to the Natural Genius or Manner of Apprehension peculiar to each Youth: But if his old Precepts will not do, he endeavours to cram the Languages down their Throats, by the Help of his darling *Ferula*, or a sullen severe Behaviour; and by this means whips his Pupils into Blockheads, and prepares their young Minds for the most slavish Subjection.

Their Want of Judgment of the Boy's Genius is not the only Misfortune that attend the Masters of Public Schools; they have prescribed a certain Course, in which they are all agreed, which spends so much Time that the most valuable Part of the Youth's Life is taken up in learning, or attempting to learn Trifles of no Signification to his future Happiness: Seven Years is the least they require to compleat a Boy in a partial Knowledge of the Classics; I call it partial, however well they may understand the Language, because they and their Masters are utter Strangers to the Spirit and Meaning of those celebrated Authors: They can render, it is true, their Words into *English*, but they can speak their noble Sentiments in no Language; and whatever Progress they have made in *Greek* and *Latin*, it is certain they often know no more of their Mother Tongue (except the mere Sound) than if they had been born in *Japan*, or at the *Cape of Good Hope*.

This is the Misfortune of most Public Schools, and the greater Seminaries of *Westminster*, *Eaton*, &c. are not free from them, and are attended with some Mischiefs not less in their Consequences than the former: There is a base Custom in *Westminster-School*, which I am surprized has not been taken notice of and remedied by the Legislature, since so many eminent Members of the Government have been brought up at that Seminary. The Custom I mean is, the tyranical Subjection under which the junior Scholars are kept by the senior: They are mere Slaves; are obliged to fetch and carry, like Spaniels; and do all the Drudgery of Menial Servants, under the Penalty of being severely beat by their Seniors: For which they have no Redress from the Masters; who both connive at and tolerate this Custom, for no better Reason than because, perhaps, they had gone through the same Discipline themselves in their Youth: This must be galling to a Boy of a generous Spirit, and can propagate nothing but the Doctrine of Slavery and Arbitrary Power.

Private Academies, as I observed, are now become much in Fashion; yet they have very few Advantages over the Public Schools, only they are not so much crouded, and therefore the Masters are more at leisure to do justice to Individuals; but they are, generally speaking, as the others, and their Method is very little better, and, for the most part, as tedious.

I should chuse to have my Son initiated in Letters after this Manner: After he had learned to read *English* distinctly, I would, instead of plunging him immediately into a *Latin* Accidence, teach him *English* grammatically; enable him to analize his Mother Tongue by all the Rules of Grammar, and make him perfectly acquainted with its natural Idiom: To fix this in his Head I would make him read and observe the Beauties of our most eminent Authors, in the different Stiles of the Bar, the Pulpit, the Stage, and Historian. He should employ at least two Years in this Manner, learning the History of his own Country, and their particular Customs and Manners. By this Time I suppose the Youth about ten or eleven Years of Age, when I would initiate him in *Latin* by teaching him to construe the most easy Authors; in the Course of which he should be taught the Difference between the

Latin and *English* Idioms: As he had learned the general Rules of Grammar, he must learn that there is no Difference in the Grammatical Construction of *Latin* and that of *English*, but that the first is declined by Termination, and the last by Article only. Thus would half the Task be over; for it is evident, that a Youth who has already learned the Principles of Grammar, need but to store his Mind with a copious Vocabulary, to learn any Language whatever. By this Means he may be able to construe any *Latin* Author in a Year's Time; and this I think is as much as is necessary for any Youth to know of *Latin* who is not designed for the Learned Professions; which he may do in three Years from his entering the Primer, as well as in a thousand. A further Advantage this Method would have, that it would be impossible for him to forget what he had learned, as long as he retains his Mother Tongue; and he must have a larger Stock of useful Ideas than if he had spent seven Years in the mere Study of *Latin;* the cramming a Boy's Head full of a Dead Language, of useless Words, and incoherent Terms, satiates his Memory and confounds his Judgment. The Ideas we receive in our early Years last longest, and have the greatest Effect upon our future Conduct. Of how much greater Advantage then would it be, to employ those Years, when the Mind is most susceptible of Knowledge, in laying up a sufficient Store of useful Ideas, which our riper Understanding and more advanced Age may enlarge, than in filling up the empty Space with mere Sound, which must remain to all Eternity the same useless Thing, a prating Eccho?

After the Youth has attained this superficial Knowledge of *Latin*, let him apply to *French*, which is learned with equal Facility: This is not only the polite Court Language of *Europe*, but is a Trading Tongue, spoke or understood in all Cities where Traffic flourishes. *Dutch, Spanish, Portuguese*, and *Italian* ought to be acquired by all who are any ways concerned in Commerce. But all these, except *Dutch*, may be acquired by the Youth's own Application, without the Help of a Master, and ought to employ his vacant Hours during his Apprenticeship. This is the Education I think sufficient, and in some measure necessary, in all Employments that are not merely Mechanical, and in the Remainder of this Tract I shall refer the Reader to this rather than make a Repetition.

53.   Education in France

THE EPHÉMÉRIDES *du Citoyen* was a sophisticated periodical published after 1768 by the famous physiocrat, Dupont de Nemours. Most of its articles treated current problems, such as agricultural productivity, the slave trade, or educational reforms. One series of articles by an anonymous writer of the 1760's (a disciple of Helvétius?) proposed a new system of education for all Frenchmen. The author does not advocate a uniform curriculum for everyone, but rather a separate educational program for each of five "classes of citizens," including the court nobility, the robe nobility, the "bourgeoisie," the artisans and small merchants, and the peasants. The principle behind all five programs is utility, a preparation for adult functions. For example, the "bourgeois" must study law or medicine, the merchant must learn accounting and sedentary habits, and even the peasant should learn the three R's. Document A below deals with the court nobility and includes a harsh criticism of the mental equipment and general public capacity of the "great lords."

Document B concerns the educational practices of the French clergy as seen through the eyes of a convinced physiocrat. The passage is a thorough indictment of the rote learning taught by an incompetent provincial clergy whose narrow scholastic training falls far short of an understanding of "the eternal and necessary laws governing the best social order." This passage perhaps reveals the mind of the physiocrat better than it does the functions of the lower clergy.

Source: *Ephémérides du Citoyen ou bibliothèque raisonnée des sciences morales et politiques,* V (1766), 156ff., 187ff., 243ff.

A.   Education of the French Court Nobility

IF I go to an ordinary school, I find there a large number of pupils engaged in receiving what is called an education. Eight or nine years must be spent in these public institutions. Then I examine the way in which this precious part of a young man's life is usually spent. For every day I find eight or nine hours sleep, which is very necessary, and about four hours for meals and recreation, which are also indispensable. Of the remaining twelve hours, I see that more than six are spent in putting Latin into French or French into Latin. I approach one of the pupils in order to find out what he is working on so diligently; it is an involved sentence, probably poorly written, by some Latin author 2,000 years ago, for, despite all their efforts, authors are liable to overlook negligences, mistakes, wordiness, and ambiguities. My young pupil tells me quite frankly that, for some years now, this is how he has spent a fourth of his life, either agonizing over the phrases the original scribbler of this Latin had meant to say or trying to put into the same language some assigned French.

Not satisfied with this, I ask my young student to tell me what the Latin or French speeches he had to translate mean, but among two hundred I scarcely find three who are in a position to tell me anything about it. Whether it be ethics, history, or poetry, they hardly remember the title. It is the *language* they are dealing with; the words and the grammatical construction absorb all of their attention, and these still tender minds do not have enough energy left to inquire into the meaning of these things. . . . [1]

The teachers themselves applaud and praise a pupil who has recited a long Latin oration without making a single grammatical error, and others are reprimanded or punished for having violated the rules of grammar. Such an education is excellent for future grammarians or Latin teachers, but is it suitable to the duties of a great lord? It seems obvious that the children of the great nobility have only a very limited need for these things, but a very urgent need for a number of others. . . .

Let us therefore examine what kinds of knowledge are indispensable, useful, or even agreeable to the great leaders of the nobility. Those they will need almost constantly when they are men should determine what they should be taught when they are children. These subjects they should learn so early and pursue so constantly that they will be familiar with the entire theory when they go out into the world and will only need to acquire experience by daily practice.

We can call all the knowledge needed by the great of the nation the knowledge of *political* and *moral economy*. By their birth

[1] Grammar schools were conducted in a similar way all over Europe. Cf. "Scheme for the classes of a grammar school" by Samuel Johnson, in James Boswell, *The Life of Samuel Johnson, LLD* (New York: Modern Library Edition, n.d.), pp. 52–53.

these people are destined to be the eye, the hand, and the voice of sovereign authority in the administration of the state. How could they carry out these important functions without being thoroughly familiar with the principles of natural law and the law of nations, without having studied the interior constitution of the monarchy, its origins and variations, without knowing about relations with other states and their good or bad influences on public tranquillity?

Ignorance of such *economic* facts is a disgrace for citizens of the first order. The positions of dignity given to them, the honors, the influence, the authority attached to their birth make ignorance all the more criminal the higher and the more considerable their rank. What a dreadful injustice to want to preside, in a position of authority, over the processes of motion in a complicated machine whose workings one does not understand! What glaring mistakes one can make! For how many evils is one responsible! How shamefully one would be exposed to the eyes of the world!

French honor is certainly still alive in that privileged class of the nation, where ambition, at least, is not extinguished, for it still aims at the most eminent positions. Excessively severe critics might perhaps tell us that it has become more and more customary to consider only the monetary value of the resulting benefits and that on the basis of that purpose alone they [the great nobles] are employing every means to obtain lucrative and honorific positions, striving only to preserve and increase them, without giving any thought to the functions and the talents these posts require. The underlings [lower officials] who actually perform these duties are left to take care of them as best they can.[2]

Perhaps the ignorance which is the necessary result of bad education has too firmly planted this fatal system. But we should like to believe that it has not yet made the alarming progress the more advanced moral critics have depicted. Enlightened great lords are still at the head of our nation, zealous and hard-working men who perform their functions and would be able to rise even higher. And most of those whose poor education, dissipation, passionate natures, or indolence have prevented them from acquiring

[2] This is a scarcely veiled criticism of the upper nobility and tends to support the view that the French nobility were attempting to monopolize the higher state offices.

the knowledge necessary for their functions are sincerely sorry they did not see the light earlier, when there was still time.

But even the most negligent and indifferent will at least not hesitate to answer the question we dare ask here. Great lords of the nation, speak up for your children! Would you like your children when they enter society to know *by themselves* all they need to know in order to perform the great functions of political administration for the glory of the king, the happiness of the nation, and consequently for their own glory and happiness? Or would you prefer them to ignore it? Would you want this to be the aim of their entire instruction and would you want them to be brought as close to these matters as their natural talents permit? Or would you prefer that this aim be completely forgotten in the planning and execution of their education? It is impossible to doubt the answer.

Economic science must, therefore, be considered as the principal subject in the education of a great lord since it is, properly speaking, the science suited to his position in life. It is vast and sublime, and, as all other sciences, it has its elementary notions, its successive developments, and its perfection. It is therefore necessary to proceed step by step.

B. *A Physiocrat on Church Education*

CHILDHOOD is but the preparation for life in society. As the organs become stronger, as the mind develops, and as the emotions unfold, our natural parents and those the law of society has added to them in order to guide, help, or replace them, must prepare us for the enjoyment of our *rights* and the fulfillment of our *duties*, teaching us the usefulness of the former and the necessity of the latter. Reason and philosophy are agreed on this principle. Religion also plays its role here, for the function of teaching children, of enlightening their minds and forming their hearts, is an essential part of the pastoral ministry.

It may seem unnecessary to prove this theoretical principle to the clergy, to tell it that the teaching of children falls within its sphere and is part of its authority. We have always seen the clergy forcefully claiming this precious and noble right. But when it comes to dealing with the practical details of these high-minded maxims, one cannot help being struck by a very obvious and most deplorable contradiction, which saddens truly religious souls as much as it offends patriotic hearts.

The French nation is by no means short of ministers of the official religion; its numerous clergy is amply provided for, showered with honors and privileges. Moreover, the revenues specially destined for its maintenance are of such a nature that they necessarily increase as the prosperity of the nation increases. The *dîme* [tithe] rises automatically with the flourishing of the state, since it represents a proportion of the primary and only true wealth and requires no capital advance and no initial outlay. If the best order of things were observed in the kingdom, agriculture and population would soon be at their highest point of perfection, and the Church would consequently enjoy the greatest opulence.

We are purposely placing these considerations at the head of the reflections which are our present concern. We present the office of enlightening the minds and forming the hearts [of the young] to the ministers of religion not only as an *obligation*, but also as a function in their *interest* in a direct and tangible way. The natural interaction between *duties* and *rights* is always such that one reaps more benefits the better he performs his functions. These two notions should never be separated if we want to enlighten and persuade.

The simple and natural laws which constitute the best order of society, then, would bring agriculture to its highest state if they were observed. This is an evident truth which is becoming ever more securely confirmed. They would assure the *dîme*-collecting clergy the greatest wealth; this too is an immediate and perfectly obvious conclusion. But these laws cannot be observed unless they are known, firmly implanted in the minds of the people, and frequently recalled. Nothing is truer than this second observation. It follows necessarily that the clergy would work for its own benefit if it spread the light, and such traits prove that an institution is founded upon the principles of order. . . .

The Church insists upon none of the duties of its ministers as emphatically as upon a continuous solicitude for the children who represent the hope of Christian society. Filled though we are with an admiration for this ministry, which we should like to communicate even to the most disdainful of our *philosophes*, we are too fond of the truth to deny that this important function is today almost always performed superficially and results in the

most profound and deplorable ignorance of the people. This ignorance begets errors, vice, arbitrary principles, corruption of
morals, misunderstanding of all the laws, and hence, all the evils
of a state in which *order* no longer rules. These evils are necessarily felt by all classes of society and especially by the clergy itself;
and they may in the end lead to doubts about its usefulness, the
sullying of its good name, and the annihilation of its revenues.

Let us go back to the first causes of this ignorance. In the first
place we will find that the pastors have replaced a paternal, attentive, continued, enlightened, kind, and solid way of teaching
with a superficial, strange, almost mercenary instruction, full of
obscurity and devoid of interest and clarity. And if we to beyond
this, we will find that the ulterior cause is the bad education of
the teachers themselves, who have never learned the great and
sublime truths and the eternal and necessary laws governing the
best possible order, who only have the vaguest notions of the
social virtues, their effects, their principles, and their indissoluble
connection with the mysteries of revealed religion and the promises and threats of the life hereafter.

This original ignorance has led to the only too obvious abuse of
reducing all teaching to dry and obscure formulas, which are
laboriously instilled for a certain time in the memories of children. But such formulas bring no light to their minds, nor any
germ of virtue to their hearts. The pastors consider it a mechanical task to teach children to repeat this obscure language word
for word, with much stuttering, and they hand this task over to
temporary vicars, who are young and poorly educated and often
perform it with the greatest indifference and the most criminal
negligence. These are sad facts. They are, perhaps, not so evident
in the capital, but they have struck us a thousand times in the
provinces. Only too often they dishonor the ecclesiastic ministry
in the eyes of honorable citizens.

The scholastic theologians, preoccupied as they are with their
abstract ideas, their words, and their disputes, enthusiastically
consider these as the essential part of religion. They have taken
over the right of drawing up the formulas for education, and were
authorized for doing so by the highest clergy. The lack of intelligence and of assiduity on the part of the lower clergy and its
vicars, as well as a desire for uniformity, seemed sufficient reason
to prescribe the curriculum in every detail and to make teaching

consist mainly of the recitation, word for word, of such memo-
rized language. In this manner, the education of children has
been reduced to cramming their memory, for a few days, with a
very thin, abridged version of scholastic theology. This method
corresponds exactly to that employed in the education of the
teachers themselves, which is limited to another, somewhat more
substantial abridgment of that same scholastic theology in barbarous language.

Having thus examined the bad state of education down to its
first principles, it is unnecessary to describe its effects in any
detail; they are only too evident and too unfortunate. The French
nation, which should be one of the best educated since its many
teachers are so well paid, so honored, and so favored by the law,
is one of the most ignorant and unpolished nations. How can it
help being vicious and unhappy, when virtue results from enlightenment and disorder from ignorance?

54. The Universities of Göttingen and Vilna

In 1784 Friedrich Gedicke, principal of a Berlin *Gymnasium* and later
superintendent of schools, was sent by the Prussian ministry of education to study the non-Prussian German universities. It was the aim of
this mission to find out how other universities were administered and
gather information about prospective professors for Prussian universities. In seven weeks Gedicke visited fourteen universities. His comments about the individual professors tell us little of the subjects
taught, since Gedicke was interested primarily in lecturing technique.
For example, he criticized Schiller, when he was professor at Jena, for
reading his lectures and using too emphatic a tone. However, Gedicke
did collect valuable information about the economic foundation of the
various universities, the number and behavior of the students, the special institutes connected with the universities, their libraries, and the
local atmosphere in general. More important, perhaps, his report confirms what Goethe had written in *Dichtung und Wahrheit:* "Each one
of the German universities has a particular character: for, as no uniform culture can pervade our fatherland, so each place clings to its
own manners and customs and adheres firmly to its own characteristic
particularities; and the same is true of the universities." [1] Gedicke thus

[1] Quoted by R. Fester in his introduction to Gedicke's report.

saw decline at Heidelberg, Altdorf, and Erfurt; stagnation at Helm-städt, Marburg, Giessen, and Erlangen; moderate conservatism at Tübingen; a new start at Jena; and great pride of accomplishment at Göttingen.

The following passage from Gedicke suggests that Göttingen was a great center of learning, especially in the humanities. The library of 30,000 volumes and good salary attracted the best scholars of the day, who in turn attracted a large, cultivated student body. We also learn that most of the students came from well-to-do families, since the tuition and fees for courses were high. Young Goethe had hoped to study at Göttingen, but his father wanted him to become a lawyer and insisted that he go to Leipzig.

Document B on the University of Vilna in Poland was written by Georg Forster, whose checkered career was quite different from the quiet existence enjoyed by most German scholars of the eighteenth century.[2] As a young man, Forster was professor of natural history at Kassel, where he became involved with freemasonry and even the Rosicrucian secret society. Since Rosicrucian mysticism led him to dabbling in alchemy, he lost his scholarly reputation as well as all his money. When Forster came to see the error of his ways, a well-paying professorship at Vilna seemed to promise a more secure existence. From an academic point of view, however, Vilna was "the wilderness": no laboratories, no botanical garden, a mediocre library, undistinguished colleagues, few students, and even fewer social diversions. Forster's description of this provincial university is in interesting contrast to Gedicke's Göttingen.

Source: Document A: *"Der Universitäts-Bereiser Friedrich Gedicke und sein Bericht an Friedr. Wilhelm II, mitgeteilt von Richard Fester," Archiv für Kulturgeschichte,* vol. I, *Ergänzungsheft* (Berlin, 1905), pp. 13ff. Document B: G. G. Gervinus, ed., *Georg Forsters sämtliche Schriften* (Leipzig, 1843), vol. VII, pp. 296ff.

A. Göttingen

THIS UNIVERSITY was founded by royal liberality and continues to be administered with that same liberality. It is better known than any other university in Germany. Its institutions and its constitution have been described in several books, especially Ritter's *Akademische Gelehrtengeschichte von Göttingen.*

Nowhere did I find the professors to have as much predilection

---

[2] This is the same Georg Forster who became leader of the Jacobins of Mainz during the French Revolution.

for their university as here. They seem to consider it a foregone conclusion that theirs is the first and foremost of all the universities of Germany and hence often speak of the others with a kind of pity and condescension. They all are, as it were, inebriated with the proud feeling of its partly real, and partly imagined, excellence. Several professors assured me quite seriously that the most famous scholars lose a considerable part not only of their celebrity but of their very usefulness when they leave Göttingen for another university (which, they claimed, was the case with professors von Selchow and Baldinger, formerly of Göttingen and now of Marburg); while a scholar of little reputation, once he comes to teach at Göttingen, will come to have a great name and reputation owing to this fact alone, since some of the glory with which they imagine their university surrounded will be cast on all those connected with it.

It is often difficult to suppress a smile when one hears some of the Göttingen scholars talk as if no light or scholarship were to be found outside the walls of Göttingen. Yet this pride in the institution has some very good effects. It fosters a certain *esprit de corps*, the like of which I have found nowhere else to the same degree. Every professor not only sees the honor of the university as his own but, conversely, his own honor and that of his colleagues as that of the University. Hence, one witnesses less intrigue, envy, jealousy, belittling, and calumny of others, which causes so much bitterness and trouble at other universities—at least they are not so evident. Here they speak more gently of the foibles of their colleagues than is usual at other universities. They are more inclined to praise and excuse all that can possibly be praised and excused. It is true that jealousies are not entirely lacking here either, but they are not expressed in as base and mean a fashion as at other universities. This is why it is more difficult here than elsewhere to find out everything one wants to know from the professors. They all are most eloquent about the excellence of their university, but equally silent and secretive about its shortcomings. It would seem desirable indeed if this *esprit de corps* which animates the professors of Göttingen and causes them to focus all their activities and all their desires on the good of the university were also present in our Prussian universities. This same *esprit de corps* also made me seek information about certain aspects from judicious and well-informed students, since I feared that the professors would not tell me everything from too loyal a regard for the honor of their university.

All four faculties are or will be staffed with more professors than they were to have originally. It is, however, understood that the full professors (*professores ordinarii*), who were not planned for at the time of the foundation, do not partake of the emoluments of the faculty. But in this respect there is a special arrangement at the Faculty of Law. The faculty as such—since the deanship rotates yearly among its members and carries out the functions pertaining to the running of the university, such as granting of degrees—consists of four professors (at present Böhmer, Pütter, Möckert, Runde). Since, however, this committee must work on a great number of law cases, the faculty has a number of nonpermanent members, who are recruited not only among the other full professors but also among associate professors (*professores extraordinarii*) and even include some simple doctors of law. These temporary members are now paid a fee for their work, which they set themselves. . . . The Faculty of Law in its widest sense, that is, counting all the professors of law, is very large indeed. It now consists of ten full professors and two associates. In addition there are a number of lecturers (*Privatdozenten*), but they are outnumbered by the professors and hence are rarely able to give a regular course. Consequently, they give a number of private courses, for which there is great demand, given the considerable number of wealthy young students. This is the reason why, despite my eagerness, I was unable to hear any of the lecturers at the Faculty of Law.

At the time of its founding, the Faculty of Theology was to have three regular members, and it has not had more for several years. However, there were four before the death of the late Professor Walch. At the moment, there are also two associate professors of theology. As at most other universities, the professor of oriental languages is not a member of the Faculty of Theology but of the Faculty of Philosophy.

The Faculty of Medicine was founded to have three members, and its deanship still rotates among the first three. However, there are four others, so that there are altogether seven full professors of medicine.

The Faculty of Philosophy was originally to have eight regular members. But now there are fifteen full professors plus six associates. In addition, there is a large number of lecturers connected with this faculty.

Among the many encouragements given to the University by the government in Hanover, the conferring of titles is one of the foremost. One or more of the members of the Faculty of Theology is usually given the title of *Konsistorialrath*. In the three other faculties the title of *Hofrath* is quite current (five professors of law, five of medicine, and ten of philosophy have received it), and three professors (Böhmer, Pütter, and Michaelis) were made *Geheimer Justizrath*. The professors seem to attach great importance to these titles, which are also given freely at other universities, except at the two Saxonian universities, where they have become rare. Even though seniority is a factor in the granting of such titles, it frequently happens that one or the other of the older professors is passed by in favor of a younger colleague—but such a preferment has no consequences for regular academic advancement. This much is certain, the government of Hanover has saved itself many a raise in salary by bestowing such inexpensive honors.

At Göttingen it is difficult to obtain accurate information about the salaries of the professors. Almost all are most secretive on this point, and generally everyone knows only his own salary and not his colleague's. Salary raises, especially, do not become public. This is because University finances are not handled in Göttingen, but in Hanover. This secrecy has beneficial effects. It prevents manifestations of jealousy and pretension. Incidentally, salaries at Göttingen are often thought to be higher than they really are. Many professors have only 300 or 400 thaler. Some of the older professors have considerably lower salaries than some of their younger colleagues. Thus, one professor, who claimed to be fully informed, assured me that the two *Geheimräthe*, Böhmer and Pütter, received no more than 800 thaler each, though this seemed unlikely to me. Some young professors have considerably more. Eichorn, for example, who was recently called from Marburg, makes 1,200 thaler. But this salary is unknown to most of his colleagues. Associate professors receive no salary at all at most universities. But here they have recently begun to pay some of them. For example, the associate professor of law, Brandis, is paid

400 thaler, and the two younger professors, Hugo and Bruhle, who were only recently hired, receive 300 thaler each.

A hard-working professor who is popular can earn a great deal here by his lectures. Compared to other universities, very few free courses are given and the fees are higher. There are no courses for less than 5 thaler and many are 10 thaler or more. In addition, many so-called private courses [*collegia privatissima*] are given, frequented by 40 to 50 students paying 3 or 4 *louis* [70 to 90 livres] for them.[1] The incomes of some of the professors are estimated at 4,000 to 5,000 thaler, or more, but of course others are not so popular and their incomes suffer.

[Several pages of remarks on the lecture techniques of individual professors follow.]

Every year two catalogues of courses are printed at Göttingen:

1. In Latin, in which the professors, by order of seniority, list their courses. This catalogue only mentions the professors, not the lecturers.
2. In German, according to subject matter. This also includes the lecturers. But the latter are only mentioned for form's sake—only rarely does one of them find a sufficient number of students for a real course. Most of them give only private lessons and so-called private courses.

The University as well as the different faculties, has more public institutes than any other university.[2] I shall discuss them briefly:

1. The most important of these institutes is the *Library*. Never, perhaps, has a public library achieved so much. The entire university owes a large part of its celebrity to it. And if, in recent times, Göttingen has formed a greater number of scholars than any other university, this is less due to the merits of the professors than to the excellence of the library and to the fact that it is more accessible than other university libraries. Many of the professors owe their literary reputation to the library alone, since it provides

---

[1] This suggests incomes of 2,800 to 4,500 livres. In France this would be roughly comparable to the income of a modest country gentleman, provincial *rentier*, or middling merchant.
[2] Gedicke uses the term "institutes" somewhat differently than it is used today.

them with the tools for their scholarship. Many young scholars have formed themselves solely by the use of this library. The example of Göttingen supports the contention that nothing is more useful for the flourishing and celebrity of a university than a large and well-planned library. The government at Hanover has spent very large sums for this purpose. It is said that over 3,000 thaler annually are spent on the library. The number of volumes is estimated at 30,000. The choice of books to be purchased is not left to the arbitrary judgment of the librarian, as is the case at most other universities, but every professor notes the books in his field he wishes purchased, and the head librarian, Hofrath Heyne, immediately proceeds to buy them. As a result, no one field is favored, and all fields are completed and expanded at the same rate.

The library is also accessible to students and faculty. Instead of being open only two days a week as at most universities, the library is open every day. Some of the librarians are there the entire day to find the books and perform other services desired. There is a folder for every professor and lecturer containing slips for book orders for himself or for his students. All these details are managed with great care. There are three main catalogues which are kept continually up to date:

1. the alphabetical catalogue in more than 100 folio volumes,
2. the subject catalogue, consisting of almost 90 volumes, and
3. the acquisitions catalogue, in which books are listed by date of purchase with full titles. All three have cross references noted in the margins.

2. The *Museum* was founded only sixteen years ago. Beginning with the purchase of Professor Büttner's natural history collection, it was later considerably increased by gifts and purchases. It contains many excellent and rare specimens of natural history. Given its short history, this collection is remarkable indeed.

3. The *Society of Learning*. Not all the professors are members, since it treats only physics, mathematics, and history. The society meets once every month. It is financed from the income of the *Gelehrte Zeitungen*, published under its auspices. Every lecturer is paid 20 thaler.

4. The *German Society* exists more in name than in fact. Once quite flourishing, it is now almost extinct.

5. The same is true of the *Historical Institute*, which owed its

existence to a quarrel of Hofrath Gatterer with the Society [of Learning]. Since the quarrel has been settled, it exists in name only.

6. An annual *prize essay* for students of all four faculties, founded five years ago, is a good incentive for many students. These prize essays, given every year by each of the faculties, have stimulated many an intelligent student and given him an opportunity to excel. There are already two professors at Göttingen who won this prize when they were students and who attracted the attention of the government by their prize-winning essays. The prize consists of a medal worth 85 ducats and the presentation is public. On the other hand, it should be said that this institution has its disadvantages for some students, leading them to work toward a single goal and stealing time from broader studies. . . .

[Gedicke goes on to discuss institutes connected with the individual faculties, such as the hospital, observatory, and church. He then broaches hiring procedures for faculty and pension plans, and furnishes some statistics on the number of students.]

Incidentally, Göttingen has the reputation of attracting students who are more civilized than those at other universities. In a certain sense this is quite true and quite understandable, given the fact that there is a smaller proportion of poor students due to the high cost of this university. Nowhere else are there as many sons of well-to-do, well-born, and wealthy parents, from whom one can as a rule expect better breeding and better manners. The majority, of course, set the tone at any university. But here the wealthy young men are the majority, as revealed by the greater number of law students over theology students. As a result, the crude and wild behavior so often present at other universities is much less evident here. Here, immorality is masked by a veil of fine manners. Whether there is really a higher level of behavior is another question. For though raucous debaucheries are less frequent here than elsewhere, there is no absence of debauched and spoiled young men whose indiscipline makes them as unhappy and useless to society as those who indulge in crude misconduct at other universities. Perhaps these finer and more subtle irregularities are all the more dangerous. The student here does not frequent beer halls but gets drunk on wine in his room all the more often. I have been told by several students that this more refined form of debauchery is much à la mode here. They assure

me that gambling is even more prevalent. Many students even
keep mistresses. All the indiscipline stemming from exaggerated
luxury is as common here as elsewhere. It is both easy and common to incur debts, and the proximity of Kassel is most alluring.
By the way, even raw excesses are not altogether lacking. During the few days that I was there, several drunken students attacked a girl in the street and then pursued her to her home
where they mistreated her to the point that her very life was in
danger.

Academic fraternities are present here as elsewhere. However,
they do not seem to be too severely frowned upon, and some
professors have even been accused of favoring this or that fraternity.

The more refined manners of the students are in a large measure due to the fact that they have easier access to the professors
than elsewhere. Every professor has set aside Sunday morning
after the sermon to talk to students. On the other hand, this
"courting," as it is called, has often degenerated into an empty
ceremony. In addition, there are Sunday assemblies at the houses
of Böhmer and Pütter, picnics and balls every other Sunday during the winter under the supervision of young Professor Böhmer,
a winter concert, and so forth. These pleasures, however, cost
money, at least indirectly, and are not found necessary at other
universities. . . .

[Gedicke describes the conduct of three royal princes at the university. He notes that there are free meals for 140 of the poorer
students.]

Hanoverian subjects are required to attend the state university,
but only for two years. The professors assured me that this ruling
is not too rigidly enforced.

B. Vilna

[Forster to Heyne,[1] December 16, 1784]

I HAVE come here resolved to fulfill my obligation and do my
work to the best of my abilities, and to the extent to which I am
furnished with the essential equipment . . . I owe a great deal of

[1] Christian Gottlob Heyne, professor of humanities at Göttingen, was
Georg Forster's future father-in-law. According to Friedrich Gedicke, who
made a study tour of the German universities for Frederick William II,
Professor Heyne was "one of the most outstanding glories" of the University of Göttingen.

gratitude to my present superiors, for they have freed me from an unfortunate situation in Kassel, where I had not conducted my affairs with the proper caution and organization and where, for the moment, I saw no possibility of extricating myself. Moreover, I am here paid a salary that I would not easily receive elsewhere. Even though this salary is adapted to the situation at this university, where all courses are given *publice* so that one cannot count on any extra income,[2] one can quite easily make ends meet with the proper economy and organization. My pen should also be able to help out once I am completely installed and can use my free time for literary endeavors. If I were fortunate enough to be a physician, I could practice here very profitably, for Professor Langmeyer is the only physician here to merit that title. Bisio, an Italian who is the professor of anatomy, has practiced here all his life and has become rich from his outrageous fees, which one was obliged to pay him since he was the only physician for so long; but he does not know anything. Since Herr Langmeyer has put a stop to advance payment for cures, Herr Bisio's practice has folded. Two Jews who received their degrees at Königsberg are the only other physicians, and one of them is a complete ignoramus, while the other, although a kindly person, has not learned very much either. But . . . for the present I am busy enough in my own field.

A new place for the botanical garden is planned, for the present one is much too small and, furthermore, unsuitable in every respect. For the natural museum, the Jesuits are willing to give their former summer dining hall, which would be large enough. My small apartment will be repaired and furnished according to my specifications as soon as the weather permits, and once I have all my books, as well as those found here, I shall have the beginnings of a decent library—better in any case then that of many professors in other universities where public libraries are not as well provided as at Göttingen.[3] The Commission of Education, the virtual head of which is the prince primate,[4] must appropriate the funds for the botanical garden and for the purchases for the museum (for its holdings do not amount to anything). But

---

[2] In German universities a professor received a salary *and* a fee from every student who took his course, cf. Document A above. In Germany these so-called *Kolleg-Gelder* are paid to this day.

[3] Cf. Document A.

[4] The prince primate was a brother of the king of Poland.

the Commission is very stingy, and it is said quite openly that the prince primate takes the money for his own use. The budget was presented to the recent Diet, which approved it without review, but a number of deputies who took a closer look found strange items of many thousands of guilders under the heading "miscellaneous expenses." They wanted to have the budget examined, but were shouted down. The money appropriated for this university amounts to 300,000 Polish guilders, or more than 16,000 ducats per year. But the primate has a predilection for the University of Cracow and takes half of this sum for that university, so that a number of things here must wait. Since, however, he is very kind to me, I hope that he will support my demands.

The number of students is quite small. Aside from six students with royal fellowships who have been studying medicine for some eight years without even having taken practical medicine and chemistry, since there has not been a hospital or a laboratory, few students are here with the intention of learning anything. Physics and natural history find an audience among the townspeople, who study them as a diversion. If anything will be able to attract students, it will be the new institutes that are planned.

I already wrote you that the observatory has beautiful instruments. They were not bought by the Commission of Education, but with a legacy of 12,000 ducats from an old lady who thereby has earned Paradise for herself. And yet it was not enough. Herr Poczebut, the kind old rector, has already spent a considerable sum out of his own purse, and the building is still unfinished. Physics as well has some good instruments; the professor is also an ex-Jesuit, but he is not as learned as the two astronomers, Poczebut and Strzecki. . . . All courses are given three times a week, each lecture being one and a half hours long. The professor of chemistry cannot teach yet, since his laboratory is only being built, and my courses also will not begin before the New Year. Everyone (I mean the workmen) works incredibly slowly and clumsily, and so far I have been unable to have a cabinet made for my minerals, so that they are not even unpacked yet. Moreover, I do not know Polish yet, which is indispensable for dealing with these people. But one must not become discouraged by such hindrances. Everything will be done eventually, but it takes time. The unwieldiness of the republican form of government can be found even in the details of domestic life. The servants here maintain a slow pace, and a man who does not deal blows in the true

Polish manner will be badly served. And I do miss our precious German cleanliness. . . .

The Bishop of Vilna, Massalski, is a most agreeable gentleman, who likes to surround himself with the members of the University. His house is the best here, and when his niece, Princess Massalska, née Radzwil, is here, the professors' wives also dine and visit there. Pride of nobility is unknown here, and the ladies of the University always consort with the nobility. Would that this were always good society! But there are always some who are well read and have good morals. I have the best relations with all of my colleagues, even though a certain amount of envy and discord exists among some of them. Herr Langmeyer is the only one I consider my friend. Since I cannot eat at home before my kitchen and my rooms are completed and since there is no carry-out shop and no inn, I have my meals at his house, and they are frugal indeed; but we see each other twice a day. He is generally esteemed here, and deserves to be, as a physician and a person; he is upright, straightforward, and without a trace of quackery.

In the winter the high court, which holds its sessions here during six months of the year, brings in many people from the provinces. Usually the marshal of the court (or highest judge) is very hospitable, gives dinners at his residence every day, also balls at night, and so forth. This is the focal point of the social life. This year the judge is a poor man and therefore lives a retiring life, but this is exceptional. Werky and Zagred, the country residences of the prince-bishop, are the summer resorts, and I must confess that I have never seen nature more beautiful in Poland, even though the forests of pine and fir always cast a hue of melancholy over everything. But then it is nature, and nature always makes for the purest enjoyment of this life.

55. Educating the Female Nobility of Russia

ONE WOULD not ordinarily look for educational institutions in a book on European prisons, but John Howard has included a short, precise description of a boarding school for girls in St. Petersburg. The school had almost 500 pupils, half nobles and half commoners, from five to fifteen years old. Classroom segregation between nobles and commoners was complete, but both groups were treated equally regarding diet, hygiene, and physical exercise. Note the difference in instruction, however. In addition to exercises in music, dancing, politeness, and needlework, the noble girls were given lessons in history, geography, and natural philosophy. No doubt these subjects were not pursued very thoroughly, but their very appearance suggests a rather enlightened curriculum. Conservative critics of Catherine II, such as Prince Schterbatov (see Document 67 in Kings and Courts), may not have thought much of this institution, but perhaps there was at least a measure of concrete reform under Catherine's verbal pose as an "enlightened despot."

Source: John Howard, *The State of the Prisons in England and Wales, With preliminary observations on some Foreign Prisons* (London, 1777), vol. II, Appendix, pp. 44–47.

ON A rising ground at a little distance from *Petersburg*, and on the south side of the river *Neva*, there is a stately pile of buildings, originally designed for a *Convent*, but ever since 1764 converted by the Empress *Catharine* the Second, into a public establishment for educating the female *nobility* of *Russia*, and a limited number of the children of *commoners*. The sleeping rooms and dining-halls in these buildings are remarkably lofty and airy, having large galleries round them; and adjoining to the buildings there are spacious gardens and lawns, which extend to the banks of the river.—The number of the children of *nobility* on this establishment is two hundred; and the number of the children of commoners or *peasants* was, till 1770, limited to two hundred and forty: but since this year it has been increased to two hundred and eighty, by a fund provided by the munificence of general *De Betskoi*, the enlightened and liberal head and director-general of this, and all the other institutions of the same kind established by her *imperial majesty*.

The principal regulations for conducting this institution are the following.—The children are admitted between five and six years of age, and continued on the establishment twelve years. They are divided into classes according to their ages, *four* of *nobles* with fifty in each class, and *four* of *commoners* with seventy in each class.—In every third year on the 21st of April, (the birthday of the Empress,) fifty children of the *nobility*, and seventy of *commoners* are taken in, to replace the same numbers discharged. —Before they rise every morning, the windows of their rooms are

thrown open to purify them with fresh air.—The *first* class
(dressed in *brown*, and consisting of children of the youngest
ages,) rise at seven in winter, and at six in summer.—After being
washed and attending prayers, they are taken into the garden
where they breakfast, and play about in the coldest weather till
nine. During their first year, each of them is allowed for breakfast, a small loaf of white bread, and a glass of milk and water;
but after their first year, they are allowed no other drink than
water.—At nine they are called back to the house, and from this
hour to eleven are employed in learning the *French* and *Russian*
languages, and in knitting, sewing &c. but care is taken to render
all the instruction they receive agreeable, nothing being taught in
this establishment by compulsion.—Twice in the week they receive lessons in dancing; and this is a part of education common
to all the classes, and never discontinued, because reckoned conducive to health.—After *eleven* they return to their play in the
garden, where they continue till noon, at which time they are
called to dinner, which consists of soup, vegetables &c. For some
months at first they are allowed meat; but they are gradually
weaned from it, till at last, while in this and the next class, it
comes to be entirely withheld from them (except in soups,) in
order to cure them of some cutaneous distempers to which at this
age they are subject, and also to prepare them for passing with
less danger through the hooping-cough, measles and small-pox.
After dinner they return to the garden, and at four, have a repast
similar to that in the morning, viz. a loaf of bread and a glass of
water. Here they continue to divert themselves till at seven they
are called to supper, which consists in winter of dried fruit, milk
and grain; and in summer of preparations of milk, and some provisions from the garden.—It may be proper to add, that they read
and write standing, and are not allowed to sit down, except to
needle-work.—In consequence of this management, and of living
so much in the air, and being used to exercise, and cleanliness and
a simple diet, they are seldom known to take cold; and become
capable of bearing the severest weather of the climate without
receiving any harm, their clothing being only a short wadded
cloak, whilst others are loaded with furs.

The *second* class (dressed in *blue*) enter it about eight years of
age, and are obliged to apply more closely to writing, drawing,
dancing &c.

The *third* class (dressed in *grey*) enter it at eleven or twelve years of age. They rise at five, in the summer, and six, in winter; but are called to the house (after breakfasting in the garden,) an hour sooner than the children in the first and second classes; because more time is wanted for instructing and improving them. They are now taught (besides drawing, dancing, turning, needle-work &c.) vocal and instrumental music. They are allowed a ball and concert every week; and a taste for books is inspired, by putting them upon copying and reciting select passages from the best authors.

The *fourth* class (dressed in *white*) enter it at fourteen or fifteen years of age. They are taught tambour-work, house-keeping, the management of a family &c. and initiated into history, geography and natural philosophy. In order to acquire a just elocution, and to exercise themselves in politeness, and vocal and instrumental music, they occasionally give balls and little operas to company from *Petersburg*.

The children of the nobility and of commoners are distinguished from one another, only by wearing a finer camlet of the colours appropriated to the different classes; and as far as diet, exercise, regimen &c. are concerned, the method of managing them is the same; but the instruction given the latter, is confined to needle-work, reading, house-keeping and such other occupations and improvements as are suitable to the humbler walks of life, for which they are intended.

The children on this foundation enjoy, as might be expected, an uncommon degree of health.—Of fifty-one children of *nobility* admitted in 1764, and fifty admitted in 1767, and fifty-two in 1770, none had died in 1781; and of fifty admitted at different times, by the particular order of the *Empress*, between 1764 and 1780, only two had died in 1781.—Of sixty children also of *commoners* admitted in 1767, and seventy in 1770, only seven had died in 1781. But of sixty admitted in 1764, thirteen had died; in consequence, it is supposed, of having been lodged in a part of the buildings which had been just erected, and therefore was not sufficiently dry.—This account I owe to the obliging information of Dr. *Guthrie*, physician to a military cadet corps of nobles, established at *Petersburg* by the *Empress*, and supposed the grandest institution of the kind in the world.

56. Rousseau's Émile

RESTIF DE la Bretonne's lamentation on the insolence of youth suggests that a new approach to child raising, associated with Rousseau's *Émile*, was widespread. In fact, Restif believes the new style of upbringing predated *Émile* and that Rousseau had only "moved with his audience" when he rejected traditional practices. Restif was convinced that the juvenile delinquency he observed in Paris was the direct result of the new freedom given children, and that the Parlement of Paris was right to suppress such works as *Émile*, which encouraged "an unruly progeny."

Source: Restif de la Bretonne, *Les Nuits de Paris or Nocturnal Spectator: A Selection*, trans. L. Asher and E. Fertig, pp. 212–215.*

Tumults—Outbursts

"WHAT A century ours is! What an age we are born in!" exclaimed Du Hameauneuf as he entered my house. "The children are leading men; hooligans, clerks, apprentice jewelers and clockmakers are usurping the nation's name and covering it with their filth, with their spite! . . . Oh, J.-J. R., I warned you of this! The Parlement, wiser than all our *philosophes*, than all our devotees, condemned your *Émile*.[1] The reason for their action was not appreciated; there was an outcry, and I believe that they were finally made to blush over it! And yet they were right! It is *Émile* that has brought us this arrogant generation, stubborn, insolent, impudent, willful, which speaks loudly, silences the elderly, and demonstrates with equal audacity first its native foolishness reinforced by upbringing and then its unripe understanding, bitter and sharp as mid-August wine.

---

* Reprinted by permission of Alfred A. Knopf, Inc. (The original French edition was published in 1788.)

[1] Rousseau's *Émile* was published in 1763. The book marked an entirely new approach to child rearing, abandoning much formal constraint and encouraging the child to explore and learn for himself.

"It isn't, oh, J.-Jacques, that your principles are bad; only that they are susceptible of abuse, and that is what the wise heads of the Parlement feared. I have seen since 1763 how the women readers of *Émile* have raised their unruly progeny! Most mothers had been giving their children to wet nurses. That was contrary to nature; but it is even more so that certain mothers should themselves nurse, and J.-J. did not say so; this omission has killed thousands of infants! . . . People determined to overthrow all the traditional practices, because some of them were wrong! Babies had been swaddled, wrapped in hard forms that cracked their ribs; girls, especially, were kept pomaded and coiffed; they were held to immobility and silence. That was wrong. J.-J. stated it strongly, because you must move your audience if you want to be heard. What was the result among the Parisians, and among those in the provinces who styled themselves *philosophes?* They left their infants stark naked; they washed them in the river, in the midst of winter (I have seen it all); they put them in a loose sack, instead of supporting the waist gently with flexible corsets like the ones on rue des Bourdonnais. Their hair flies free now in hideous, disgusting fashion. They are no longer restrained, instead they climb all over you with their filthy feet. When you visit their parents they make noise enough to deafen you, and at the very moment when their father or mother is on the point of answering some important question of yours they choose instead to satisfy some childish query from their dear son or their darling daughter. It is fifteen or twenty years now since this style of upbringing, supposedly patterned after J.-J. (for *Émile* was only the incidental cause and not the beginning), came to Paris; and we can see its effects already! . . . Come, come with me, my friend, let me show them to you!"

"What in the world has happened?" I asked him.

"You saw nothing this morning; you stayed in your room. But come with me."

I followed him, and we walked to the Palais.

From the Pont Saint-Michel I heard some noise. "What is it?" I asked Du Hameauncuf. But he did not answer. As I watched I caught sight of a young man fleeing along the Quai des Orfèvres, with the whole horde of locksmiths', jewelers' and clockmakers' boys in pursuit. They overtook him on the quay. "Ah, gentlemen, what do you want with me? I am a plain citizen, I came to watch like you did. . . ." He was given no time to say more. A police clerk who bore him a grudge had chalked the terrible sign on his clothing. He was assaulted; he was thrown to the ground. Du Hameauneuf and I mingled with the mob and we were fortunate enough to save the poor man, insulting him all the while. We gave him the word under our breath, and, struggling, he came along with us.

We went through the halls of the Palais de Justice. There was another incident. A chalk-marked woman was undergoing a cruel whipping by the clerks. Again, we succeeded in freeing her. The poor woman was exhausted. But as soon as she understood that she could leave she regained all her strength. There is nothing like terror to set a pace. . . . Finally the late hour sent everyone away. We visited the Marquise, and we delighted again in the sight of her. . . . Alas! we did not know that this joy was soon to be denied us!

We told her what we had just seen. She moaned at the tale, and her sincere sorrow intensified our own. We spoke of nothing else.

Du Hameauneuf returned to the Palais. All was calm. Youngsters and thieves alone had caused the rioting; the men had taken no part in it. I would not speak of these troubled days, except that I want to vindicate the nation.

I told the Marquise, "It's those fifteen- to twenty-year-old adolescents raised according to J.-J. who do all the harm. Oh, people of France, return to your old stern ways, and change only the abuses!"

IX

Religion and the Churches

ONE DOES not think of the eighteenth century as an "age of faith." Yet the century produced enough evangelicals, revivalists, and enthusiasts to escape the charge of religious stagnation. Such revivalist movements were found more frequently on the fringes than in the bosom of the established churches and their activities were greeted with skepticism and even alarm by clerical and secular authorities. In France, the convulsionaries of St. Medard threatened to drive Jansenism outside the bounds of orthodoxy in the 1730's, while a millenarian Protestantism born in the hills of the Cévennes was suppressed by armed force. Less episodic, though scarcely less charged with emotional fervor, was a "religion of the heart" opposing the more formal theological and liturgical practices of the established churches.

Pietism in Germany and Methodism in England reflected this tendency. Both movements stressed man's role as a blind instrument of God, as opposed to the more autonomous individual of the *philosophes*, latitudinarians, or Catholics. Methodism in particular placed great emphasis on arousing religious emotion by forensic sermons, large camp meetings, hymn singing, and violently demonstrative conversions. The selection from John Wesley (Document 57) makes this characteristic clear. Methodism was also concerned with everyday human behavior, insisting even more on the avoidance of worldly pleasures than on charity and brotherhood. In this it resembled early Calvinism. The selection from the German Pietist, Spener (Document 58), shows the application of such asceticism to business life. In one way, however, Wesley parted company with Calvinism; he considered education beyond the minimal capacity to read the catechism and Scriptures as superfluous and even dangerous. Hard work was far better for the child's soul than book learning.

Much of early Methodism was autocratic, anti-intellectual, downright superstitious, and even callous. Yet it had an emotional appeal to which many responded readily, not only on the level of hysteria, but on the more edifying level of moral purpose and direction. Undoubtedly Methodism met a community need by exhorting its membership to abandon Gin Lane for a more wholesome existence. More important, Methodism, with all its faults, touched the tragic side of man's

existence in a way the traditional churches did not. Whether it acted
to divert the poor of England from more direct action for political and
social reform is a much harder question to answer.

The episcopate, Anglican or Catholic, was becoming increasingly
aristocratic. This tendency was not destined to vitalize the religious
zeal of the upper clergy, especially since many younger sons seemed
less willing to accept their assigned berth than a century before. The
career of the Bishop of London (Document 59) lacks a certain spiritual dimension. Moreover, clerical absenteeism and laxity—perennial
problems in the Church—became graver faults in a society undergoing
increasing social stress. The absenteeism of the Archbishop of Rouen,
for example, resulted in the prelate's loss of touch with the social
problems of his diocese and an analysis of local conditions lacking in
subtlety or foresight (Document 60).

The middling clergy of town and cathedral chapter was much more
likely to be functional and socially conscious. Canons like Abbé Baston, while hardly men of great vision, were nevertheless conscientious
as administrators, teachers, or dispensers of local charity. The cathedral
chapter served as a real bond in a society where the social ties were
loosening. Its relations with the parish priest and the poor of town and
country deserve more study.

More striking in retrospect than signs of clerical negligence were
examples of religious prejudice. State religions were still firmly in place
almost everywhere. Religious tolerance was honored in the drawing
room, not in parliaments, governments, or courts of law. In France,
Protestants had no legal standing whatsoever, and in England Catholics
could neither vote nor hold office. Jews were confined to ghettos,
frequently outside the city, and excluded from public office and guild
membership. The religious tolerance of Joseph II in the Hapsburg
Empire was exceptional and ephemeral.

Behind these laws were the popular prejudices of centuries, many
times stronger than the governments that promulgated them. The
Calas affair at Toulouse in 1761 was one example of religious hysteria.
The Gordon Riots in 1780 (Document 62) were more violent and
destructive, but the English Parliament resisted popular pressure more
courageously than the magistrates of Toulouse. At times it seemed that
all the efforts of the *philosophes* to end such bigotry were in vain.

The Age of Enlightenment was also an age of healers, alchemists,
astrologers, and other charlatans. Not only the poor and ignorant, but
many of the well-to-do and even educated were attracted by such
fraudulent miracle workers. Their affront to common sense and their
persistent popularity seem extraordinarily. Cagliostro was the most famous, with his elixir of love and youth, followed by Mesmer's animal
magnetism, Böttcher's alchemy, and Dr. Graham's curious "celestial
bed." Perhaps the courting of charlatans was little more than a passing
fad for bored members of the upper class, but for others this interest in
the occult may reflect deeper psychological needs.

57. John Wesley

JOHN WESLEY, the founder of English Methodism, was converted by a disciple of Count Zinzendorf, the German Pietist. The first short selection from Wesley's *Journal* (Document A) describes his visit to Herrnhut [Hernhuth], Zinzendorf's religious colony in Saxony. Herrnhut appears to possess a tolerant, almost genteel atmosphere, with a great emphasis on singing. By contrast, in Document B Wesley describes the rash of conversions near Everton in great detail. Apparently he saw nothing excessive or strange in these violent "deliverances," which left pews and benches in a shambles.

Wesley's impetuous will and energy are evident in the very cadence of his *Journal*. In the fifty-three years after his conversion he traveled 224,000 miles and preached over 40,000 sermons, some of them to audiences of 20,000 people. His *Journal* indicates a wide variety of listeners—farmers of Meldred, colliers of Gateshead, gownsmen of Cambridge, officers and gentlemen of Morpeter. Wesley spoke anywhere, at any hour, to any number of people—on table tops in the open air, in the streets at night, in churches, hospitals, pubs, court houses, and private homes. He saw himself as the perpetual knight-errant in the service of God's Word. There was also a touch of the miracle worker, as when Wesley suggested he had cured a young girl of madness or when he prayed for relief from the heat of the sun and was "answered."

Source: *The Works of the Rev. John Wesley, in ten volumes* (New York, 1826), vol. I, p. 204; vol. II, pp. 426–429.

A. August, 1738

TUESDAY, AUGUST 1, At three in the afternoon, I came to Hernhuth, about thirty English miles from Dresden. It lies in Upper Lusatia, on the border of Bohemia, and contains about an hundred houses, built on a rising ground, with ever-green woods on two sides, gardens and corn-fields on the others, and high hills at a small distance. It has one long street, through which the great road from Zittau to Lobau goes. Fronting the middle of this street is the orphan-house; in the lower part of which is the apothecary's shop, in the upper, the chapel, capable of containing six or seven hundred people. Another row of houses runs at a small distance from either end of the orphan-house, which accordingly divides the rest of the town (beside the long street) into two squares. At the east end of it is the Count's house, a small plain building like the rest; having a large garden behind it well laid out, not for a show, but for the use of the community.

We had a convenient lodging assigned us, in the house appointed for strangers; and I had now abundant opportunity, of observing whether what I had heard was enlarged by the relators, or was neither more nor less than the naked truth.

I rejoiced to find Mr. Hermsdorf here, whom I had so often conversed with in Georgia; and there was nothing in his power which he did not do, to make our stay here useful and agreeable. About eight we went to the public service, at which they frequently use other instruments with their organ. They began, as usual, with singing: then followed the expounding, closed by a second hymn; prayer followed this; and then a few verses of a third hymn, which concluded the service.

Wednesday 2, At four in the afternoon was a love-feast of the married men, taking their food with gladness and singleness of heart, and with the voice of praise and thanksgiving.

Thursday 3, (and so every day at eleven), I was at the Bible Conference, wherein Mr. Miller, (late master of a great school in Zittau, till he left all to follow Christ), and several others, read together, as usual, a portion of Scripture in the original. At five was the conference for strangers, when several questions concerning justification were resolved. This evening Christian David came hither. O may God make him a messenger of glad tidings.

On Friday and Saturday (and so every day in the following week), I had much conversation with the most experienced of the brethren, concerning the great work which God had wrought in their souls, purifying them by faith: and with Martin Dober, and the other teachers and elders of the church, concerning the discipline used therein.

Sunday 6, We went to church at Bertholdsdorf, a Luthern village about an English mile from Hernhuth. Two large candles stood lighted upon the altar; the Last Supper was painted behind it; the pulpit was placed over it, and over that a brass image of Christ on the cross.

The minister had on a sort of pudding-sleeve gown, which covered him all round. At nine began a long voluntary on the organ, closed with a hymn, which was sung by all the people sitting, in which posture, as is the German custom, they sung all that followed. Then the minister walked up to the altar, bowed, sung these Latin words, *Gloria in excelcis Deo;* bowed again, and went away. This was followed by another hymn, sung as before, to the organ by all the people. Then the minister went to the altar again, bowed, sung a prayer, read the Epistle, and went away. After a third hymn was sung, he went a third time to the altar, sung a versicle, (to which all the people sung a response), read the third chapter to the Romans, and went away. The people having then sung the Creed in rhyme, he came and read the Gospel, all standing. Another hymn followed, which being ended, the minister in the pulpit used a long extemporary prayer, and afterwards preached an hour and a quarter on a verse of the Gospel. Then he read a long intercession and general thanksgiving, which before twelve concluded the service.

B. *May, 1759*

ABOUT THIS time the work of God exceedingly increased under the Rev. Mr. Berridge, near Everton. I cannot give a clearer view of this, than by transcribing part of the journal of an eye witness.

"Sunday, May 20, being with Mr. B——ll at Everton, I was much fatigued, and did not rise: but Mr. B. did, and observed several fainting and crying out, while Mr. Berridge was preaching: afterwards at Church, I heard many cry out, especially children, whose agonies were amazing: one of the eldest, a girl of ten or twelve years old, was full in my view, in violent contortions of body, and weeping aloud, I think incessantly, during the whole service: and several much younger children were in Mr. B——ll's view, agonising as they did. The Church was equally crowded in the afternoon, the windows being filled within and without, and even the outside of the pulpit to the very top; so that Mr. B. seemed almost stifled by their breath; yet feeble and sickly as he is, he was continually strengthened, and his voice, for the most part, distinguishable, in the midst of all the outcries. I believe there were present three times more men than women, a great part of whom came from far; thirty of them having set out at two in the morning, from a place thirteen miles off. The text was, *Having a form of godliness, but denying the power thereof.* When the power of religion began to be spoken of, the presence of God

really filled the place: and while poor sinners felt the sentence of
death in their souls, what sounds of distress did I hear! The greatest number of them who cried or fell, were men: but some
women, and several children, felt the power of the same almighty
Spirit, and seemed just sinking into hell. This occasioned a mixture of various sounds; some shrieking, some roaring aloud. The
most general was a loud breathing, like that of people half strangled and gasping for life: and indeed almost all the cries were like
those of human creatures, dying in bitter anguish. Great numbers
wept without any noise: others fell down as dead: some sinking in
silence; some with extreme noise and violent agitation. I stood on
the pew-seat, as did a young man in the opposite pew, an able-
bodied, fresh, healthy countryman: but in a moment, while he
seemed to think of nothing less, down he dropped with a violence
inconceivable. The adjoining pews seemed to shake with his fall:
I heard afterwards the stamping of his feet; ready to break the
boards, as he lay in strong convulsions, at the bottom of the pew.
Among several that were struck down in the next pew, was a girl,
who was as violently seized as he. When he fell, Mr. B——ll and
I felt our souls thrilled with a momentary dread: as when one
man is killed by a cannon-ball, another often feels the wind of it.

"Among the children who felt the arrows of the Almighty, I
saw a sturdy boy, about eight years old, who roared above his
fellows, and seemed in his agony to struggle with the strength of
a grown man. His face was as red as scarlet: and almost all on
whom God laid his hand, turned either very red or almost black.
When I returned, after a little walk, to Mr. Berridge's house, I
found it full of people. He was fatigued, but said he would,
nevertheless, give them a word of exhortation. I stayed in the next
room, and saw the girl whom I had observed so peculiarly distressed in the Church, lying on the floor as one dead, but without
any ghastliness in her face. In a few minutes we were informed of
a woman filled with peace and joy, who was crying out just before. She had come thirteen miles, and is the same person, who
dreamed Mr. B. would come to her village, on that very day
whereon he did come, though without either knowing the way or
the place to it. She was convinced at that time. Just as we heard
of her deliverance, the girl on the floor began to stir. She was then
set in a chair; and after sighing awhile, suddenly rose up, rejoic-
ing in God. Her face was covered with the most beautiful smile I

ever saw. She frequently fell on her knees, but was generally running to and fro, speaking these and the like words, 'O what can Jesus do for lost sinners! He has forgiven all my sins! I am in heaven! I am in heaven! O how he loves *me*! And how I love him!' Meantime, I saw a thin, pale girl, weeping with sorrow for herself, and joy for her companion. Quickly the smiles of heaven came likewise on her, and her praises joined with those of the other. I also then laughed with extreme joy: so did Mr. B——ll, (who said it was more than he could well bear.) So did all who knew the Lord, and some of those who were waiting for salvation: till the cries of them who were struck with the arrows of conviction, were almost lost in the sounds of joy.

"Two or three well-dressed young women, who seemed careless before, now felt the power of God, and cried out with a loud and bitter cry. Mr. B. about this time retired, and the duke of M——, with Mr. A——ll, came in. They seemed inclined to make a disturbance, but were restrained, and in a short time, quietly retired. We continued praising God with all our might: and his work went on as when Mr. B. was exhorting. I had for some time observed a young woman all in tears; but now her countenance changed. The unspeakable joy appeared in her face, which, quick as lightning, was filled with smiles, and became of a crimson colour. About the same time John Keeling of Potton, fell into an agony: but he grew calm in about a quarter of an hour, though without a clear sense of pardon.

"Immediately after, a stranger well-dressed, who stood facing me, fell backward to the wall; then forward on his knees, wringing his hands, and roaring like a bull. His face, at first, turned quite red, then almost black. He rose and ran against the wall, till Mr. Keeling and another held him. He screamed out, 'O what shall I do, what shall I do? O for one drop of the blood of Christ!' As he spoke, God set his soul at liberty; he knew his sins were blotted out: and the rapture he was in seemed too great for human nature to bear. He had come forty miles to hear Mr. B., and was to leave him the next morning; which he did with a glad heart, telling all who came in his way, what God had done for his soul.

"I observed about the time that Mr. Coe (that was his name) began to rejoice, a girl, eleven or twelve years old, exceeding poorly dressed, who appeared to be as deeply wounded, and as desirous of salvation as any: but I lost sight of her, till I heard the joyful sound, of another born in Sion: and found, upon inquiry, it was she, the poor disconsolate, gypsy-looking child. And now did I see such a sight, as I do not expect again on this side eternity. The faces of the three justified children, and I think of all the believers present, did really shine: and such a beauty, such a look of extreme happiness, and, at the same time, of divine love and simplicity, did I never see in human faces till now. The newly justified eagerly embraced one another, weeping on each other's necks for joy. Then they saluted all of their own sex, and besought both men and women to help them in praising God. . . .

"The violent struggling of many in the above-mentioned Churches, has broken several pews and benches. Yet it is common for people to remain unaffected there, and afterwards to drop down in their way home. Some have been found lying as dead on the road: others, in Mr. B.'s garden; not being able to walk from the Church to his house, though it is not two hundred yards. . . ."

58. Pietism and the German Merchant

THE FOLLOWING letter is taken from a manual of business correspondence, a practical guide for the budding merchant, containing forms of invoices, contracts of all kinds, conversion tables for foreign currencies, and other business papers. This is a letter from a theologian and suggests that Pietism had some hold on German merchants. Notice that this letter to a young apprentice contains only the vaguest kind of practical business advice (be friendly, obedient, helpful, honorable in all money matters), but insists that every minute of a young apprentice's day reflects religious devotion. But it is a devotion closely tied to the avoidance of worldly pleasures and wasted time. Neglect is the worst of sins; obedience to masters and application to craft the greatest of virtues. The letter insists that the apprentice's God-given occupation is an integral part of a life dedicated to divine service. The whole tenor of the letter implies that worldly success will probably follow such an attitude, though God's honor and the salvation of the soul are, of course, more central.

Historians usually associate the complex interrelation between religion and capitalism with Reformation Calvinism.[1] We should not forget to look for it in later centuries as well.

[1] It is only necessary to mention the names of Max Weber and R. H. Tawney and the voluminous literature they evoked on this relationship.

Source: Paul Jakob Marperger, *Der allzeit fertige Handels-Korrespondent* (Hamburg, 1707), pp. 665ff.

Letter of Advice from a Father to His Son
Who is Apprenticed to a Merchant,
As It Was Composed by the World-Famous Theologian,
Dr. Spener [1]

DEAR SON,

Your letter and your wishes for the New Year have pleased me. May GOD, to whom we direct all our wishes, fulfill them in a way that enhances HIS glory, benefits my office, and is profitable to all of my family. May HE also let you enter a year—or rather all of your years as HE has foreordained for you in this world—spent so that the divine light and power in your soul are increased every day through the Holy Spirit. May all your acts be guided by HIS grace and be pleasing to HIM. May HE also grant you as much of health and the other good things of life as HE knows to be beneficial to you. This is my daily wish for you and your brothers and sisters. If such a wish is to be effective, you must add your daily heartfelt prayers and walk before GOD as it is pleasing to HIM. Your main concern, now and all your life, must be to serve your heavenly Father, since you know that this is what HE expects of you. Read also, whenever you find time, in the Holy Bible and other edifying works, and listen attentively to the word of GOD in the sermons, so that your good beginning in the knowledge of GOD may be further and further advanced and imprinted ever more firmly in your soul.

This does not require much reading, but it does require that you reflect diligently upon what you have read. Reading only one verse in the morning, but thinking about it all day long as you are working, is more useful than reading the whole chapter without further thought. Choose, therefore, one of these verses and apply it to your whole day, using it according to what it contains. If it speaks of GOD's kindness, you should keep this kindness before your eyes all day long; if it is something you should do, ask yourself if you have done so hitherto and make a resolution on that day to lead your life accordingly henceforth. In this manner you

[1] Philipp Jacob Spener (1635–1705) is often called the "Father of German Pietism."

will achieve more knowledge [of God] and become confirmed in it. Be sure to pay particular attention to prayer, saying your prayers morning and evening, before and after meals, but always with deep attention and remembering in your heart at all times to whom you are speaking, to whom you are presenting yourself.

Do not think, however, that such prayers are sufficient, but remember faithfully that Christians should pray continually, so that, when you go to work, you ask GOD for the grace necessary for the completion of your task. Even during your work you should frequently lift up your heart to GOD, beseeching HIM to look upon you graciously, to protect you from all sin, to grant you the strength to do HIS will, to remit your faults for the sake of HIS Son, and other such short prayers. These require no art, but once you have become accustomed to them, a good inspiration will let you find the words with which to pray in all simplicity. Having begun, while still at home, to pray from the heart in your own words, do not give up such praying, but perfect yourself in it, since you can believe that the more intimately you are in the habit of speaking to GOD, the more grace you will obtain from HIM.

On the holy Sunday especially, you should spend as much time as you can find in religious practices, foregoing more and more the common habit, which sets aside Sunday as a day of pleasure and gaiety. You should seek your pleasure in GOD and in spiritual matters, since it is certain that these are the most pleasurable. Such time as you can find outside the church service you should employ in praying, reading, singing, and thinking about the kindnesses GOD has bestowed upon you during the past week and about the evils from which HE has protected you, thanking HIM for all such kindnesses and asking HIS forgiveness if you have sinned, and finally making a firm resolution to please GOD in the coming week. If you thus sanctify the Sunday, you will surely always have a blessed week and grow in Christianity in such a way that you shall have nothing to regret in all eternity. Remember also, however, that piety consists not only of reading, hearing, or praying, but of actions themselves. Oh my child, be sure to make it a habit to resolve upon arising, as soon as you are saying your prayers, to avoid sinning that day and to please GOD in all your activities, because such is the wish of your Heavenly Father, who has given you the occupation in which you are engaged so that you may learn to make all your life into a divine service. This means that you are never happier than when you think about your activities at the end of the day and find that you have done what is good, and that you are never more unhappy than when you realize that you have failed to do what is good or actually done what is evil.

Always remember that any time spent in this world during which we do not have GOD before our eyes or do something in HIS honor is wasted. In order to serve HIM faithfully at all times, remember that wherever you are GOD is with you, seeing and hearing everything you think, say, or do. This thought will often keep you from doing evil and spur you on to do good; it will even be the reason for all the good you do.

Next to GOD, you must think of your parents, diligently praying for them, and remembering what they are doing for you. For this you must always give thanks to GOD, and you must be careful to follow the advice they are constantly giving you and to act in such a way that they do not feel sorrow or shame because of you, but rejoice and praise GOD for you. This is the best gratitude you can show to them.

Since the Heavenly Father has led you from the house of your parents to that of another master, you must remember that you now owe this master and his wife all that you owe your parents: you must love them with all your soul and obey them, not just from fear of punishment, but from the bottom of your heart. To be in a position to do something to their advantage or to forestall any disadvantage to them should be your greatest joy, just as if it were your own advantage.

In words and deeds you must act meekly and respectfully toward them, and in your service you must never fail to do anything, willfully or through neglect. You will do this the more conscientiously if you realize that the good or evil you do to them is seen by GOD as if it were done to HIM. Likewise, if you always serve your masters as you would serve Christ Himself, and from the bottom of your heart, your service will be easier for you; not to mention that you will more easily gain your master's good will in this fashion. This also, but above all GOD's will, is to be considered. For this reason you must pray as devotedly for your masters as for your parents, considering their well-being as if it were your own.

Regarding the journeymen from whom you must also learn, not only custom but also GOD's order of things require that you submit to them, since GOD has placed them in a more advanced position than you. Being helpful and accommodating, as you should be, will win you their affection, which will be to your advantage and also afford you a good conscience. As for the rest of the domestics and your fellow apprentices, be friendly and agreeable with all of them, and do everything that is asked of you, so long as it is not against GOD or your masters. But do not ever let yourself be seduced into doing or participating in anything with the domestics and apprentices (even with the journeymen) harmful to your masters behind their backs; for the loyalty you owe them must be more important to you than the favor of the others, which will not profit you in the long run.

Be diligent in your work, pay attention to everything, and remember always that the profession you are learning now will not only be the means of earning a livelihood for the rest of your life but also that of serving GOD and your fellow man. Remember also that, to a large extent, it depends on you whether you will be a useless person or whether you will amount to something in this world. Therefore, you must pray to GOD with all your heart for His Holy Spirit, and also expend all possible effort and care during your years of apprenticeship.[2]

As to all other people you have to deal with, be friendly, respectful, modest, and serviceable with everybody; for such virtues are pleasing to GOD and also recommend a young person to people. Be not afraid of work when you can do a Christian good turn to anyone. Do not consider your own profit in such a case, but always show that it is your pleasure to be serviceable. Be trustworthy in your business house, and if money or valuables are placed into your keeping, consider it as great a sin to defraud by even a single *heller* as with a large sum, since GOD judges the intention, not the quantity. Be extremely cautious, so that you will not cause damage through carelessness. If you should have bad luck, however, do not try to deny it or put the blame on others, but show your trustworthiness by an open confession.

Do not engage in much social intercourse with your fellow apprentices unless you have to, except if you are sure of their

---

[2] This is a good example of blending free will with God's will.

Christian character. As a general rule, you must avoid bad company like the plague; but if you have an hour of leisure, it is always better to spend it in the company of people older than yourself, from whom you can learn something. Beware of gambling as of the very devil, for these are the ropes by which he pulls so many into temporal and eternal ruin. Remember always that food and drink are given to us by GOD for our sustenance and health, that we should use them for our pleasure and not abuse them through excess and wantonness. Be especially careful to avoid nibbling of fruits, since, taken at the wrong time, they are often hazardous to our health, which, being the most important of the worldly goods, must be carefully tended to.

Concerning a general rule for your behavior in this world toward yourself and others, everything can be sealed by your never varying acceptance of GOD's will. In this manner you will suffer patiently if HIS will should impose any misfortune upon you, and especially if you should be wronged by others, which also cannot happen without HIS consent. In that case also, you must learn to be patient, and you must believe that it is most salutary to a young man to learn in his youth to endure and suffer patiently; for by such suffering our own will, the most prominent feature of the Old Adam, will be most effectively broken, and such characters will, in their further lives, be able to do more than those who have never learned to suffer anything.

This, my dear son, is what your father, who desires your temporal, spiritual, and eternal welfare has deemed useful to send you for this time as a help to your memory, especially in your present state.

59. The Late Lord Bishop of London

The Annual Register was the informed Englishman's almanac, containing articles ranging from politics, foreign affairs, and trade statistics to travel accounts, poetry, and character sketches. In this issue of 1787, the Register has reprinted an obituary from the Gentleman's Magazine on the late Robert Lowth, Bishop of London.

The brief genealogy indicates that the bishop came from a modest line of clergymen and apothecaries and that his father had been chaplain to the Bishop of Winchester. His father's reputation at Winchester, an education at New College, Oxford, and the fortunate patronage of the Cavendish family launched young Lowth on a successful career in the Anglican Church. Advancement followed regularly: Lowth passed from bishopric to bishopric until he succeeded to London at the age of sixty-six. The obituary applauds the bishop's literary merits, his taste in the arts, and reminds the reader that he "conversed with lettered elegance, with very courtly suavity and ease. That his morality was religious, and his religion Christian need not be doubted"—nor, we might add, dwelt upon.

Source: "Characters," *The Annual Register* (London, 1787), pp. 35-37.

*Some Account and Character of the Late Robert Lowth, D. D.,
Lord Bishop of London;
Extracted from the Gentlemen's Magazine for November 1787*

HIS FAMILY were originally from the county of Lincoln. His great grandfather was Mr. Simon Lowth, rector of Tylehurst, in the county of Berks; his grandfather William Lowth, an apothecary in the parish of St. Martin, Ludgate, and burnt out, with great loss, at the fire of London in 1666. His father was William Lowth, of St. John's College, Oxford, and chaplain to Dr. Mew, bishop of Winchester, in which church he had a prebend, and the living of Boniton, in the county of Hants, well known by his Commentaries on the prophetic writings, and other learned works. He died in 1732, leaving two sons, the late bishop of London, and Charles Lowth, an eminent hosier in Paternoster-row, F. A. S.[1] 1756, and his collection of prints was sold after his death, 1770.—His Lordship was born in 1711. Winchester was the school which has the boast of breeding this very learned and virtuous man. From thence he was removed, on the same foundation, to New College, Oxford, where he proceeded M. A. 1737, and was created D. D. by diploma in 1754. His fame for classical accomplishments and Oriental literature was there soon and greatly established, and was never unaccompanied with credit, yet more enviable, of private worth, and manners at once delicate and brave. These were such recommendations as were sure to force their way with those who were themselves most commendable. The hereditary virtue

[1] Fellow of the Antiquarian Society.

of the Cavendishes is not more certain than their lineal readiness
to distinguish the virtue of others. Mr. Lowth was chosen as the
tutor of the Duke of Devonshire. He went abroad with him, and
brought home such a return as was to be expected from kindred
honour and well reciprocated use. When the duke became lord-
lieutenant of Ireland, Dr. Lowth went with him, and, as first
chaplain, had the first preferment which government there got in
their disposal. That was no less than the bishoprick of Kilmore.
But Lowth's mind at that time being set on objects even higher
than mitres, many family and friendly charms, and some pursuits
in literature, which particularly endeared the preference of his
native country, an exchange was sought for, and, what very
rarely happens, was no sooner sought for than found. There was
at that time a Mr. Leslie, with the same eagerness to get into
Ireland as Lowth had to get out of it. He agreed to accept Kilmore, Lowth succeeding to what he relinquished, a prebend of
Durham and the rectory of Sedgefield. Butler was then Bishop of
Durham; and when he collated Lowth to these preferments, he
expressed a well-natured exultation on this double gratification of
mutual wishes; and perhaps allowably, with a secret preference
to superior talents. To this resultless plea who can help being
partial? And how is the jurisdiction of a bishop to get more fa-
vourably distinguished than by all his ostensible favours being
possessed by distinguished men? Such was the good effect of the
first kindness from the Duke of Devonshire; but it was not the
last. Merit, when to be rewarded by the meritorious, is sure of no
penurious reward. In the administration formed by the late Duke
of Cumberland, Lowth's friends participating largely, he was the
first bishop that they made. On the bench of bishops, as every
where else, the first step is the hardest. From thence each other
advance follows with comparative ease, tho' his first bishoprick
was St. David's, to which he was appointed in May, 1776, on the
death of Bishop Squire. He went to Oxford on the September
following, on the translation of Bishop Hume from thence to the
see of Salisbury; and in April 1777, when London lost Bishop
Terrick, he was succeeded by Dr. Lowth. He entered on this high
office with expectations singularly splendid. He brought with him
a literary character of the first order, to decorate the diocese; and
he promised to serve it as Terrick had done, with temper and
discretion, both most exemplary; with the same amiable manners,

with the same useful zeal. These expectations he did not disappoint. He was as good as his word. He could not be better. Not one of his predecessors ever had claim to more desert, and was more spontaneously devoted to the claims of deserving men. His patronage need have no more said about it, than that it provided for two such men as Dr. Horsley and Mr. Eaton. His literary character is better known from its own efforts than by any thing now to be said about it. Few men attempted so much, and with more success. A victory, and on the right side, over such an adversary as Warburton, is no small distinction. His triumphs in Hebrew learning were yet more gratifying. Witness his learned Praelections on its poetry, while he held the poetry professorship, from 1738 to 1748, at Oxford. They were published in 1763, and translated into English by Mr. Gregory in 1787. But perhaps the most enviable, as the most useful atchievements, are what refer to his own language; which owes to him what nothing said in it can ever pay, the First Institutes of Grammar, printed in 17—; and, in his Translation of Isaiah, the sublimest poetry in the world.—His obligations to the colleges where he received his education are admirably expressed in his judicious, complete, and learned Life of their Founder, 1758; reprinted, with additions 1759. His gratitude to the university at large was not more finely worded in that elegant vindication of her in his letter to Bishop Warburton, p. 64.—His personal manners and opinions had in them nothing particular. That his morality was religious, and that his religion was Christian, need not be doubted. He conversed with lettered elegance, with very courtly suavity and ease.—His taste in the arts was highly refined, and of the objects in which the imagination loves to revel, landscape scenery appeared to interest him most. . . .

60. *An Archbishop's Reaction to a Grain Riot*

VIOLENT DISORDER is rarely greeted by contemporaries with patient understanding and dispassionate analysis. The reaction of Monseigneur Nicolas de Saulx-Tavanes, grand almoner of the queen at Versailles, to the Rouen grain riots of 1752 was no exception. Indeed, the archbishop's acquaintance with his diocese was largely limited to his sumptuous country residence at Gayon, at least twenty miles from the city of Rouen. Under these circumstances, one would hardly expect a thorough account of the riots. One might only have anticipated a more sympathetic approach to the problems of marginally employed textile workers.

There was little understanding of any kind in the archbishop's observations to his courtier friend, the Duc de Luynes. The riots, provoked by hysterical women spinners, encouraged and led by outside troublemakers, and even joined by respectable citizens, resulted in indiscriminate pillaging of the city's grain magazines. For such "sedition" there could be only one solution, a firm demonstration of force and authority.

The cost of episcopal absenteeism is to be measured not only in terms of loosening ties between upper and lower clergy, but also in the failure of the Church to respond constructively to growing stresses in French society. A prelate like Tavanes was not callous but remote, not uncharitable but unaware.

Source: Duc de Luynes, *Mémoires sur la cour de Louis XV, 1735–1758* (Paris, n.d.), vol. XI, pp. 499ff.

Versailles, April 26, 1752

I HAVE spoken to the Archbishop of Rouen [Nicolas de Saulx-Tavanes] about the sedition at Rouen, and he gave me a number of details. He said that, although it is very possible that the cloth had been cut on the looms and the workers laid off, this is not what started the revolt. Trade in linen and cotton cloth is very important in Rouen, amounting to 27 or 28 million per year. In order to maintain this trade, rules must be established and observed with exactitude. One rule is that the women spinners must not sell their thread to individual merchants but only to the manufacturers on specified days of the week. But often a woman needs money immediately and brings her thread to a merchant who refuses to buy it. She then complains loudly, claiming that she will die of hunger and that she cannot wait until the day specified. Other women join her. Very soon people get excited and it is enough for one to say, "They are trying to starve us to death," to bring about a revolt. These women are joined by a number of vagrants who, after having been all over the kingdom, have come to Rouen. This gathering soon made its decision; they decided to pillage the grain magazine of the Cordeliers, which they promptly proceeded to do.

There are neither troops nor a commanding officer at Rouen. M. de Luxembourg, the governor [of the province], is absent. The First President of the *Parlement* commands fifty "bourgeois" who do not perform regular service. What is needed is a regular patrol for the nightwatch and better police measures, including one or two regiments of regular infantry in the faubourgs of the city. However, these regiments should not be garrisoned in the city itself, because they might impede commercial activities. Barracks might be built in the faubourgs at the expense of the municipality.

The news from Rouen indicates that the disturbance has abated. Ten to twelve rioters have been arrested, although others have posted placards threatening fire if their comrades are not released. Over 40,000 pounds of wheat have been pillaged from the four principal magazines of the city . . . as well as from those belonging to individuals, including the almshouse. . . . A regiment of infantry and the mounted police have arrived. There has been some firing and some men have been killed. What seems so terrible to me is that well-to-do people—among others a man with 800 livres *rente*—have participated in the pillaging of grain.

61. *The Cathedral Chapter*

WE KNOW less about the Catholic Church than about other institutions in France. Emphasizing the deep gulf between a privileged, wealthy episcopate and a conscientious, poor parish clergy, historians have neglected the middling clergy of the cathedral chapter, teaching order, seminary, or even monastery. Here is Abbé Baston's reflection on his own cathedral chapter of Rouen, and, although like many memoirs it has the earmarks of an apologia, it is nevertheless informative. Baston's observations suggest a whole range of utilitarian good works and charities performed by local cathedral chapters. When Alfred Cobban concludes that "whoever won the Revolution, the poor lost," [1] he is thinking in part of the reduction of charity forced upon such cathedral chapters by Revolutionary legislation. On the other hand, Abbé Baston suggests that an expenditure of one tenth of the chapter's revenue on charity is very high. Given the condition of the poor at Rouen during the winter, one wonders. Equally noteworthy is the administration of

[1] *A Social Interpretation of the French Revolution*, p. 170.

the chapter's landed property and the treatment of tenant farmers, who were able to buy the chapter's farms during the Revolution. Is this an indication of lenient leases, as the abbé says, or a lack of deep loyalty to the chapter, or both? Yet however skeptical we may be of Abbé Baston's own interpretations, the response of his cathedral chapter to the plight of the poor of Rouen should be sharply contrasted to that of the Archbishop of Rouen, Monseigneur Nicolas de Saulx-Tavanes, in the preceding document.

Source: Abbé J. Loth and C. Verger, eds., *Mémoires de l'abbé Baston, chanoine de Rouen, d'après le manuscrit original*, vol. I, *1741–1792* (Paris, 1897), pp. 267ff.

THE [CATHEDRAL] chapter of Rouen, among the largest and the most illustrious of the kingdom, was also one of the most distinguished in membership. The old nobility and the high robe aspired to it, even though its share of temporal assets was not as great as many others. The *septennium* of the universities,[1] one of the least excusable ways to membership, had forcibly introduced a number of professors of literature, who might well have lacked the necessary ecclesiastic qualities. However, with the exception of one man who did not resist the schism,[2] they all exhibited both talent and exemplary piety as well as the most amiable character. The chapter was presided over by a priest who honored this office as much as the office honored him. To prove the value of this testimony, I shall add that he was among those whose Jesuit leanings had prejudiced him against me. His bias soon vanished, however, and he came to respect me. He told me this himself.

The duties of a canon absorb the better part of the day if he performs them conscientiously. There were few canons at Rouen who did not add good works to their obligations of public prayers. Only charity obliged them to undertake these works, which were for the benefit of their fellow men. Some spent the hours when they were not needed for the choir in the confessional; others took to the pulpits to preach the Word of God in their town or in the other towns of the diocese, as well as in Paris and even at court. By turns they took part in the administration of

---

[1] This expression designates the right of the universities to give their clerical professors a canonate in certain chapters after seven years of teaching.
[2] I.e., accepted the Civil Constitution of the Clergy during the Revolution.

hospitals, or helped with the completion of important municipal projects. They devoted themselves to teaching young clerics at the bishop's see, to the administration of the diocese, to the enforcement of discipline in religious communities; they lent a helping hand to the evangelical work of foreign or national missions. Some of them sat as judges on the law courts; some were authors of distinction, shone in the academies, thrived on profound erudition, or enjoyed the gentle aroma of poetry.

Piety did not suffer because of these various occupations. There was not one scandal, only eminent virtue. It was truly a majestic office [to be a canon], worthy of our religion and the God it worships. The rules were followed with great exactitude, even though it might be said that they were not strict, dispensing the elder canons and those who were legitimately engaged in other pursuits from being present on certain occasions. Yet these worthy elders often gave more heed to their zeal than to their strength and were the first to appear at exercises in which they did not have to participate. There were rules even for external things: a canon who appeared in his place of residence dressed other than in a long robe would have been censured by the chapter assembly at the request of the supervisor. The chapter of Rouen had chaplains, cantors, and an orchestra, but the canons did not discharge their obligation of singing the praise of God on these assistants. Even if their voices were disguised by others which were stronger and more melodious, they still rose toward the throne of the Eternal with a fervor that compensated for their weakness and ineptitude. All the masses were celebrated by a canon with the assistance of two others. None of them had, or could have, a vicar to replace him; only a bishop or a canon of the cathedral was permitted to celebrate the Sacrifice of the Redemption upon the high altar. . . .

Speaking of interest, I do not remember having noticed a single instance in which the canons of Rouen showed themselves dominated by that base and crippling egoism which places individual interest above the general welfare. The first consideration in all discussions was the honor of the company; and far from working only for themselves or for their own generation, the present members thought of their successors, the canons yet to be born, much as childless couples who hope to have children will tenderly and carefully work for the life these children will have with them and after them. The canons would rather have injured themselves than prejudiced those who would take their places a hundred years hence. Somehow they feared their criticism, their complaints, and especially their justified reproaches. If such solicitude is estimable in men who are the first in a long natural succession, i.e., in fathers, grandfathers, great-grandfathers, and ancestors, does it not call for even greater admiration if it directs the actions of men who perpetuate themselves through strangers whom they do not even adopt themselves but who are given to them and whom they cannot refuse?

The chapter of Rouen had two kinds of property: common property and property belonging to the individual prebends called *canonical* or *individual* property. The latter was administered by the individual titularies, but I do not know how. The former was managed by a canon who had the title of *steward*, and he rented [the property] out under the supervision and consent of the whole chapter. The rent contracts were never publicly auctioned and the revenue could easily have been augmented if the rent contracts had been auctioned to the highest bidder.[3] In England I knew an old priest who for many years rented the right of collecting the *dîme* for the chapter in his parish for 800 francs, and he told me that his profit was 100 *louis* (2,300 livres). Even though he lived in poverty, he was happy that he was cheating the "gentlemen of the chapter." The good man was wrong; he was not cheating them. They knew the approximate value of the revenue, but they wanted a priest who had to distribute alms in his parish to have ample resources. Those who rented land from us were treated almost as favorably. They [lease terms] were rarely changed and rent increases were so slight compared to what they could have been that, when the Revolution came and a temporary law took them away from us, most of them [the renters] had acquired enough wealth to purchase the domains they had rented from us.[4]

The chapter I am praising here had one rather wealthy ward which was to remain a perpetual minor: it was the *workshop* [*fabrique*] of the cathedral church. The chapter was not accountable to anyone for the proceeds of this workshop, and it could have

---

[3] Auctioning to the highest bidder was the common manner of leasing larger properties in France.
[4] Were the farms restored? Not unless the new owners agreed. Or was the *abbé* hopeful of a change in the law?

put part of them into its own coffers without lacking justification for doing so. But no guardian ever acted with more care, caution, and delicacy. While the stipends of the chapter had a lay administrator, those of the workshop were administered by a canon chosen from among the wealthiest and most distinguished, whose only reward for this rather burdensome office was the satisfaction of performing well. This canon was the natural defender of his ward. And where did he plead in its behalf? Before the chapter. He often asked the chapter to provide for its needs, and the chapter did not lend in order to be paid back; it gave. If urgent needs made a loan necessary, the chapter stood security. Its honesty and loyalty were so well known by the public that the only formality the lenders asked was to have the terms of the loan inscribed in the register of the chapter, usually without even asking for a copy. Whenever the question arose whether an expense should be borne by the cathedral church and its workshop or by the company [i.e., the chapter], the canon who was the guardian or "intendant" of the workshop always claimed that the company should pay. He did not even have to argue the point to have his way; usually the "company" laughed, decided against its own interest, and paid. "It is for the Church," the canons said, "we must not keep too close an accounting."

Reading over what I have written, I notice that I still have a great many things to say in its [the chapter's] honor. What charity! What eagerness to help the unfortunate! I do not only speak of the poor in the countryside where we had property and tax rights [dîmes]: no priest depending on us ever wrote in behalf of the needy of his parish without obtaining what he asked. I also speak of the poor of the town. In this particular region of France almost all the winters are hard. When the river overflows, its waters bring misery to the most crowded, industrious, and indigent quarters of the town. If the water is changed into a solid mass by freezing, all work in the very active port must be suspended. The frost stops the spinning wheels and looms and all the occupations which provide a livelihood for the women and older children. These unfortunate people, who in the good season do not exhibit the prudence of the ant or earn enough to lay anything aside, can only find resources in the indefatigable charity of their pastors, and the pastors can only find help in public charity.

So the [religious] corporations contribute. . . . Alas, I am expressing myself as if these happy times were still here! They are over. The locusts and a swarm of other idle animals have destroyed to the roots the plant which gave subsistence to the widow who can no longer spin, the orphan who will perhaps never spin, the father of a family, who is lying on a bed of straw of want and illness. It is passed, the time when religion, rich in worldly goods, gave to those who asked and also to those who could not or dared not ask. . . . On such occasions the chapter of Rouen took the lead in the good work by virtue of its zeal and generosity. Its coffers, mediocre though they were, provided help which would have wiped out misery and all that goes with it if other purses had been opened in the same proportion for the benefit of the needy. I am not exaggerating when I say that a tenth of the common property was expended in this common charity.[1]

62. The Gordon Riots—London, 1780

RELIGIOUS PREJUDICE could take a violent and ugly turn. The riots that made London a madhouse for a full week can be ascribed to many causes. They reflected the grievances of London laborers toward Irish immigrants, the zeal of certain Methodists, the proganda of political associations, the inadequacies of the London police system, and even the desperation of the city's poor, venting their frustrations in burning, looting, and drinking. But one cause stands out above the rest—the fear of "popery." Despite the efforts of more enlightened reformers, a mild relief measure for English Catholics became the excuse for a mob attack on Catholic chapels, shops, and residences, ending in general breakdown of municipal law and order. The outburst was not spontaneous. It was "mobilized bigotry," the culmination of handbill hawking by the Protestant Association of London. The inflammatory nature of this organization's propaganda can be seen in this "Appeal":

> To tolerate Popery is to be instrumental in the perdition of immortal souls now existing . . . and . . . to provoke the vengeance of an holy and jealous God, to bring down destruction on our fleet and armies, and ruin ourselves and our posterity.[2]

[1] One would like to know the total revenues of the chapter and how they were spent.
[2] Quoted in Eugene C. Black, *The Association* (Cambridge, Mass., 1963), p. 155.

By such broadsides, popery was identified with sedition and associated in the popular mind with war with France and failure to pacify the American colonies. Wild rumors circulated that 20,000 Jesuits were hiding in an underground network in the Surrey bank of the Thames waiting to flood the city.

Sir Nathaniel Wraxall, M.P., was in the London streets during these June days and, like other observers, stamps the riots with a Hogarthian quality. He also compares the firm, courageous reaction of George III with Louis XVI's "weak" response to street disorders in Paris nine years later. Although Wraxall insists that the Parliamentary opposition had no part in the disorders, there is little doubt that the Gordon Riots served to condemn all efforts at Parliamentary reform and strengthen the hand of conservatives. Reform was on the defensive in England even before the French Revolution associated almost all political change with a threat to English national security.

Source: Sir Nathaniel W. Wraxall, *Historical Memoirs* (Philadelphia, 1845),[1] pp. 116–121.

I was personally present at many of the most tremendous effects of the popular fury, on the memorable 7th of June, the night on which it attained its highest point. About nine o'clock on that evening, accompanied by three other gentlemen, who, as well as myself, were alarmed at the accounts brought in every moment, of the outrages committed; and of the still greater acts of violence meditated, as soon as darkness should favour and facilitate their further progress; we set out from Portland-Place, in order to view the scene. Having got into a hackney-coach, we drove first to Bloomsbury-square; attracted to that spot by a rumour generally spread, that Lord Mansfield's residence, situate at the north-east corner, was either already burnt or destined for destruction. Hart Street and Great Russel-Street, presented, each, to the view, as we passed, large fires composed of furniture taken from the houses of magistrates or other obnoxious individuals. Quitting the coach we crossed the square, and had scarcely got under the wall of Bedford House, when we heard the door of Lord Mansfield's house burst open with violence. In a few minutes, all the contents of the apartments being precipitated from the windows, were piled up, and wrapt in flames. A file of foot soldiers arriving, drew up near the blazing pile; but, without either attempting to quench the fire, or to impede the mob, who were indeed far too

[1] The *Historical Memoirs* were first published in 1816.

numerous to admit of being dispersed, or even intimidated, by a
small detachment of infantry. The populace remained masters;
while we, after surveying the spectacle for a short time, moved on
into Holborn, where Mr. Langdale's dwelling house and warehouses afforded a more appalling picture of devastation. They
were altogether enveloped in smoke and flame. In front had assembled an immense multitude of both sexes, many of whom
were females, and not a few held infants in their arms. All appeared to be, like ourselves, attracted as spectators solely by curiosity, without taking any part in the acts of violence. Spirituous
liquors in great quantity ran down the kennel of the street, and
numbers of the populace were already intoxicated with this beverage. So little disposition, however, did they manifest to riot or
pillage, that it would have been difficult to conceive who were
the authors and perpetrators of such enormous mischief, if we
had not distinctly seen at the windows of the house, men, who,
while the floors and rooms were on fire, calmly tore down the
furniture, and threw it into the street, or tossed it into the flames.
They experienced no kind of opposition, during a considerable
time that we remained at this place; but, a party of horse guards
arriving, the terrified crowd instantly began to disperse; and we,
anxious to gratify our farther curiosity, continued our progress on
foot, along Holborn, towards Fleet-market.

I would in vain attempt adequately to describe the spectacle
which presented itself, when we reached the declivity of the hill,
close to St. Andrew's church. The other house and magazines of
Mr. Langdale, who, as a catholic, had been selected for the blind
vengeance of the mob; situated in the hollow space near the north
end of fleet-market, threw up into the air a pinacle of flame resembling a volcano. Such was the brilliant and beautiful effect of
the illumination, that St. Andrew's church appeared to be almost
scorched by the heat of so prodigious a body of fire; and the
figures designated on the clock, were as distinctly perceptible as
at noonday. It resembled indeed a tower, rather than a private
building, in a state of conflagration; and would have inspired the
beholder with a sentiment of admiration allied to pleasure, if it
had been possible to separate the object, from its causes and its
consequences. The wind did not however augment its rage on this
occasion; for the night was serene, and the sky unclouded, except

when it became obscured by the volumes of smoke, which, from time to time, produced a temporary darkness. The mob, which completely blocked up the whole street in every part, and in all directions, prevented our approaching within fifty or sixty yards of the building; but the populace, though still principally composed of persons allured by curiosity, yet evidently began here to assume a more disorderly and ferocious character. Troops, either horse or foot, we still saw none; nor, in the midst of this combination of tumult, terror, and violence, had the ordinary police ceased to continue its functions. While we stood by the wall of St. Andrew's church-yard, a watchman, with his lanthorn in his hand, passed us, calling the hour, as if in a time of profound tranquillity.

Finding it altogether impracticable to force our way any further down Holborn-hill, and hearing that the Fleet prison had been set on fire; we penetrated through a number of narrow lanes, behind St. Andrew's church, and presently found ourselves in the middle of Fleet-market. Here the same destruction raged, but in a different stage of its progress. Mr. Langdale's two houses were already at the height of their demolition; the Fleet prison on the contrary was only beginning to blaze, and the sparks or flaming particles that filled the air, fell so thick upon us on every side, as to render unsafe its immediate vicinity. Meanwhile we began to hear the platoons discharged on the other side of the river, towards St. George's Fields; and were informed, that a considerable number of the rioters had been killed on Black-friars bridge, which was occupied by the troops. On approaching it, we beheld the king's bench prison completely enveloped in flames. It exhibited a sublime sight, and we might be said there to stand in a central point, from whence London offered on every side, before, as well as behind us, the picture of a city sacked and abandoned to a ferocious enemy. The shouts of the populace, the cries of women, the crackling of the fires, the blaze reflected in the stream of the Thames, and the irregular firing which was kept up both in St. George's Fields, as well as towards the quarter of the mansion-house, and the bank;—all these sounds or images combined, left scarcely any thing for the imagination to supply; presenting to the view every recollection, which the classic description of Troy or of Rome, in the page of Virgil, or of Tacitus, have impressed on the mind in youth, but which I so little expected to see exemplified in the capital of Great Britain.

Not yet satisfied, and hearing that an obstinate conflict was going on at the bank, between the soldiery and the rioters, we determined, if possible, to reach that spot. We accordingly proceeded through St. Paul's church-yard towards it, and had advanced without impediment to the poultry, within about sixty paces of the mansion house, when our progress was stopped by a sentinel, who acquainted us that the mob had been repulsed in their attempt upon the bank; but, that we could penetrate no further in that direction, as his orders were peremptory, not to suffer the passage of any person. Cheapside, silent and empty, unlike the streets that we had visited, presented neither the appearance of tumult, nor of confusion; though to the east, west and south, all was disorder. This contrast formed not the least striking circumstance of the moment. Prevented thus from approaching any nearer to the bank, finding the day begin to break, satiated in some measure with the scenes which we had witnessed, and wearied by so long a peregrination, which, from our first alighting near Bloomsbury square, had all been performed on foot; we resolved to return to the west end of the town. On Ludgate hill we were fortunate enough to meet with a hackney coach, which conveyed us safely back, about four o'clock in the morning.

X

Kings and Courts

EIGHTEENTH-CENTURY court life was a web of personal intrigue, shifting factions, and place seeking, half hidden under the glitter of pageantry, ceremony, and proper décor. Here the play of personalities seemed more pronounced, if only because alliances of families or cliques were so transitory. At the center of this decorous, giddy world was the monarch, object of flattery, persuasion, and plot, the person whose fancy or whim could make or ruin a career overnight.

The court of Versailles was the most famous. A number of circumstances had contributed to make it the most elegant and probably the most corrupt in Europe. They included the Bourbon policy of drawing the upper nobility to Paris to strip them of local influence, the Ludovican reputation of Versailles as the backdrop of royal éclat, the social supremacy of French manners and etiquette, and, not least important, the absolutist claims of the French monarch. To be close to the king or his mistress meant to be near the springs of fortune—pensions, offices, preferments, not to mention such subsidiary advantages as a good marriage market, the best connections for placing one's children, and the most felicitous surroundings to dramatize one's rank and prestige. For this was a world that still placed pedigree and the valor of ancestors high in the scale of virtue. In such an environment an illustrious noble name could win a fortune by marriage or royal favor, and a rich commoner could gain an office and a coat of arms by adding a measure of technical competence to the more traditional procedures of intrigue and maneuver.

Versailles has not yet found its Sir Lewis Namier. What was the configuration of these shifting alliances of families? How did they affect policy at a given moment? Historians still have but a hazy picture of these factions clustering around Belle Isle, Chauvelin, Choiseul, Du Barry, Artois, Polignac—while contemporary memoir writers seem scarcely more precise about their operations and impact. But the cumulative effect seems clear enough. Madame Campan leaves little doubt about the disastrous effects of someone like Marie Antoinette assuming an active role in royal appointments. Her observations and those of the Comtesse de Boigne confirm the impression of a monarchy in rapid decline.

The English court was something else. Court intrigue there was, but the Parliamentary and local political activity of the English landed aristocracy tended to offset the dangers of family connection and influence with a good measure of political experience and administrative competence. Nevertheless, Document 64 from Horace Walpole makes it clear that the royal will or whim was still decisive and that ministers were removed by intrigues "in high places."

The Russian case seems different again. Unlike Louis XVI, Catherine II was not only theoretically absolute but also active and arbitrary. At St. Petersburg, if we can believe Prince Schterbatov, not even court etiquette could provide a certain recognized procedure for office seeking. Property laws were regularly flaunted. Corruption of officeholders, wholesale bribery, and theft suggest the later novels of Gogol and Turgenev—a nation without a constitution, a despotism tempered only by inefficiency and corruption.

63. The King's Coucher

COURT ETIQUETTE was originally designed to exalt the dignity of kingship, to add luster and a touch of the superhuman to the viceroy of God on earth. Here we discover court etiquette leading to opposite results. Poor Louis XVI, naturally somewhat gross and infantile, is made ridiculous by the ceremonial *coucher*. Madame de Boigne was not opposed to the formalities of the court, but this royal performance she found personally painful and most degrading to the crown of France. Reading this, one grasps the real tragedy of hereditary kingship. We even suspect that it was not the ceremony that degraded Louis, but quite the reverse.

Source: Comtesse de Boigne, *Mémoires* (Paris, 1907), vol. I, pp. 55ff.

THE KING [Louis XVI] went to his *coucher*. The so-called *coucher* took place every evening at half past nine. The gentlemen of the court assembled in the bedroom of Louis XIV (but Louis XVI did not sleep there). I believe that all those who had been presented at court were permitted to attend.

The king came in from an adjoining room, followed by his domestic staff. His hair was in curlers, and he was not wearing his decorations. Without paying attention to anybody, he stepped behind the handrail surrounding the bed, and the chaplain on duty was given the prayer book and a tall taper stand with two candles by one of the valets. He then joined the king behind the handrail, handed him the book, and held the taperstand during the king's prayer, which was short. The king then went to the part of the room where the courtiers were, and the chaplain gave the taperstand back to the first valet who, in turn, took it over to a person indicated by the king. This person held it as long as the *coucher* lasted. This distinction was very much sought after. Hence, in all the salons of the court, the first question asked of persons coming back from the *coucher* was: "Who had the taper holder?" The choice as always and everywhere, rarely met with approval.

The king had his coat, vest, and finally shirt removed. He was naked to the waist, scratching and rubbing himself as if alone, though he was in the presence of the whole court and often a number of distinguished foreigners.

The first valet handed the nightshirt to the most qualified person; to the princes of the blood, if any were present, for this was a right and not a favor. If it was a person with whom the king was on familiar terms, he often played little tricks before donning it, missed it, passed it, and ran away, accompanying this charming nonsense with hearty laughter, making those who were sincerely attached to him suffer. Having donned the nightshirt, he put on his robe and three valets unfastened the belt and the knee buckles of his trousers, which fell down to his feet. Thus attired, hardly able to walk so absurdly encumbered, he began to make the round of the circle.

The duration of this reception was by no means fixed; sometimes it lasted only a few minutes, sometimes almost an hour; it depended on who was there. If there was no "sparker," as the courtiers among themselves called a person who could make the king talk, it lasted hardly more than ten minutes. One of the most skillful of these sparkers was the Comte de Coigny. He was always careful to find out what the king was reading at the time and always managed to steer the conversation to a subject where he thought the king would be able to shine. Hence, he was often given the taperstand, and his presence was unwelcome to those who hoped the *coucher* would be short.

When the king had enough, he dragged himself backward to an easy chair which had been pushed to the middle of the room and fell heavily into it, raising both legs. Two pages on their knees seized his shoes, took them off, and dropped them on the floor with a thump, which was part of the etiquette. When he heard it, the doorman opened the door and said, "This way, gentlemen." Everybody left, and the ceremony was over. However, the person who held the taperstand was permitted to stay if he had anything special to say to the king. This explains the high price attached to this strange favor.

64. Horace Walpole on George III's Accession, 1760

EIGHTEENTH-CENTURY England spawned a host of memoir and letter writers, beginning with Lord Chesterfield, Lady Montague, Lord Hervey, Fanny Burney, not to forget such intellectual giants as Gibbon and Hume. But, by sheer quantity alone, the correspondence and memoirs of Horace Walpole deserve special attention.[1] No doubt, Macaulay's charge that Walpole has given posterity more drawing room "trifles" than solid social analysis has much truth. But it was Walpole himself who said: "I am no historian; I write casual memoirs; I draw characters; I preserve anecdotes." [2] In this self-appointed role, Horace Walpole had no peer.

Walpole's description of the accession of George III demonstrates his talent for the portrait. That he overemphasized the influence of mother and favorite in 1760 seems probable. That Pitt was his hero, while Bute and Newcastle provoked his caustic criticism, is certain. Nevertheless, the passage demonstrates the important role still to be played in English policy-making by court influence and by the king himself. In 1760, royal "prerogative" was on the offensive, and no ministry could survive without the support of the king.

Source: Matthew Hodgart, ed., *Horace Walpole: Memoirs and Portraits* (New York, 1965), pp. 102–106.*

Accession of George the Third

GEORGE THE Second, contradicting the silly presages drawn from parallels, which had furnished opposition with names of unfortunate Princes, who were the second of their name, as Edward,

[1] W. S. Lewis and W. H. Smith, eds., *Horace Walpole's Correspondence* (New Haven, Conn., 1939–, 34 vols.).
[2] Quoted in G. P. Gooch, *Courts and Cabinets* (New York, 1946), p. 193.
* Reprinted by permission of The Macmillan Company of New York.

Richard, Charles, and James, terminated his career with glory both to himself and his people. He died, crowned with years and honours, and respected from success, which with the multitude is the same as being beloved. He left a successor in the vigour of youth, ready to take the reins, and a ministry universally applauded, united, and unembarrassed by opponents.

No British monarch has ascended the throne with so many advantages as George the Third. Being the first of his line born in England, the prejudice against his family as foreigners ceased in his person. Hanover was no longer the native soil of our Princes; consequently, attachment to the Electorate was not likely to govern our councils, as it had done in the last two reigns. This circumstance, too, of his birth, shifted the unpopularity of foreign extraction from the House of Brunswick to the Stuarts. In the flower and bloom of youth, George had a handsome, open, and honest countenance; and with the favour that attends the outward accomplishments of his age, he had none of the vices that fall under the censure of those who are past enjoying them themselves.

The moment of his accession was fortunate beyond example. The extinction of parties had not waited for, but preceded, the dawn of his reign. Thus it was not a race of factions running to offer themselves, as is common, to a new Prince, bidding for his favour, and ready each to be disgusted if their antagonists were received with more grace; but a natural devolution of duty from all men to the uncontroverted heir of the Crown, who had no occasion to court the love of his subjects, nor could fear interrupting established harmony but by making any change in a system so well compacted. The Administration was firm, in good harmony with one another, and headed by the most successful genius that ever presided over our councils. Conquests had crowned our arms with wonderful circumstances of glory and fortune; and the young King seemed to have the option of extending our victories and acquisitions, or of giving peace to the world, by finding himself in a situation so favourable, that neither his ambition nor moderation could have been equitably reprehended. The designs and offences of France would have justified a fuller measure of revenge; moderation could want no excuse.

A passionate, domineering woman, and a Favourite without talents, soon drew a cloud over this shining prospect.

Without anticipating events too hastily, let it suffice to say that the measure of war was pushed, without even a desire that it should be successful; and that, although successful, it was unnaturally checked by a peace, too precipitate, too indigested, and too shameful, to merit the coldest eulogy of moderation.

The first moment of this new reign afforded a symptom of the Prince's character; of that cool dissimulation in which he had been so well initiated by his mother, and which comprehended almost the whole of what she had taught him. Princess Amalie, as soon as she was certain of her father's death, sent an account of it to the Prince of Wales; but he had already been apprised of it. He was riding, and received a note from a German *valet-de-chambre*, attendant on the late King, with a private mark agreed upon between them, which certified him of the event. Without surprise or emotion, without dropping a word that indicated what had happened, he said his horse was lame, and turned back to Kew. At dismounting he said to the groom, "I have said this horse is lame; I forbid you to say the contrary."

Mr. Pitt was the first who arrived at Kensington, and went to Princess Amalie for her orders. She told him nobody could give him better counsel than his own. He asked if he ought not to go to the Prince? She replied she could not advise him; but thought it would be right. He went. I mention these little circumstances because they show, from Mr. Pitt's uncertainty, that he was possessed with none of the confidence and ardour of a man who thinks himself a favourite.

From Kew the new King went directly to Carleton House, which belonged to the Princess Dowager; ordering his servants and the Privy Council to wait for him at Saville House, then his own residence; and adjoining to Leicester House, where the Princess usually lived. The Duke of Cumberland went to Leicester House, and waited two hours; but was sent for, as soon as the King knew it, to Carleton House, where he determined to stay, and avoid the parade and acclamation of passing through the streets: at the same time dismissing the guards, and ordering them to attend the body of his grandfather.

To the Duke of Cumberland he marked great kindness, and told him it had not been common in their family to live well together; but he was determined to live well with all his family. And he carried this attention so far as to take notice to the Duke after Council, that his friend Mr. Fox looked in great health. And again, when the Privy Council had made their address to his

Majesty by the mouth of the Archbishop, it not being thought decent that the compliment on the death of his father should be uttered by the Duke, the King remarked it, and expressed an apprehension that they had put a slight upon his uncle. Nor would he suffer the name of his brother, the Duke of York, to be mentioned in the public prayers, because it must have taken place of that of the Duke of Cumberland.

At that first Council, the King spoke to nobody in particular but his former governor, Lord Waldegrave. His speech to them he made with dignity and propriety. In whatever related to his predecessor he behaved with singular attention and decency, refusing at first to give the word to the guard; and then only renewing what the late King had given. He sent to Princess Amalie to know where her father's will was deposited. She said one copy had been entrusted to her eight or nine years before; but thinking the King had forgotten it, she had lately put him in mind of it. He had replied, "Did not she know, that when a new will was made, it cancelled all preceding?" No curiosity, no eagerness, no haste was expressed by the new King on that head; nor the smallest impediment thrown in the way of his grandfather's intentions. A Gentleman of the Bedchamber was immediately dismissed, who refused to sit up with the body, as is usual. Wilmot and Ranby, the late King's physician and surgeon, acquainted the King with two requests of their master, which were punctually complied with. They were, that his body might be embalmed as soon as possible, and a double quantity of perfumes used; and that the side of the late Queen's coffin, left loose on purpose, might be taken away and his body laid close to hers.

In his first Council the King named his brother the Duke of York, and Lord Bute, of the Cabinet. As no notice was taken of Lord Huntingdon, it indicated an uncertainty whether he, who had been Master of the Horse to the King when Prince, or Lord Gower, who had held that office under the late King, should fill the post. To the Speaker of the House of Commons, the King said it should not be his fault if that assembly did not go upon business earlier in the day than they had done of late; a flattering speech to an old man attached to old forms.

The King's speech to his Council afforded matter of remark, and gave early specimen of who was to be the confidential minister, and what measures were to be pursued: for it was drawn by Lord Bute, and communicated to none of the King's servants. It talked *of a bloody and expensive war, and of obtaining an honourable and lasting peace.* Thus was it delivered; but Mr. Pitt went to Lord Bute that evening, and, after an altercation of three hours, prevailed that in the printed copy the words should be changed to *an expensive but just and necessary war;* and that after the words *honourable peace* should be inserted, *in concert with our allies.* Lord Mansfield and others counselled these palliatives too; but it was two o'clock of the following afternoon before the King would yield to the alteration. Whether, that the private Junto could not digest the correction, or whether to give an idea of his Majesty's firmness, I know not; but great pains were taken to imprint an idea of the latter, as characteristic of the new reign; and it was sedulously whispered by the creatures of the Favourite and the Mother, that it was the plan to retain all the late King's ministers, but that his Majesty would not be governed by them, as his grandfather had been. In confirmation of part of this advertisement, the King told the Duke of Newcastle and Mr. Pitt that he knew their attachment to the Crown, and should expect theirs, and the assistance of all honest men.

Mr. Pitt was too quick-sighted not to perceive what would be the complexion of the new reign. His favourite war was already struck at. He himself had for some time been on the coldest terms with Lord Bute; for possession of power, and reversion of power could not fail to make two natures so haughty, incompatible. It was said, and I believe with truth, that an outset so unpromising to his darling measures made Mr. Pitt propose to the Duke of Newcastle a firm union against the Favourite; but the Duke loved intrigues and new allies too well to embrace it. And from that refusal has been dated Mr. Pitt's animosity to Newcastle; though the part the latter took more openly and more hostilely against him afterwards was sufficient cause for that resentment. Whether these two men, so powerful in Parliament and in the nation, could have balanced the headlong affection that attends every new young Prince, is uncertain. I think they could. A war so triumphant had captivated the whole country. The Favourite was unknown, ungracious, and a Scot: his connection with the Princess, an object of scandal. He had no declared party; and what he had was insignificant. Nor would he probably have dared to stem such a body of force as would have appeared against him. At least the union of Pitt and Newcastle would have checked the torrent, which soon carried everything in favour of Prerogative. Newcastle's time-serving undermined Mr. Pitt, was destructive to himself, threw away all the advantages of the war, and brought the country to the brink of ruin.

65. The Court at Versailles

AMONG THE many memoir accounts of the court at Versailles, the reflections of Madame Campan, lady in waiting to Queen Marie Antoinette, are reliable and revealing. Madame Campan was no political analyst, but her minute observations on court etiquette and the royal preoccupations at Versailles and Marly may tell us more about the shortcomings of the French monarchy than volumes on the procedures of the royal council.

The document demonstrates the effects of the young queen's meddling in the affairs of state. Apparently well-meaning, but weak-willed and incapable of judging men, Marie Antoinette let herself be used by court factions, especially by the Polignac family. The queen's remark that one of her protégés, newly appointed to the London embassy, "could do neither harm nor good," is pitifully naïve. Worse, it demonstrates almost criminal corruption in the highest echelons of the royal administration.

Source: Madame Jeanne Louise Henriette (Genet) Campan, *Memoirs of Marie Antoinette* (New York, 1910), Memoirs of the Courts of Europe Series, vol. III, pp. 171ff.

THE INFLUENCE of the Comtesse de Polignac increased daily; and her friends availed themselves of it to effect changes in the Ministry. The dismissal of M. de Montbarrey, a man without talents or character, was generally approved of. It was rightly attributed to the Queen. He has been placed in administration by M. de Maurepas,[1] and maintained by his aged wife; both, of course, became more inveterate than ever against the Queen and the Polignac circle.

[1] Jean Frédéric Phélippeaux, comte de Maurepas, adviser of Louis XVI in 1774. Although responsible for the choice of Jacques Turgot as controller-general of finances, Maurepas was, in every other respect, an aged mediocrity.

The appointment of M. de Ségur to the place of Minister of War, and of M. de Castries to that of Minister of Marine, were wholly the work of that circle. The Queen dreaded making ministers; her favourite often wept when the men of her circle compelled her to interfere. Men blame women for meddling in business, and yet in courts it is continually the men themselves who make use of the influence of the women in matters with which the latter ought to have nothing to do.

When M. de Ségur was presented to the Queen on his new appointment, she said to me, "You have just seen a minister of my making. I am very glad, so far as regards the King's service, that he is appointed, for I think the selection a very good one; but I almost regret the part I have taken in it. I take a responsibility upon myself. I was fortunate in being free from any; and in order to relieve myself from this as much as possible I have just promised M. de Ségur, and that upon my word of honour, not to back any petition, nor to hinder any of his operations by solicitations on behalf of my *protégés*."

During the first administration of M. Necker,[2] whose ambition had not then drawn him into schemes repugnant to his better judgment, and whose views appeared to the Queen to be very judicious, she indulged in hopes of the restoration of the finances. Knowing that M. de Maurepas wished to drive M. Necker to resign, she urged him to have patience until the death of an old man whom the King kept about him from a fondness for his first choice, and out of respect for his advanced age. She even went so far as to tell him that M. de Maurepas was always ill, and that his end could not be very distant. M. Necker would not wait for that event. The Queen's prediction was fulfilled. M. de Maurepas ended his days immediately after a journey to Fontainebleau in 1781.

M. Necker had retired. He had been exasperated by a piece of treachery in the old minister, for which he could not forgive him. I knew something of this intrigue at the time; it has since been fully explained to me by Madame la Maréchale de Beauvau. M. Necker saw that his credit at Court was declining, and fearing

[2] Jacques Necker, controller-general during the War of the American Revolution, earned wide popularity for financing the war without new taxes. By enormously increasing the public debt, he prepared the way for national bankruptcy in 1789.

lest that circumstance should injure his financial operations, he requested the King to grant him some favour which might show the public that he had not lost the confidence of his sovereign. He concluded his letter by pointing out five requests—such an office, *or* such a mark of distinction, *or* such a badge of honour, and so on, and handed it to M. de Maurepas. The *ors* were changed into *ands;* and the King was displeased at M. Necker's ambition, and the assurance with which he displayed it. Madame la Maréchale de Beauvau assured me that the Maréchal de Castries saw the minute of M. Necker's letter, and that he likewise saw the altered copy.

The interest which the Queen took in M. Necker died away during his retirement, and at last changed into strong prejudice against him. He wrote too much about the measures he would have pursued, and the benefits that would have resulted to the State from them. The ministers who succeeded him thought their operations embarrassed by the care that M. Necker and his partisans incessantly took to occupy the public with his plans; his friends were too ardent. The Queen discerned a party spirit in these combinations, and sided wholly with his enemies.

After those inefficient comptrollers-general, Messieurs Joly de Fleury and d'Ormesson, it became necessary to resort to a man of more acknowledged talent, and the Queen's friends, at that time combining with the Comte d'Artois and with M. de Vergennes, got M. de Calonne [3] appointed. The Queen was highly displeased, and her close intimacy with the Duchesse de Polignac began to suffer for this.

Her Majesty, continuing to converse with me upon the difficulties she had met with in private life, told me that ambitious men without merit sometimes found means to gain their ends by dint of importunity, and that she had to blame herself for having procured M. d'Adhémar's appointment to the London embassy, merely because he teased her into it at the Duchess's house. She added, however, that it was at a time of perfect peace with the English; that the Ministry knew the inefficiency of M. d'Adhémar as well as she did, and that he could do neither harm nor good.

[3] Charles-Alexandre de Calonne, one of the last controllers-general before the French Revolution. His attempt to raise new taxes by convoking the Assembly of Notables in 1787 and appealing to the privileged was both desperate and futile.

Often in conversations of unreserved frankness the Queen owned that she had purchased rather dearly a piece of experience which would make her carefully watch over the conduct of her daughters-in-law, and that she would be particularly scrupulous about the qualifications of the ladies who might attend them; that no consideration of rank or favour should bias her in so important a choice. She attributed several of her youthful mistakes to a lady of great levity, whom she found in her palace on her arrival in France. She also determined to forbid the Princesses coming under her control the practice of singing with professors, and said, candidly, and with as much severity as her slanderers could have done, "I ought to have heard Garat sing, and never to have sung duets with him."

The indiscreet zeal of Monsieur Augeard contributed to the public belief that the Queen disposed of all the offices of finance. He had, without any authority for doing so, required the committee of *fermiers-généraux* [4] to inform him of all vacancies, assuring them that they would be meeting the wishes of the Queen. The members complied, but not without murmuring. When the Queen became aware of what her secretary had done, she highly disapproved of it, caused her resentment to be made known to the *fermiers-généraux*, and abstained from asking for appointments —making only one request of the kind, as a marriage portion for one of her attendants, a young woman of good family.

66. The Court of Weimar

IN MANY ways, the Duke of Weimar resembled King Louis XVI. He was lazy, childish, inarticulate, and spent hours eating and reviewing his honor guard of thirty-three men. He strikes us as a complete bore, saved from the fate of the Bourbon king by the absence of an intriguing and powerful Versailles. Weimar was small, and the political vulnerability incurred by such an existence was limited. Instead of assuming tragic proportions, the duke lends Weimar an air of German comic opera.

[4] The royal "tax farmers" acted as private banking enterprises and advanced the royal government a sum of capital in return for the privilege of collecting the indirect taxes. The tax farmers were usually very wealthy and a target for much social criticism.

Source: *The Memoirs of Charles Lewis Baron de Pollnitz*, vol. I, pp. 180ff. Anonymous contemporary translation.

[1729]

THE DUKE of Weimar spends very little Time in his Capital, but commonly resides at a Seat which he has caus'd to be built about a League out of Town. He has given it the Name of *Belle-Vue*, because of the fine Prospect which it commands from the Apartments of the first Storey. The House is small and not very commodious, so that the chief Beauty of it is its Situation, which is very charming. The Gardens which are begun upon very good Plans will be beautiful when finish'd, as well as the Pheasant-Walk and Menagerie, where there are Turkeys and all sorts of Fowl.

The Duke of *Weimar's* Name is Ernest-Augustus. He is the eldest of the Ernestine Branch which lost the Electorate when *Charles* V was Emperor. He marry'd a Princess of Anhalt-Cothen, who I have been told, was a Lady of distinguish'd Merit. She dy'd and left him a Son and three Daughters.

The young Prince is about ten Years of age. He can neither hear nor pronounce well, and is withal of a very tender Constitution. The Physicians say it signifies nothing, and that as he grows up he will acquire a Freedom of Speech. But I question it, and am apt to think rather that those Disciples of *Aesculapius* will send him into the other World. The only Hopes of any Male Issue of Weimar are founded upon this Child. The Duke of Saxe-Eysenach who is the next a-kin has no Children; so that the Dominions of Weimar and Eysenach too are ready to devolve to the Family of Saxe-Gotha. The Duke of Weimar's Subjects teaze him very much to marry, but the Prince does not seam to be in a Humour to satisfy them; for I have often heard him say that he can't bear the mention of Marriage.

No body presumes to go to *Belle-Vue* without being sent for, except only on *Mondays* when poor People are permitted to go thither with their Petitions which they deliver to the Secretary, and he gives them to the Duke. Persons of Quality whether Foreigners or others that have a mind to speak with the Duke, apply for it to the Marshal of the Court, but are seldom admitted to an Audience.

The Duke has rarely any other Company at *Belle-Vue* but two young Ladies whom he calls his Maids of Honour, and three young Women, Citizens Daughters, who go by the Name of his Chamber-Maids; a Major of his Troops, and the Officer of his Guard, who is a Lieutenant or an Ensign. I had forgot to mention the Baron *de Bruhl* who is the Duke's Favourite and his Master of the Horse.

'Tis with these Persons that the Prince passes his Time. He wakes early in the Morning, but makes it late before he rises; for he takes his Tea in Bed, and sometimes plays on the Violin. At other times he sends for his Architects and Gardeners, with whom he amuses himself in drawing of Plans. His Ministers also come to him while he is in Bed to talk upon Business. About Noon he gets up, and as soon as he is dress'd, sees his Guard mount, which consists of 33 Men, commanded by a Lieutenant or an Ensign. He exercises his Soldiers himself, and corrects them too when they commit any Fault. This done he takes the Air, and at two or three o'Clock sits down to Table, where the two Maids of Honour, the Master of the Horse, the Major, the Officer of the Guard, and even Foreigners, if any happen to be there, are of the Company. The Dinner holds a long while, and 'tis sometimes three, four, and five Hours before they rise from Table. The Glass never stands still hardly, and the Duke talks a great deal, but the Conversation is commonly on Subjects that are not very agreeable. When Dinner is over they drink Coffee, after which the Duke retires for a few Minutes, and then plays at Quadrille with his two young Ladies and the Major; but sometimes he does nothing but smoak Tobacco, and he often retires to his Chamber where he amuses himself with Drawing, or else playing on the Violin till he goes to Bed.

There scarce a Week passes but the Duke gives an Invitation at least once or twice to all the Persons of Quality of the Court, and all the Officers of his Troops, at which time there are two great Tables spread, where they dine, play, sup, and afterwards dance till next Day.

The Duke's Troops consist of a Battalion of 700 Men, a Squadron of 180 Troopers, and a Company of Cadets on Horseback. His Infantry consists of pick'd Men. Since the famous *Bernard de Weimar* who was Pensioner to Lewis XIII, King of *France*, no Duke of *Weimar* had so many Troops, and really they must be chargeable to the Duke, whose Revenues 'tis said don't exceed

400,000 Crowns. This Prince has made a Treaty with the King of Poland whereby he engages to assist the King with his Battalion whenever his Majesty thinks it necessary for his Service; in which Case the King promises to give that Battalion the same Pay as he does his own Troops. Mean time the Duke is obliged to clothe them all according to the Pattern which is sent to him from Dresden; and indeed their Clothes are very rich, especially those of the Officers and Cadets, which are so bedaub'd with Gold and Silver Lace that a Foreigner who comes to Weimar cannot but admire it.

The Duke's Family is very numerous, for besides the Prince his Son and the three Princesses his Daughters, he has a Sister, and a Mother-in-law, who is a Princess of Hesse-Hombourg: Meantime he has a numerous Court, and may boast that of them are Persons of very great Merit.

67. Corruption at St. Petersburg

PRINCE SCHTERBATOV wrote this scathing criticism of the Czarina Catherine II in the 1780's, but prudently refrained from publishing it during his lifetime. Although the prince translated parts of Fénelon, Montesquieu, Beccaria, and even Pope's *Essay on Man*, he was convinced that the despotism of the empress resulted from the "unstable" moral teachings of the *philosophes*. On the one hand, he objected to Catherine's "liberalism" in permitting a translation of Voltaire, so detrimental to "Christian law." On the other hand, he condemned her "despotism" in flaunting the "laws of the realm."

After devoting considerable space to the Czarina's well-known voluptuousness and her succession of lovers, Prince Schterbatov expands on the nefarious effects of luxury, flattery, and corruption at court. He then proceeds to treat the arbitrary interference of the empress in ordinary legal procedures, the corruption of local officials, and the venality of office. The prince even condemns Catherine's encouragements to education as superficial bids for personal fame.[1] Only by a return to the "Divine Law" could Russia be saved from such despotism. Perhaps Schterbatov saw himself as a Russian Fénelon, hoping to fashion a monarchy limited by a higher Christian law, but preserving class privileges and even censorship.

[1] See Document 55 on the education of noble girls at St. Petersburg in the section on Education.

Source: Kurt Stählin, ed. *Fürst Mikhail Schterbatov, "Über die Sittenverderbnis in Russland"* (Berlin, 1929), trans. [into German] Ina Friedländer and Sergei Jacobsen, pp. 110ff.

Chapter IX. The Reign of Catherine II

IT HAS been said that women are more inclined to autocracy than men; of the empress it can be said that she is a woman among women. Nothing upsets her more than to be told in the course of a discussion of public affairs that the laws are opposed to her will. She will immediately answer: "Can I not order this despite the laws?" Never has she found anyone who has dared to reply that as a despot she can, but that to do so would impair her glory and the confidence of the people. Many examples prove her despotism: 1) There was the time when Talysin's villages were given back to Marya Pavlovna Naryshkina, even though the villages were Talyzin's property by the contracts of sale and his actual possession. 2) Then, there was the law case of the children of Prince Boris Vassilevitch Golyzin regarding the illegally confiscated villages of Strechnov belonging to their great-grandfather. The Senate recognized the illegality of the confiscation and sent a report asking for permission to restitute the property to the rightful heirs. The report was signed "So be it," and this seemed to do justice to the heirs. Later, this "So be it" was interpreted by the Private Council as meaning "The confiscation is to be upheld." 3) Akim Ivanovitch Apuchtin reported to her on behalf of the War Commission concerning the retirement of a major general. He was given the order to grant this retirement without a promotion in rank; and when he objected that the law stipulated unequivocally that major generals were to be promoted on retirement, she answered that she was above the law and did not wish to give him this reward. Such examples from the ruler surely inspire similar autocracy and injustice in the great lords. Groaning under such iniquities, Russia gives daily indications that the example of the ruler is contagious.

Such thinking, especially when found in a public figure ruled by favorites, necessarily breeds partiality and injustice. I could cite many examples of both, but it is enough to cite the example of Sacharov. Because she accused him of "bad morals," his [property] case was not heard [in the court] but sent to the archives—

as if bad morals should be treated along with a case involving
villages. In such a case, even a corrupt person might have justice
on his side. This is not an occasion for judging "morals," but a
man's property claims, exclusive of everything else. Regarding the
claims of Wachmeister to his grandfather's domains in Livland,
which had been illegally confiscated as the departments of the
Senate testified, it was decided nevertheless that the domains
should be ceded to General Brown, who has them to this day.
Count Roman Larionovitch Voronzov, known all his life as corrupt, was named governor of Vladimir, but this did not keep him
from taking bribes as usual. This fact was known to the empress,
who reprimanded him mildly by sending him a large purse. Only
after his death, when the ruin of the local population was complete, was the order given to investigate his conduct as governor.
Although the ruinous oppression had lasted for seven years, only
the last two years were investigated. Such examples occur frequently and must surely encourage the subjects to adopt similar
procedures in their own interest. . . .

Can it be true that the ruler who controls most of the wealth of
the country is rapacious? It must be so, for I cannot qualify the
new habit of selling rank for money, so severely criticized by all
political writers, in any other way. There are a great many examples for this. Lukin, the corrupt and rapacious farmer-general,
gave the court 8,000 rubles for a public school from money he had
stolen, and was made a captain. Prokofej Demidov had been in
court for beating a secretary of the Commission of Law and had
continually committed defiant and impudent acts unacceptable to
any orderly government; he received the rank of major general in
exchange for a gift of money for the foundlings' home and another one of 5,000 rubles for public schools. He was thanked
publicly in the newspapers. As if the ruler were unable to found
institutions of public usefulness without taking money from corrupt individuals, and as if corrupt morals could be redeemed with
money!

This example became even more contagious. All ranks have
grown venal, and offices are no longer given to the most qualified
but to the highest bidder, who repays himself by taking bribes
from the people. Nobles wealthy from robbing the Crown are
given high rank. For example, Loginov used to be a farmer-
general. As such, he was not only a thief but was convicted of

embezzling a commission. Yet he was given a military rank. Faljeev, who always charged three times the market price when furnishing supplies to the ruler, not only received a military rank and nobility but also made all his accomplices officers. Trade has become contemptible, unworthy characters have entered the nobility, thieves and scoundrels are rewarded, corruption is being encouraged—all this with the knowledge and encouragement of the ruler. How, under these circumstances, can we expect justice and unselfishness from the lower courts?

This autocratic ruler governs by acts directly related to her craving for fame. The many institutions she founded, which seem to be made for the benefit of the people, are in reality nothing but signs of her lust for fame. Were she really interested in the welfare of the state, she would also give some attention to the operation of these institutions after their founding. But satisfied with establishing them and convinced that she will be eternally honored by future generations, she gives no further thought to their development and does not intervene if abuses arise. Witness the foundlings' home, the convent for the education of noble daughters, the refounding of the military academy, etc. In the first institution, many children have died, and, even after twenty years, it has furnished hardly any artisans. The second institution has produced neither educated nor well-mannered girls, except to the extent in which nature herself has endowed them. Education in this establishment consists in the playing of comedies rather than in the improvement of heart, manners, and mind. Those educated in the third institution graduate with little knowledge and a complete dislike for obedience of any kind.

XI

An Age of Reform?

THE DEGREE of social penetration of the Enlightenment is very difficult
to measure and appraise. Daniel Mornet in his brilliant, pioneering
work on the intellectual origins of the French Revolution investigated
the avenues of dissemination of ideas, ranging from reading clubs and
academies to private libraries and village cahiers, and concluded that
even peasants were influenced by some of the reformist ideas of the
philosophes, especially those regarding public education and civil
equality.

One can also examine the lawmaking process, its phraseology, apparent aims, and application. For example, the remonstrances of the Paris
Parlement contain substantial quantities of natural-rights vocabulary
and even specific proposals for civil-rights legislation. Given the privileged position of the magistrates and their increasing leadership of the
French nobility in the second half of the eighteenth century, this is
especially interesting. The French nobility was a privileged class, and
privileged classes rarely abdicate their advantages unilaterally. Did
these nobles of the robe believe it possible to defend civil liberty and
limited monarchy without legislating civil equality? Did they really
understand the implications of abolishing *lettres de cachet* and guaran-
teeing individual civil rights? Was their espousal of constitutional government expedient, consciously philosophical, or simply an unconscious reflex to the clichés of their own salons and clubs? No doubt
motivation differed with each magistrate. And when the Revolution
broke out, not a few noblemen were shocked by the application of
their own ideas.

The state of the prisons and of criminal law is a good indicator of
social concern with human improvement. John Howard's survey of
European prisons and workhouses does not produce an edifying picture, and no doubt he was not permitted to see the worst examples.
The lash of the *knoot* whip in St. Petersburg, the mastiff in an inquisi-
tional prison in Madrid, the galley prisoners of the pope at Rome, the
torture machines in a dungeon at Hamburg do not suggest great strides
of Enlightenment. On the other hand, it appears that most of the
French, Dutch, and German prisons were reasonably orderly, healthy,
and free from sadism and brutality. No doubt workhouse conditions

for women and children were far from ideal, but probably no worse than conditions in textile mills outside.

English criminal law exacted the death penalty for theft, including horse-stealing and many minor felonies, though it is noteworthy that many death sentences were commuted to transportation (see Howard's Table V for the Norfolk circuit). Of course, Howard was not permitted to see the notorious French "interrogation"—judicial torture—in operation. The inimitable Restif de la Bretonne informs us quite forcefully of the human relics who survived it. Restif's description of a public execution on the Place de Grève, complete with hucksters and jeering spectators, is even more horrendous. No wonder bandit chiefs like the famous Cartouche became Parisian folk heroes. All in all, European criminal procedure was still a long way from the ideals of Beccaria or Bentham.

Given Europe's prodigious economic and social problems in the eighteenth century, freedom of expression may seem like a luxury. But freedom of the press was an important vehicle for reform as well as an end in itself. Here England clearly led the way. Not that the right of political and social criticism was firmly established in the face of the formidable common-law doctrine of "seditious libel." Yet the Wilkes case marked an important stage in a long battle for freedom of expression, punctuated by the abolition of general warranties of arrest in 1765 and the Fox Libel Act in 1792. In the same years the English press developed enormously in quantity, quality, and self-confidence. The semiliterary journals of Defoe, Addison, and Steele or the hired papers of Walpole, had to make room for more popular and openly political newspapers such as *The North Briton, The Morning Chronicle, The Public Advertiser,* and *The Morning Post.* The indispensable organs of modern political life were growing apace.

In striking contrast with England, the French political press before 1789 was nonexistent except for a few mediocre journals such as the *Gazette de France* and the *Journal de Paris.* To be sure, the clandestine press, consisting of brochures, pamphlets, and news sheets largely printed abroad, had a certain circulation, but always at the risk of imprisonment to those who distributed them. The relative freedom accorded to the major *philosophes* should not blind us to the fact that for hundreds of minor news peddlers France was a police state.

Two groups of Europeans seemed almost totally forgotten by reformers of any stripe or inspiration. They were the Jews and the serfs of eastern Europe. Deplorable as their legal status and living conditions were, the most modest efforts at alleviating them met with either indifference or active opposition. Both groups were considered outcasts, another breed of men, deprived of the minimum protection that "citizenship" afforded the most ordinary European tradesman, artisan, or free peasant. To these men the French Revolution would offer the first glimmer of hope, but it would be another half century before their legal disabilities ended throughout Europe.

Some historians have regarded the eighteenth century as an "age of reform." Perhaps English social history substantiates such an assessment if we survey it closely. But it is difficult to apply such an epithet to the Continent. For an age of reform must be something more than an age of reforming ideas. Institutional changes and laws promoting human betterment were too few to label the period before 1789 one of reform. On the contrary, one is struck by the singular incapacity of most European governments to meet the growing demographic, social, and economic problems of the century.

68. A Remonstrance of the Parlement of Paris

IN RECENT years, European historians have placed great emphasis on the "aristocratic reaction" of the eighteenth century. In France the *parlements*, or sovereign courts of appeal, led by noble magistrates of the robe, increasingly resisted royal edicts by asserting their power of judicial review. By the eve of the French Revolution, the Parlement of Paris was not only attempting to block all royal tax reform, but also appealing to the public and employing a vocabulary that smacked of the rights of man. Given the privileged status of its noble members and the special position of the Parlement itself, this remonstrance, or formal protest to the king, suggests a very dangerous policy. It might also be argued that many of the members of the Paris Parlement were sincere liberals, and their allusions to consent theory and the specific condemnation of the famous *lettres de cachet* should not be regarded as hypocritical propaganda. Was the nobility, in Paris at least, infected by the Enlightenment?

The following remonstrance was delivered to Louis XVI on March 13, 1788.

Source: Jules Flammermont, ed., *Remonstrances du Parlement de Paris au XVIIIme siècle* (Paris, 1898), vol. III, pp. 713ff.

SIRE,
It is the duty of your Parlement to keep a constant watch over the needs of the people and the rights of the sovereign: the people may be led astray by factions, and kings are only too exposed to rash advice. Your Parlement speaks of liberty to kings and of submission to the people. It gives dignity to this submission by its example, and it gives firmness to authority by its principles. In a

word, Sire, it is your Parlement's function to attach royal authority to justice and public liberty to loyalty. To do this has always been its aim and its reward in times of stress.

Still penetrated with these sentiments, still desiring to merit the benevolence of our kings and to ensure the liberty of our fellow citizens, we have come to the steps of the throne in order to bring before Your Majesty the most baneful error that can befall a sovereign; we have come, Sire, to invoke your justice, your wisdom, and your humanity against the use of the *lettres de cachet*.

These terrible words make every heart beat more slowly and throw all thinking into confusion. In terror, everyone hesitates, looks around him, and does not dare to explain himself; and the mute people hardly dares raise its thoughts to the inconceivable power which disposes of men without judging or even hearing them, which arbitrarily casts them into impenetrable darkness and keeps them there, in a place where the light of day often does not penetrate any more than the eye of the law, the cry of nature, or the voice of friendship. The people does not dare think of that power whose very essence is mystery and whose only justification is force; of that power which is exercised with impunity by ministers, underlings, and police spies; of that power, finally, which from the ministers down to the last tool of the police, forms a formidable chain of oppressors over our heads before which all the laws of nature and of state must remain silent.

No indeed, Sire, the laws of nature and the laws of the state shall not accuse your Parlement, the living law at the steps of the throne, of a guilty silence.

Man is born free, and his happiness depends on justice. Liberty is an inalienable right. It consists of being able to live according to the laws. Justice is a universal duty and precedes the very laws, which presuppose it and must direct it, but can never exempt kings or subjects from this duty.

Justice and liberty! These, Sire, are the principle and the aim of every society, these are the unshakeable foundations of all power and, happily for the human race, the admirable connection between these two goods is such that without them there is no reasonable authority and no solid obedience.

The use of the *lettres de cachet* reverses all these ideas. It reduces justice to a chimera, liberty to a word. It goes against

reason, it is contrary to the statutes, and the motives by which
one tries to justify it are only pretexts contradicted by the evidence.

It goes against reason; it is patently repugnant to human nature, to the nature of monarchy, and to the elementary notions of
morality.

But such, precisely, is the essential character of the *lettres de
cachet*.

It is not in human nature to be self-contained. For man, self-
containment is a state of war, in which deviousness or force alternately command and in which justice, being without sanction,
has no power. It is, therefore, in man's nature to unite with his
fellow men and to live in society, submitting to general agreements, i.e., laws. But agreements which would subject him without protecting him would no longer be laws, they would be fetters. Force can impose these fetters, weakness or madness can
bear them, but force does not create obligations, and weakness or
madness cannot make commitments; all legitimate submission is
voluntary by its very principle. A guilty citizen has consented in
advance to the judgment that condemns him. Men who would say
to other men: "Do, by all means, pass an arbitrary judgment; we
consent if, upon a word from your lips, a letter from your hand,
we lose our fortune, our liberty, our wives, our children, and even
the right to defend ourselves. . . ," men, we contend, who would
speak thus would surely be insane. The consent of the people to
the use of the *lettres de cachet*, therefore, would be incompatible
with reason, but reason is the natural state of man as of society, so
that the use of the *lettres de cachet* is repugnant to human nature, which is reasonable as well as sociable.

Is it said that this usage is founded upon the nature of mon-
archical power? The answer to this is not very difficult to find.

Kings rule by conquest or by the law. If the victor misuses his
conquest, if he violates the rights of man, if the conquest is not
changed into a capitulation, if it is force which administers the
fruits of victory, it will not give the conqueror subjects, but
slaves. Kings who rule by law must come back to principles. Reason does not permit kings to order that which it would not permit
peoples to consent to.

And how could reason tolerate such a reversal of morality?

Fortunately, Sire, the guardian principles of the human race
are not in need of proofs, they are self-evident. It is evident that

justice must protect weakness against power. It is evident that the scales must be balanced between the rich and the poor.

It is evident that dishonor and punishment must follow a crime after it has been judged, but then only.

If there were a power which could arbitrarily put a stop to legal procedures, which could make distinctions among offenders, protecting some and giving up others, it is evident that such a power, by compromising the justice of the sentences, would add the notion of partiality to that of the example.

And if this power were to constantly favor a certain class of citizens to the exclusion of all others, it is evident that the law, no longer having the function of punishing such and such crimes but such and such classes of society, would completely destroy the sense of justice and innocence in these proscribed classes, keeping them in a perpetual state of terror and degradation.

These incontestable truths can be applied directly to the use of the *lettres de cachet*. Two men meet, one of them is weak, the other powerful, one is poor, the other rich. The poor man can say to himself: If this man offends me, if he attacks my honor, my liberty, my life, the laws assure me of their support. But the laws deceive me: perhaps authority will feel differently about it, and in that case authority will have its way. But if I offend him, I shall be apprehended, imprisoned, dishonored, abandoned, punished; that same authority will be mute, these same laws will be inexorable. Where, then, is justice? Is misery, then, a crime? Does simple humanity no longer mean anything? Is a simple man, a poor man, no longer a citizen? The statutes are as opposed to the *lettres de cachet* as the principles. At all times ambition, vindictiveness, flattery, and cupidity have besieged the throne, but at all times the laws have also warned the sovereigns and defended the people, if not with equal success, at least with equal energy; and this continuous struggle between arbitrary power and liberty has not extinguished the sense of liberty in the minds of people and of kings. The last Estates General held in Blois has beseeched the king to limit the *lettres de cachet* to his entourage, to use them not to remove these men from their business, their homes, and their families, but only to keep them away from his palace and to deprive them of his "presence," without depriving them of justice. It is a maxim of our monarchy that no citizen can be imprisoned without a warrant from a judge. All the kings of the first two dynasties have recognized this maxim. Hugues Capet already found it when he came to the throne; all the statutes of the realm have confirmed it under the third dynasty. It has instituted the only distinction among prisoners our laws allow, that between prisoners for crime and prisoners for debts. The Ordinance of 1670, finally, conforming in this respect to all the previous ordinances, has given the official stamp to this maxim by stipulating that prisoners accused of crimes must be interrogated within twenty-four hours after their imprisonment; but this stipulation is a useless, derisory precaution as long as the *lettres de cachet* continue to be in use.

Thus the rights of the human race, the fundamental principles of society, the most enlightened reason, the most cherished interest of legitimate power, and the most elementary notions of morality and legality all unanimously condemn the use of the *lettres de cachet*.

69. Reform of Prisons and Penal Law

JOHN HOWARD was one of a prolific breed of English single-causers. Howard devoted his life to prison reform and began his campaign by an extensive fact-gathering tour of European prisons. In 1777 he published two substantial volumes of his findings, and selections from his reports on conditions in France, Germany, and Russia are presented here.

Howard was rather favorably impressed with Paris prisons, which he found reasonably clean and airy and where prisoners were given exercise, medical attention, clean linen, and adequate food. German prisons were equally clean and airy, even heated in winter, and the newer ones contained no dungeons. "Engines of torture" appeared occasionally, however, much to Howard's chagrin and apparently contrary to English experience. The German "houses of correction" seemed well-organized and, not unlike the English workhouses, their inmates were diligently occupied in spinning, knitting, weaving, or "rasping logwood." Russian treatment of debtors seemed very harsh and, although capital punishment was restricted to crimes of treason, public punishment by the *knoot* whip often resulted in death.

Throughout his work, Howard maintained that conditions in English prisons were inferior to those in most prisons on the Continent. More important, he implied that continental Europeans were more inclined to adjust the punishment to the gravity of the crime. The number of crimes that involved the death sentence in England was considerable, as the table from the Norfolk circuit shows. Only after historians have studied European legal systems more intensively and comparatively can we be more conclusive about the relative justice and equity of the criminal law. It would appear, however, that Whig praise of English criminal law before the Benthamite reforms of the early nineteenth century was not altogether justified.

Source: John Howard, *The State of the Prisons in England and Wales, With Preliminary Observations on some Foreign Prisons* (London, 1777), vol. I, pp. 105–107, 114–115, 484; vol. II, pp. 40–43.

Germany

THE GERMANS, well aware of the necessity of *Cleanliness* in Prisons, have very judiciously chosen to build them in situations most conducive to it; that is, *near Rivers:* as at *Hanover, Zell, Hamburgh, Bremen, Cologne, Mentz* and many other places.

In the Gaols that I saw there were but few prisoners, except those called, improperly, *Galley-Slaves.* One cause of this, here as in Switzerland, is a speedy trial after commitment.

The Galley-Slaves have every where a Prison to themselves. They work on the *Roads,* the *Fortifications, Chalk-Hills,* and other public service; for four, seven, ten, fifteen, twenty years, according to their crimes: and are cloathed, as well as fed, by the Government. At *Wesel,* which belongs to the KING of *Prussia,* there were ninety-eight of these slaves: they have two pounds of bread a day, and the value of three halfpence English every day they work.

I saw no under-ground dungeons in any of the new Prisons in *Germany:* nor indeed in any new Prison abroad. At *Lunenburg* the dungeons are disused: and instead of them are built additional rooms up stairs: one for each prisoner. And in most of the Gaols each criminal is alone in his room; which is more or less strong, lightsome, and airy, as the crime he is charged with is more or less atrocious.

One often sees the doors of sundry rooms marked *Ethiopia, India, Italy, France, England,* &c. In those rooms, parents, by the authority of the Magistrates, confine for a certain term dissolute children: and if they are inquired after, the answer is, they are gone to *Italy, England,* &c.

I do not remember any Prison in *Germany* (nor elsewhere abroad) in which *Felons* have not, either from the public allowance, or from charities, somewhat more to live on than bread and water. In some places a person goes on market-days with a basket for prisoners: and I have seen him bring them a comfortable meal of fresh vegetables. But there are separate Prisons in which confinement for a week or two on bread and water is all the punishment for some petty offences. Perhaps, when a condemned criminal is only to live a day or two, such diet may be more proper than the indulgence with which the *Germans* treat prisoners, after sentence of death, which is commonly executed within forty-eight hours. The malefactor has then his choice of food, and wine, in a commodious room, into which his friends are admitted; and a Minister attends him during almost all his remaining hours. . . .

The Prison at HANOVER was built about thirty years ago. It is situated on the river *Leyna*. There are eleven strong rooms, about ten feet square, and ten and a half high; with a bed of solid stone in each, eleven inches from the ground, and nine inches higher at the head. Over these are larger apartments for debtors &c. The rooms are warmed by stoves in winter. Criminals have a small chain: they are allowed straw to lie on, and two coverlids. When I visited the Prison there were seven criminals and one debtor. The Keeper sells no liquors, but has a salary. In the Council-Chamber are all the various Edicts in frames. There is a Torture-Chamber, but I with pleasure learned that the two cruel engines had not been used for four years.

LUNENBURG. I found the criminals here employed on a different work from any I had before seen: digging stone from a large chalk-hill called *Kalck-Berg*. Others were preparing it for the kiln, grinding, sifting, packing &c. in the warehouses. The casks are about three hundred weight. It is sent to *Hamburgh* and other distant places, as it makes an excellent cement. Many other men were employed; but the criminals, of whom there were thirty-one, had a chain of about four pounds. Their allowance was a pound and half of bread, and three halfpence in money: provisions much cheaper than in England.

At HAMBURGH *Felons* in the *Bütteley* were all in irons. The common method of execution is decollation. The Executioner, who is Gaoler, shewed me the sword which, he said, he had made use of eight times.

Among the various engines of torture, or the question, which I have seen in *France* and other places, the most excruciating is kept and used in a deep cellar of this Prison. It ought to be buried ten thousand fathom deeper. It is said the inventor was the first who suffered by it: the last was a woman, not two years ago. . . .

TABLE V

An ACCOUNT of the Number of Criminals Condemned to Death; Executed; and Sentenced to Transportation: with their respective Offences: from the Year 1750 to 1772 Inclusive; within the several Counties &c. in the NORFOLK CIRCUIT.

Years	Petty Treason and Murder	Burglary and House-breaking	Robbery in Highway & Dwelling	Horse-stealing, &c.	Forgery	Returning from Transportation	Six other Crimes	Condemned to Death	Executed	Reprieved for Transportation	Grand Larceny	Petty Larceny	Seven other Crimes	Sentenced to Transportation
1750	2	3	8	8	—	—	—	21	10	8	24	3	—	35
1751	—	6	4	6	—	—	—	16	12	12	24	—	—	36
1752	3	3	3	15	1	—	3	28	11	13	28	1	2	44
1753	2	4	2	11	—	—	2	21	6	10	18	1	—	29
1754	—	9	2	17	1	—	4	33	13	20	29	1	4	54
1755	—	2	4	7	—	—	1	14	2	9	20	1	1	31
1756	—	2	2	7	—	—	6	17	1	16	18	1	—	36
1757	1	8	5	11	—	—	2	27	6	12	34	—	1	46
1758	—	2	6	15	—	—	1	24	5	23	31	1	2	57
1759	—	2	3	8	—	—	—	13	3	15	12	2	—	29
1760	—	5	3	3	—	—	—	11	3	11	15	—	1	27
1761	1	1	2	2	—	—	2	8	2	4	13	—	1	18
1762	1	1	1	1	2	1	1	8	2	3	10	—	—	15
1763	3	3	1	5	—	—	1	13	5	6	19	1	2	27
1764	—	4	2	8	—	3	2	19	3	10	16	1	4	29
1765	—	4	2	14	—	—	—	20	1	19	29	1	2	52
1766	2	8	4	14	—	—	2	30	4	17	27	—	1	45
1767	2	6	2	14	—	—	6	30	5	38	34	—	—	72
1768	—	1	1	10	—	—	4	16	5	16	35	1	2	55
1769	2	9	1	4	—	1	1	18	6	11	22	—	2	34
1770	—	5	5	12	—	1	1	24	7	17	18	—	—	35
1771	1	4	1	6	—	—	4	16	5	11	30	—	2	43
1772	—	1	1	4	—	—	1	7	—	7	17	—	1	25
Total	20	93	65	202	4	6	44	434	117	308	523	15	28	874

Russia

IN *Russia* the peasants and servants are bondmen or slaves, and their lords (or masters) may inflict on them any corporal punishment; or banish them to *Siberia* on giving notice of their offence to the police. But they are not permitted to put them to death. Should they, however, die by the severity of their punishment, the penalty of the law is easily evaded.

Debtors in this country are often employed as *slaves* by government, and allowed twelve *roubles* yearly wages, which goes towards discharging the debt. In some cases of private debts, if any person will give sufficient security to pay twelve *roubles* a year, as long as the slave lives, or till the debt is paid off; as also to produce the slave when he is demanded; such person may take him out of confinement: but if he fails to produce him when demanded, is liable to pay the whole debt immediately.

There are no regular gaolers appointed in *Russia*, but all the prisons are guarded by the *military*. Little or no attention is paid to the reformation of prisoners.

There is no capital punishment for any crime but treason: but the common punishment of the *knoot* is often dreaded more than death, and sometimes a criminal has endeavoured to bribe the executioner to kill him. This punishment seldom causes immediate death, but death is often the consequence of it.

The governor of the *police* at *Petersburg* was so kind as to fix a time for shewing me all the instruments commonly used for punishment—the axe and block—the machine (now out of use) for breaking the arms and legs—the instrument for slitting or lacerating the nostrils—and that for marking criminals, (which is done by punctuation, and then rubbing a black powder on the wounds)— the *knoot* whip—and another called the *cat*, which consists of a number of thongs from two to ten.

The *knoot* whip is fixed to a wooden handle a foot long, and consists of several thongs about two feet in length twisted together, to the end of which is fastened a single tough thong of a foot and half, tapering towards a point, and capable of being changed by the executioner, when too much softened by the blood of the criminal.

August 10, 1781, I saw two criminals, a man and a woman, suffer the punishment of the *knoot*. They were conducted from

prison by about fifteen hussars and ten soldiers. When they arrived at the place of punishment, the hussars formed themselves
into a ring round the whipping-post, the drum beat a minute or
two, and then some prayers were read, the populace taking off
their hats. The woman was taken first, and after being roughly
stript to the waist, her hands and feet were bound with cords to a
post made for the purpose, a man standing before the post, and
holding the cords to keep them tight. A servant attended the
executioner, and both were stout men. The servant first marked
his ground and struck the woman five times on the back. Every
stroke seemed to penetrate deep into her flesh. But his master
thinking him too gentle, pushed him aside, took his place, and
gave all the remaining strokes himself, which were evidently
more severe. The woman received twenty-five, and the man sixty:
I pressed through the hussars, and counted the number as they
were chalked on a board; and both seemed but just alive, especially the man, who yet had strength enough to receive a small
donation with some signs of gratitude. They were conducted back
to prison in a little waggon. I saw the woman in a very weak
condition some days after, but could not find the man any more.

70. *Judicial Torture and Public Execution*

ONE OF the great horrors of criminal-law procedure was judicial torture, euphemistically called the "interrogation" in France. How normal this procedure seemed can be gathered from an article in a ruling
of the Imperial Diet of 1731 which states:

> It is an abuse not to accept artisans [into a guild] who have been
> imprisoned and examined because of a suspected crime but proven
> innocent *by the test of torture or other legal means* and exoner-
> ated by the authorities.[1]

Equally gruesome were the public executions. Restif de la Bretonne
describes both the results of torture and a public execution. Perhaps
the greatest horror was the reaction of the spectators who watched
criminals broken on the wheel as if they were actors in a comic opera.

[1] Our italics. See Document 35.

Source: Restif de la Bretonne, *Les Nuits de Paris or Nocturnal Spectator: A Selection*, trans. L. Asher and E. Fertig, pp. 7–8, 189–191.*

The Broken Man

I WENT home by way of rue Saint-Antoine and the Place de Grève. Three murderers had been broken on the wheel there, the day before. I had not expected to see any such spectacle, one that I had never dared to witness. But as I crossed the square I caught sight of a poor wretch, pale, half dead, wracked by the pains of the interrogation inflicted on him twenty hours earlier; he was stumbling down from the Hôtel de Ville supported by the executioner and the confessor. These two men, so completely different, inspired an inexpressible emotion in me! I watched the latter embrace a miserable man consumed by fever, filthy as the dungeons he came from, swarming with vermin! And I said to myself, "O Religion, here is your greatest glory! . . ." I saw the other as the wrathful arm of the law. . . . But I wondered: "Have men the right to impose death . . . even on the murderer who has himself treacherously taken life?" I seemed to hear Nature reply with a woeful no! . . . "But robbery?" "No, no!" cried Nature. "The savage rich have never felt they devised enough harsh safeguards; instead of being friends and brothers, as their religion commands, they prefer the gallows. . . ." This was what Nature said to me. . . .

I saw a horrible sight, even though the torture had been mitigated. . . . The wretch had revealed his accomplices. He was garroted before he was put to the wheel. A winch set under the scaffold tightened a noose around the victim's neck and he was strangled; for a long while the confessor and the hangman felt his heart to see whether the artery still pulsed, and the hideous blows were dealt only after it beat no longer. . . . I left, with my hair standing on end in horror. . . .

Execution by Torchlight

The crier had announced a death sentence during the day. "It would be a horrible thing, this proclamation of death sentences,

* Reprinted by permission of Alfred A. Knopf, Inc. (Originally published in French in 1788.)

except for the necessity of an example! But considering that necessity it is not horrible enough. When there is an execution the
whole city should be set shuddering; bells should toll the culprit's
appearance, and that dreadful moment when he meets his fate.
They talk of the unceremonious way executions are carried out in
England—that is a greater horror still. And we find that the number of convicts executed there, not to speak of the two-thirds more
whom the king reprieves, is three-quarters greater than the count
of executions in France! But it is no less true that our vile scandal-
mongers, with their savage joy and the comments they allow themselves, are in conflict with humanity, with reason, with religion,
with the value of the execution of death sentences. . . . Look at
those wretches, listen to them (this is clearly Du Hameauneuf
speaking), and you will be outraged by their dissipation, their ma-
liciousness, their barbarous jubilation!"

We were proceeding toward the Place de Grève. It was late,
and we thought the execution over. But the gaping mob proclaimed the contrary.

"Let us go on," Du Hameauneuf continued, "since the opportunity offers itself; let us observe the great hideousness of crime and
the great severity of civil law on the one hand, and the great
beauty of religion on the other! When a culprit rides by in the
fatal tumbrel, I see only the consoling minister as he strives to
restore to Nature the monster who has violated her."

As he spoke, I caught sight of some movement on the steps of
the Hôtel de Ville. It was the first of the three convicts going to
meet his end! . . . When the penalty is too great for the crime it is
an atrocity and the effect is lost; it inspires not dread, but outrage.

The man was broken on the wheel, as were his two companions. I could not endure the sight of that execution; I moved
away; but Du Hameauneuf watched it all stoically. I turned to
look at something else. While the victims suffered, I studied the
spectators. They chattered and laughed as if they were watching
a farce. But what revolted me most was a very pretty girl I saw
with her sweetheart. She uttered peals of laughter, she jested
about the victims' expressions and screams. I could not believe it!
I looked at her five or six times. Finally, without thinking of the
consequences, I said to her "Mademoiselle, you must have the
heart of a monster, and to judge by what I see of you today, I
believe you capable of any crime. If I had the misfortune to be
your sweetheart, I would shun you forever."

As she was no fishwife, she stood mute! I expected some unpleasant retort from her lover—he said not a word. . . . Then, a few steps away, I saw another young girl, drenched in tears. She came to me, leaned upon my arm, hiding her face, and she said, "This is a good man, who feels pity for those in anguish!"

Who was that compassionate girl? . . . A poor thing who had abandoned herself to the procurers on the Quai de la Ferraille! I looked at her; she was tall and attractive. I led her to the Marquise's shelter without waiting for Du Hameauneuf.

Then I went to her house; she was in, and I reported what I had done. Then my friend appeared. He was overwhelmed with respect and feeling for the priest, the confessor of the guilty men.

71. John Wilkes and Freedom of the Press

AT THE beginning of George III's reign a new debate arose over freedom of the press. Among many published criticisms of the policies of the new king and his minister was a sharp attack on the king's speech of 1763 by John Wilkes in the April issue of his journal, *The North Briton*. Already under heavy fire, the ministry retaliated with a whole series of arrests bearing the charge of "seditious libel."

The Wilkes case brought to light two vital issues affecting freedom of expression. First, did the government have the right to issue general warrants of arrest on the signature of a secretary of state, a procedure not essentially different from that used in France for *lettres de cachet?* Here, the resolution came quickly. In 1766, the House of Commons condemned all future use of general warrants.

The second issue was more complex. At the Wilkes trial, Lord Mansfield defined liberty of the press as freedom from prior restraint, subject to penalties of common law for abuse of that liberty, adding that the "truth" was no defense but actually aggravated the libel. Subsequently, the libertarians of the eighteenth century demanded that 1) the determination of seditious libel be made by citizen jurors and not by royally appointed judges, and 2) the truth should constitute an adequate defense. Before 1800 it did not occur even to the most radical English constitutional reformers, with the possible exception of Jeremy Bentham, that the whole concept of "seditious libel" might be overthrown.[1]

[1] See Leonard Levy, *The Legacy of Suppression: Freedom of Speech and Press in Early American History* (Cambridge, Mass., 1960), pp. 144–149 and *passim.*

Issue No. 45 of *The North Briton* is, therefore, more than an example of a new kind of political journalism; it marks an important milestone in a basic controversy over legal limits to freedom of expression.

Source: *The North Briton. By John Wilkes, Esq., C. Church and others. Illustrated with Useful and Explanatory Notes, and a Collection of all the Proceedings in the House of Commons and Court of Westminster against Mr. Wilkes* . . . (London, 1772), vol. II, pp. 247ff.

Numb. XLV. Saturday, April 23, 1763

The following Advertisement appeared in all the Papers on the 13th of April

THE NORTH Briton makes his appeal to the good sense, and to the candour of the English nation. In the present unsettled and fluctuating state of the *administration,* he is really fearful of falling into involuntary errors, and he does not wish to mislead. All his reasonings have been built on the strong foundation of *facts,* and he is not yet informed of the whole interior state of government with such *minute precision,* as now to venture the submitting his crude ideas of the present political crisis to the discerning and impartial public. The Scottish minister has indeed *retired.*[1] Is His influence at an end? Or does He still govern by the *three* wretched tools of his power,[2] who, to their indelible infamy, have supported the most odious of his measures, the late ignominious *Peace,* and the wicked extension of the arbitrary mode of *Excise?* The North Briton has been steady in his opposition to a *single,* insolent, incapable, despotic minister; and is equally ready, in the service of his country, to combat the *triple-headed, Cereberean* administration, if the Scot is to assume that motley form. By Him every arrangement *to this hour* has been made, and the notification has been as regularly sent by letter under His Hand. *It therefore* seems clear to a demonstration, that He intends only to retire into that situation, which He held before He first took the seals; I mean the dictating to every part of the king's administration. The North Briton desires to be understood, as having pledged himself

[1] The Earl of Bute, prime minister and favorite of George III.
[2] The Earls of Egremont and Halifax, and G. Grenville, Esq. (note in document).

a firm and intrepid assertor of the rights of his fellow-subjects, and of the liberties of Whigs and Englishmen.

Genus orationis *atrox, & vehemens, cui opponitur, lenitatis & mansuetudinis.* CICERO

"The *King's Speech* has always been considered by the legislature, and by the public at large, as the *Speech of the Minister.* It has regularly, at the beginning of every session of parliament, been referred by both houses to the consideration of a committee, and has been generally canvassed with the utmost freedom, when the minister of the crown has been obnoxious to the nation. The ministers of this free country, conscious of the undoubted privileges of so spirited a people, and with the terrors of parliament before their eyes, have ever been cautious, no less with regard to the matter, than to the expressions of *speeches,* which they have advised the sovereign to make from the throne, at the *opening* of each session. They well knew that an honest house of parliament, true to their trust, could not fail to detect the fallacious arts, or to remonstrate against the daring acts of violence committed by any minister. The speech at the *close* of the session has ever been considered as the most secure method of promulgating the favourite court-creed among the vulgar; because the parliament, which is the constitutional guardian of the liberties of the people, has in this case no opportunity of remonstrating, or of impeaching any wicked servant of the crown.

"This week has given the public the most abandoned instance of ministerial effrontery ever attempted to be imposed on mankind. The *minister's speech* of last Tuesday is not to be paralleled in the annals of this country. I am in doubt, whether the imposition is greater on the sovereign or on the nation. Every friend of his country must lament that a prince of so many great and amiable qualities, whom England truly reveres, can be brought to give the sanction of his sacred name to the most odious measures, and to the most unjustifiable public declarations, from a throne ever renowned for truth, honour, and unsullied virtue." I am sure all foreigners, especially the king of Prussia, will hold the minister in contempt and abhorrence. He has made our sovereign declare, *My expectations have been fully answered by the happy effects which the several allies of my crown have derived from this salutary measure* of the definitive Treaty. *The powers at war with*

*my good brother, the king of Prussia, have been induced to agree
to such terms of accommodation, as that great prince has approved;
and the success which has attended my negotiation, has necessarily
and immediately diffused the blessings of peace through every
part of Europe.* The infamous fallacy of this whole sentence is apparent to all mankind: for it is known that the king of Prussia did
not barely *approve,* but absolutely *dictated,* as conqueror, every
article of the terms of peace.[3] No advantage of any kind has ac-
crued to that magnanimous prince from *our negotiation,* but he
was basely deserted by the *Scottish* prime minister of *England.*
He was known by every court in Europe to be scarcely on better
terms of friendship *here,* than at *Vienna:* and he was betrayed by
us in the *treaty of peace.* What a strain of insolence, therefore, is
it in a minister to lay claim to what he is conscious all his efforts
tended to prevent, and meanly to arrogate to himself a share in
the fame and glory of one of the greatest princes the world has
ever seen. The king of *Prussia,* however, has gloriously kept *all* his
former *conquests,* and stipulated security for his allies, even for the
elector of Hanover. I know in what light this great prince is considered in Europe, and in what manner he has been treated here;
among other reasons, perhaps, for some contemptuous expressions
he may have used of the *Scot:* expressions which are every day
ecchoed by the whole body of *Englishmen* through the southern
part of this island.

The *Preliminary Articles of Peace* were such as have drawn the
contempt of mankind on our wretched negotiators. All our most
valuable conquests were agreed to be restored, and the *East-India
company* would have been infallibly ruined by a single article of
this fallacious and baneful negotiation. No hireling of the minister has been hardy enough to dispute this; yet the minister himself has made our sovereign declare, *the satisfaction which he felt at
the approaching re-establishment of peace upon conditions so
honourable to his crown, and so beneficial to his people.* As to the
entire approbation of parliament, which is so vainly boasted of,
the world knows how that was obtained. The large debt on the
Civil List, already above half a year in arrear, shews pretty clear
the transactions of the winter. It is, however, remarkable, that the
minister's speech dwells on the *entire approbation* given by parliament to the *Preliminary Articles,* which I will venture to say,

[3] The Peace of Paris, 1763, ending the Seven Years' War.

he must by this time be ashamed of; for he has been brought to confess the total want of that knowledge, accuracy and precision, by which such immense advantages, both of trade and territory, were sacrificed to our inveterate enemies. These gross blunders, are, indeed, in some measure set right by the *Definitive Treaty;* yet the most important articles, relative to *cession, commerce,* and the Fishery, remain as they were, with respect to the *French.* The proud and feeble *Spaniard* too does not Renounce, but only Desists *from all pretensions, which he may have formed, to the right of fishing*—where? Only *about the island of* Newfoundland—till a favourable opportunity arises of *insisting* on it, *there, as well as elsewhere.* . . .

"In vain will such a minister, or the foul dregs of his power, the tools of corruption and despotism, preach up in *the speech that spirit of concord, and that obedience to the laws, which is essential to good order.* They have sent the *spirit of discord* through the land, and I will prophecy that it will never be extinguished but by the extinction of their power. Is the *spirit of concord* to go hand in hand with the Peace and Excise, through this nation? Is it to be expected between an insolent Exciseman, and *a peer, gentleman, freeholder, or farmer,* whose private houses are now made liable to be entered and searched at pleasure? *Gloucestershire, Herefordshire,* and in general all the *cyder* counties, are not surely the *several counties* which are alluded to in the *speech.* The *spirit of concord* hath not gone forth among them, but the *spirit of liberty* has, and a noble opposition has been given to the wicked instruments of oppression. A nation as sensible as the *English,* will see that a *spirit of concord* when they are oppressed, means a tame submission to injury, and that a *spirit of liberty* ought then to arise, and I am sure ever will, in proportion to the weight of the grievance they feel. *Every legal attempt of a contrary tendency* to the *spirit of concord* will be deemed a justifiable resistance, warranted by the *spirit of the English constitution.* . . .

The *Stuart* line has ever been intoxicated with the slavish doctrines of the *absolute, independent, unlimited* power of the crown. Some of that line were so weakly advised, as to endeavour to reduce them into practice: but the *English* nation was too spirited to suffer the least encroachment on the antient liberties of this kingdom. "The *King of England* is only the first magistrate of this country; but is invested by the law with the whole executive power. He is, however, responsible to his people for the due execution of the royal functions, in the choice of ministers, &c. equal with the meanest of his subjects in his particular duty." The personal character of our present amiable sovereign makes us easy and happy that so great a power is lodged in such hands; but the *Favourite* has given too just cause for him to escape the general odium. The *Prerogative* of the crown is to exert the constitutional powers entrusted to it in a way not of blind favour or partiality, but of wisdom and judgment. This is the spirit of our constitution. The people too have their *prerogative*, and I hope the fine words of Dryden will be engraven on our hearts:

Freedom *is the English Subject's* Prerogative.

72. The French Press Before 1789

THE *Gazette de Paris*, the *Mercure*, and the *Journal de Paris* formed almost the entire French press before the Revolution. Restif de la Bretonne comments below on the first French daily, the *Journal de Paris*, published after 1777. It was four pages in length, one of which was half covered with the title, and cost 24 livres for an annual subscription—well beyond the reach of an artisan with 400 livres income. "Political opposition," writes Eugène Hatin, "existed in books, in the *Encyclopedia*, in the discourses of Rousseau, and the tragedies of Voltaire; it was everywhere, except in the newspapers." [1]

Source: Restif de la Bretonne, *Les Nuits de Paris or Nocturnal Spectator: A Selection*, trans. L. Asher and E. Fertig, pp. 209–211.[*]

The Journal de Paris

IN THE evenings at the Marquise's we usually read the newspapers. These are the ones to which she subscribed: The *Mercure*, the *Journal de Paris*, the *Petites affiches*, the *Affiches de*

---

[1] Eugène Hatin, *Histoire du journal en France, 1631–1853* (Paris, 1853), pp. 48–49.
[*] Reprinted by permission of Alfred A. Knopf, Inc. (Originally published in French in 1788.)

province, the *Journal de physique*, the *Année littéraire*, the *Lunes du Cousin Jacques*, the *Ami des enfants*, the *Feuille de Normandie*, and the *Affiches de Guyenne*. Tonight I will only discuss the *Journal de Paris*. Du Hameauneuf told us of its origin in these words:

"In 1775 or 1776, a M. du Rosoi, author of *Henry IV*, a lyric drama which had forty performances at the old Théâtre des Italiens, published a *Gazetin de Paris* which had no success at all. There you have the father of the *Journal de Paris*. It's like seeing a good peasant whose son has become Minister of State. The progeny was born in 1777, several months after the death of its father. As for its mother, she is still around and in good health; she is my neighbor and seems to be doing well; she is the head of a littérateur who frequently visited the printer of the poor *Gazetin*. The grandfather of the paper is English, though I don't know his name, for it is claimed that several London papers gave M. du Rosoi the idea for his *Gazetin*. The origin, then, is foreign, and the birth is not noble—which doesn't prevent hizzonor-monsieur le *Journal de Paris* from being a great nobleman." We laughed a bit at the Marquise's over this storytelling manner which was peculiar to Du Hameauneuf.

"The *Journal de Paris*," he resumed apropros of an article which he had just read, "is very useful and could be even more so if it had an industrious contributor who would turn up worthwhile news, but as it is now, it contents itself with whatever comes its way. Certainly the task is easier this way and brings in no less, for even as it is, it arouses a daily curiosity; but it should be possible for diligence never to run idle. The government might draw an inconceivable advantage from this paper by arranging it better than it does. I would like to see a column on the second or third page regularly devoted to short reports on debates within the government; I would like the book announcements to be purely expository, with these words: 'In three months we will give the public's reaction to this work.' This should be done without fail, for it is easily enough accomplished. I would like the article on entertainment to occupy only the last page, and its useless filler cut back on the occasion of a new play; care should be taken not to print the endless number of insignificant letters which stuffs the paper when there are so many important things to be said! The *Journal de Paris* should report all the public events of the previous day: such-and-such a case tried—civil as well as criminal—without an analysis; such-and-such a meeting, at the lecture hall or the clubs, or even the Freemasons; every accident, without exception—it is easy enough to learn of them, and the *Journal* brings in enough to go to that expense.

"What use is the half-page devoted to title? '*Journal de Paris*' in small type and the meteorological observations reduced to the smallest possible space—all that need take but an inch. I would like to see this important paper keep a tight rein on lawyers, solicitors, notaries, bailiffs, professors, merchants—even more exalted personages—by reporting their misdeeds without mentioning their names, up to the third offense when it would be required to do so."

73. *The Paris Police and the Clandestine Press*

THE NINETEEN volumes of *Archives de la Bastille* published by François Ravaisson between 1866 and 1904 contain a small fraction of the thousands of dossiers deposited in the Paris state prison between 1659 and 1769. Every prisoner who passed through the Bastille had a dossier. Such a dossier might include the minutes of interrogations, statements by witnesses, letters from informers (anonymous and otherwise), the decisions of a police commissioner regarding the release of a prisoner, petitions, and other matters.

One item, dated November 3, 1766, relates to a Swiss dealer in clandestine literature named Rodolphe Etter. From this we learn that he had spent over two years in the Bastille (1759–1761), probably as a result of the events described by the Countess de Chastenay in Document 73. In 1766 he was again arrested for peddling clandestine manuscripts. Between January and November, 1766, Etter had commissioned forty manuscripts to a copyist at 3 livres per copy. He had then sold these manuscripts for an average of 10 livres, making a profit of about 280 livres. If nothing else, these figures show that there was a certain interest in this kind of literature.

Paris was full of men like Etter. They dealt not only in individual manuscripts and brochures but also in clandestine newspapers. Since the official newspaper, the *Gazette de France*, was heavily censored, the clandestine newspapers were very popular. Publications such as the *Gazette de Hollande*, the *Courrier du Bas-Rhin* (printed in Utrecht), the *Gazette de Cologne,* the *Courrier de l'Europe* (printed in London), and about a dozen others were regularly smuggled into France and sold for between 30 and 40 livres per year.[1] The *Archives de la Bastille* is full of reports concerning the seizure of such materials and the imprisonment of individuals like Etter.

Another group, clandestine reporters, the so-called *gazetins,* worked for the police. They went everywhere: to winehouses, to fashionable salons, to the theater, to the stock exchange, to fires, accidents, and public gatherings of all kinds, and they reported all the events, rumors, and the mood of the people to the police. During the years 1742 to 1747, the lieutenant general of the Parisian police made a daily digest of these reports and sent them to the minister.[2] These letters have been published and show clearly that no detail was too small to escape the interest of the police authorities.[3] It should be added that the Paris police also employed three thousand spies and informers.[4]

Apologists for the Old Régime in France have often pointed to the freedom of the pen enjoyed by the more prominent *philosophes.* It is well to remember that countless lesser journalists and pamphleteers soon discovered the limits to such freedom.

Source: François Ravaisson, ed., *Archives de la Bastille* (Paris, 1866–1904), vol. XVII, pp. 299–301.

Countess Belfont de Chastenay to Bertin,[5] June 21, 1759

PLEASE FORGIVE me for troubling you again, but I feel that under the circumstances I must, and I also feel that I would rather tell you my fears than to be haunted by them. Unless I am mistaken, I have everything to hope from your indulgence. Here, then, is what happened.

Yesterday, at about two o'clock in the afternoon when I was at the table with my husband and one of our friends and relatives, my chambermaid brought me a manuscript entitled: *State of the Affairs of the Kingdom, of the Revenues of the King, of his*

---

[1] Eugène Hatin: *Les gazettes de Hollande et la presse clandestine aux XVIIme et XVIIIme siècles* (Paris, 1865).

[2] Comte de Maurepas, who at that time was *sécrétaire de la maison du roi.*

[3] A. de Boislisle, ed., *Lettres de M. de Marville, lieutenant de police au ministre Maurepas (1742–1748)* (Paris, 1896, 3 vols.). Some undigested reports of the *gazetins* were also published in the *Révue rétrospective* between 1834 and 1897.

[4] Boislisle, *Lettres de Marville,* vol. I, p. x. The police had a regular budget of 1 million livres per year for these spies.

[5] *Lieutenant de police* of Paris in 1757, controller-general in 1759.

Personal Expenditures, plus Remarks about the Government, etc, or some such title. The maid told me that the individual who wanted to sell it was no doubt a foreigner, because she could not understand his speech very well.

I told her to let him enter. He was wearing a redingote and I asked him from which country he came. "Alsace," he replied. I spoke German to him, but his accent was anything but Alsatian. I told him that I was surprised to find such a manuscript in his hands and asked him if he sold many of them. He said that he was afraid to take risks except with foreigners. I asked him: "Have you written this?" and he replied: "Yes, Madam." "But," I said, "if you cannot speak French, how can you write it so well?" He answered only with a movement of his head. I asked him how much he wanted for this manuscript. "Nine livres," he answered, "but Madam can give me as much as she likes; I would give it to her if I dared; it is for the sake of the country and in the hope of obtaining the honor of her protection." I told him that right now I could not tell if his work was authentic, that he could come back Thursday at three o'clock at the latest, that I should look the manuscript over, and that, since he wrote so well, I would put him to work on some German papers. He promised to come back tomorrow. I did this in order to have time to communicate my observations to you. They are the following:

It seems to me that a foreigner who is nothing less than an Alsatian cannot possibly possess the secrets of the state, its finances, its resources, and the rest. Moreover, the man might be sent by some enemy who knows that we are related to the house of Brandenburg, since the great-aunt of the king of Prussia married a Chastenay. All in all, it seems to me that this manuscript is suspect, and I did not want to buy it. If it is of interest to you, you may so inform me, and if someone is insidiously trying to ruin me, you are herewith notified. I am a naturalized French citizen, and I shall always make it my duty to report faithfully anything that might be directed against my sovereign. This manuscript peddler is coming tomorrow between two and three o'clock; if it is important to you to find out more, please let me know your intentions by one of your men, or by a note, otherwise I shall dismiss the man and the manuscript.

Marginal Note from Bertin to d'Hemery [1]

This is the same manuscript as that of M. de Nantouillet. If we have this kind of newsmonger followed for a few days, we should find out where the depot is and who is the author of this non-sense. Comtesse de Chastenay has been informed that I will send someone tomorrow before two o'clock so that he can speak to her before that man arrives. She is firmly convinced that people who have a personal grudge against her have sent him to set a trap for her. I am just as convinced that it is nothing so extraordinary; but if we follow the traces of that character, we might be able to find out. Moreover, he has told Madame de Chastenay that he would inform her of even more secret things to which he has access.

74. *The Legal Disabilities of the Jews*

IN 1750, there were about 3 million Jews in a population of about 150 million Europeans. Half of these lived in Poland and most of the rest in other parts of eastern Europe. Those in central Europe were concentrated in large towns, such as Vienna, Berlin, Frankfurt-am-Main, and Leipzig. Smaller Jewish colonies settled in Holland, England, Italy, and France, especially in Alsace.[2]

In all of these countries, the age-old legal disabilities remained in full vigor. The Jews lived in crowded ghettos, excluded from the guilds, professions, landownership, and large-scale enterprise. Only a minority achieved wealth and position, including the so-called court Jews and a few international bankers.[3] Most Jews eked out meager livings as peddlers, horse dealers, or petty moneylenders, lowly occupations compounding popular distrust and contempt. "Ghetto life," writes a modern authority on Jewish history, "produced the bedraggled, unkempt

---

[1] Inspector in charge of the Luxembourg quarter, where Madame de Chastenay lived.

[2] See Abraham Leon Sachar, *A History of the Jews* (New York, 1937), p. 249.

[3] Cf. Lion Feuchtwanger's *Power*, a fascinating historical novel about Josef Süss Oppenheimer, who rose to unprecedented heights in the service of the Duke of Württemberg and died an ignominious death after his fall from power.

type, hunted in appearance and obsequious in demeanor, the type by which the world judged the Jew and his Judaism. Europe made the Jew into a caricature and then scorned him for playing the part." [1]

These legal disabilities remained unchanged until the French Revolution and were not finally eradicated until after 1848 in central Europe. Joseph II of Austria was the only ruler to take major steps toward ending them, and all his work was undone when he died. A bill attempting to make the English Jews full citizens in 1753 met with such fierce opposition that it was withdrawn a year later. Frederick II and Voltaire were outspoken anti-Semites. Lessing, the German dramatist, shocked the literary circles of Berlin by his friendship with Moses Mendelssohn, a brilliant Jewish philosopher. Lessing's drama *Nathan the Wise* was one of the first efforts to teach Gentiles what Jews were like. Their complete segregation had made the Jews seem "foreign" and even sinister.

The restrictions on the Jews were enforced. The following Ordinance of 1682 "policed" the Jews in Leipzig during the annual fair. In 1710, when Marperger wrote his treatise on fairs, this ordinance was his guide.

Source: Paul Jakob Marperger, *Beschreibung der Messen und Jahrmärckte,* Appendix to Chapter XII, p. 231ff.

Ordinance Concerning the Jews of the City of Leipzig, de anno *1682*

WE, BY the grace of God, Johann Georg III, Duke of Saxony, Jülich, Cleve, and Berg, Marshal and Elector of the Holy Roman Empire . . . having heard the report of a commission charged with studying certain shortcomings in the commerce of our good city of Leipzig, and this commission having also submitted an ordinance concerning the Jews, who were found to be useful to commerce and the community, do therefore confirm the said ordinance, which reads word for word as follows:

1. No Jew shall be permitted to trade in this place unless he bring a certificate from his authorities stating that he is an honest tradesman; at least he shall be required to produce a sufficient and authoritative statement to that effect.
2. None shall lodge in the faubourgs (except the Jews dealing in horses, whereof more below), under penalty of 20 reichsthaler.

[1] Sachar, *op cit.,* p. 254.

3. An arriving Jew, whoever he may be, and without exception, shall be given a registration form at the gate through which he enters and shall inscribe his name, and any other name by which he may be known, as well as his place of residence and the hour of his arrival under penalty of 20 reichsthaler.

4. This form he shall be required to take to the customhouse within twenty-four hours, or, if it should be closed, as on a Sunday or holiday, he shall take it to the appointed custom officials, stating at the same time whence he has come, what his business is, whether he has come to buy or to sell, whether he has any associate and who this associate is, where he intends to take lodgings, etc. All of this shall be written down on his certificate of entry in view of his future expedition, under penalty of 20 reichsthaler.

5. Within the same delay he shall also report to the municipal court in order to pay his *Schutzgeld* (Jew tax) under a special penalty of 20 reichsthaler; all this in accordance with the edict concerning the Jews which was published *anno* 1675 on the occasion of the New Year's fair and has been in observance ever since.

6. The certificate of entry, the receipts about the payment of the *Mauth* or *Schutzgeld*, as well as the yellow badge must be carried by every Jew at all times, and he shall be under obligation to present them upon request; and at any time to any apparitor or constable or else be liable to paying the said apparitor or constable 1 reichsthaler. Should he fail to obtain a certificate of entry within twenty-four hours or to present himself at the customhouse, he shall be liable to a penalty of 40 reichsthaler.

7. No Jew shall pack his wares with that of another, unless he has declared his associate upon his registration form or gate paper, under penalty of 30 reichsthaler.

8. The Jews shall declare their wares properly at their arrival and departure and pay the weighing fee, under penalty of their confiscation.

9. None shall buy his wares here in such a way that they are delivered to him free of charge outside the city gates; neither shall he have any taken out by a Christian, be he a local man

or a stranger. And even though a Christian who has participated in such a fraud will be punished by a high penalty in
money if he is found out, he shall not only be freed of his
penalty if he reports the fraud to the customhouse afterward
but shall also be given 10 per cent by the Jew. Likewise, if the
servant or boy of the Christian discovers such knavery without
his master's knowledge, the servant or boy shall also be entitled to 10 per cent from the Jew. In the same manner, a Jew
who discovers such a misdemeanor of another Jew to the
customhouse shall enjoy this reward and be exempt from the
penalty he may have incurred.

10. All Jews shall eschew the buying of stolen or suspicious goods
    and any dealings with the helpers, wives, children, or servants
    of shopkeepers and hucksters, the penalties to be fixed.

11. Jewish women shall conform to all the above regulations, as
    shall Jewish servants, under the penalties stipulated for each
    of them.

12. Since the Jewish women as well as Jewish servants usually pay
    only half of the *Mauth* [Jew tax], it shall remain so as to the
    women; but no Jew shall be permitted to keep a manservant
    unless he can produce a sworn statement showing that the
    said man is in his service and his keep and that the said man
    is not engaged in trade, either for himself or for another. None
    shall be considered a boy if he is over thirteen years old, and
    all must be presented at the customhouse.

13. No Jew who is unable to produce a certificate from his au-
    thorities or prove in some other way that he is a dealer who
    does considerable business here, or at least buying and selling
    amounting to 600 reichsthaler, which he is able to pay, shall
    be tolerated here; or at least, he shall not be permitted to return
    after he has been here once, under penalty of imprisonment
    at his own expense and until he leaves town.

14. None of the Jewish brokers shall be admitted here unless he
    has been chosen by the principal Jews, but even then there
    shall only be two or three, or at most four of them, according
    to the circumstances. Each one will have to pay 3 or 4, or at
    least 2 reichsthaler at the customhouse and, besides, pay a per-
    centage of his profits if he establishes any brokerage business.
    Those who are excluded shall not engage in any brokerage;

otherwise they shall pay at least as much as if they had done 600 reichsthaler worth of business.

15. The jewelers shall appear at the customhouse in order to declare their anticipated revenue; but this assessment should be made as if the said revenue amounted to 800 reichsthaler. Those who have already made their declaration shall be so assessed until their contract expires, but must pay taxes on the full amount.

16. Jews who are dealing in feathers do not declare more than the value of their feathers, but the authorities must see to it 1) that they have proper stores here, 2) that they bring considerable quantities and/or sell 600 reichsthaler worth of wares here, and 3) that they do not bring feathers from infected localities.

17. Those who want to sell used clothing shall not be admitted here, neither those who want to deal in suspicious furnishings.

18. The horse dealers may remain outside of the town, but they shall also report to the customhouse within twenty-four hours and duly state their intentions and everything else. None of them shall have more than one Jewish manservant, the others must be Christians. If such horse dealers intend to do any other business here, they shall also pay the appropriate fees and likewise always carry their identifications and badges; all this under the penalties stated for these infractions.

19. Since it frequently happens that various Jews produce passes from local and other gentlemen, especially from Bohemian gentlemen, stating that they have come on behalf of these gentlemen and asking therefore to be exempt, it must be stated that no Jew shall be exempted because of a pass, but shall be made, like any other Jew, to register in due form and to pay his fees, also to comply with the regulations concerning the Jews in all particulars, under the penalties stated.

20. Those who arrive claiming that they do not intend to trade here but are only passing through on their way to another town where they intend to visit their friends, shall be requested to prove this or else to pay the fee for a trading permit. If, after due investigation, they have been passed free for this time, they shall not be permitted to use the same pretext again, or else they will be liable to a certain penalty over and above the trading fee.

21. Jewish musicians shall not engage in any other business here; however, they shall have to pay 1 ducat per person.

22. Before their departure, the Jews shall report to the custom-house with their certificate of entry and the receipt for their *Mauth*. If they have not yet done 600 reichsthaler worth of business, they shall account for the rest. Likewise, other Jews, such as jewelers, feather dealers, brokers, court financiers, and buyers shall do the same, and thereupon receive their certificates of release. But those who do not comply with these regulations or depart without their certificates of release shall, if they ever return, either not be tolerated at all or else be fined 50 reichsthaler per person, without exception.

23. All of the Jews shall conform to the regulations laid down on April 22, 1668, as well as to the above-mentioned ordinance dating from the New Year's fair of 1675 in all the particulars that have not been amended or clarified by the present ordinance, nor shall they be permitted henceforth to act against the said ordinances.

We herewith confirm, by virtue of our sovereign power and authority, the foregoing ordinance concerning the Jews through the present letter-patent, wishing to see it enforced in all its particulars, without any infractions whatsoever, as long as it is not prejudicial to us, our heirs and descendants, as well as to our high privileges, the authorities of our country, and our justice. We therefore reserve to us and our heirs and descendants the right to alter, supplement, amend, or nullify it, if we see fit to do so in good faith and of our own free will.

In witness thereof we have signed this letter by our own hand, and caused our greater seal to be affixed to it.

Done and given at Dresden, October the second, 1682

JOHANN GEORG, ELECTOR

75. *Abolition of Serfdom in Russia*

BORN a member of the Russian gentry, Aleksandr Radishchev had been sent to study at the University of Leipzig by the czarist government. Upon his return in 1771, he entered a career in the government service.

Two years later, the Pugachev Revolt swept the Volga Valley, burning manor houses and killing gentry until it was finally suppressed by the Russian army. This dramatic event turned Radishchev's attention to the plight of the Russian peasantry. In 1790, he published *Journey from St. Petersburg to Moscow*, in which he thoroughly examines the evils of serfdom and advocates gradual abolition. The book, a selection of which is printed below as Document 75, earned Radishchev the death sentence for "sedition" from Catherine II, subsequently commuted to ten years in Siberia. Released in 1801, Radishchev became a member of Alexander I's reformist commission, but it was soon apparent that the new czar would not abolish serfdom, even by gradual stages. In fact, serfdom would remain a distinctive institution in Russia and the Hapsburg Empire for another half century.

Source: Aleksandr Nikolaevitch Radishchev, *A Journey from St. Petersburg to Moscow*, trans. Leo Wiener, ed. Roderick Page Thaler, pp. 151–156.*

. . . But, to return to our more immediate concern with the condition of the agriculturists, we find it most harmful to society. It is harmful because it prevents the increase of products and population, harmful by its example, and dangerous in the unrest it creates. Man, motivated by self-interest, undertakes that which may be to his immediate or later advantage, and avoids that from which he expects no present or future gain. Following this natural instinct, everything we do for our own sake, everything we do without compulsion, we do carefully, industriously, and well. On the other hand, all that we do not do freely, all that we do not do for our own advantage, we do carelessly, lazily, and all awry. Thus we find the agriculturists in our country. The field is not their own, the fruit thereof does not belong to them. Hence they cultivate the land lazily and do not care whether it goes to waste because of their poor work. Compare this field with the one the haughty proprietor gives the worker for his own meager sustenance. The worker is unsparing in the labors which he spends on it. Nothing distracts him from his work. The savagery of the weather he overcomes bravely; the hours intended for rest he spends at work; he shuns pleasure even on the days set aside for it. For he looks after his own interest, works for himself, is his own master. Thus his field will give him an abundant harvest; while all the fruits of the work done on the proprietor's demesne

* Reprinted by permission of the Harvard University Press.

will die or bear no future harvest; whereas they would grow and be ample for the sustenance of the citizens if the cultivation of the fields were done with loving care, if it were free.

But if forced labor brings smaller harvests, crops which fail to reach the goal of adequate production also stop the increase of the population. Where there is nothing to eat, there will soon be no eaters, for all will die from exhaustion. Thus the enslaved field, by giving an insufficient return, starves to death the citizens for whom nature had intended her superabundance. But this is not the only thing in slavery that interferes with abundant life. To insufficiency of food and clothing they have added work to the point of exhaustion. Add to this the spurns of arrogance and the abuse of power, even over man's tenderest sentiments, and you see with horror the pernicious effects of slavery, which differs from victory and conquest only by not allowing what victory cuts down to be born anew. But it causes even greater harm. It is easy to see that the one devastates accidentally and momentarily, the other destroys continuously over a long period of time; the one, when its onrush is over, puts an end to its ravages, the other only begins where the first ends, and cannot change except by upheavals which are always dangerous to its whole internal structure.

But nothing is more harmful than to see forever before one the partners in slavery, master and slave. On the one side there is born conceit, on the other, servile fear. There can be no bond between them other than force. And this, concentrated in a small range, extends its oppressive autocratic power everywhere. But the champions of slavery, who, though they hold the sharp edge of power in their hands, are themselves cast into fetters, become its most fanatical preachers. It appears that the spirit of freedom is so dried up in the slaves that they not only have no desire to end their sufferings, but cannot bear to see others free. They love their fetters, if it is possible for man to love his own ruination. I think I can see in them the serpent that wrought the fall of the first man. The examples of arbitrary power are infectious. We must confess that we ourselves, armed with the mace of courage and the law of nature for the crushing of the hundred-headed monster that gulps down the food prepared for the people's general sustenance—we ourselves, perhaps, have been misled into autocratic acts, and, although our intentions have always been good and have aimed at the general happiness, yet our arbitrary behavior cannot be justified by its usefulness. Therefore we now implore your forgiveness for our unintentional presumption.

Do you not know, dear fellow citizens, what destruction threatens us and in what peril we stand? All the hardened feelings of the slaves, not given vent by a kindly gesture of freedom, strengthen and intensify their inner longings. A stream that is barred in its course becomes more powerful in proportion to the opposition it meets. Once it has burst the dam, nothing can stem its flood. Such are our brothers whom we keep enchained. They are waiting for a favorable chance and time. The alarum bell rings. And the destructive force of bestiality breaks loose with terrifying speed. Round about us we shall see sword and poison. Death and fiery desolation will be the meed for our harshness and inhumanity. And the more procrastinating and stubborn we have been about the loosening of their fetters, the more violent they will be in their vengefulness. Bring back to your memory the events of former times. Recall how deception roused the slaves to destroy their masters. Enticed by a crude pretender, they hastened to follow him, and wished only to free themselves from the yoke of their masters; and in their ignorance they could think of no other means to do this than to kill their masters. They spared neither sex nor age. They sought more the joy of vengeance than the benefit of broken shackles.

This is what awaits us, this is what we must expect. Danger is steadily mounting, peril is already hovering over our heads. Time has already raised its scythe and is only awaiting an opportunity. The first demagogue or humanitarian who rises up to awaken the unfortunates will hasten the scythe's fierce sweep. Beware!

But if the terror of destruction and the danger of the loss of property can move those among you who are weak, shall we not be brave enough to overcome our prejudices, to suppress our selfishness, to free our brothers from the bonds of slavery, and to re-establish the natural equality of all? Knowing the disposition of your hearts, I am sure that you will be convinced more readily by arguments drawn from the human heart than by the calculations of selfish reason, and still less by fears of danger. Go, my dear ones, go to the dwellings of your brothers and proclaim to them the change in their lot. Proclaim with deep feeling: "Moved to pity by your fate, sympathizing with our fellow men, having come to recognize your equality, and convinced that our interests are mutual, we have come to embrace our brothers. We have abandoned the haughty discrimination which for so long a time has separated us from you, we have forgotten the inequality that has existed between us, we rejoice now in our mutual victory, and this day on which the shackles of our fellow citizens are broken shall become the most famous day in our annals. Forget our former injustice to you, and let us sincerely love one another."

Such will be your utterance; deep down in your hearts you already hear it. Do not delay, my dear ones. Time flies; our days go by and we do nothing. Let us not end our lives merely fostering good intentions which we have not been able to carry out. Let not our posterity take advantage of this, win our rightful crown of glory, and say contemptuously of us: "They had their day."

That is what I read in the mud-stained paper which I picked up in front of the post hut as I left my carriage.

Upon entering the hut I asked who were the travelers who had stopped there immediately before me. "The last traveler," the postilion told me, "was a man about fifty years old; according to his traveling permit he was going to Petersburg. He forgot and left a bundle of papers here, and I'm forwarding them to him right now." I asked the postilion to let me look through the papers, and, unfolding them, I discovered that the piece I had found belonged with them. By means of a good tip I persuaded him to let me have the papers. Upon examining them I found that they belonged to a dear friend of mine; hence I did not consider their acquisition a theft. Up to the present, he has never asked me to return them, but has left me free to do with them what I pleased.

While they were changing my horses, I examined with great interest the papers I had acquired. I found a large number of articles in the same vein as the one I had read. Everywhere I recognized the spirit of a charitable man; everywhere I saw a citizen of the future. It was clear above all else that my friend was deeply disturbed by the inequality of the estates. A whole bundle of papers and drafts of laws referred to the abolition of serfdom in Russia. But my friend, realizing that the supreme power was not strong enough to cope with a sudden change of opinions, had outlined a program of temporary legislation leading to a gradual emancipation of the agriculturists in Russia. I will sketch here the main lines of his scheme. The first law provides for the distinction between rural and domestic serfdom. The latter is abolished first of all, and the landlords are forbidden to take into their houses any peasant or anybody registered in the last census as a village dweller. If a landlord takes a peasant into his house as a servant or artisan, he at once becomes free. Peasants are to be allowed to marry without asking their masters' permission. Marriage license fees are prohibited. The second law has to do with the property and protection of the peasants. They shall own individually the plot that they cultivate, for they shall pay the head tax themselves. Property acquired by a peasant shall belong to him, and no one shall arbitrarily deprive him of it. The peasant is to be reinstated as a citizen. He shall be judged by his peers, that is, in courts in which manorial peasants, among others, are to be chosen to serve. The peasant shall be permitted to acquire real estate, that is, to buy land. He may without hindrance obtain his freedom by paying his master a fixed sum to release him. Arbitrary punishment without due process of law is prohibited. "Avaunt, barbarous custom; perish, power of the tigers!" says our legislator. —Thereupon follows the complete abolition of serfdom.

European Currencies, 1760

The principal currencies referred to in this volume are as follows:

English Money
1 pound = 20 shillings
1 shilling = 12 pence

French Money
1 livre = 20 sous
1 sou = 12 deniers
1 *écu* = 3 livres
1 *louis d'or* = 23 livres

Florentine Money
1 *scudo* = 7 *lire*

Imperial Money
1 reichsthaler = 2 gulden
1 gulden = 60 kreutzer
1 groschen = 3 kreutzer
1 Imperial ducat = 4 gulders,
20 kreutzer

The above currencies had the following equivalents in French livres:

1 English pound = 23 livres or 1 *louis d'or*
1 Florentine *scudo* = 5.68 livres
1 Imperial reichsthaler = 3 livres or 1 *écu*
1 Imperial ducat = 6.50 livres

The French livre in 1760 was very roughly equivalent in purchasing power to the American dollar today (1968), if it is understood that the subsistence income was about 500 livres in 1760. Agricultural products were, of course, cheaper than today, while all manufactured items were much more expensive. Consumption habits were consequently quite different. Nevertheless, one can establish a meaningful scale of incomes beginning with the artisan at 500 livres, the country gentleman at 10,000 livres, and ending with the city merchant and grand seigneur with revenues of 50,000 livres and more.

Chronology, 1700 to 1789

1701–1714	War of the Spanish Succession
1703	St. Petersburg founded by Peter the Great
1709	Last nationwide famine in France
1713	Papal bull condemning Jansenist doctrine
1714	Death of Queen Anne; crown of England to House of Windsor: George I (1714–1727)
1715–1774	Louis XV of France
1719	Defoe's *Robinson Crusoe*
1720	South Sea Bubble; collapse of John Law's financial schemes in France
1721	Sweden relinquishes Baltic provinces to Russia by treaty; Montesquieu's *Persian Letters*
1722	Table of ranks issued by Czar Peter the Great
1721–1742	Ministry of Robert Walpole in England
1726–1743	Ministry of Cardinal Fleury in France
1727	Death of Isaac Newton; first indemnity acts in favor of nonconformists in England
1727–1760	George II
1730–1736	Count Zinzendorf's colony of Moravian Brethren at Herrnhut
1732	Voltaire's *Letters Concerning the English Nation*
1733	Kay's "flying shuttle" patented
1735	First use of coke for smelting iron by Darby in England
1738	Wesley organizes first Methodist association
1739	Austro-Turkish war ends; Anglo-Spanish war begins
1740	Frederick II seizes Silesia and precipitates War of the Austrian Succession (1740–1748); Richardson's *Pamela*
1740–1786	Frederick II of Prussia
1745–1790	Leopold I, Grand Duke of Tuscany, an "enlightened despot"

1745–1764   "Reign" of Marquise de Pompadour, mistress of Louis XV
1745–1746   Suppression of the second Jacobite rising in Scotland
1748   Montesquieu's *Spirit of the Laws*; Hume's *Philosophical Essays Concerning Human Understanding*
1749   Diderot's *Letter on the Blind*; Fielding's *Tom Jones*
1750   New *vingtième* tax in France, an effort to tax the privileged; Rousseau's *Discourse on the Arts and Sciences*
1751   Diderot's *Encyclopedia*, vol. I
1754   Condillac's *Traité sur les Sensations*
1756   Prussia allies with England, France with Austria in the "Diplomatic Revolution"; Seven Years' War begins
1757–1761   William Pitt the elder leads the war cabinet in England
1758   Helvétius's *De l'Esprit*
1759   Capture of Quebec by the English; Lisbon earthquake
1760   Rousseau's *Julie, ou la Nouvelle Héloïse*
1760–1820   George III
1761   Capture of Pondichéry by the English
1762   Rousseau's *The Social Contract* and *Émile*
1762–1796   Catherine II of Russia
1763   John Wilkes case begins in England; French lose Canada and India to English by Treaty of Paris; Prussia retains Silesia by Treaty of Hubertsburg
1764   Voltaire's *Philosophical Dictionary*; expulsion of the Jesuits from France
1765   Hargreaves's spinning jenny; James Watt invents steam engine
1768   Captain Cook's first voyage to the South Seas
1769   Russia occupies Rumanian principalities; Arkwright's "water frame" patented
1770   Raynal's exotic book on the "Two Indies"; ministry of Lord North begins in England; the Boston Massacre
1771   Maupeou reforms in France
1772   First partition of Poland
1773–1774   Pugachev's peasant revolt on the Volga

1774   Accession of Louis XVI and return of *parlements;*
            Goethe's *Werther*
1774–1776   Turgot's efforts at fiscal reform in France fail
1776   English colonies in North America declare independ-
            ence; Adam Smith's *Wealth of Nations;* Gibbon's
            Decline and Fall of the Roman Empire, vol. I
1778–1783   France joins American colonies against England
1778–1787   Recession in France
1779   Crompton's mule jenny
1780–1790   Joseph II of Austria, "enlightened despot" who at-
            tacked the privileged classes and freed the serfs
1780   Gordon Riots in London
1781   Rousseau's *Confessions*
1782   Recognition of American independence by England
1783   Invention of the puddling process; Lavoisier's analysis
            of water; Russia annexes the Crimea
1784   Beaumarchais' *Marriage of Figaro;* Herder's *Philoso-
            phy of the History of Mankind*
1785   Catherine II increases noble privileges in Russia; the
            Diamond Necklace Scandal in France
1786   Mozart's *Marriage of Figaro*
1787–1792   Russo-Turkish War
1787   Meeting of the Assembly of Notables in France and
            refusal of the privileged to accept tax reforms
1788   Kant's *Critique of Practical Reason*
1789   Bentham's *Introduction to the Principles of Morals
            and Legislation;* outbreak of the French Revolution
            amidst severe depression

Selected Bibliography

M. S. Anderson, *Europe in the Eighteenth Century, 1713–1783* (New York, 1961).

P. Ariès, *Centuries of Childhood* (London, 1962).

J. Blum, *Lord and Peasant in Russia from the Ninth to the Nineteenth Century* (Princeton, N.J., 1961).

W. H. Bruford, *Germany in the Eighteenth Century: The Social Background of the Literary Revival* (Cambridge, 1955).

G. R. Cragg, *The Church and the Age of Reason, 1648–1789* (London, 1960).

D. Dakin, *Turgot and the Ancien Régime in France* (London, 1939).

M. T. Florinsky, *Russia: A History and an Interpretation* (New York, 1953, 2 vols.).

F. Ford, *Robe and Sword. The Regrouping of the French Aristocracy after Louis XIV* (Cambridge, Mass., 1953).

D. George, *London Life in the Eighteenth Century* (London, 1925).

L. Gershoy, *From Despotism to Revolution, 1763–1789* (New York, 1944).

D. V. Glass, and D. E. C. Eversley, eds., *Population in History: Essays in Historical Demography* (London and Chicago, 1965).

J. Godechot, *France and the Atlantic Revolution* (New York, 1965).

G. P. Gooch, *Louis XV, the Monarchy in Decline* (London, 1956).

H. Heaton, *Economic History of Europe* (New York, 1948).

H. Holborn, *A History of Modern Germany*, vol. II, *1648–1840* (New York, 1963).

R. A. Knox, *Enthusiasm, A Chapter in the History of Religion* (New York, 1961).

J. Kulischer, *Allgemeine Wirtschaftsgeschichte des Mittelalters und der Neuzeit*, vol. II (Munich and Berlin, 1928–29).

C. E. Labrousse, and R. Mousnier, *Le XVIIIme siècle: Révolution intellectuelle, technique et politique, 1715–1815* (Paris, 1953).

J. Lindsay, ed., *The New Cambridge Modern History*, vol. VII, *The Old Regime, 1713–1763* (Cambridge, 1957).

P. Mantoux, *The Industrial Revolution in the Eighteenth Century* (London, 1955).

D. Marshall, *The English Poor in the Eighteenth Century* (London, 1926).

S. T. McCloy, *The Humanitarian Movement in France in the Eighteenth Century* (Lexington, Ky., 1957).

G. E. Mingay, *English Landed Society in the Eighteenth Century* (London and Toronto, 1963).

L. B. Namier, *The Structure of Politics at the Accession of George III* (New York, 1957).

R. R. Palmer, *The Age of the Democratic Revolution*, vol. I, *The Challenge* (Princeton, N.J., 1959).

J. H. Plumb, *England in the Eighteenth Century* (London, 1953).

——, *Men and Places* (London, 1963).

H. Rosenberg, *Bureaucracy, Autocracy, and Aristocracy: The Prussian Experience, 1660–1815* (Cambridge, Mass., 1958).

G. Rudé, *The Crowd in History, 1730–1848* (New York, 1964).

A. L. Sachar, *A History of the Jews* (New York, 1937).

P. Sagnac, *La Formation de la société française moderne*, vol. II (Paris, 1930).

H. Sée, *Economic and Social Conditions in France During the Eighteenth Century* (New York, 1927).

B. H. Slichter van Bath, *The Agrarian History of Western Europe*, A.D. *500–1850* (New York, 1963).

A. de Tocqueville, *The Old Regime and the French Revolution* (New York, 1927).

Index

DOCUMENTARY HISTORY OF WESTERN CIVILIZATION
Edited by Eugene C. Black and Leonard W. Levy

ANCIENT AND MEDIEVAL HISTORY OF THE WEST

Morton Smith: ANCIENT GREECE

A. H. M. Jones: A HISTORY OF ROME THROUGH THE FIFTH CENTURY
Vol. I: The Republic
Vol. II: The Empire

Deno Geanakoplos: BYZANTINE EMPIRE

Marshall W. Baldwin: CHRISTIANITY THROUGH THE CRUSADES

Bernard Lewis: ISLAM THROUGH SULEIMAN THE MAGNIFICENT

David Herlihy: HISTORY OF FEUDALISM

William M. Bowsky: RISE OF COMMERCE AND TOWNS

David Herlihy: MEDIEVAL CULTURE AND SOCIETY

EARLY MODERN HISTORY

Hanna H. Gray: CULTURAL HISTORY OF THE RENAISSANCE

Florence Edler de Roover: MONEY, BANKING,
AND COMMERCE, THIRTEENTH THROUGH SIXTEENTH CENTURIES

V. J. Parry: THE OTTOMAN EMPIRE

Ralph E. Giesey: EVOLUTION OF THE DYNASTIC STATE

J. H. Parry: THE EUROPEAN RECONNAISSANCE: Selected Documents

Hans J. Hillerbrand: THE PROTESTANT REFORMATION

John C. Olin: THE CATHOLIC COUNTER-REFORMATION

Orest Ranum: THE CENTURY OF LOUIS XIV

Thomas Hegarty: RUSSIAN HISTORY THROUGH PETER THE GREAT

Marie Boas Hall: NATURE AND NATURE'S LAWS

Barry E. Supple: HISTORY OF MERCANTILISM

Arthur J. Slavin: IMPERIALISM, WAR, AND DIPLOMACY, 1550-1763

Herbert H. Rowen: THE LOW COUNTRIES

C. A. Macartney: THE HABSBURG AND HOHENZOLLERN DYNASTIES
IN THE SEVENTEENTH AND EIGHTEENTH CENTURIES

Lester G. Crocker: THE AGE OF ENLIGHTENMENT

Robert and Elborg Forster: EUROPEAN SOCIETY IN THE EIGHTEENTH CENTURY